American Lives

The Stories of the Men and Women Lost on September 11

by the staff of *Newsday* and the Tribune Company

Introduction by Jimmy Breslin

CAMINO BOOKS, INC. Philadelphia

Manufactured in the United States of America

1 2 3 4 5   05 04 03 02

Library of Congress Cataloging-in-Publication Data

American Lives: the stories of the men and women lost on September 11 / the staff of Newsday *and the Tribune Company.*
>   *p.   cm.*
>   *ISBN 0-940159-77-5 (trade paperback: alk. paper)*
> *1. Victims of terrorism—New York (State)—New York—Biography. 2. Victims of terrorism—Virginia—Arlington—Biography. 3. September 11 Terrorist Attacks, 2001. 4. World Trade Center (New York, N.Y.)—Biography. 5. Pentagon (Va.)—Biography. 6. New York (N.Y.)—Biography. 7. Arlington (Va.)—Biography. I. Tribune Company. II.* Newsday *(Hempstead, N.Y.)*
>   *HV6432 .A525 2002*
>   *973.931'092'2—dc21*   *2002003962*

Cover and interior design: Adrianne Onderdonk Dudden

This book is available at a special discount on bulk purchases for promotional, business, and educational use. For information write to:

Publisher
Camino Books, Inc.
P.O. Box 59026
Philadelphia, PA 19102

www.caminobooks.com

To the survivors of the lost

Contents

Preface

Even as it happened, the attack on the World Trade Center was almost impossible to believe. It was a story of incredible destruction that very quickly became a story of heroism. It was a story most editors and reporters wished they didn't have to cover.

As clouds of debris hung on the wind and fell to the scarred earth, the roll call of the lost blew across the wounded nation. Within hours, *Newsday* began assembling the stories that emerged. Two days after the attack, the chronicles of the lost became a continuing feature in the paper. They are the heart and soul of this book.

Space limitations made it impossible to include all the stories that have been published in *Newsday* and other Tribune Company newspapers, and some of the pieces presented here have been modified and updated since they first appeared. All those lost at the World Trade Center and the Pentagon and in the planes that were hijacked on September 11 deserve mention, and an extensive listing appears at the end of the book.

The stories we have selected are representative of those who perished. They represent a mosaic of American lives.

The people in the pages that follow came from the amiable streets of small towns and the blaring avenues of big cities. They were window washers and investment bankers, waiters and stockbrokers, cops and firefighters. Some came from families that have lived here for generations, others were immigrants from Africa and Europe and Central America, in search of freedom and futures. They danced to salsa beats and did volunteer work and coached Little League. They were mothers and fathers and brothers and sisters. They talked at the dinner table about today and dreamed about tomorrow. They held their children tightly.

There are few celebrities among them, and it is easy to describe the lost as ordinary people. But they were no more ordinary than the rest of us. All were remarkable in the framework of their own lives, the worlds they moved in, the people they touched. A man who gave shelter to a destitute single mother and made her his life and raised a family with her. A firefighter who gave his bone marrow to a stricken child thousands of miles away. A woman who taught math in Uzbekistan and was about to teach it in New York City. A janitor who refused retirement because he loved life and the dignity of work.

This book also contains pieces by *Newsday* columnists Paul Vitello, Shaun Powell, Dennis Duggan and Jimmy Breslin, and an introduction by Breslin, who hears the city crying but celebrates its courage.

We would like to thank the families of the lost for their help. *Newsday* is donating its profits from the book to charities associated with helping these families. The Long Island Mentoring Partnership provides a school-based mentoring program that addresses both the short-term and the long-term needs of children experiencing trauma as a result of the events of September 11. Safe Horizon (Queens) operates programs, in eight schools, that are designed to reduce students' trauma and offer lessons in personal and social healing.

And we dedicate this book to those who lived the American Lives that fill it. Their stories needed to be told. They need to be remembered.

Harvey Aronson
Editor, *American Lives*

American Lives

Introduction

JIMMY BRESLIN

I stand on the street corner in the darkness and wait for her, but for another day she is not here.

But already she is part of the story of the thousands missing when the planes hit the top floors of the World Trade Center and caused the silver towers to become black smoke and inside the smoke were orange and red flames and if you looked up, there were falling people outlined against the silver tower sides. If you were close, you heard the

THUMP!

DEAD!

THUMP!

DEAD!

of the bodies as they hit cement.

By night, Kevin Madden of Aon Insurance was in tears at his kitchen table. Fate had caused him to be out of his office then and alive now. "Lucy Fishman," he said. Everyone loved her. She hadn't been heard from. Nor would she. Nor would a couple of hundred others.

My friend Helen Rosenthal sat through the night. She finally called. "Josh is missing," she said.

They all were spirits in the sky. At the end, there were 3,000 of them. And the memory of them is in the pages of this book. They are not missing here. They are alive and laughing and smiling and in love and needed, and you mourn for the loss. They form one of the necessary books of my time. It is a memorial to read of them. Forget these stone sculptures. Your children and grandchildren won't know what they're about. But let them read and learn of all the working people, in uniform or out, who were turned into dust in the dark sky.

And now I stand on the street corner and wait for her.

I don't remember the first time I saw her. I know the hour, between 5:45 and 6 a.m., because I already have finished swimming at the health club and she comes walking along on her way to the gym for her exercise.

The street was West 68th between Columbus and Broadway and I am walking down from Columbus and she is walking up from Broadway. In the darkness of the end of winter nights, she kept her eyes fixed straight ahead and her face showed resolve and a little apprehension upon seeing somebody walking toward her.

I stepped into the street and crossed to the other side.

She was young and had short black hair and a face filled with energy. She had a fast stride. Quick, quick, quick. I never more than glanced at her because I wanted to put her completely at ease. I walked across the street and went home.

That went on for a long time. One morning, I was late or she was early and I was still on Columbus Avenue, almost at the corner of 68th Street, when she came around the corner with her fast walk. People who barely recognize each other and suddenly meet at a strange place exhibit warmth. She smiled a little and her lips said hello, but I did not hear her voice. I nodded.

From then on, when we would see each other on the familiar 68th Street, she would smile and I'd nod or smile back. But I still went to the other side of the street.

This went on through so many months of darkness and cold and morning rain, when we both walked with heads down, and then at times when the sky lightened and spring arrived and after it, summer heat. Always, a smile and a nod and then I parted and she went on.

I never spoke to her, nor did she ever speak to me. I never got her name or where she was coming from at such an hour and what job she was going to for the rest of the day. It had to be a good job, I figured. She is up this early and at an expensive health club. She smiled. I nodded. Month after month.

On the September morning, she passed me and I passed her and I was in the bedroom when the plane hit the first tower and I looked out the bedroom window and saw the black smoke and the necklace of flames around the top floors of the tower facing me. I put on work clothes and went downstairs and got on what was maybe the last Number 2 train going downtown. It is an express and it got me there in time to be on Liberty Street, a half block from the south tower when it exploded.

"Run."

"Run."

I turned one corner and here was a firefighter standing alone. He said he just barely got out.

He said, "I have a daughter in college in Baltimore. I love her."

He started to cry. And I started to cry. It was the first time I ever cried on a job in my life.

I did nothing but go to the trade center each day.

When I went back to the health club in the early hours, I was doing it for a week, maybe ten days, when I realized that I had not seen her. Suddenly in the morning I noticed that she was not walking on the street at about 6 a.m.

I began to look carefully into the morning dimness to see if she was down the block someplace, not yet crossing Broadway, or if she was still coming down Broadway from uptown. I never knew where she came from; she just materialized on the street, walking so quickly. And now I did not see her all last week.

I found myself irritated. "Where is she?" I said aloud.

The days and nights of my working life had become one of hurt women asking in strained voices for lost men, and so many young men in tears standing in a hospital doorway and asking if the woman of their lives might possibly be inside.

And there was nobody. Not in the wreckage at the World Trade Center, nor at the hospitals. The morgue was empty. There were 6,453 listed as missing, all of them in the sky forever from the moment the building blew up.

And this young woman no longer passes me going the other way in the morning.

Not only do I not know her name, but I never saw her with anybody else. I have no one to ask.

On the 14th day since the catastrophe, I was around the corner on West 68th Street at the appointed hour. She was not there. She was not in the dimness on the other side of Broadway. When I reached the corner and looked uptown on Broadway, she was not one of those coming through the light of the outdoor newsstand on the corner of 69th.

She was not here in my morning.

I stood on the corner in front of the Food Emporium supermarket and looked for several minutes. Maybe she moved, I thought. Maybe she got married to some nice guy. Or maybe some nice guy she is married to found a new job and they moved. Maybe she has a new job and her hours changed. Maybe she comes to exercise later in the morning. Maybe there is a pleasant reason for her not being here in the morning. Maybe she will simply be here tomorrow and not have the slightest idea why I am upset.

Right now as I stand on the street corner in the early morning, this young woman, whose name I do not know, whose voice I have never heard, is part of the overwhelming anxiety of the days of my September in the city.

The butcher from the supermarket came out, holding a container of coffee.

"What are you looking for?" he said.

"Somebody."

"They'll come," he said.

"I hope so," I said.

The mornings turned into days and weeks and they marked three months with somber announcements and it was meaningless to me. Worry about today and tomorrow. I certainly never thought of her anymore.

I am turning onto Broadway at the same hour, five of six, and it is now 14 weeks since the catastrophe and I am about to go inside the supermarket and buy a paper and I happen to glance up Broadway.

Deep in the January darkness, moving along quickly. An arm swinging. I stand there and I watch as she comes closer. It is the left arm swinging. Here she is, walking quickly. Quick, quick.

Here coming out of the shadows is the face, smiling as she sees me. She comes right up to me.

"Where have you been?" I say to her.

For an instant she doesn't understand.

"I thought you were gone," I said.

Now she knows. Her face changes.

"Oh, I'm sorry. I'm sorry."

"What am I supposed to think? You disappeared like the others."

"I'm so sorry. I just stopped coming. I had two friends who were missing and we went looking for them. We had pictures and everything. I just didn't want to go anyplace else."

She starts to leave with a smile.

"One thing."

She stops.

"I'm glad you're alive."

She turns and walks off, quickly.

When I went upstairs, my wife looked at me and said, "What's the matter?"

"I just saw a ghost," I said.

Jimmy Breslin is a columnist for Newsday.

Little Brother, You're MVP in Our Hearts

SHAUN POWELL

Scott Powell

DAMN. This was one instance where I wished he had the instincts of Emmitt Smith, the peripheral vision of Gale Sayers, Spud Webb's ability to soar three times his own height, and a sudden burst at the finish, like Carl Lewis.

Had he possessed all four skills, we'd be sitting here right now, rehashing his amazing dash to destiny, and playfully wondering why he never showed this to anyone before.

You see, I teased my brother because he wasn't the greatest athlete. In fact, I always reminded Scott that he wasn't quick enough to beat his brother out of the womb.

His identical twin, Art, squeezed ahead in the first official race of their lives. Minutes later, their mother gave birth to a backfield. Scott grew up, grew healthy, and yet when it came to sports, remained a kid—both in his approach and, unfortunately, in his ability. He loved to take his turn with the Whiffle ball bat, no matter how often he whiffed, which was plenty. He played football in the backyard, always steering clear of the big old oak tree and never forgetting that any contact with the hedges meant he was out of bounds. Still, he was easy to tackle from behind and tough to throw to when you had to score before dinner.

And basketball. I mean, it was a little painful and a lot funny to see him put the ball through the hoop. A field goal is what they call it, and yet he stood a better chance of kicking one than swishing one.

So very early, it was evident that Scott wasn't going to be Scott Skiles or Scott Stevens or Jake Scott, not even Dennis Scott. He peaked quickly, around age 12, just past Little League and not quite long enough for junior high. Give him credit for recognizing his limits, and us for constantly riding him about them.

As it turned out, we weren't looking in the right place. His athletic ability was all in the fingers. They were as nimble as Walter Payton's feet. He used them to play the drums, so well he could put on a show with the bongos or a snare. His fingers could strum a guitar, too, so beautifully that you couldn't help but hum along. Mostly, he was best on a piano. Those fingers did gymnastics on the keys, bouncing between the black and the white, always in harmony, always in sync.

Music became his passion and a good part of his life. For many hours every day, while we were out playing catch, he was inside playing tunes. He and his brother were never discovered soon enough for us, but in time, some record labels did notice. He began producing melodies for singers during weeknights and playing the clubs on weekends. It supported him for more than a decade, until his fingers grew restless and discovered computers.

When it came to keyboards, he was no different on a Dell than on a Steinway. In a remarkably short time, he knew just about every circuit, software, chip and chat room. He gained enough knowledge to create a new career. By now, you figured he'd left sports behind, when in truth, he knew it like never before.

I've met very few people who could carry such an intelligent and lengthy conversation about boxing, basketball and football, three sports that completely escaped him as a kid. He knew the Redskins would turn into a comedy troupe the moment Daniel Snyder bought them and became king. He knew about the WBC and the IBF and more letters in boxing than I know in the alphabet. Plus, I can honestly say he was one of the few who didn't believe, from the start, that Chris Webber and Juwan Howard would make any Washington fan forget Elvin Hayes and Wes Unseld.

The last time we laughed hard was while we sat and watched the Wizards play. The game was hilarious enough. But we found humor in real topics that night: our kids, people we knew, things we did, stuff we saw on TV. It was a typical moment that captured his only mood. He was fun, peaceful, provocative.

He was also my little brother and best friend. Scott Powell arrived at work on time at the Pentagon on September 11. When the plane hit, a woman who sat across from him watched Scott jump over a desk.

Then, through the smoke, she was certain Scott saw the exit down the hall.

He tried. He just couldn't run fast enough, or far enough, into my arms.

Shaun Powell is a columnist for Newsday.

1
Last Phone Calls

The calls came mostly on cell phones but over land lines, too. At the start, they came from the airliners flying into chaos. Then the first plane hit the towers and swirls of black smoke changed the Manhattan skyline and the world beyond. And the ether crackled with words of reassurance in the face of death, words of courage and caring, words of disbelief and fear, words of love.

"My God," a husband told his wife, "they're jumping out of windows."

"I'm safe," a son told his father. "It's not my building"— and then the second plane struck.

"I just want to tell you how much I love you," a daughter told her mother.

"Take care of my dad," a young man on the threshold of tomorrow told his girlfriend. "The two of you, love each other."

They were words to remember.

They were last words.

ROBERT DEANGELIS JR.
"Robert, There's Another Plane Coming."

Moments before 9 on September 11, Denise DeAngelis picked up the ringing telephone at the brick house on Peach Grove Drive in West Hempstead. "Denise, honey, I can't believe what my eyes are seeing!" her husband, Robert, said from his office on the 91st floor of the World Trade Center, Tower Two. "I can't believe what's going on."

"What's wrong, Robert? What's wrong?"

"Denise, my God, they're jumping out the windows; they're jumping out the windows."

"Robert?"

"Go and turn on the TV, Denise!"

She turned on the TV in their living room. The sky was a brilliant blue over the Manhattan skyline, but a noose of black smoke swirled around the first tower, which had been hit minutes earlier.

"Denise! My God, three people right in front of me just jumped out of the window of that building."

She watched the TV and saw the second jet speed left-to-right across the screen. She screamed into the phone. "Robert, there's another plane coming. Get out of the building. Get out of the building!" There was no answer as the skyscraper erupted into flames.

"I love you," she said.

Denise never heard from him again, but she still beeped him in the days that followed, every hour on the hour, because she hoped it might help rescuers locate him. They found his body a month later.

Family and friends wondered whether Robert, 47, a fire district commissioner on Long Island, got into trouble by helping others. That seemed like something he would do, they agreed. He had evacuated to the 78th floor with the others after the first jet hit, but then he had gone back up to the 91st floor when Port Authority officials said everything was clear. When he got back, he answered the phones. He took a call from the elderly mother of his secretary, Maureen Cunningham. "Don't worry," he told Dorothy Cunningham, of Glendale, Queens. "Maureen's out. Everyone's out."

"But what about you?"

"I'm all right," he said. "I'm answering the phones so people can call to see if people are OK."

His first wife, Diane, had died of breast cancer in 1994, but then, three years ago, he and Denise married. They were the same height—5 foot 5—and everyone was glad DeAngelis had found someone again. It was Denise's first marriage. "He was a small man, but with such a big, big character," Denise said. He was also a fitness buff, very strong, and he never ate junk—although he always kept a dish of candy on his desk for others, said his colleague Robert Resch. His brother Paul said Robert's friends, including some who played football with him at West Hempstead High, kidded him with a nickname that was founded in respect. They called Robert DeAngelis "Little Giant."

In New York, DeAngelis was a purchasing manager, buying the massive equipment and materials needed for engineering and construction projects managed around the world by the Washington Group International. His latest assignment was a $705 million hydroelectric project in the Philippines. A former altar boy, he remained a devout Roman Catholic and attended 7 a.m. mass on most weekday mornings. Sometimes he arrived so early the priest let him open the church doors.

Nothing unusual happened early on September 11. Robert ran his usual five miles through the leafy neighborhood, where he lived with Denise and his two daughters, Lisa and Jenna. It was such a clear day. Then he left home, attended the 7 a.m. mass at St. Thomas, got on a bus for Jamaica and boarded the train into Manhattan.

An hour or so later, in the brick house on Peach Grove Drive, the telephone rang.

PAUL ANDREW ACQUAVIVA
"I Know My Husband Is Dying."

The moments have not come often, but when they do, Courtney Acquaviva wonders how she is going to get through the pain. "Just recently, I walked into his closet," she said. "I had to dust his shoes off because he's not wearing them anymore. How do you wrap your mind around it?"

Her best friend of 13 years is gone. Her husband, Paul Acquaviva, was her partner in life, the one who would always be there to get her over the humps in life. In a matter of minutes, she became a single mother with a 3-year-old child and a baby boy on the way. "When the Oklahoma bombing happened, I was so bent out of shape," said Courtney Acquaviva, 30, from Glen Rock, New Jersey. "I felt for those people, but you don't think it can happen to you. Then, it does, and it's too much."

Acquaviva, 29, worked atop Tower One on the 103rd floor. He was the vice president of corporate development at eSpeed, a subsidiary of Cantor Fitzgerald. He was an athlete, playing both varsity basketball and football for Wayne Valley High School in New Jersey and intramural sports in college.

He had been a brilliant student with a lengthy list of achievements—National Honor Society in high school, several college scholarships and awards, Phi Beta Kappa at Rutgers University and a law degree from Columbia University, among other distinctions. And he was gorgeous. But the stuff of their 13-year friendship went beyond looks and a printed scroll of accomplishments. "His looks drew me to him," she said. "His personality kept me with him."

Their romance began with all the giddiness of a typical teen romance story. They met at a party in high school. She was a senior and he was a junior. He passed her in a doorway and that was it, she said. Courtney went home and looked him up in the yearbook. She found out where his locker was and altered her routes to class. The two began dating shortly afterward.

Acquaviva attended Rutgers University, and she attended Douglass College of Rutgers. He was one of those gifted students who did well without much struggle, she said. She remembered taking a class together and studying for hours to do well on an exam. Her husband, she said, simply read the material and aced the test. "This is the way his mind was," his wife said, chuckling. "It was very difficult to win an argument with him."

On September 11, he called her twice from his office after the planes struck the towers. He told her that he loved her. The cell phone was breaking up. She told him that she loved him and that their daughter, Sarah, loved him. Then the line went dead. Courtney Acquaviva shut off the TV, scooped her crying daughter off the bed and played dolls with her. "I said to myself, 'I know my husband is dying . . . but I can't be there for him. I can't comfort him,'" she said through tears. "All I can do is take care of his children."

Courtney Acquaviva has just begun to truly grieve her husband's death, she said. She had to be strong for Sarah and the baby boy, Paul Andrew, who was born December 29, 2001. Now, the memories are spilling over and the loss is too large to comprehend. But the traces of her husband still can make her smile through the grief.

Every now and again, she discovers mementos of their daily life. The tags her husband tore off his recently dry-cleaned clothes and randomly tossed about the bedroom turned up in her shoe the other day. And every once in a while, she'll find his chicken-scratch writing in the middle of a note pad by the phone. "I'll laugh, because I get it," she said. "He's still around. I'll say to him, 'You're still playing your tricks.'"

She remembers their last vacation in the Bahamas, the week before September 11. Her husband and her daughter, Sarah, swam and built sand castles together. Courtney Acquaviva savors that moment by the oceanside bar—she sipping a virgin daiquiri and her husband drinking his cocktail. They smiled, she recalled, and told each other that life couldn't get any better.

MADELINE AMY SWEENEY
"I See Water and Buildings. Oh My God!"

Her message was chilling, but the flight attendant's voice on the phone was remarkably calm. "This plane has been hijacked," Madeline Amy Sweeney told Michael Woodward, an American Airlines manager on the ground at Logan International Airport.

Sweeney, a 35-year-old mother of two young children with 12 years of experience, often sought weekend duty so she could spend more time during the week with her family in Acton, Massachusetts. On this Tuesday, though, she was one of nine flight attendants on the doomed Flight 11 out of Boston, and she told Woodward that two of them had already been stabbed. "A hijacker also cut the throat of a business-class passenger, and he appears to be dead," she said.

Sweeney apparently saw only four of the five hijackers. All four were Middle Eastern, Sweeney told Woodward. Three of them, she said, had been sitting in business class, and "one spoke English very well." It isn't clear where Sweeney was on the plane, but even as she was relating details about the hijackers, the men were storming the front of the plane and "had just gained access to the cockpit." Then, she told Woodward, the plane suddenly changed direction and began to descend rapidly. "At that very point, Sweeney tried to contact the cockpit but did not get a response," according to the FBI's investigative report.

Woodward then asked Sweeney whether she knew her location. The reply: "I see water and buildings." The water she saw was the Hudson River, and the buildings were the New York City skyline. "Oh my God! Oh my God!"

Then the conversation ended.

Officials at the airline and the FBI didn't want to discuss the conversation. But Sweeney's account, combined with other information about the takeover, probably was invaluable to the investigation. "She was very, very composed, very detailed," said one official familiar with the call. "It was impressive that she could do that."

ANDRE FLETCHER
"Turn On Your Radio"

As Zakary Fletcher edged through backed-up rush hour traffic on his way to downtown Manhattan on September 11, columns of gray smoke rising from the skyline caught his eye. Instinctively, the off-duty firefighter called his twin brother on his two-way cell.

"Andre, do you know anything about a job that's happening in the city?"

Zakary recalled his brother's response: " 'Where are you, under a rock or something? Turn on your radio. Two planes have hit the World Trade Center.' "

Andre Fletcher, a member of Rescue Company 5 on Staten Island, had just crossed the Verrazano-Narrows Bridge on his way to the blazing lower Manhattan towers. "Be careful," Zakary told him. "I know you rescue guys think you're such hot-shots. I'll see you at the job."

Zakary never saw or heard from his brother again.

Zakary is convinced Andre never thought twice about rushing into the hellish scene. "He was the type of person who would act first and think after,"

he said. "He was so gung ho, so very aggressive. He was the ideal rescue fireman."

Andre, the father of Blair, 12, was scheduled to be off that day but was filling in because of a manpower shortage within his unit. He was also scheduled to be promoted to fire marshal—a promotion his brother said he would receive posthumously.

Out of uniform, Andre was the all-round athlete who played both football and baseball for the New York Fire Department. And he spent a lot of time in Wyandanch, Long Island, where he lived until recently, and in the Bushwick section of Brooklyn, where he and his brother grew up, trying to instill discipline and focus in the lives of neighborhood kids. "He gave a lot of his time and resources to anyone who asked," Zakary said.

Even as kids, both he and his twin were smitten with the idea of becoming firemen, Zakary said. A fire station was down the block from the elementary prep school they attended, he recalled. It was hard to pay attention whenever the alarms sounded at the firehouse. "On field trips to the firehouse, we were overwhelmed with excitement," he recalled. "We heard stories of how firefighters rescued people, how they were big and brave but gentle. We were awed by that."

Both brothers were on the Long Beach Police Department's waiting list of new recruits, Zakary said. Andre was sixth in line. The pay was attractive, Zakary said, adding that "we always were looking to do better." But he doubts Andre would have followed through. "He absolutely loved being a firefighter."

BRADLEY HODGES VADAS
"Dad, I Gotta Go. There's Smoke in Here Now."

Donald Vadas was at a neighbor's home in Norwalk, Connecticut, when the first cellphone call came from his son, Bradley. The stockbroker who worked on the 89th floor of the south tower described a surreal scene: a plane had smashed into the north tower of the World Trade Center.

" 'Don't worry, I'm safe. It's not my building. But it's bizarre, Dad, people are jumping out of the windows,' " Donald Vadas recalled his son saying. The elder Vadas went into his house and flicked on CNN.

"I saw the second plane hit and I knew exactly what was going on. My son is on the 89th floor, and the plane looked like it hit at about the 60th or so. At 9:14, my son called again. He said, 'Dad, this is probably going to be our last conversation. I just want to tell you how much you mean to me, what a great dad you are. I love you.' Then we talked a little about love, and he said, 'Dad, I gotta go. There's smoke in here now.' He was crying; he was scared. I had to get outside after that. I couldn't control myself."

Later, Donald Vadas learned his son had also left a short voice-mail message for his girlfriend, Kris McFerren. The two had been going together for nine years and planned to marry. "He told her, 'Take care of my dad; the two of you, love each other,'" Donald Vadas said.

Vadas grew up in Weston, where his mother, Connie Taylor, still lives. He was a 1986 Boston College graduate and joined the brokerage firm Keefe, Bruyette and Woods, working his way up to a senior vice president. The rewards flowed: Vadas split his time between a waterfront home in Westport—he loved to fish and ride jetskis—and a home in New York City. "He achieved a lot in his 37 years—and no one gave him anything. He ate a lot of spaghetti in college," Donald Vadas said. "What a great son he was."

CAROL RABALAIS
"Take Care of My Kids."

Soon after arriving from Jamaica 12 years ago, Carol Rabalais got divorced. The breakup left her as sole provider for her three children, Kerene, now 20, Samantha, 11, and Selvyn, 14. She put food on the table and paid the rent for her two-room flat in Brooklyn by taking temporary jobs or working for minimum wage, minding other people's children at a day care center. "Things were hard for her," said Rabalais' sister, Patricia Tate of the Bronx. "Sometimes she couldn't pay her bills, but her family was always there for her. She never believed in taking handouts from the system."

Rabalais hoped to put those struggles behind her when she landed her dream job in the spring. She was assistant to her boss and head of her unit at Aon, the insurance company with offices on the 98th floor of Tower Two. "She was very excited about this job," Tate said. "She came here, and she was hell-bent on making it. She had just gotten to where, as a single mother, she could provide for her kids. Then this happens."

Right after the first tower was struck, Rabalais phoned her mother, Mary, in the Bronx, her sister said. "She said, 'Mom, take care of my kids,' and the phone went dead." After calling Tate's daughter, Marsha, 10 minutes later, Rabalais phoned her mother a second time. "'Mom,'" Tate quoted her sister, "'The building is falling apart. They just crashed into my building. Oh my God.'"

Rabalais' daughter, Kerene, worked part-time for Aon on the same floor as her mom. Kerene, a student at New York Technical College, was running late the morning of the attack. Her mother left their Crown Heights home without her, and she caught a later train into the city. Tate said Kerene was just about to enter the revolving door of the World Trade Center when the first jetliner struck. She ran away from the building, Tate said, then tried to get back in to search for her mom. She was turned away. She watched in horror as the second plane hit.

Tate said her sister loved life, and much of hers revolved around her church, the New Life Tabernacle in Brooklyn. As many as three times a week, Rabalais would attend services and Bible study. Her sister, Tate said, "was a forgiving person, never one to hold a grudge. If I was mad with her, she'd say, 'Get over it, that was yesterday.'"

"She was the light in the darkness," Tate said. "She always made you feel warm, made you feel like you're somebody."

STACEY LYNN PEAK
"Mom, We May Be Trapped."

She left the small town where she had been a flag girl and runner-up for high school prom queen. But even in her most harrowing moments atop the New York City skyline, Stacey Peak did not forget Tell City, Indiana, or the people she loved who live there.

When the phone rang early that Tuesday morning, her mother, Bobbie Peak, thought it might be Stacey, who normally called four times a week. On the line, Stacey, an energy broker at Cantor Fitzgerald, spoke so quickly, with so much chaos in the background, that her mother could barely hear her.

"Mom, there's a fire in our building and we may be trapped," Stacey said before she was disconnected. "I just want to tell you how much I love you."

"I'll never forget that," her mother said.

Peak came from Tell City, a town of 8,000 where many work in factories or on farms. Her two sisters, Judy Rhoads and Toni Peak, still resided there. One brother, Phillip, lived in Georgia, and Mike was in Colorado. After a year at state college, Peak moved home with her mother, waitressing while earning her math degree nearby in Evansville, then working in a clerical job for a local coal company.

That did not satisfy her, however, and she abruptly moved to New York eight years ago to become a nanny on Long Island. She returned home, then moved again, to Louisville, where she learned to be an energy broker. In 1997, she accepted a similar position in Houston, and two years ago, in New York. "She did everything that we were too afraid to leave a small town and do, and did it," said Stephanie Tsantis, a friend.

Peak, who was 36, enjoyed acting and yoga classes, and the people she met in Manhattan, where she lived alone. But she always kept Tell City close by. She visited each Christmas and had been home in August for an annual festival. When her brothers entered her apartment on East 22nd Street after the tragedy, they found a mug of coffee out and the television on for John John, her terrier, and Weber, her cat. A birthday card from her mother, sent a week before, stood on a table.

"It just broke their heart," Bobbie Peak said. "She had pictures of our family all over the place, because she did miss home. She's a small-town girl. It looked like she had gone out to get a loaf of bread."

TITUS DAVIDSON
"I Heard a Rumbling in the Background"

Titus Davidson was the kind of dad who liked to stay in touch. Indeed, his 25-year-old daughter Tanya Dale said with a laugh, he called every day—"to the point where it was annoying."

But as she sat in front of her TV, watching with horror as the Twin Towers burned, she was unable to get him on the phone. Dale was frantic with worry by the time Davidson, a 51-year-old security guard at Morgan Stanley, called her from the 41st floor of Tower Two, where he was helping firefighters escort workers to safety.

"He was so calm," she said. "He said, 'I love you,' and then I heard a rumbling sound in the background. He called my name three times, and it disconnected." Staring in shock at the TV screen, Dale watched the tower where her father worked crumble.

The oldest boy in a family of 16, Davidson left Clarendon, Jamaica, at 22 with little more than his hopes for success in America. Like many Jamaican immigrants, Davidson settled in South Brooklyn and went straight to work—first as a cook in a Jamaican restaurant in Flatbush, then as a construction worker before he became a security guard. Her father read everything he could get his hands on, from her college textbooks to motivational tomes. "He had a lot of dreams," she said. Some of them, like making it big in business, never came true. So he lived through Tanya, watching with pride as she graduated first from Columbia University and later from Hunter College, where she earned a master's degree in social work.

Davidson and Tanya's mother, Desreen Dale, lived together for a year but never married. After their breakup, Davidson trekked up to Dale's home in the Bronx every week, where he showered his only child with "unconditional love," said Dale, who remembers him as a quiet man with a beautiful smile and an easy disposition. "I can't remember him shouting once at me," said his daughter. He was also, she added, as much of a hero as the firefighters who died in the attacks. "I want people to remember the security guards," she said.

STEVEN JACOBSON
"Get Me Out of Here. Send Help."

Victor Arnone remembers the time in 1984 when his good friend and WPIX-TV colleague Steve Jacobson told him, "You'll remember these as the good ol' days." He was right, Arnone says now.

Jacobson, 53, was atop Tower One when the planes hit on September 11. A transmitter engineer, his job was to keep the TV station broadcasting, no matter what. That's what he did on numerous occasions. That was his job. "The biggest sin for a transmitter man is to go off the air," Arnone said. During the 1993 bombing of the World Trade Center, Jacobson was at the top of the tower. He stayed until 3 or 4 a.m. to keep the transmitter working, Arnone said, and once he walked crosstown through a blizzard to fix the transmitter and keep the station on the air.

On the morning of September 11, Arnone was at an emergency transmitter on a roof at 42nd Street and could see the World Trade Center go up in smoke. "I'm working on this, to get on the air, and I'm watching this. I know my buddy's in there," Arnone said. A brief conversation moments earlier with Jacobson had horrified Arnone. He knew his friend of 23 years was trapped. Jacobson told him it was too hot to leave the room. "Get me out of here. Send help," he said, before the line cut off.

An accomplished amateur radio operator, Jacobson was known throughout the ham radio world by his call sign, N2SJ. When not working, he and Arnone would hook up with other radio operators to discuss just about anything, from technical problems to classical music. Often, these light-hearted discussions among the ham radio friends would lead to "roasts," with Jacobson as the recipient. "For old-timers like us, it's a part of our lives," Arnone said.

Jacobson was known for his dry sense of humor and, as Arnone called them, "Steveisms," such as "Wherever you go, there you are." One of his favorite sayings was "It's nobody's business," according to Arnone, and Jacobson used it freely—whether about his tendency not to use turn signals when he drove or as a retort when colleagues surprised him with a birthday banner.

Also known for his hats, Jacobson was often called "Indiana Jacobson" by his colleagues atop the World Trade Center when he wore his leather jacket and wide-brimmed hat. The tight-knit group of transmitter engineers were all close friends and knew each other well, Arnone said. "We all help each other out."

Jacobson left behind a wife, Deborah, and two daughters, Rachel and Miriam, whom he would routinely take to visit his mother in Washington Heights. Jacobson used to call her daily. "She misses him terribly," Arnone said. His voice breaking, he said, "Excuse me. It's just that I miss him so much, too."

2
Love Stories

Their stories are made for songs and poetry and music that make us laugh and cry.

The story of a husband and his wife who took sick. He carried her in her weakness, he shared her tears of pain. "He loved me so much," she says, wondering how she can go on without him. "For better or for worse, that's what he would tell me. For better or for worse."

The story of a couple whose transatlantic courtship led to marriage. She was his soul mate and now he sees her in the darkness, feeling her touch, breathing in her scent, seeking her in dreams.

The story of two men who nurtured a garden of roses and daylilies and eggplants, white and lustrous. Now the one who is left tends the beds of winter and waits for spring.

Stories of the human heart. Love stories.

KATHERINE WOLF
She Lives Still in His Dreams

He dreamed about her—his wife, his soul mate—a month ago.

She, Katherine Wolf, was perched on the end of their bed. He, Charles Wolf, was sitting in a chair facing her.

He told her how much he loved her, and they embraced. It was an embrace that felt so real that he could feel the texture of her skin, inhale her smell, that same smell he tried futilely to keep in her pillowcase for weeks after she died.

"It felt so real," Wolf's 47-year-old husband says wistfully.

On September 11, Wolf, 40, went to work at Marsh & McLennan on the 97th floor of Tower One and perished instantly, her husband thinks, when the first plane struck.

"It's a great comfort for me that she didn't suffer," says Charles, who now lives alone in Manhattan, save for the company of his cocker spaniel.

The couple met by chance in the basement of First Presbyterian Church on Fifth Avenue in the summer of 1988. She was a piano prodigy who had started playing at the age of 3 and studied at the Royal College of Music in London. A piano accompanist in London, Wolf played with an amateur operetta group, the Philbeach Society. Charles sang with the Village Light Opera Group in Manhattan. The two companies had an exchange, and so in the summer of 1988, they crossed paths.

"Who is that woman?" he asked a colleague from the opera company he sang in. "I have got to get to know her." They knew in an instant, with that brief encounter in the church basement. "Essentially, it was all over except the formalities." After one year of a transatlantic relationship, they were married, and she moved into his 12-by-18-foot studio apartment in Greenwich Village.

He's doing well, he says reassuringly. His life is moving forward without the evening glass of wine and conversation they liked to share at Susie's Chinese Restaurant across the street or at LaMargarita.

He's the head of a neighborhood merchants and residents association and is running his home-based catalog Internet business. Still, there are those moments, flashes of pain, uncontrollable sobbing.

"People tell me that I'm doing marvelously well," he says. "That doesn't mean it doesn't hurt. I miss her terribly. I mean, she was my soul mate."

Their relationship was never perfect. But he knew he could be with no other.

Recently, he found his wife's dream journal. The last entry was dated August 10, he says, and he reads it:

"I held a long tubular atom bomb with a pointed end and then I released it. I told the people I needed to tell that I had released the bomb. Another bomb was on its way to our house. I could see its lights on the radar screen. It could track by smell. I remembered how to trick it. The bomb did not go off but it hit where I had just been sitting. I could see the bomb in the shape of a paper plane with a sort of break in the end to stop it from going off. Charlie was with me."

And with that, Charles Wolf breaks into a deep, long sob.

PETER CARROLL
A Soul Mate for Better and for Worse

He carried her from room to room when she was too weak to move. He cooked her favorite steak dinner to help her gain back the weight she had lost. And when she cried because she couldn't bear the pain, he cried along with her.

Since his wife, ToniAnn, was diagnosed with a rare nerve disorder in January 2001, Pete Carroll left her side as little as possible. And when the 42-year-old firefighter had to go to work, he called constantly, often just to tell her he loved her. So when his wife didn't get a phone call on the morning of September 11, she knew something was wrong. Carroll's company, Squad 1 of Park Slope, was one of the first to reach the Twin Towers after they were attacked that morning. His body was found in the wreckage two days later.

"My world is gone," his wife said. "I'm just totally, totally lost."

The Staten Island couple had had only a year and a half of marriage, but it was the real thing, she said. "We were soul mates," she said. "Guys in the firehouse said they never saw him smile so much till he was with me."

When she became sick with fibromyalgia and chronic fatigue syndrome, she wondered at first whether her husband would stick around, she said. "He told me that he loved me so much," she said. "'For better or for worse,' that's what he would say to me. 'For better or for worse.'"

Despite the difficulties of caring for his new bride, the last year was a high point in Carroll's life, said his sister, Pat Dagata. "He was very happy," she said. "When he married ToniAnn, it seemed like he had finally found the right one for him. They were very happy together."

Between them, the couple had six children from previous marriages. Carroll had four—Nicole, 20, Michael, 17, Peter, 8, and Christopher, 6. ToniAnn's children, Anthony DeNiro, 19, and Dana DeNiro, 17, also considered Carroll a father, she said.

Since they first got together, in 1996, ToniAnn said, she never imagined her life without Carroll. "I always thought I would die before him," she said. "I don't know how I'm going to go on . . . You're finally together and you find happiness, and then that happiness is taken away from you."

The couple had looked forward to Carroll's retirement in 2002, after 20 years with the fire department. "That's what his dream was, to retire, buy a house by the water. I would have my own garden to plant flowers, and he would go fishing," she said. "We were looking forward to our old age together, no doubt about it."

DAVID GARCIA
A Life He Never Imagined

Deborah Garcia was a 17-year-old freshman at SUNY Cortland, walking across campus, talking to herself, when she was startled by a voice from behind talking back at her.

"I said what a nice day it was, the sun was shining, and he said, 'Yes, it is a nice day, isn't it?'" she recalled. The voice belonged to her future husband, David Garcia, then a 20-year-old junior.

"And that's how we met," she said. "We've been together ever since."

David Garcia was lost from the 97th floor of the World Trade Center's Tower One, where he was working as a consultant for Marsh & McLennan.

It was not unusual for Garcia, 40, to strike up conversations with complete strangers, his wife said. "It's typical for him to talk to anybody who was standing near him. It doesn't matter what race they are, it doesn't matter if they're wearing a suit or have holes in their pants," she said. "He found everyone interesting and worthy of conversation."

Of course, meeting Deborah was different. That chance conversation in 1981 led to a 20-year love affair that included the couple's marriage in 1987 and the birth of their two sons, Davin, 8, and Dylan, 4. It's a life Garcia never imagined having, his wife said. Legally blind because of a degenerative eye disease, his life initially seemed like an uphill struggle.

"When he was younger, he was angry about it," she said. "He never thought he would get married or have children, because he didn't want to burden anybody with it. He didn't think he'd have a successful life."

But Garcia proved himself wrong. After graduating from SUNY with a degree in mathematics and computer science, he became a computer programmer, working for several companies before going into business for himself as a consultant. Because his eyesight prevented him from driving, he took the bus to the train station every morning.

The family lived in Freeport, where Garcia took his sons to the beach and helped out with their Little League teams. Though he couldn't drive a car, he did take his sons out on his boat. The Garcias traveled abroad, to Japan and Spain, where he had family, and went on skiing trips to Vermont and camping trips to Maine.

Many who met Garcia did not notice his disability. "Most people didn't know he was blind until they went to shake his hand," his wife said.

It was love that gave Garcia the confidence to live his life the way he did, she said. "He just developed an appreciation of everything that life had to offer, so he no longer had to focus on what was wrong," she said. "We just had so much love between us that he was confident that his life would be rich, no matter what the circumstance, and his sons would be there to help him."

Just days before the attacks on the World Trade Center, his wife said, "We had even looked at each other . . . and said, 'God, things are so good that it's almost hard to believe.'

"I said, 'You spoil me.' And he said, 'It's my pleasure.'"

MICHAEL LEPORE
He Tended to His Garden and His Partner

The white eggplants Michael Lepore planted in his garden are ripe to splitting. But Lepore is not there to make his special low-fat eggplant Parmesan.

It's a month after the destruction of the World Trade Center, and Lepore's partner of 18 years, David O'Leary, watches the smooth, white orbs from the windows of the pair's dream house in Bronxville.

"We were waiting for his white eggplants to be ripe enough," says O'Leary, 43. "They're still there. It's just so hard to go out and do anything with them."

Everything has been difficult for his friends and family since Lepore was lost, O'Leary says. Lepore, a project analyst at insurance company Marsh & McLennan, took care of those he loved just as he did the flowers and vegetables in his garden.

Since Lepore's father died when he was 14, his mother and three younger brothers had come to rely on him.

"He was like a brother and at the same time a father," says the youngest brother, Anthony, who is 11 years younger than Michael. "He was our leader."

Michael would pick up his brother from school, ferry him to after-school activities and help him with homework. Michael even made it to Anthony's basketball games when their mother was working. "He'd sit with all the mothers," Anthony recalls. "He'd just be having a grand old time."

Lepore's mother, Jean Lepore-Carlucci, says she has lost a son and a friend. "He was like my buddy. I could talk to him about everything and anything."

As an adult, Lepore went out of his way for friends, and even for strangers. He loved connecting job-seekers with employers and was an incorrigible romantic when it came to matchmaking. He could even take credit for his mother's second marriage, having introduced her to her husband.

And around the house, O'Leary says, "he just organized everything. He did all the cooking—I did the cleanup. He made the grocery shopping lists—I just pushed the carts. Michael took care of everything, and it allowed me to just take care of him."

The two felt they led a "charmed and lucky life." Both successful professionals, they had just filled their modernist ranch house with the Mission-style furniture they collected. Lepore loved to cook sumptuous Italian meals for friends and family, and the house was always packed on Christmas and Thanksgiving.

O'Leary had just been promoted to controller at the publishing company Penguin Putnam, and the couple celebrated on the Friday before the attacks. When O'Leary arrived to pick up Lepore from the Bronxville train station that night, he was greeted with a splendid sight. Lepore was sitting on a bench with a huge bouquet of flowers, a bottle of champagne, a bottle of O'Leary's favorite wine and two skim lattes. He was reading a book and smoking a cigar.

"To see him at the train station, just surrounded by all this stuff . . . " O'Leary says. "That will always stay in my mind."

The couple were looking forward to the next phase of their lives together. "Life was just starting to get much easier for us," O'Leary says. "We were getting established in what we were doing career-wise. We were really starting to settle in on the good part of life."

On the morning of September 11, the couple drank coffee on their patio, as usual, with their three cocker spaniels, and looked out upon Lepore's carefully tended garden, with its beds of daylilies, rose bushes, vegetable patch and rock garden.

"It was a beautiful morning," O'Leary says. "I was noticing how he just looked so wonderful."

Since that day, friends have pitched in to keep up Lepore's pride and joy—raking, digging, pruning and putting in bulbs to bloom in the spring.

ALEXIS LEDUC
He Took Her into His Home—and His Heart

Isa Rivera ended a stormy marriage in 1997 when she took her newborn son and walked out of her first husband's home in the Bronx. Seeking refuge with family, Rivera pounded uptown pavements, stopping at cousins' houses, only to be turned away at their doors.

A destitute single mother, Rivera found shelter in a hallway of a drug-infested apartment building in the Bronx, where she stayed with her baby, Adolfo Rodriguez, for two weeks until one of her co-workers, Alexis Leduc, caught wind of her shoddy living arrangements and intervened.

"He found me there and asked me what I was doing," Rivera said. "I told him that my family didn't want me. . . . He gave me $125 and told me to find a room in Manhattan." Rivera hesitated, not knowing the ins and outs of the busy borough, but Leduc, who had just separated from his first wife, volunteered to be Rivera's personal guide.

A few weeks later, he became her roommate. "He said we could live together until we figured something out," she said. "We were roommates for about three months. Then we became husband and wife."

The couple would have celebrated their 24th wedding anniversary on January 25, 2002.

Leduc, 45, a maintenance supervisor for the 95th to 97th floors of Tower One, spoke to his wife the morning of September 11 while she was doing her bills, the couple's daughter, Cindy, said. "He said that Tower One was on fire. She told him to get out, but he said no, because the Port Authority police told him to stay in the building."

The Puerto Rican–born Leduc, who came to New York City with his family while still a child, was an enthusiastic collector of cards and model cars. Every weekend, the couple trooped to a hobby shop on 34th Street to buy another antique model car for Leduc's extensive collection—his favorite, a 1932 Cadillac that he painted black. "He has over 500 antique die-cast cars," Cindy Leduc said.

Rivera said her husband was never one to scrimp when it came to his collections. "As much as he could afford, he would buy," she said. And when he couldn't spare the cash, his wife would, because "he deserved it because he was a good man, husband, father and provider," she said.

Boxes upon boxes of baseball, football and basketball cards sit in Leduc's Bronx apartment. Rivera remembered her husband and their son, Elvis, sprawling out on the floor thumbing through price indexes to find out the book value of their Mickey Mantle or Billy Martin cards.

"He told me he didn't have a childhood," Rivera said. "He told me he loved his toys." She remembered her husband's boyish exuberance every time he finished putting together one of his model cars. "He would come into the room and yell, 'Look at my beautiful car,'" she said. "I liked the fact that he was into all of those things because he enjoyed himself so much."

With his children, Leduc played the role of "father, and friend," Cindy Leduc said. He would sit them down in front of the television to watch wrestling pay-per-views and would never hesitate to give stern lectures about the importance of an education, something he never received.

"He was everything to me," Cindy Leduc said.

LAURA RAGONESE-SNIK
She Opened Up His World

Thank goodness Laura Ragonese-Snik was forward and outgoing, her husband, John, said. If she hadn't asked him straight out if he wanted to continue seeing her after their first date, their relationship might have ended as quickly as it started.

Shy and reserved, John Snik was nervous about meeting the successful New York businesswoman his brother had fixed him up with. He was 38, rarely dated and had never been married. He spent his weekends reading books and renting movies.

Then he took Laura bowling. To his surprise, the vivacious 35-year-old single mother had a great time.

"She asked me, did I have a good time, and I said, 'Yeah,'" John recalled. "And she said, 'Do you want to see me again?' So I said, 'Oh, sure.'"

Two years later they were married. They called each other after arriving at work every morning. Laura commuted from their Bangor home to Manhattan, where she worked for Aon Corporation on the 101st floor of the south tower of the World Trade Center. She was on the phone with John when a plane hit the north tower.

"Something just happened," she told him. "There's been an explosion. I have to go."

Months after the tragedy, John still had to fight back tears when he talked about her. He shares his grief with Laura's son James, 16. And he takes comfort in the good fortune that brought him and Laura together.

She pulled him out of a shell, he said. She taught him to dance.

It was like Laura to do that. John said she was always upbeat and outgoing. Growing up in Brooklyn, she won the lead in her high school's production of *South Pacific*. As an adult, she sang in her church choir in East Stroudsburg and performed in a local production of *A Christmas Carol*. She encouraged a love of music and theater in

James by taking him to Broadway shows on their frequent trips to New York.

She loved the city and her job. Of course, John can't help but shake his head at the irony. She handled disaster claims for Aon.

"Every time there was a plane crash," he said, "she'd get a call."

NURUL and SHAKILA MIAH
They Always Lived Side by Side

Shakila Miah's father, Sharif Chowdhury, urged his daughter to switch jobs, to find something more stable than the temporary position she held on the computer help desk at Marsh & McLennan. But for Shakila Miah, there was one major attraction to working on the 97th floor of the World Trade Center's Tower One—she was just four floors above her husband, Nurul Miah, Marsh's director of audio-visual technology.

"They got out of work at the same time, they'd go to lunch at the same time," said Chowdhury. "After marriage, my knowledge is they never separated. They always lived side by side."

On September 11, both Nurul, 36, and Shakila, 26, were lost when a plane hit their building.

Little more than a year earlier, the couple were married in a traditional Bengali Muslim ceremony attended by hundreds of friends and family in Virginia. Both were originally from Bangladesh, and many of the couple's peers have arranged marriages. But the couple had what's referred to as a "love match."

"They fell in love," said Nur I. Miah, Nurul's brother. After the couple met at a mutual friend's wedding, they started dating, and Shakila told her father about her beau. The next step was a meeting between the two families, where the Miah clan—including his five younger siblings, parents and cousins—came down from New York and New Jersey to meet the Chowdhurys in Virginia.

"The boy was very nice," said Chowdhury. "He captured all of our hearts with his behavior. Everybody liked him."

After the wedding, Nurul proudly brought his bride to their apartment in Bay Ridge, which he had entirely remodeled—the floors were varnished, the walls replastered and new furniture filled the rooms.

As the oldest of six children, Nurul grew up knowing his behavior would be an example to his two brothers and three sisters. When he was a child of 12

and the family lived in Dhaka, Bangladesh, he would shop for the family's groceries while his father was out at work, said his brother. The small boy would return from the stores, a couple of miles from home, laden with bags of rice, vegetables and lentils.

"He went through a struggle in life, and he wanted the best for us," said Nur. "We just followed in his footsteps."

After the family moved to New York when Nurul was 21, he worked his way up to his position at Marsh. He also was a part owner of a pizza parlor in midtown Manhattan.

Though he worked hard, Nurul found time for his favorite hobby—hunting. He would take weekend trips to Virginia and upstate New York, returning with deer, mountain goats and sometimes bears. He would distribute the meat among the couple's friends and relatives. Nurul loved it so much that Nur joked that the prenuptial agreement said his wife had to let him go.

Shakila had her own hobbies. She had taken up photography and loved to sing the songs of the Bengali poet Rabindranath Tagore. And, her father said, "She was always very much intelligent. I always take her advice when I go to do something."

On Labor Day weekend, the Chowdhurys visited their daughter and son-in-law in Brooklyn. It was a busy three days—the couple had arranged trips to the beach, to an apple-picking orchard, to the South Asian stores in Queens, to an Indian concert and to friends' houses.

As the family crossed the Brooklyn Bridge in the Miahs' new Jeep, Shakila pointed out the Twin Towers to her parents.

"She was telling me, 'Dad, I work in this tower, on the 97th floor,'" he recalled. "And she was saying it very proudly, that she works in this tower."

JOSH VITALE
Love Was Always There

Josh Vitale and his fiancee, Ina Weintraub, had been best friends since their first awkward encounter at a junior high school party in Syosset.

"He liked me, but he was very chubby then, and I didn't like him back," Weintraub recalled.

Though she now considers him the love of her life, Weintraub said, "I'm having a harder time missing my best friend since I was 12 than anything else."

Vitale worked at Cantor Fitzgerald as a trading sales clerk, on the 104th floor of the World Trade Center's Tower One. He was lost in the September 11 terrorist attacks.

Vitale and Weintraub, both 28, were engaged in May 2001, on Mother's Day, and were to marry on July 3, 2002. Two months before the attack, they moved into a new apartment together in Great Neck.

The couple's path to commitment was a nontraditional one, however. Over their years of friendship, it never seemed the right time for romance. Then, two years ago, Vitale broached the subject.

"He basically laid it on the line that he had been in love with me for so many years, and if he didn't say anything he would always regret it," Weintraub said. "At first I was mad because he had waited so long."

Weintraub didn't speak to Vitale for three months.

"It was a really long three months," she said. "Then I knew . . . From when we first got together, we knew we were getting married."

In retrospect, she said, "Everybody around us saw it except us. Everyone—my parents, his parents, and we were like, 'No, we're just friends.' And when we finally did get together, everyone was so happy."

In their new apartment, she said, the couple was "on cloud nine."

The past few months had been full of realizations for Vitale, said his fiancee. At one time, she said, "Josh wanted the Porsche and the mansion, but in the last few months, he figured out that that doesn't make a person rich," she said. "It's more the relationships and the love that you have. That's what makes you rich and successful."

Everything in Vitale's life was "clicking," Weintraub said. He had just passed the exam to become a trader, he loved his job at Cantor Fitzgerald, and he was looking forward to starting a family.

"He just couldn't wait," she said, "for his future to begin."

TEDDINGTON HAMM MOY
A Very Serious Affair

 She was in the aisle seat on a plane to Taiwan, and Teddington Hamm Moy was the quiet young man sitting by the window. She took in his dark business suit, the briefcase propped beside him, his steady, thoughtful gaze.

"He looked like a very serious guy," Madeline Lew Moy said.

But over the course of that summer 27 years ago on a student trip to Asia, she saw different sides to the man in the window seat. He was a joker. He was a dancer. He was a romantic.

And she found they had even more in common. Both were Chinese-American, though from opposite coasts of the United States. Their families were from the same village, Toi Son, in Canton, and spoke the same dialect. Both were brought up to respect their parents and the traditions of their culture. He worked in his father's grocery store in Washington, D.C.'s Chinatown when he was a kid, and she helped her mother out with the family's sewing shops in San Francisco.

A week before they returned to America, the man she now knew as "Ted" gave her an orchid for her hair and asked her to dance with him. In Hong Kong, they shopped together and picked out a gold crucifix for him. And when they were back at their respective homes, Moy became serious again. "Serious about the fact that he loved me and he wanted to get to know me more," Madeline said.

She felt the same way. "We more or less were writing love notes to each other three or four times a week. We talked on the phone for hours."

Moy visited her in California that year, 1975, and the next. In 1977, when he came to visit, he asked her to come home with him to meet his family. And in 1978, when he graduated from the University of the District of Columbia, he moved to San Francisco to be closer to his sweetheart.

He courted her with dinners and movies, as well as nights out dancing to the disco music they both loved—Dionne Warwick, Olivia Newton-John, Diana Ross, the Village People.

In 1980, Madeline's mother chose a "good luck day" in the Chinese calendar, July 12, and they married. They eventually settled in Silver Spring, Maryland, outside Washington.

Though his family's Chinese culture was important to him, Moy, 48, was passionately devoted to the United States. He was a civilian employee of the Department of Defense, working for the procurement department and then as a program manager for information-management support. He collected flags and pictures of eagles and wore an American flag tie every Fourth of July. Last Independence Day, he entertained his children, Jessica, 19, and Daniel Ted, 14, by dressing up in shorts and a shirt emblazoned with the Stars and Stripes, and a floppy brimmed hat like Uncle Sam's.

"He said, 'You're going to see me wear this for the rest of my life, every Fourth of July,'" said his wife.

But that turned out to be his last Fourth of July. Moy was killed when a hijacked plane hit the part of the Pentagon housing the accounting department, where he was part of an elite management-training program.

Madeline is grateful for one thing—the gold crucifix necklace the couple shopped for together on that student trip to Asia 27 years ago was returned to her intact.

"So there's hope that he's gone up to heaven and he's having eternal life," she said. "And he's trying to tell me he's OK."

DENNIS COOK
A Recovered Ring Completes a Circle of Life

Little more than a month after losing her husband in the attack on the World Trade Center, Dana Cook marked what would have been her sixth wedding anniversary. The day's sadness was relieved by an act of human kindness.

"I received a key found by a New York City police officer," she said. "On the key ring, there was our wedding band."

Her husband, Dennis Cook, 33, worked on the 104th floor of Tower One as a bond salesman for Cantor Fitzgerald for six years. He and Dana, of Colts Neck, New Jersey, would have celebrated their anniversary on October 28. Instead, his widow found some solace in the band that marked their life together.

Dana explained that her husband was a golfer and would place the wedding band on his key ring during a game to gain a more comfortable grip on his clubs. "The officer was able to trace it because my husband also had one of those little supermarket discount tags with a bar code attached to the key ring," she said.

She called and thanked the officer, Richard Conte, who worked in a digging and recovery unit that sifted through items found in the rubble at the site. Conte had sent the key ring with the wedding band to the city property clerk as required. "But it began to bother me knowing it would just be sitting on a shelf," Conte said.

Eventually, he obtained permission from his superiors to track down the owner on his own time. "I found out who Dana's father was. He worked near the precinct, so I brought it to him personally," Conte said. Al Palladino, her father, then brought the ring to Dana and her two daughters, Sophia, 3, and Lindsay, 6 months. "Dennis was a great father, a family man and loving husband," said his wife.

MARIA ABAD
She Always Had a Smile

In 1970, Maria Rose Abad was a clerk for the summer at Merrill Lynch. Rudy Abad was her supervisor. "I fell in love with her from a distance," he said. "She was a scrawny little thing—90 pounds—but there was something very sweet-looking about her."

Because he was her supervisor, he wasn't able to ask her on a date, though he did take her out on her last night at the job. After that, their friendship grew, with long chats on the telephone. But Maria still wouldn't date him. "I was hoping for more, but I was content," he said. "I think after a couple of years she realized that what she felt for me wasn't just friendship."

When they finally wed, in 1974, he said, "We had a Cinderella marriage. Everyone knew that we were the happiest couple you'd ever meet. We lived for each other." Even after 26 years of marriage, the couple still had "quality time" together after dinner every night. "We would sit on the couch and I would massage her feet," he said. "She would love that. She'd say it was the best part of her day. For me, if it made her happy, it made me happy."

Meanwhile, her career took off. From a start as an administrative assistant at Keefe, Bruyette and Woods 23 years ago, she became a senior vice president and the highest-ranking woman in the company. She was in her 89th-floor office in Tower Two on the morning of September 11 and called her husband after the plane hit. "She said, 'We're on the 88th floor, we're waiting for a fire marshal to come up and bring us down,'" Rudy Abad said. "That was the last I've heard from her."

Abad attributes his wife's success in part to her intelligence—she graduated summa cum laude from Queens College and was awarded membership in the Phi Beta Kappa Society. But even more, he said, she was successful because she worked hard, loved her job and maintained a positive attitude. "In the 30 years that I knew her, I never heard her say a single negative thing about anybody," he said. "Every morning I woke up, she had a smile. She never had a bad day, or never showed it if she did."

Rudy Abad, at 56, has already retired, and said that Maria, 49, planned to retire at the end of this year. The couple, who never had children, looked forward to traveling for six months a year. They planned to go "everywhere," he said—Bali, Vienna, Rome, Switzerland and especially Hawaii, where they had vacationed for several years. Now, he said, he doesn't know what he'll do.

"I can't think about what could have been," he said. "I can only look back to what was and try to get some happiness out of that, painful as it is."

STEVEN CAFIERO JR.
From E-mail with Love

Donnamarie Striano couldn't understand why her Internet pen pal, Steven Cafiero Jr., was looking for love online.

"He was a beautiful-looking man," she said, judging from the photos he sent her over their one-year correspondence. He was funny and sensitive, with a rippling physique, the result of years of competitive bodybuilding. So why, she asked, couldn't he just go to a bar and meet a girl?

"Donna," he wrote back, "I couldn't pick up a girl if she had a handle."

Won over by his humor, Striano, of Manhasset, agreed to meet him in person in 1998. They hit it off—"He was by far the funniest person I met in my life," she said. A year and a half later, she moved into his apartment in Whitestone, where he had grown up.

A gourmand whom his girlfriend dubbed "Mr. Zagat," Cafiero, 31, loved eating out in Manhattan and often talked of moving there. "He always liked the city," said his mother, Grace Kneski, who raised him alone after she and his father, Steven Cafiero of Glenville,

New York, were divorced. But Whitestone was convenient to Manhattan and more affordable, so there he stayed, close to his pals from the neighborhood.

From touch football to arm wrestling to golf, Cafiero loved sports of all kinds. He still bowled in the local league and maintained a "200-and-something average," said Gene Camp, who knew Cafiero for 10 years. Cafiero belonged to the New York Arm Wrestling Association, which Camp founded, and competed regularly, taking second place in the 1995 Empire State Arm Wrestling Championships.

But to those who knew him, his personality was as memorable as his athleticism. "He was a hell of a nice guy," Camp said. His mother described Cafiero as a very loving, very caring son. She remarried and moved out to Calverton in 1990, but the two still managed to see each other nearly every week. In June 2001, he threw her a surprise 50th-birthday party at a restaurant in Oakdale, complete with balloons and champagne.

He brought that same thoughtfulness to his relationship with Striano, surprising her with trips to the Poconos and Las Vegas, and with home-cooked, candlelight dinners. "He was the only man I ever knew who went out shopping for cookbooks," she said. They intended to marry but were in no rush, she said. In a way, they already had a family: two cats and a much-adored pug named Nelson, whom Cafiero even took out on summer boating expeditions.

A former limousine driver who had managed a cell-phone store across the street from the World Trade Center, Cafiero was ecstatic when he landed a job in August as a client specialist at Aon Corporation in Tower Two. "Steve wanted to be corporate," Striano said. "He didn't know whether he was going to like insurance, but being up on the 92nd floor was like heaven." He had been on the job only three weeks when the trade center was attacked.

MARCIA CECIL-CARTER
Her Smile Filled His Heart

The weekend before September 11, Marcia Cecil-Carter saw her month-old grandson, Zion Owens, for the first time. "She just fell in love from the moment she saw him," said her husband, Ondre Carter. "For those two days, we just played with him all day." But on Tuesday morning, Cecil-Carter was running late for work at Carr Futures, on the 92nd floor of Tower One, where she was a reconciliation clerk. "I wanted to tell her, 'Stay home, and I'll stay home, and let's play with the grandson,'" said Carter. "It just never came out. I wish I would have said it."

At 34, Cecil-Carter had not expected to be a grandmother. But when she heard that her daughter, Amber, was pregnant at 17, she took it in stride, her husband said. After all, she had given birth to Amber when she herself was 17, having graduated from high school in her native Chicago while pregnant, and she went into a Navy boot camp just months after the birth. "She was a strong person," said Carter. "She really focused on life and what she had to do to survive, for her and her daughter."

Yet life was a joy to Cecil-Carter, her husband said. "She had this heart-filling smile," he said. "When she smiled, it just filled your heart. You knew everything was going to be OK."

Carter said he was as enthralled with his wife as he was when they first met, on a street in Brooklyn five years ago. "To me, she had a gasping beauty," he said, describing her green eyes and long brown hair. "Even when she would get up in the morning, I used to be like, 'Wow. She's so beautiful. She's so beautiful, and she's mine.'"

The couple have a 4-year-old son, Devonte. The night before Cecil-Carter was killed, they stayed up all night talking about their past and future together, as they tended to do a couple of times a week. "We'd go to work tired," Carter said. The couple had already achieved some of what they'd set out to do, buying a house and traveling to Hawaii. But there were more plans for the future—a chain of gourmet popcorn stores they hoped to open and, possibly, another child.

Carter calls his wife "my only true friend that I've ever had in my life. I'm just honored that I got to spend the time with her that I did. God blessed me."

BABITA GUMAN
Her Memory Is Engraved

 Babita Roopnarain and her family had just arrived in the United States from their native Guyana. The family was without transportation, so when they ran into another family at the airport that they knew from back home, they gladly accepted a ride home to the Bronx.

As it turned out, said Deodat Guman, Babita, the young high-schooler he'd been eyeing during the drive, lived across the Grand Concourse from where he lived with his family.

Guman recalled how he and his Dewitt Clinton High School mates habitually visited nearby Walton High looking to pick up girls. To his surprise, he bumped into Babita, who unbeknownst to him was a student there. "Don't I know you from somewhere?" he asked her. Guman said he walked the pretty, young high school senior home. They dated for six years, then walked down the aisle.

Babita, 33, was memorialized in a Hindu ceremony at her Bronx home three weeks after the offices on the 97th floor of Tower Two, where she'd worked for Fiduciary Trust Company International as a computer technician, were destroyed in the attacks. She'd been with the company for just over a year, her husband said.

Nearly every step of the 16-year journey with his wife had been the most joyful imaginable, Guman said. She was a take-charge go-getter, he said, the glue that kept their household and, to a great extent, his life together. She saw to it that the bills got paid, stayed on top of the family's investments and took care of most of the day-to-day domestic tasks, including being there for their two girls, Christina, 8, and Melissa, 6.

At the same time, she held down a demanding full-time job while taking graduate classes in computer science at Pace University. "She was the type of person who went after what she wanted, never allowing anything or anyone to get in her way," her husband said. "She was something else."

Babita Guman came to America in 1983. After graduating from Walton, she earned a degree in computer science from Long Island University's Brooklyn campus. With her sights set on becoming a teacher, she was scheduled to take a board of education test the week following the attacks, her husband said. If the way she raised her own children was any indication, he said, his wife would have been a no-nonsense teacher. A stickler for education, she made sure the children cracked the books before they cranked up a game. Her credo was work before play.

In great part, that attitude fueled Guman's unrelenting determination to get ahead, to have some of the nicer things in life, her husband said. Plans were jelling to move up from their one-bedroom Bronx starter home to a five-bedroom place in a

Westchester suburb, he said. Had it not been for his wife, Guman said, he could not imagine where he'd be today. He was a wild, directionless high school dropout when they first met, he said. But she helped him get on track, coaxing him to take the General Education Development high school equivalency diploma exam and coaching him for it along the way. Then she pointed him toward trade school, where he learned to fix diesel engines.

He put his wife on such a pedestal, Deodat Guman said, that he decided to keep her memory alive by etching a portrait of her onto his body. The tattoo, a head shot covering the left side of his back from the middle of his rib cage to his neck, has a backdrop of the Twin Towers. "It's my way of immortalizing her," he said.

CURTIS NOEL and AISHA HARRIS
In Two Promising Lives, at Long Last Love

For two years, Curtis Noel and Aisha Harris led intertwined lives. With all they had in common, the only surprising thing about their relationship is that it took so long to get off the ground.

Both 22, they lived a little more than a mile and a half apart in the South Bronx and met three years ago through mutual friends. Harris, who wasn't dating anyone at the time, started going out to parties and clubs with the group while she continued her search for the elusive Mr. Right. "She was looking for someone with their head screwed on straight, someone who had goals," said her mother, Arvette Harris.

At the time, Aisha Harris was studying physical therapy at Long Island University's Brooklyn campus. Harris loved to shop and spent hours keeping up with the high school friends who turned to her for advice. But ambition and focus mattered. "She used to cram so much living into a short time," said her mother. "Seven days a week, she was doing something."

If Harris wanted her life to go somewhere, so did Curtis Noel. Like Harris, he lived with his parents, immigrants from Trinidad who instilled the value of family and hard work in their youngest son. "He was brought up to do the right thing," said Noel's best friend, Garvin Richardson.

Noel was a quiet young man with a sly sense of humor who loved to play the clown, especially with his mother. "I used to call him my little wretch," she said, because of his fondness for tricks, like pretending he was going to kiss her and then licking her face. He also loved reggae and hip-hop music and worked as a DJ team with Richardson at neighborhood parties. But Noel had a steady job as a switch operator at General Telecom, was studying telecommunications at Manhattan Community College and dreamed of owning his own home.

"What about Curtis?" Arvette Harris asked her daughter when she complained about the shortage of responsible men. "Sounds like you're looking for the same thing."

It took a year for the penny to drop. When it did, it dropped with a vengeance. "It was obvious to me that they were just crazy about each other," said Harris' mother. The couple took vacations together in Florida and the Caribbean and were constantly visiting each other's house.

Harris switched her major to telecommunications after a summer internship at General Telecom turned into a customer service job. Noel was taking night classes and looking into buying a condo in Brooklyn. The two had discussed marriage and their future, said Harris' mother, but they both wanted to get financially established first. "For people so young, they had everything on the ball," she said.

Recently promoted to switch operator, Harris was working at her boyfriend's side on the 83rd floor of Tower One when terrorists flew a plane into their building. Richardson, who worked at a nearby General Telecom office, used the company two-way phone to talk to his best friend one last time.

Noel was choking on the smoke but "sounded calm," Richardson said, even after he was told that the south tower had collapsed. "He was trying to be strong" for Harris, Richardson said.

DOUG IRGANG
An Underground Romance

Every morning, Doug Irgang took the same Lexington Avenue express train to go to work at the Sandler O'Neill & Partners financial firm, where he did institutional sales.

A neatly dressed strap-hanger, Irgang would stand in the crowded cars, seemingly absorbed by the stories in the *Investor's Business Daily* that he subscribed to.

But while he read about equities trading or the NYSE, Amex and NASDAQ indexes, Kristin Ladner, another passenger on the same daily ride, looked at the back of his folded paper for the usual feature story.

One such morning, while she, a Manhattan teacher, was reading a story on educational issues, Irgang moved his paper and their eyes met.

A conversation started. From then on, they looked forward to meeting every morning. They had a lot in common and liked each other. She liked, for example, that he remembered to ask about her ill father.

Soon, after she scribbled her phone number on his paper, they started dating.

In December 2000, he got on his knees and proposed marriage by the lighthouse in Montauk, where they liked to spend weekends.

They were to be married in Arizona the following December and then fly away for a honeymoon in Hawaii. But Irgang, 32, an Upper East Side resident who grew up in Roslyn, was at work on September 11 on the 104th floor of Tower Two.

He called his mother, Joanne, in Manhasset, to say he was OK. Then he called Ladner and, unable to reach her, left a voice-mail message. When she learned of the attack on the towers, Ladner sat waiting for a second call that never came.

In describing the man she had planned to marry, Ladner said, "For a businessman in New York, he was not that type of person who is jaded by life. He loved his job, but it didn't define him in any way."

MICHAEL HANNAN
The One She Was Looking For

They met in Montauk during a carefree summer between college years. Michael Hannan was Andrea LaMarche's first love; she was his.

But after dating for two years, the couple parted company. She transferred to a Maryland college and then moved around the country. He earned his bachelor's degree at SUNY Oswego and started his career in finance at Marsh & McLennan.

Despite their breakup, the two never lost touch. Even if it was just as friends, "He was always somebody that I wanted to be part of my life," she said.

One day, when Andrea was living in Houston, she hung up after an hour-long conversation with Michael to find her close girlfriend staring at her.

"I was laughing, and I guess my whole face was just lit up," she recalled. "My girlfriend looked at me and she said, 'Andrea, this is what it should all be about. This is what you should be looking for.' I said, 'You're right.'"

The two reunited after five years apart. They were married in 1999 and settled in Lynbrook, his boyhood home. Hannan, the 34-year-old father of two who had worked his way up to become assistant vice president in the New York Finance Center, a division of Marsh & McLennan, was lost in the attack on the World Trade Center. He worked on the 98th floor of Tower One.

Although he loved his work, his wife said he saw the money he earned as a means to enjoy life rather than to acquire material goods. Hannan would sooner choose a weekend in the Adirondacks with friends over a much-needed new couch. "I love to describe him as somebody who cared so much more about doing rather than having," she said. Whether it was canoeing down a mountain stream or playing softball at the Silver Point Beach Club in Atlantic Beach, "He had a real zest for life, and he was so much fun to be around," his wife said. "That was just kind of contagious."

Hannan cherished his daughters, 5-year-old Rachel and 18-month-old Alexandra, his wife said. His favorite time of the night was bedtime, when he would tuck his girls under their covers, read them a book, and then snuggle.

"He was a big snuggler," she said.

IAN SCHNEIDER
He Made Every Day a Party

When Ian Schneider began to romance the woman he would marry, his playfulness drew her to him immediately.

"He told me every day would be a party and I was always invited, and that's kind of how it was," Cheryl Schneider said. "He packed in as much as he could."

They both had worked at Cantor Fitzgerald then, but she left to raise their children, Rachel, 11,

Jake, 9, and Sophie, 7. When Schneider, 45, a senior managing director, walked through the doors of their Short Hills, New Jersey, home at the end of the day, the children fought for the right to jump first into his arms.

On September 11, Schneider called his wife to tell her he planned to evacuate his office on the 104th floor of the World Trade Center.

"He told me a plane hit the building, that it rocked like never before, that he was OK, that I would hear some things on the news, that I shouldn't worry," Cheryl said.

He was a large man, 6 feet, 2 inches tall, with an equally big heart and expansive wit, those who knew him said. He'd organize outlandish office pools, betting, for example, on which professional athletes might get arrested. Schneider also would run out to assist children injured in the sports leagues he coached, whether or not they were on his team.

"You could know him for a minute, and you felt like you knew him for years," said Jill Bloom, a family friend.

In his love for sports, Schneider coached three teams in a season—soccer, softball or baseball—and rooted fervently for the Yankees with his best friend, Howie Kessler of Smithtown.

A Brighton Beach native with a thick Brooklyn accent, Schneider spent an entire game years ago badgering outfielder Oscar Gamble to throw a baseball to him in the stands. Near the end of the game, Gamble finally heaved a ball his way. And Schneider dropped it.

Stories like that, and wild laughter, echoed through his home in Short Hills, where 20 people gathered on the Thanksgiving Day after the attack.

"I made a toast at the beginning of dinner and let everyone know that he would always be with us and be part of us and not to be afraid to talk about him," Cheryl said.

His wife imagined him carving their turkey as he always did, messily in their first years of marriage, then exquisitely of late, even if a quarter of the bird disappeared into his mouth before making it to the table. Then he'd gripe about a lack of leftovers.

Bloom said her husband, Bryan, misses coaching with Schneider, who would talk personally with each child after a game. She misses his quick wit, the way Schneider would respond when she called early on a Sunday and asked if he was sleeping. "No," he'd answer. "I had to get up to answer the phone."

HAROLD LIZCANO
One Last Kiss, One Last Present

On September 11, Harold Lizcano kissed his new wife goodbye. Then he looked back, turned around and kissed her again. That night, when Lizcano didn't return to their East Elmhurst apartment, his wife, Emily, thought of that unexpected second kiss as a last gift.

But weeks later, she opened his American Express bill and saw a single charge from the Shubert Theater. It was for two tickets for the musical *Chicago*. She called the box office. "When the guy said it was for November 4, I yelled out, 'That's my birthday!'" said Emily.

Lizcano, 31, had been an accountant for Carr Futures on the 92nd floor of Tower One. At first, she said, "It felt like September 11 all over again." Then she felt thankful. "I'd prefer to go through this pain than for him to be in my shoes . . . I don't think he would be able to handle it."

She had always been the stronger of the two. As one of five kids, she had constant family support. Lizcano, a Queens native, was raised by his mother, Sonia Mira of Woodside. In spite of their differences, the couple, who were friends for three years after meeting at work, fell in love. "He was so pure and honest and loving, there was never any malicious intent at all," she said.

They had a June wedding, a Hawaiian honeymoon and deep spirituality. Raised in the Catholic Church, Lizcano was described as a true gentleman. Though he didn't like to send flowers—they die too quickly, he said—three weeks before their wedding, a dozen of the biggest, reddest and most rare roses arrived at his wife's desk.

What about the Broadway show? Emily decided to go with her father.

HARRY RAINES
After 20 Years, They Still Held Hands

He wasn't into rose petals or serenades, but Harry Raines was a true romantic, his wife said. It was the simple, little things that he paid attention to that won his wife's heart over and over again. "Harry would go to bed 10 minutes or so before me and lie down on my side of the bed so that I would be warm," said Lauren Raines. "To me, that's more romantic than flowers."

And if success is measured by how one appreciates one's family, Harry Raines, 37, was a prosperous CEO.

"Everyone knew he was father of the year," Lauren said of his attention to his three children, Jillian, 8, Kyle, 6, and Kimberly, 2. Every day during the summer, after getting home from his job at Cantor Fitzgerald, Raines would eat dinner on the front lawn of his Bethpage home as he watched his children play.

Weekends were spent playing ball, splashing in the pool or roller skating. Anything to be together. "Even those neighbors that didn't know his name knew he was the guy with the dog and the kids," Lauren said. Artwork by his children and pictures of the family wallpapered the walls of his office.

The couple were friends from childhood, but it was not really love at first sight. From the time Lauren was 15 until she was 22, Harry would constantly ask her out on dates, only to be rebuffed. Finally, her friends persuaded her to give it a try. More than 20 years later, Lauren said they were still holding hands as they took their evening walks. The Raineses would have celebrated their 21st anniversary a month after terrorists attacked the trade center.

It's been hard for the children and Lauren since the attack, but she keeps close to her the memory of the love that her husband had for them. "I know I was blessed," she said. "I knew he was head over heels in love with me and a dedicated husband and father."

PATRICIA MASSARI
That Day, They Learned She Was Pregnant

On the morning of September 11, Louis and Patricia Massari had a special reason to get up early. Louis ironed Patricia's clothes so she wouldn't be late for work, while Patricia did a home pregnancy test in the bathroom. The result was positive.

"She cried, I cried, we talked," said Louis. "I was overwhelmed with excitement, and at the same time . . . was like, 'What do we do? What do we do?'"

They were both only 25 years old. They had been married two years. And they were both trying

to finish school while working full time. As he saw his wife off to her job as a working capital analyst at Marsh & McLennan that morning, Louis said, "Don't worry—everything will be OK."

That was the last time he saw Patricia, though he was speaking to her on the phone when the first plane hit Tower One, where her office was on the 98th floor. "The last thing I heard from her was 'Oh, my God,'" he said. Then the phone went dead.

Later that day, Louis said, he was glad he had ironed her outfit that morning.

"When I talked to investigators who asked me what she was wearing, I was able to describe it to a T," he said.

Though the pregnancy was not planned, Louis said, there was no doubt that the couple would have had the baby. As well as mourning his wife, Louis is now left mourning the child he had only begun to imagine.

"I would switch spots with her tomorrow," he said. "Because then our family could go on."

The Massaris had known each other since they were 15, growing up in the same neighborhood of Glendale. As teenagers, Louis said, "I thought she was cute, she thought I was cute." They started dating when they were 19, and were married four years later, in 1999.

"Our first year of marriage was very nice, and then the second year got very busy," he said. The demands of work and school and of trying to save enough money to move out of her parents' house made it difficult for the couple to find time for each other.

Two days before the attack, however, the Massaris went to a church picnic together.

"Sunday was kind of a day that you could say we rekindled our lost time with each other," he said. The couple played basketball together and learned how to play bocce. "We hugged and kissed and did the things you do when you first start dating."

Now, Louis said, "I feel cheated that I'm not going to be able to have more of those. I miss her a lot."

GANESH LADKAT
A Party of One

She cooked his favorite dishes. Rice. Shrimp curry. Kheer, an Indian sweet.

She bought a fruitcake, his favorite, in his honor.

Then Sonia Ganesh Ladkat, 25, spread out the food on the kitchen table of her

Somerset, New Jersey, apartment and celebrated what would have been her husband's 28th birthday. Alone.

"We used to cook together every night, so it was really hard for me to go in the kitchen and cook," she said. "But I wanted to celebrate his birthday." It was just two months after the attack on the trade center, where Ganesh K. Ladkat worked for Cantor Fitzgerald's eSpeed division on the 103rd floor of Tower One.

"It was very difficult," she said, her voice trailing off.

Less than a year after she was married in India and set foot in this country for the first time, Sonia Ladkat is left alone, living in a land where she knows of no life without her husband.

Both of their families live in Pune, a city in the western state of Maharashtra. The couple met five years ago, when they were taking computer courses at the prestigious Indian Institute of Technology University in Pune. She was 19; he, 21. They saw each other frequently at study sessions and in class. But they didn't get along at all.

"We always had arguments and things like that," she said. "If I said something, he used to say the opposite."

Upon graduation, the two started missing those grade-school-like fights and soon found themselves seeing each other after work, grabbing dinner, going to movies, meeting with friends—until the day Ladkat told her he was moving to the United States to work in Boston.

"I was like, 'OK, I'm happy for you.' And then we realized when he was going that we weren't going to see each other anymore," she said. "And then things were different."

That realization changed everything.

After Ladkat moved to Boston in 1998, the two spoke frequently and chatted online, though they never saw each other. They talked about getting married and discussed the engagement with their parents, who agreed. Then, 2½ years after Ladkat left India, he returned to Pune for their wedding, a grand traditional Hindu event attended by more than 1,000 guests.

In January 2001, Sonia moved to Boston with her new husband, starting a life in a new country they hoped to raise a family in. They moved to New Jersey in June after he landed a job at Cantor Fitzgerald. "It was his dream to work at the World Trade Center," she said.

In New Jersey, they settled into the rhythms of their new life. She would drop him off at the train station at 7:30 a.m. He would return home at 6 p.m. They passed their evenings cooking together, renting movies, both Hindi and English, and working out at the gym together. On weekends, they would go to the Hindu temple in Bridgewater.

"After marriage, we weren't away from each other for even a single day," she said. "I was having fun. The most important thing was, I was with Ganesh. I never felt homesickness. I never missed India, being with him."

Now, even though she has no family here, she said she is determined to remain in the United States. "I'm going to stay here, because I have all my last few memories here," she said. "I don't want to leave these memories."

3
FDNY

So many of us took what they do for granted. We heard the sirens, saw the polished trucks speeding through the city streets and overlooked the fact that a firefighter's job is to rush into fire and smoke and crumbling buildings. To go willingly into harm's way. To rescue people.

It is a noble calling that in many cases is handed down through generations of those who serve in the FDNY. Father to son, brother to brother. A New York fire chief explained a century ago that "the nobility of the occupation thrills us and stimulates us to deeds of daring, even of supreme sacrifice."

More than 340 firefighters died in the line of duty at the World Trade Center. No one can take what they do for granted ever again.

BRIAN HICKEY
He Never Lost Sight of the Job

Death seemed everywhere on that June day in 2001. Captain Brian Hickey and his wife, Donna, had just finished burying two of his men from Rescue 4. They had been killed with another firefighter in a hardware store blaze in Astoria. Hickey himself bore the wounds of the blast that had blown him into a ceiling at that fire. A sense of mourning cloaked the city. But the captain, who always knew who he was and who he wanted to be, told his wife to take heart.

"Everyone's got to die one day; it's inescapable," he told her. "I hope I go that way."

Three months later, the Rescue 4 captain was lost, along with other members of his company, in the cascade of flame, stone and metal that once was the World Trade Center. Outside his firehouse in Woodside the following week, a thousand New Yorkers lit the dark with candles, said Hail Marys and sang "The Star-Spangled Banner." Inside, Donna Hickey remembered her husband's words and said she was going to be OK. She said she was at peace, knowing that he had meant what he said.

Hickey had said the same thing in a different way at his dining room table months before during an interview about fire protection. "Young guys always think they're going to live forever. But you can never lose sight of what our job really is."

Hickey's job as a city rescue captain was to pull people out of burning buildings, to haul them out of holes and out of wrecked cars, and out from under the tracks of subway trains and the fuselages of crashed planes. He presided over a company of men so admired that buffs all over the country line up to bid at auction for their cast-off garments.

He described his calling in *FDNY: Brothers in Battle*, a movie he made with his younger brother Ray, a television editor who died of cancer soon after the film aired.

"I have no ambition in this world but one, and that is to be a fireman," Hickey quotes a turn-of-the-century New York fire chief, Edward Crocker, as the film opens. "The position may, in the eyes of some, appear to be a lowly one; but we who know the work which a fireman has to do, believe his is a noble calling. Our proudest moment is to save . . . lives. Under the impulse of such thoughts, the

nobility of the occupation thrills us and stimulates us to deeds of daring, even of supreme sacrifice."

Hickey found his calling when he was 18 years old and a friend invited him to the Bethpage volunteer firehouse. He put off going to college to join. "It's a brotherhood, it's a camaraderie, it's a club that you belong to," he said in the interview. "Ask a young firefighter why they joined and they'll say, 'I want to fight fires, I want to save lives.' But it's not really your main reason for doing it. It's to belong to the club and do something exciting."

The fun stopped on the night of May 25, 1978, when a man who had just been fired from a swimming-pool store got drunk and torched the building. Two members of Hickey's department were trapped in the blaze and died. "I was 24 at the time," he said. "I changed. I went down a different road as far as what I thought was important and not important. . . . You don't realize until you're older what our job really is," he said. "You realize it's more dangerous."

Twenty-three years later, a gas can spilled by a teenager seeped into the basement of a hardware building-supply store in Astoria and onto some electrical wiring, bursting into flames on Father's Day. Hickey had led four of his men into the building with a water can and demolition tools when the chemicals in the basement exploded, hurling them against the ceiling. Hickey and three of the men managed to escape as the floor collapsed beneath them. But Firefighter Brian Fahey was not so lucky.

As a dazed and wounded Hickey struggled to regain his bearings, his radio crackled with a mayday from Fahey, who was trapped in the basement. Fire crews launched a frenetic effort to pull him out of the inferno but were driven back. The driver of Hickey's rig, Harry Ford, lay dead on the sidewalk under toppled masonry. Another firefighter, John Downing, was found nearby.

A preliminary probe concluded that this was one of the few fatal fires in city history that couldn't be chalked up to poor training, or misplaced resources, or anything other than freak bad luck. Hickey was philosophical—except for one thing.

"The only thing that hurt him, hurt him deeply," his wife said, "was that he couldn't save their lives. He had no control."

The firefighter's wife says her husband had prepared her for the possibility of widowhood from the very beginning of their marriage, and she had accepted it. "This was a calling. This is his calling. He knew the dangers and was never, never afraid, because his heart was in the job. It's his life. He was one of the fortunate people who go through this life never questioning, 'What am I going to be, what am I going to do?'

"I'm very proud of him. He's a hero. It's a big loss for the city of New York."

Then she laughed, a deeply happy laugh.

"But I had him."

TERRENCE FARRELL
A Hero by Any Definition

The first time Chantyl Peterson met the man whose blood runs through her veins was a late summer day in 1994. She was a 6-year-old girl from Nevada with long blonde hair and a frilly pink dress. Firefighter Terry Farrell, whose bone marrow saved her from deadly blood cancer, was big and kind, handsome in his dress uniform.

As cameras flashed on the 87th floor of the World Trade Center, Farrell took her in his arms, and his voice gave way as he asked, "Is she beautiful, or what?"

In November 2001, Chantyl, now a healthy, horse-crazy, 13-year-old A student, was back in New York, slumped in the seventh pew of St. Patrick's Church in Huntington, gazing at the casket of the stranger who had become a second father to her.

"Hero" was the word for Farrell back in 1994, when he donated his bone marrow to a little girl thousands of miles away. And the word was used again at the funeral, after he perished trying to save others in the devastation of the World Trade Center.

But her husband never aspired to be a hero, said Nora Farrell. Not seven years ago when he gave Chantyl her life back. "I'd hope that people would do that for me if my children needed help," he said afterward. And not on September 11. "He was just a regular guy and he was happy with that," Nora said. As for the lives he saved, "He thought anyone else would have done the same."

A firefighter in the city's elite Rescue 4 unit in Woodside, Queens, and assistant chief in the suburban Dix Hills volunteer department, Farrell loved it, said his wife, whether he got paid or not. At night, she recalled, "His radio would go off, and I didn't even know he was gone . . . He would come back and shower, but still the smell of smoke that was on his body and in his hair—that's what would wake me up."

Farrell had hurt his hand earlier in the year with an electric saw, and he found the months of surgery and recovery frustrating—especially when he heard of an explosion on Father's Day in Astoria, Queens. Three firefighters died, including two from Rescue 4.

"He was sorry he wasn't there," Nora said. "They're all like that. . . . As soon as the bandage came off, he was back."

On a trip in July 2001 to Baltimore for a firefighter's convention, Farrell insisted on spending the whole time selling T-shirts for the families of the firefighters killed in Astoria, leaving his wife and two children, T.J., 14, and Rebecca, 8, to explore the city without him. Nora took the opportunity to do some early Christmas shopping for her 45-year-old husband, a man who asked for only two things every year—a pair of boots and a pair of work pants.

She did well. She found a beautiful wooden box for his department pins and honors and, as a stocking stuffer, a calendar featuring models wearing firefighter's gear. She got the calendar autographed by the models themselves at the convention.

"I was all set for Christmas for him," Nora said. But without her husband of "16 wonderful, glorious years," the holidays were tough. Every day has been tough.

"My son's doing excellent in school," Nora said. "It's just that he's not part of the school. He just wants to come home. I guess he wants to check on me. . . . My daughter, she makes us laugh. She doesn't want to cry in front of people, so she doesn't cry. . . . But she does cry at night."

Everywhere she looks, Nora sees reminders of her husband—the deck and sewing room he built for her, the basement he finished for the kids, fire-chief cars like the one he drove.

"And," she said, "I have his pants hanging on my bicycle, just the way he left them."

DANIEL LIBRETTI
A Chef Whose Specialty Was Firefighting

Every New York City firefighter has at least one second job, it seems, unless he is home taking care of the children while his wife works. But few moonlighting stints have brought as much joy to the department as that of Rescue Company 2 firefighter Daniel Libretti, 43, whose Crown Heights brethren feasted on the same crepes and souffles he prepared on off days as a pastry chef at the top-rated Manhattan restaurant La Caravelle.

"I don't know the names of half the things he made for us—I'm a simple guy," said Pete Romeo, a longtime friend and company member, who helped carry Libretti's remains from the rubble of the World Trade Center a month after the attack. "But all the rich people are paying a lot of money for the food we were eating. He'd do the meal from start to finish. You didn't have to help him. I guess it's a chef thing."

Still, there was no easier way to torment Libretti than to tell him he was a terrific cook. He wanted to be known as a good firefighter.

And he was—one of the best, his peers say, who spent 15 years in East New York's Ladder Company 103, for a time the city's busiest firehouse in its worst neighborhood.

No precinct in the city had a higher murder rate when Libretti got himself assigned there at the height of the crack epidemic in the early 1980s. Gaunt addicts roamed the streets breaking into anything that wasn't locked behind concertina wire, toppling telephone poles to scavenge the copper cable. The back wall of the firehouse was a popular spot for executions. Libretti and his fellow firefighters were called out an average of 30 times a night, typically to burning crack houses—heavily barricaded, decaying buildings that were littered with dirty needles and salted with booby traps. Sometimes they managed to rescue the children who too often were left untended in those buildings. Sometimes a person would stagger over from the bar across the street with a bullet wound or a broken beer bottle sticking out of his belly after a fight. Tending to them was part of the job, too, because there weren't enough police to go around.

"There wasn't a lot of good happening anywhere around us," recalled Romeo, who met Libretti at that firehouse in 1985. "You just try to go and help. You're the hope in the neighborhood."

For an aggressive firefighter like Libretti, this harsh place was heaven, with his co-workers, a cast of characters who called themselves "The Men's Club" as they went out each night amid the gun battles, helping wherever they could. Before they turned in at night, Libretti would take orders for breakfast.

Libretti was a character, too, friends say, a man who could fit in as easily at the Ritz as on the corner of Bergen Street and Schenectady Avenue, a happy man brimming with energy, a patient man who loved people. Over morning coffee, he'd tell his wife, Dolores, he was thinking of building a deck, and she'd come home from work to find it half completed. He had a thing for winemaking, too: red, white, you named it, he'd make it, calling his label Ridgewood Estates after the street in Elthingville, in Staten Island, where he and his wife lived.

Life gradually improved in East New York and, two years ago, Libretti moved up to Rescue 2 looking for more action. He was already much admired there, said company member Duane Woods—for both his firefighting and his cooking.

Before Libretti joined Rescue 2, the company called themselves the "Pudding Heads," because their favorite cook at the time made chocolate pudding after every meal. "When Danny got here, he said, 'I got something better for you,' and he made up some chocolate mousse from scratch," Romeo said. "So then we became the 'Mousse Heads.' We got a little bit of class."

After Libretti died, someone tried to keep his dessert tradition going, but it didn't work. "It was all lumps in it, like mousse hash," Romeo said sadly. "You gotta do the right thing with the chocolate."

JOHN FANNING
He Warned This Day Could Come

John "Jack" Fanning knew about danger. In a career with the New York Fire Department that spanned 31 years, he once plunged into the treacherous East River to rescue the passengers of a helicopter that had crashed. Another time, he saved a boy dangling from cables in an empty elevator shaft between the third and fourth floors of a burning building in the Bronx.

Fanning also knew about terrorism, both first-hand and as a trained expert. When a truck bomb exploded at the World Trade Center in 1993, Fanning was among the first firefighters to respond. In 1995, he was deployed with New York City's Urban Search and Rescue Team to Oklahoma City after the bombing of the Alfred P. Murrah Federal Building and to Puerto Rico after Hurricane

Marilyn. A battalion chief, he headed the department's Hazardous Materials Operations Unit and represented the city on the Federal Emergency Management Agency's Incident Support Team at the 1996 Summer Olympics in Atlanta.

And Fanning, 54, was supervising the first firefighters responding to the September 11 terrorist attack on the World Trade Center when, his family was told, he died while trying to save others inside the towers.

The irony is that he practically predicted the tragedy only a few months earlier in what now seems like eerily prescient testimony. Fanning was one of the FDNY's leading experts on anti-terrorism and served on a national anti-terrorism panel at the Harvard University School of Government. In May 2001, he was invited to testify before a Senate Appropriations subcommittee, where he warned that much more needed to be done to prepare major cities for an attack. "Whatever the scale," he told the senators, "firefighters and other responders will be there within minutes, some quite possibly becoming victims themselves."

He'd known about the danger his whole life. Born in Brooklyn and raised in Jackson Heights, Queens, Fanning quit college to follow his father into firefighting, where he rose to the rank of battalion chief by 1994.

The honors he received never went to his head. "He was a loving husband, a loving father and a very humble person," said his wife of 15 years, Maureen McDermott-Fanning, a registered nurse and mother of the couple's two sons, Sean, 13, and Patrick, 5. "In spite of his medals and credentials, he was just a regular guy."

Both Sean and Patrick have autism. About two weeks before his death, Fanning and his wife discussed establishing a trust to build a residential home on Long Island for autistic children. Family members plan to complete that mission in his memory.

His sons from a previous marriage, Ryan and Jeremy, called their father the bravest man they've ever known. "The regard for his life wasn't there," Ryan said. "It was for other people's lives." His daughter Jacqueline, 22, said her father was looking forward to her wedding the following April. A week before the attack, he had e-mailed her the name of the song he wanted the two of them to dance to at the wedding: "Forever Young," by Bob Dylan.

PETER GANCI
He Ignored His Own Order to Flee

Peter Ganci was the kind of guy who wouldn't dream of letting on that he was the highest-ranking uniformed officer in the New York City Fire Department.

"I'm a fireman," the department chief would tell people who asked about his profession.

Ganci died as he lived, working side by side with his troops as they dug out survivors of the blast at the World Trade Center. "He was in the war zone," said his son, Christopher Ganci, 25. "He wanted to be with the guys."

The 54-year-old firefighter had always been that way. In the Farmingdale Fire Department as a volunteer. In the 82nd Airborne as a paratrooper. And in the New York City Fire Department, where he served for 33 years and was decorated repeatedly for bravery.

"He loved the brotherhood and the camaraderie," said Ganci's son, Peter III, 27. "It got in his blood, and he wouldn't leave."

Friends described Ganci as a man who had a passion for clamming, crabbing and golf outings, who was a straight shooter in conversation, who valued his job as much as his family.

"He could be speaking with the president or a cab driver and he would respect them the same," said a friend who had known Ganci since their childhood in Farmingdale.

Eyewitnesses said that immediately after a jet struck the first tower, Ganci rushed to the scene from his command post in downtown Brooklyn and started the rescue effort. He was in the basement of Tower One when it collapsed. Rubble caved in on him, but he dug himself out.

Ganci directed the mayor, the fire commissioners and others to clear out of the area because it was apparent that the second tower would fall. But he ignored his own order, as did the Reverend Mychal Judge, the city fire department's chaplain, and William Feehan, first deputy commissioner of the fire department. "I'm not leaving my men," Ganci said, according to firefighters on the scene.

Peter and Christopher knew their father was probably inside the building when it collapsed. That's just the way he was.

Later that day, New York City police came to the home where Ganci lived with his sons, his daughter, Danielle, 22, and his wife, Kathleen, to deliver the news that he was lost.

The day after, Peter Ganci's sons stayed outside the house to greet the firefighters, neighbors and family who came to pay their respects.

"Your father was a hero," said a woman standing off to the side of the sons.

Peter looked at the ground and mumbled, "That doesn't do me any good, though."

VERNON CHERRY
A Renaissance Man in Tune with the World

A pioneer black firefighter, Vernon P. Cherry showed he belonged, serving almost 30 years among the ranks of New York City's bravest. But his zest for life and living radiated far beyond the walls of Ladder Company 118 at the base of the Brooklyn Bridge in the city's largest borough.

Cherry, who was about a month shy of 50 when he perished on September 11, was the company's official vocalist. His melodic tenor voice could be heard at most firefighters' functions, including medal ceremonies and funerals. And with his five-piece band, the Starfires, Cherry performed at weddings and bar mitzvahs.

But Cherry, a longtime court reporter, was as well known and well liked in the halls of justice as he was in wedding halls.

"He was one of the most outgoing, friendly, nonpretentious persons I had ever met," said State Supreme Court Justice Alice Schlesinger, who first met him during the late 1980s, when they worked Small Claims Court together.

As he waited for cases to come before the bench, Cherry would take it upon himself to answer questions, going beyond what he was supposed to do. "He hated just to do nothing," Schlesinger said of Cherry, adding that her family and his family—including Joanne, his wife of more than 30 years, and three children—became close. "He was just a terrific guy."

Cherry's mother, Fannie Mae, now 82 and a resident of Woodside—where as a widow she single-handedly raised six children—noticed that he liked to sing at an early age, said his daughter, Selena Daniel of Woodbridge, New Jersey. Some-

how managing to obtain discount music lessons for her son, Fannie Mae took him each week from the family's Woodside home to the Brooklyn Academy of Music for voice instruction.

He graduated from Aviation High School in Long Island City. While working for the New York City Transit Authority fixing tracks, he took several civil service exams, Daniel said. He thought a city job would bring his family the stability he didn't have as a child.

Her father was something of a Renaissance man, Daniel said. He was a scholar, a historian and a genealogist. And he loved to rummage through thrift stores, where he acquired some of his most treasured finds, including musical instruments, artwork and golf clubs. "He couldn't pass up a good deal," Daniel said, amused that he had two sets of golf clubs, a right-hand set and a left-hand set. "He lived his life to the fullest," she said.

Cherry's daughter recalled how once, in a supermarket, her father tipped the bag boy $20 and told him to keep up the good work and stay out of trouble. The boy reminded Cherry of himself as a youngster, she said.

When the family lived in Coney Island, her father had close friends among virtually all the ethnic groups in the community, including Russians and Jews, she said. And during his years as a court reporter, Schlesinger recalled, Cherry regularly went out of his way to help people fight their cases. For instance, when some people couldn't afford needed transcripts, Cherry would type the material and send it to them for free.

Cherry, who had planned to retire at the end of the year, was working the 9 a.m. to 6 p.m. tour September 11. His was among the first companies dispatched to the scene. His daughter was told that Cherry went straight into one of the blazing towers to save lives.

ANGEL JUARBE JR.
A Winner on Reality TV and in Real Life

Angel Luis Juarbe Jr. was the type of guy who would roam the streets of the South Bronx picking up stray dogs and taking them home. He was so diligent in his self-appointed task that at one point his family had five dogs, all named "Butchie."

Juarbe, 35, a firefighter with Ladder Company 12, loved animals, liked being out in the wilderness and found joy in spending time with his family. He was also proud to be a firefighter and helped turn the station house, in Manhattan's Chelsea, into a homey place where neighborhood children hung out, but only after they assured him they had completed their homework.

"He picked up a stray cat and took it to the firehouse," said his older sister, Susan Juarbe, a court officer, also of the Bronx. "When he got there, a few of the officers were telling him it was a typical firehouse—you work, you watch TV, you do your shifts. Now they have a cat and a fish tank, and kids who come to visit."

Juarbe, a health-conscious man who this year was picked to model for the firefighters' calendar, also was outgoing and did not fear adventure. About three years ago, he sold his beloved Mustang to pay for a trip to Africa, so he could see animals wander freely through the Serengeti Desert. In the same spirit, he had applied for several television reality shows with the hopes of representing New York and his firefighting comrades.

This summer he got a call to go to Los Angeles and audition for the Fox show *Murder in Small Town X*, and was picked. In the reality show, contestants had to solve a fictional murder in a small town. In the first week of September, he got his brothers, Charles and Edgar, and his sister, Jessica, and their relatives and neighbors together in the Wales Avenue building where he lived all his life, to see the show. His mother cooked the flavors of her native Puerto Rico for the occasion.

They watched in suspense as he competed to solve a mock crime in a small Maine town. They were surprised to see him pass the first rounds, earn the respect of other contestants and win the grand prize, $250,000 and a new Jeep Liberty.

They hugged and cried. He promised to throw a block party, where he was to announce that he would use part of the money for a scholarship fund for his nephews and nieces. There, Juarbe would also hand the keys to the sport utility vehicle to his father, Angel Sr., and would give his mother, Miriam, the down payment for the family's first home.

But he was just finishing his shift on the morning of September 11 and rushed to the World Trade Center after the terrorist attack. He was last seen running inside one of the towers after helping to evacuate the Marriott hotel.

After several hours, Juarbe's brothers, who are police officers, called the family and said they were fine. Juarbe was never heard from.

JOSEPH FARRELLY
"Love You, Joe."

 He seemed like a man who knew life was precious. His work as a firefighter let him see up front the tenuous link between life and death. Perhaps that's why Captain Joseph Farrelly left behind such a legacy of love.

Children at Public School 3 in Staten Island knew him as "Fireman Joe," who came to their school to teach them about fire safety. Dozens of foster babies, drug-addicted at birth, felt his kind touch and reassuring words. His wife, Stacey, has boxfuls of romantic notes and cards to remind her of his love for her and the children, sent through their 25 years together.

Stacey Farrelly said her husband left her love notes and roses throughout their marriage, and not just on Valentine's Day or their anniversary. She would find his heartfelt thoughts on a sticky note on the dashboard of her car or on the back of a receipt on the kitchen table in their Staten Island home. Stacey found what was to be his last love note when she got home September 11.

"Dear Stace," he wrote, "I can't begin to tell you how much I love you. Words are inadequate. Already, I can't wait to get home. Hope you had a good time today. Love you, Joe."

The note was a final testament to their life together.

The 47-year-old firefighter, who was with Engine Company 4 on South Street in Manhattan, was believed to be in a tower lobby when the building collapsed.

Farrelly's love for his children was evident in the time he spent with them, either at Little League games, at the Boy Scouts or at home. His oldest son, Ryan, 20, said his father "never argued, never cursed, never got angry." Ryan's childhood memories include camping trips with his parents, his brother Devin, 18, and their sister Julianne, 11, where they were taught to live in harmony with nature. "He liked to go anyplace where it was relaxed," said Ryan.

Farrelly and his wife also were foster parents to many drug-addicted babies over the years. In 1986, his wife said, she and her husband were watching a TV show on "border" babies who were addicted to drugs and needed stable environments. "I turned to Joe and said, 'We can do that. We can take a baby.'"

For the next seven years, the Farrellys took in newborns and nursed them through their addictions, returning them after six months to foster or adoptive parents. Stacey Farrelly said her husband loved the babies. "He used to like doing the nighttimes," his wife said. "He would talk to them and tell them not to worry, that they would have a good life."

LEON SMITH JR.
He Lived His Childhood Dream

 Leon Smith Jr. knew his calling early.

He was a third-grader when he told his mother in no uncertain terms that he wanted to be a fireman. The youngster often disappeared, Irene Smith said, but she always knew where to find him: hanging out in the firehouse across the street from the family's former home in the Crown Heights section of Brooklyn.

Punishment didn't dissuade him. "I was fighting a losing battle," she said. So much so that her husband pleaded the case for letting him be. "At least you know he's safe there," the late Leon William Smith Sr. would tell his wife.

Since September 11, Irene Smith has found emotional refuge and solace at Ladder Company 118, the Brooklyn Heights firehouse where her only child fulfilled his childhood dream for almost 20 years.

At least twice a week, she shares home-cooked meals with the Ladder Company 118 crew, four of whose members—including her son—died at the World Trade Center. "We eat and talk and spend time together," she said, sobbing. "They give me the strength I need to go on and I give them the strength they need to keep going. All of Ladder 118 are my sons now, my extended family."

Smith, who nicknamed all of his fellow Ladder Company 118 crew members, went by the name of "Express" because he always said his beloved truck should be among the first to arrive when dispatched to a fire. Smith called his fire truck his "girlfriend." He washed it every chance he got, his mother said. And when he was off tour, his crew knew they'd better spruce up Smith's "girlfriend" before he returned or they'd hear from him. His mother said he did practically all the mechanical work on Number 205, the truck he drove to the World Trade Center with five others aboard.

After high school, Smith took pretty much all of the civil service exams available. While on the waiting list for about a year, he worked for the Department of Sanitation as well as the Traffic Department. The Corrections Department called first, but he decided right before his interview that it wasn't for him. "He couldn't take being closed in."

Irene Smith recalled that her son was mechanically inclined from an early age. He used to build miniature racecars with tiny working engines, she said. "He loved working with his hands and had the patience of a saint. I can see him now, walking around the house with that remote control."

She can also still hear her son's boisterous laugh and conjure up images of his giving ways. Once he came home from school without his coat, and when she asked what had happened to it, he told her he had given it to a kid who didn't have one because he had three. Occasionally, she said, "I'd hear a knock at the door and I'd open it to see several neighborhood kids standing there, grinning. He would say, 'I invited them, Mamma.' I didn't have any money, but I couldn't refuse them."

Smith was separated from his wife, Marilyn, the mother of his three children. His twin daughters, Tiffany and Yolanda, 18, are in their first year at Johnson C. Smith University in Charlotte, North Carolina. A third daughter, Nakia, 25, and her 2-year-old son, Mekhi, live in Bedford-Stuyvesant. A student at Manhattan Community College, Nakia was preparing to attend a class just blocks from the Twin Towers when news of the attack forced her to cancel her trip into Manhattan. Buildings on the campus were damaged by debris from the crumpled skyscrapers.

The last time his mother spoke to her son, she asked him when he planned to retire. "He said, 'I can't retire until my twins get out of college. Then maybe I'll think about it.'

"Leon was my hero," his mother said. "When my husband passed, I told Leon I'd lost my right arm. He said, 'No, you haven't, Mamma, I'll always be here for you.'"

ORIO PALMER
His Specialties: Stickball and Firefighting

At breakfast time, Orio Palmer would pop in a Rascals CD and do goofy dances around his Valley Stream kitchen singing "It's a Beautiful Morning." The kids laughed and called him the Music Man.

The New York City fire battalion chief, who'd had it tough growing up in the Bronx, would take the neighborhood kids out fishing on days off, just because he'd never gotten to do that himself as a boy.

He was determined to teach all the kids stickball, too, an almost-lost art he mastered at their age. And when he and his wife, Debbie, were invited to a Halloween toga party, a white sheet wasn't enough for Palmer: He had to wear a pink one, put high heels on his sandals and arrive as the "Boy Toy from Troy."

On their refrigerator, Debbie Palmer still keeps the saying her husband taped there before he led the men of his Manhattan battalion to the World Trade Center September 11: "Live while you're alive." Sixteen members of Battalion 7 were lost along with Palmer, 45.

Palmer joined the fire department 20 years earlier at Engine Company 46 in the Bronx. He transferred to firehouses in Brooklyn and Queens as he worked his way up the promotional ladder before landing with Battalion 7 on West 19th Street in Manhattan. That battalion protects the Empire State Building, Madison Square Garden and Pennsylvania Station.

Palmer became known to hundreds of co-workers as an instructor for firefighters studying for promotional exams. He also used his teaching skills to write articles for the fire department newspaper on safety topics, such as the dangers of buildings with separate up and down "scissor" staircases, and ways to communicate in tunnels and buildings when radios fail.

Palmer's community tended his family after the attacks. Complete strangers sent cards and letters of support, and neighbors dropped off meals and groceries. The mail carrier left bagels on the doorstep, and tradespeople called asking if there was anything they could fix. At school, teachers and guidance counselors took the Palmer kids—Dana, 14, Keith, 12, and Alyssa, 9—under their wing. Even the sanitation crews carried the family garbage cans up the driveway and left them neatly by the side of the house.

"They just want to do any little thing," his wife said. "What I've learned is that there is a lot more good in the world than bad."

WILLIAM LAKE
Any Life Was Worth Saving

The horse was on its knees, smoke-sick and frozen with fear, when Billy Lake and his partners found it in the burning barn.

They had followed the whinnying they'd heard from outside the inferno at the Bergen Beach stables in south Brooklyn. The men decided it was time to go when the horse refused to budge, but Lake was just as stubborn.

"He said, 'No, I ain't leaving that horse,'" recalled Rescue 2 firefighter Clifford Pase of the June 2000 arson that killed 21 of 24 horses. "So we put straps on him, rigged him up and dragged him out. And Billy gave him oxygen, and he survived."

That horse was just one of many animals rescued over the years by Lake, who once performed mouth-to-snout resuscitation on a dog he'd pulled out of frozen Prospect Park Lake, comrades remembered at a wake in his lifelong neighborhood of Bay Ridge, in Brooklyn.

A Harley-Davidson lover, too, Lake was remembered by 700 motorcyclists from all over the tri-state area who rode to the firehouse in a memorial benefit.

But Lake, 44, was better known for his passionate dedication to saving human lives. The 20-year veteran had suffered hearing loss from rescue scuba dives, and chemicals encountered on another call had burned the skin of his hands. Lake wanted to put in at least another five years before taking retirement, said his former wife, Dorothy Lake, with whom he had reconciled.

"His saying was, 'Pain is just weakness leaving the body,'" she recalled.

Retired firefighter Richard Evers, a friend, remembered Lake's intense commitment when the two went to Oklahoma City as part of a rescue and recovery team.

A group of federal Drug Enforcement Administration agents was standing vigil at the Oklahoma site, refusing to budge until their partner was brought out of the wreckage. They pointed to the spot where he'd been when the building blew, a perilous, hard-to-reach spot beneath what firefighters came to call the "Mother Slab" of precariously dangling concrete.

Lake, Evers and their partners went to work and got the agent's remains out within a couple of hours. They stood silently at attention as the dead man's colleagues carried him away.

"This was just one of the victim removals we were involved in, but for some reason we took this very personal," Lake recalled in a diary-type account called "Random Thoughts on Oklahoma," an experience he said "made you proud to be an American."

A month after the trade center attack, another group of recovery workers stood at attention as Lake's own company members carried his flag-wrapped remains from the wreckage. They circulated that essay at his wake.

Lake's recovery brought closure, at least, to a grueling month of uncertainty for his 7-year-old son, Kyler. The boy had finally called Evers, his godfather, demanding to take part in the recovery effort.

"He didn't think they were doing a good enough job," Dorothy Lake said. "Every night, he kept saying, 'Daddy's waiting for me.'"

THOMAS GARDNER
A Nature Lover and a Natural Comic

He had tackled tenement fires in Harlem and chemical spills in Queens for his living, but Thomas Gardner spent his days off teaching children for free at the Bronx Zoo.

The 39-year-old firefighter earned a college degree in biology and education during his 17 years with the New York City Fire Department and planned a second career as a high school science teacher.

"His first love was science and nature and animals," Gardner's wife, Liz, said from their home in Oceanside, where Gardner, 39, had an occasional job as a substitute teacher before joining Haz-Mat Company 1.

As a single man, Gardner had nursed injured birds back to health as a member of Volunteers for Wildlife. That hobby gave way to fatherhood, and Amy, 9, and Christopher, 6, are keeping only frogs at home right now, their mother said.

As a firefighter, Gardner had specialized training on a spectrum of toxic threats, including anthrax, and flew to many parts of the country teaching law enforcement agencies to handle those dangers.

A hockey fan, he played the game in Long Beach with a lifelong group of friends from all over Long Island. He also had a gift for comedy. Before joining the fire department, he worked briefly as an administrative assistant at NBC, and sold jokes to Joan Rivers, Phyllis Diller and Henny Youngman.

Haz-Mat Company 1 friend John Larocchia is himself a stand-up comic who had begun a radio show on Long Island's tiny WGBB. Gardner played his straight man on the show. And the two had just finished a treatment for a TV comedy on firemen.

Gardner had endured building collapses, burns and other firefighting injuries during 12 years with Engine Company 59 in Harlem. Firefighters in Squad 288, which shares a Maspeth firehouse with Haz-Mat Company 1, had been pestering him to join them because of his experience. On September 11, 18 people were lost from those two companies, the worst losses in the department citywide.

"He felt a tremendous amount of guilt being in Haz-Mat, because they don't go to fires—he was always struggling with whether he was in the right place," Liz Gardner said. "He was always the person that people went to to help solve a problem."

MICHAEL KIEFER
Firefighting Was All He Talked About

Bud Kiefer doesn't know exactly how it started.

It may have begun when Michael was 3. On weekends while his wife worked, Kiefer kept his son entertained by taking him to the local firehouse. "Maybe that stuck," he said. "I think it's just something that's in you, it's just part of your makeup. This was all he ever talked about."

Whatever the origin, Michael Kiefer was crazy about firefighting. Growing up, the boy would set up imaginary fire scenes on his Franklin Square block, enlisting his younger sister Lauren as his probationary firefighter. He drew "FDNY" on all his schoolbooks and read firefighting manuals for fun.

When he was old enough to ride a bike, Michael would chase fires he heard about over a police scanner. At least once, a police officer had to escort him home when a fire took the boy into a rough neighborhood.

In his teens, he joined the Franklin Square junior firefighters' organization and quickly became its chief. But the quiet neighborhood didn't satisfy Michael's craving for adventure, his father said. He joined the Malverne association, and then—still in search of action—joined the Freeport volunteer firefighters. He later switched to the Hempstead department.

Kiefer's devotion to firefighting was nearly matched by his interest in religion, his parents said. Even as a teenager, Kiefer attended mass with his mother every Saturday and served as a eucharistic minister at St. Catherine of Sienna Church in Franklin Square.

One of the priests there likes to tell a story about him, his mother said. "One of the priests had known how religious he was," she recalled. "So he said, 'Did you ever think of becoming a priest?'"

Though his mother said he had briefly considered the clergy, his response was firm. "You save the souls," he told the priest. "I'll save the bodies."

After graduating from St. Mary's High School in Manhasset in 1994, Kiefer joined the fire cadet program at John Jay College of Criminal Justice, which ended in a job with the New York City Fire Department as a paramedic.

Kiefer's dream was now within reach. After working as a paramedic for about a year and a half, he took the promotional exam to become a firefighter.

"By this time, he'd been studying all his life," his father said. "Every book he had in his bedroom has something to do with the fire department."

Kiefer scored 100 percent on both the physical and written exams. In December 2000, Kiefer became a "probie," or probationary firefighter, and joined the Engine Company 280/Ladder Company 132 firehouse in Crown Heights. It was a dream assignment, his father said. "He knew he wanted to go to Brooklyn. That was where all the action was."

As Kiefer headed toward the burning World Trade Center on the morning of September 11,

many pieces of his life were coming together. His family, which also includes another sister, Kerri, had no doubt that Kiefer, 25, planned to marry his girlfriend, Jamie Huggler.

"He finally met the person he wanted to spend the rest of his life with," said his mother, Pat Kiefer. "I guess he was saving for a ring."

DURRELL PEARSALL
A Fearless Teddy Bear Who Kept the Beat

 When Durrell Valentine Pearsall joined his friends in the Emerald Society Pipe Band on trips to Ireland to play, old men would stare in amazement at the olive-skinned, 300-pound drummer, saying, "God bless your size!"

But the Irish half of the Rescue Company 4 firefighter knew more songs from that land than anyone else in the New York City Fire Department, it seemed, and was hammy enough to sing them all.

"We'd be somewhere blowing off some steam and he'd jump up and start an Irish song, and we'd all join in on them," recalled his bandmate and fellow Rescue 4 firefighter, Liam Flaherty. "He was a job icon. He was larger than life."

But if "Bronko" Pearsall's loss has been so keenly felt by the band that a special memorial is likely, it is stirring reaction in many other quarters. Captain of the fire department's football team, a Nassau fire safety educator and a decorated Hempstead firefighter, Pearsall is remembered as a fearless Gentle Ben, a "teddy bear," a "puppy dog," who always made time for kids.

The Hempstead Fire Department is raising money to endow an athletic scholarship at Long Island University's C.W. Post Campus in memory of its former offensive tackle, who played there from 1988 to 1991.

Bronko, 38, grew up in Hempstead playing on fire trucks as the son of Durrell Pearsall Sr., a 57-year member of that fire department. His mother, Carmela, nicknamed him after 1930s football great Bronko Nagurski, because he was so big she thought his destiny lay in sports.

Pearsall graduated from C.W. Post in 1992, thinking he'd be a gym teacher. He coached junior varsity sports in New Hyde Park for a year before joining the city fire department. But all along, he'd been a Hempstead volunteer firefighter. He received two medals of valor, for pulling a woman out of a burning apartment window and for crawling under a car to free a trapped child, said Deputy Chief George Sandas.

In the city, he put his football skills to use as co-captain of the department team, enduring the annual loss to the police department's team at a charity game for the Widows and Orphans Fund.

He had a way about him that made people want to be near him, many friends recalled. So when Pearsall got a Screen Actors Guild card and a spot opposite legendary Jets coach Bill Parcells in a Tostitos commercial two years ago, friends from the band and the team trekked to Brother Jimmy's Bar on Third Avenue in Manhattan to watch it.

There lay Bronko on a football training table with the coach, munching away on Tostitos. There sat Bronko on the bench, rocking to the Rascals song "Groovin."

"We all jumped up and cheered," Flaherty said.

MICHAEL WEINBERG
His Sister Worked in the Towers

Firefighter Michael Weinberg, 34, of Maspeth, was off duty, eagerly anticipating a 9:08 a.m. tee time at Forest Park Golf Course on September 11, a perfect, sunlit day for golf. As he waited at the clubhouse for his starting time, Weinberg heard reports that a plane had crashed into the World Trade Center.

Weinberg had two reasons for throwing his clubs into the back of his sport utility vehicle and rushing into lower Manhattan. First was his loyalty to the New York City Fire Department. Second was his devotion to his sister, Patricia Gambino, who worked on the 72nd floor of Two World Trade Center. "They saw him running to the car, flying out of there," said Gambino, a Morgan Stanley employee.

"He flew . . . For the life of me, I don't know how he got there so quickly," said Gambino, who managed to escape the inferno by taking an elevator from her office down to the 44th floor, a main elevator lobby. Then she worked her way down the stairs and walked away.

Weinberg apparently stopped at his station house—Engine 1, Ladder 24, at 142 West 31st Street—and drove to the complex with the Reverend Mychal Judge, the fire department's chaplain, and Captain Daniel Brethel of Farmingville, who died alongside Weinberg as they sought cover under a truck when the towers collapsed. The family believes that Judge administered last rites to Weinberg before they both perished.

Weinberg grew up in Maspeth and attended St. John's University on a baseball scholarship. A center fielder, he was named Big East Most Valuable Player in 1988, according to his father, Morton Weinberg. Weinberg then joined the Detroit Tigers organization, playing Triple A baseball in both Niagara Falls and Fayetteville, North Carolina. An avid all-round athlete, Weinberg also worked as a lifeguard and trainer.

Handsome and well-built, Weinberg modeled and was featured in the fire department's calendar. "Everywhere he went, people would say he was striking, but he was more beautiful inside," said Gambino, adding, "He was just an incredible human being and that's why he is with God now."

WILLIAM WIK
He Knew the Risks and Tried to Help

The rescue workers who pulled William Wik from the World Trade Center ruins figured he was a firefighter. He wore the same gloves as the five firemen he was found with, and a flashlight and radio lay near his body, his wife said.

But Wik, 44, worked on the 92nd floor of Tower Two for Aon Corporation and apparently had volunteered to help emergency workers when he was killed. His wife, Kathleen Wik, counts herself among the lucky because his body was recovered and properly buried a few days after the attack.

"I got him back because he helped the firemen," Kathleen Wik said. "That was my gift for his bravery."

Wik was an assistant director in risk-management services for Aon—a job he had started in May 2001. He spent his weekends and free time with his children—Tricia, 16, Katie, 12, and Danny, 8—and whatever athletic or musical activities they were involved in. "At this point in our lives, our hobbies were the kids," Kathleen Wik said.

New York City police officers delivered Wik's wallet and wedding band to his Yonkers home. His wife said her own farewell to her husband, touching the rose tattoo on his upper left arm before his funeral.

She laughed about the tattoo, something her husband had done in his youth that he tried to hide under long-sleeved shirts as an adult.

"No one would believe he had a tattoo because he looked so conservative," Kathleen Wik said. "He was quiet and unassuming." Now she plans to get a similar rose tattoo of her own.

ROBERT MCMAHON
A Man of Many Charms

Sorting through photos for her husband Robert's wake in November 2001, Julie McMahon was struck by how hard it was to find an image of him standing alone. The Woodside firefighter always seemed to be hugging or kissing or goofing around with one or another of the 2,000 people who would later come to mourn him—and he was always in motion.

Carpenter, photographer, golfer, chef and volunteer at a camp for sick kids, McMahon had also just finished gutting and renovating the family home in preparation for the birth of their second child. Patrick Robert McMahon was born on January 6, 2002.

"He looks like my husband around the eyes," said Julie, nursing the new baby while speaking on the phone. "He kind of brought us a new focus and allowed me to have something positive in my life for the first time in a while. But it's bittersweet, too." The couple's older son, Matthew Clifford McMahon, turned 2 in February 2002.

Her husband, Julie said, "had a very special way of making everyone feel like a friend. . . . He put so many things in his life of 35 years that most people will never put into 70 years."

Working at Manhattan's Ladder Company 20 on Lafayette Street is a job with many charms for a firefighter, and McMahon sampled most of them during his nine years with the department.

Little Italy is part of its territory, and that meant sweet sausage from Dom the butcher and fresh pasta from Raffetto's. McMahon knew the merchants of the neighborhood by name and would pick up extra mozzarella and ravioli to take home

to his wife in Woodside. McMahon's lasagna was highlighted two years ago in a *GQ* magazine article on "guy food."

"You've got to use fresh Italian parsley," he told *GQ*. "It's the fresh ingredients women love."

SoHo also comes under Ladder 20's protection, and McMahon was working toward a bachelor's degree in fine arts, studying painting and photography. During his years on Lafayette Street, he witnessed the neighborhood's transformation from industrial district to style center at close range.

"He loved being so close to all the galleries," his wife said. "Going in to do fire inspections, he got to see some really neat places."

McMahon also had a big heart. After the younger brother of a friend died of leukemia, he volunteered for two weeks as a counselor at Happiness Is Camping, a special camp for kids with cancer, in Blairstown, New Jersey. There, he met Julie, a pediatric cancer nurse at Memorial Sloan-Kettering Cancer Center, who quickly won his heart. The two married $2^1/_2$ years ago, but they continued helping out at the camp and formed tight bonds with a number of the kids there, who stayed in touch with them year-round.

"I've gotten so many phone calls from concerned children since this happened," Julie McMahon said. "They were calling to comfort me as well."

GLENN WINUK
A Lawyer Drawn to Firefighting

He was a partner in a law firm, but Glenn Winuk had another passion.

"He worked hard to be an attorney and a partner in a good law firm," said his brother, Jay, "but his passion, his real passion, is firefighting. From the time we were in grade school, sharing a bedroom together, this was his thing."

Winuk, a Jericho native and former member of that community's volunteer fire department, was last seen by his colleagues heading toward the Twin Towers from the Broadway office of Holland & Knight shortly after the two airliners struck the World Trade Center. Witnesses said the 40-year-old attorney took gloves and a mask from passing firefighters and headed toward the disaster scene, just a block and a half away.

It was the same thing he had done in 1993, when terrorists set off a bomb in the center's basement. It was the same thing he had done countless times over 20 years as a Jericho firefighter. It was the last time his colleagues saw him.

"He was clearly on his way to go help," Winuk's brother, Jay, said. "He may have just jumped in and started working. He was there very soon after the planes, and probably sometime before the towers fell."

Jay Winuk said Glenn, 40, had been drawn to firefighting since his early childhood, when he and his brothers, Jay and Jeff, would take turns on the fire pole at the New York City firehouse where their uncle, firefighter Harold Einhorn, was stationed.

Winuk, a graduate of Hofstra Law School, was a former member of the Jericho Fire Department, where he had served for 20 years and had reached the rank of lieutenant. He received his undergraduate degree from SUNY Oneonta. He lived in Manhattan and had worked at Holland & Knight for 13 years.

Jericho Fire Chief David Ginzburg said that Winuk was extremely loyal and always eager to help. "It's no surprise to hear that he ran right in there," Ginzburg said. "He probably just looked for somebody who needed help getting out of the building."

Jay Winuk said he tried to call Glenn immediately after watching live images of the second plane striking the second tower. "My hope initially was that I would have a chance to talk to him before he went down there," Jay said. "But if I had got him on the phone, it wouldn't have stopped him from going."

DENNIS CROSS
He Shared the Danger with His Men

Dennis Cross wasn't the type to linger outside a burning building. At the beginning of his 37-year career with the New York City Fire Department, Cross had asked to be transferred to a busy company because he wanted to respond to more fires. His wife, JoAnn, knew this. So did his lifelong best friend, Brian O'Flaherty, a fellow battalion chief.

When O'Flaherty rushed to the World Trade Center on September 11, he knew Cross was already there. When the south tower crumbled around him, O'Flaherty knew Cross was most likely deep in the building. "When I am in the ambulance and leaving the scene, I had this bad feeling that Dennis did not make it," said O'Flaherty, 59, from his home in Rockville Centre, where he was recovering from his injuries. "He would go in as far as anybody."

Watching television that day at home in Islip Terrace, JoAnn Cross knew, too, that her 60-year-old husband was lost. "He had a saying that he loved. He'd say, 'Take care of men, and men will take care of you,'" she said. Part of taking care of his men, she said, was to go into the fires with them.

While some men his age left the department or considered retiring, Cross—the chief of Battalion 57—spent his free time running, biking and lifting weights to make sure he was fit enough to extend his career as long as possible. "He loved the job, and he was damn good at it," his wife said. "He didn't want to ever retire."

O'Flaherty called Cross "one of the most knowledgeable chiefs in the department," but said Cross never wanted to go for the promotion to deputy chief because that meant fewer chances to charge into burning buildings and less attachment to his men. "He knew that corner of Bedford-Stuyvesant where he worked better than probably anyone in the department," O'Flaherty said. "The department doesn't know what it has lost."

"He wanted to be a fireman since I met him when I was a kid," said JoAnn Cross, who met her future husband through friends when she was 12 and he was 15. Three years later, they started dating. Cross took the firefighter's exam after high school, then fought in Vietnam with the Army. Upon returning home, he married JoAnn and was assigned to Engine Company 2 in Manhattan. He and JoAnn raised three daughters, Lisa, Laura and Denise.

Cross and O'Flaherty grew up together in Queens, where they used to talk about their dads, both firemen, who both died young. They worked together 11 years, at Ladder Company 105 and Ladder Company 102, both in Brooklyn. Although they never worked together after 1979, the two men stayed close, spending time with each other's family, skiing upstate and sailing in Cross' boat on the Great South Bay.

When he was frustrated with things at work, such as a requirement that all firefighters wear masks (he thought it gave a false sense of security), Cross would unwind on a jog with his wife or by throwing the baseball with his son Brian, 29, a city firefighter.

O'Flaherty likes to think that his friend is in heaven, talking about firefighting with Cross' father, who died from a heart attack after battling a major fire when Cross was 13. "He probably told his father all the new tactics they now use in the department," O'Flaherty said. "They probably laugh at it all, because nothing has changed. The fireman still crawls into the building to put out the fire the same way as 50 years ago."

RAYMOND DOWNEY
"He Did What He Had to Do"

Some things you learn about people only after they've gone. For the family of Raymond Downey, the manila folder was like that.

Downey headed the New York City Fire Department's special operations command and was one of the most decorated firefighters in the city. From his ruddy complexion to his habit of running into smoky buildings without a mask, Downey seemed to many of his colleagues to represent the very essence of what it meant to be a firefighter—so much so that some of them jokingly called him "God."

But he never boasted about his accomplishments to his family, never reveled in the praise that seemed to follow him wherever he went.

Except for the manila folder he carried in his briefcase, that is. The folder was the only indulgence Downey allowed himself. He stuffed it with letters and accolades from a 39-year career and gave it a label in a small, tidy script: "That A Boys."

His wife, Rosalie, found the folder after Downey was lost in the World Trade Center attack. "He never complimented himself," she said. "He always just did what he had to do."

But the people who knew the 63-year-old chief, the firefighters who worked with him, didn't share Downey's reluctance to cite his achievements.

His knowledge of how buildings fall apart was so legendary that at national firefighting conferences, whole rooms would go quiet when he walked in. "He was idolized," said Hal Bruno, chairman of the National Fallen Firefighters Foundation.

His expertise was sought not only within the five boroughs of New York City but at disasters around the country. Downey directed recovery work at the Oklahoma City disaster and in the 1993 bombing of the World Trade Center. He also helped pioneer an urban search-and-rescue program that mobilizes local firefighters to respond to disasters nationwide.

Fellow firefighters said Downey had a knack for instantly assessing a disaster scene and coming up with a novel solution. In Oklahoma, one of the biggest obstacles to rescuers was a giant concrete slab they had dubbed "Mother" that dangled precariously amid the wreckage. Downey thought the slab should be cinched up against the side of the building. Engineers and other experts disagreed, offering their own suggestions. In the end, "We eventually did what Ray told us to do," said Gary Marrs, the recently retired chief of the Oklahoma City Fire Department.

Downey also made frequent trips to Washington, serving on a congressional advisory panel on domestic terrorism. In an interview with *Newsday* in 1997, he warned that the next war would be fought in an urban setting. For Downey, said Joe Allbaugh, director of the Federal Emergency Management Agency, "it wasn't a matter of if, it was a matter of when."

An ex-Marine, Downey joined the department in 1962 and served in two midtown ladder companies before joining Brooklyn's Rescue 2, an elite unit charged with rescuing endangered firefighters. In 1972, he was promoted to lieutenant and assigned to an engine-and-ladder company in East Harlem that earned the nickname "the Fire Factory" because it fought so many blazes.

In 1980, after advancing to captain and serving in other units, Downey returned to Rescue 2 as its leader.

"He was the best fire officer I've ever known," said John Barbagallo, a retired firefighter who worked in Rescue 2 with Downey. "And when you have a good leader, you'd follow him into hell."

To his five children—Fire Lieutenant Chuck Downey of Commack, Fire Captain Joseph Downey of West Islip, Ray Downey Jr. of Babylon, Marie Tortorici of Deer Park and Kathy Ugalde of Deer Park—Downey was a strict yet loving father who kept his work separate from his family life and encouraged them to channel their energy into sports. When they were growing up, Downey would sometimes work longer shifts just so he could make it to a son's wrestling match or a daughter's soccer game.

"He always had that Marine attitude—that tough exterior," said his son Ray, a physical-education teacher. "But once you got behind that, he really was a softie."

Downey was last seen in the Marriott hotel after the first tower had collapsed. He may have been heading to the second tower to evacuate firefighters when it came down, Chuck Downey said.

It may seem darkly ironic that a man who achieved international acclaim for his familiarity with rubbled disasters would himself die in one. But to his family and friends, it makes perfect sense. When a situation turned deadly, Downey would often order his men out just as he was running in.

Sometimes, Rosalie Downey says, she still talks to her husband, a man she met more than 40 years ago when they flirted through a glass partition in a Manhattan bank. She asks him why he didn't stay out when he led other firefighters to safety that day.

But, she says, she knows better than that. "Then I tell myself, Ray would have never lived with himself."

4
Lost Promises

The death toll spread across the fabric of the future—snuffing out so much promise, so many goals left unachieved, so many children left fatherless and motherless. More than 3,000 children from at least 555 communities as far away as Australia lost a parent. A father who wanted nothing so much as to start a special school for autistic children like his son. Or a mother who was "on a rocket going up"—rising from waitress to stockbroker and all the while keeping her two sons at the center of her life.

The lost promise was numbing. A 21-year-old two months out of college who had just started training at an investment firm and had the world in front of him, a benefits specialist who was on the way to becoming a pastry chef, a young woman who captured the thoughts and emotions on the faces of her fellow commuters in her sketchbook but whose life was cut short before she could prove herself as an artist.

And a young economist who exuded love. During her memorial service, a storm was gusting. Then the people who knew her started talking about her joy for life. And sunlight flooded the church.

RICHARD ARONOW
He Dreamed of a School for Autistic Kids

For Richard Aronow, the joys of life were simple and basic. They centered on his family and a dream for the future: establishing a school for autistic children like his son.

"Richard's deep love for his family governed his life," said his wife of nearly 13 years, Laura Weinberg. "He quietly devoted himself to his autistic son and concern for his future." Their son, William, was 4 on the day of the attack, and Laura said the couple shared a dream of someday starting a special school staffed by experts in the field, "which could teach Willie and other autistic children.

"Willie began to learn sign language through talented teachers at home this summer," she said, noting that her husband also started to pick up the skill and knew a number of signing gestures. One day, when her husband was leaving for work, she said, he and Willie both signed their goodbyes. "It was heartening to see," she said.

Aronow, 48, of Mahwah, New Jersey, was a deputy chief in the legal department of the Port Authority who worked on the 66th floor of the trade center's Tower One. He had worked at the PA for 18 years. "He was an ethical and knowledgeable lawyer," his wife said. "He made friends with and coached people on all sides of any deal." She said he was very proud of his achievements, especially of working on regional development projects for the Port Authority.

Though William has great difficulty with spoken language, he often reached out to his father, who "made great efforts to help his son develop," Weinberg said.

Aronow was a student of history with a particular interest in Asia, and he was a world traveler for many years. With his wife and son, he had visited such places as Hong Kong and Thailand. Though recently they had stayed closer to home for the sake of William's health, they still loved to take trips together, even if just to a nearby park or river, or to the Twin Towers.

On the morning of September 11, Aronow kissed his wife goodbye as she dozed and left for his job. Around 9 that morning, his son saw a flash of the unfolding disaster on television. He walked to his room, looked up at the woman who was watching him and made the sign for sad.

CARRIE PROGEN
Portrait of an Aspiring Artist

By day, Carrie Progen worked as an administrative assistant at Aon's offices high atop the World Trade Center. But her real work began on the subway ride home, when the 25-year-old artist got out her sketchbook to capture the subtle shifts of thought and emotion she saw playing across the faces of her unsuspecting fellow commuters.

"It's like she had two lives," said her boyfriend, Erik Sharkey. They met in 1995 at Brooklyn's Pratt Institute—she was studying illustration; Sharkey was working on a film degree—and began dating a year later. Progen's day job was just that, he said, a way to pay the bills while she worked as a freelance illustrator and tried to figure out how to break into the art world. At night, she spent long hours painting in the tiny one-bedroom apartment they shared in Fort Greene.

In high school, Progen told her older brother Matthew's art teacher, "You've got the wrong Progen in your class, because I'm the one who's going to be an artist." After graduating, she set out, with typical gumption, to be just that. New York, with its high rents and relentless competition, is a hard proving ground for struggling young artists. Both Progen and Sharkey ended up grudgingly taking office jobs to support their artistic endeavors—he produces videos for corporate clients such as Lehman Brothers. But that didn't sour her enthusiasm for life in the big city.

"We were always laughing and going out, always spontaneous," said Sharkey, a Bronx native who turned Progen, originally from Ashburnham, Massachusetts, into a Yankees fan. One of her favorite activities was people-watching at jazz clubs and quintessentially New York events like the Mermaid Parade in Coney Island and the Festival of San Gennaro in Little Italy. "She wanted to soak up that atmosphere," he said.

Being here was the culmination of Progen's small-town dreams. "She wanted to have an exciting life, and she wanted diversity," her boyfriend said. The daughter of an assistant district attorney, Progen came from a very traditional family, but "she had her own goals," said her mother, Kathy Progen. "She had her own way of thinking about everything." Still, said Sharkey, for Progen to go from Ashburnham, population 5,000, to New York was "gutsy."

That was her hallmark. A martial arts enthusiast who spent 10 to 12 hours each week studying jeet kune do, Progen challenged herself to be the best in her class by taking on her male classmates, "and she didn't want them to pull any punches," Sharkey said with a laugh. "She was tough."

But not with him. Living with Progen was like "the slumber party that never ended," Sharkey said. "We always talked about growing old together." Her mother said that Progen didn't want kids, but was set on being "the favorite aunt" to her 1-year-old nephew, Kael.

That plan was cut short by the September 11 attacks on the trade center. Sharkey, who worked nearby at the World Financial Center, spoke with his girlfriend after the first plane hit. She said she was evacuating, but she failed to make it down from her office on the 100th floor before the south tower collapsed.

"It's like a huge part of me has gone with her," Sharkey said. For him, one of the hardest things to bear is the knowledge that Progen's life was cut short before she got the chance to prove herself as an artist. "One of her dreams was to have a really good Manhattan art show," he said. So he put together a posthumous exhibit of her work on November 17, 2001, at Anderson's Martial Arts Academy in Manhattan, the studio where she studied. Said Sharkey, "I wanted to give her a night for her."

HECTOR TIRADO JR.
An Orphan Who Looked After His Siblings

 At the age of 30, Hector Tirado Jr. was a rookie firefighter—a "probie," still on probation—when he ran into Tower One. But his short life had been fuller, and harder, than many twice as long.

At 15, orphaned along with his three younger siblings, Tirado took the weight of the world on his shoulders. His mother had died several years earlier, and, when he lost his father, Tirado moved the family in with their uncles and aunt. "He would not go to sleep until his brothers had eaten,"

recalled his uncle, Robert Tirado, 49. "We would tell him, 'Hector, we'll take care of that. Why don't you go to bed? You have work tomorrow.' But he wasn't like that." After a difficult upbringing, Tirado was accustomed to looking out for the younger kids, his uncle said. "Hector was a very sad little boy," he said. As Hector got older, he said, "He told us he never wanted to be without a family."

At 18, when he graduated from high school, Tirado got a job as a waiter, and moved his small family—his brothers, Angel and Sean, and sister, Marina—to an apartment in the East Bronx. A year later, he had a family court declare him legal guardian to his three siblings. "His goal was to have all his brothers together and try to build up the family," his uncle said.

There were tough times and large hurdles to overcome, his uncle said. Tirado's brother Sean was at one point placed in a group home because of his truancy from school, for instance. But when Tirado became their guardian, "It made a difference, because the kids never got into trouble anymore," his uncle said. After a couple of years, Tirado's grandparents offered to take in the younger children.

Tirado joined the U.S. Army and was posted in Panama. He returned a year later, and met his future wife, Sheneque Jackson. They had five children, ranging in age from 6 to 13 when he died—Devon, Denzel, Ronald, Ashley and Hector III. "He was very happy in that time," said his uncle. "They sort of became the family that he really wanted." The couple divorced five years ago, his uncle said, and the children now live with their mother in Ohio.

Tirado had always worked, his uncle said. Since he was in high school, when he worked in a shoe store and did construction jobs, "Hector was always employed. People liked him, so he always had a job," his uncle said.

But it was only in the past couple of years that Tirado found his calling. It was about two years ago that he became an emergency medical technician, and then, 1½ years ago, he became a firefighter at Engine Company 23 on Manhattan's West Side. "He loved being a firefighter," his uncle said. "He said, 'I'm beginning to live. I feel so full of energy.'"

And indeed, things were looking up for the young man who had spent so many of his years taking care of others. He planned to finish college and then go to medical school to become a doctor. He had just bought a co-op in the East Bronx. And, his uncle said, "He told me that he wanted to meet the woman of his dreams.

"He was sort of at the beginning of his life," his uncle said. "He was at that point in his life that he was beginning to live and see that there's more to the world than just sadness."

JENNIFER FIALKO
She Beat Hodgkin's and Eased Others' Pain

 Jennifer Fialko was such a survivor, her roommate Linda Hannan said, that she couldn't possibly be missing.

The three years after her Hodgkin's disease subsided into remission were the most fulfilling of Fialko's life. She started a home-based therapeutic oils business, hoping to ease the pain of other cancer sufferers with alternative therapies, the same way she eased her own. She lived her life more fully and simply—spending time with friends and family, becoming a vegetarian and practicing yoga. "She really looked at her illness as a gift," said her mother, Evelyn Fialko, of River Edge, New Jersey.

The Teaneck, New Jersey, resident had just met a man who she told her brother was the love of her life, and corresponded with him in Chicago by phone and e-mail. And after taking computer classes, Fialko, 29, started a new job with the client-services department at Aon Corporation in August 2001.

When the first plane hit Tower One on September 11, Fialko ran the city block across the 92nd floor of Tower Two to the west side of the building and felt the explosion's heat through the window. At 8:59 a.m. she called her new love and said, "I've got to get out of here." At 9:03, the second plane hit the tower she was in.

Her father, Robert, said his daughter lived a full life. Fialko had been a co-captain of the field hockey and softball teams at River Dell High School in Oradell, New Jersey, was fluent in Spanish and Portuguese and had traveled in Europe and South America. She played field hockey on a team as an adult. But Robert Fialko said he is most grateful for his daughter's sweet spirit and indomitable generosity.

During her illness, she stuck Post-it notes with cheery messages on them in her mother's date-book to take Evelyn Fialko's mind off the doctor's appointments she penciled in. When Jennifer recovered, she visited other cancer patients in hospitals to listen and to comfort. "'You are worthy without any proof.' She used to say that all the time," Robert Fialko said. "I think her goal was to cure the world."

MARINA GERTSBERG
They Thought She Was Safe Here

 Marina Gertsberg seemed to have everything going for her: brains, beauty, athletic and musical skills and an unaffected charm that won her instant friends. She also had an adventuresome spirit.

This led her parents, Roman and Anna, to worry often about the safety of their only child. "Marina wanted to go back to Odessa to see the place where she was born," her mother said. "But I told her this is not a good time. It's not safe there now." The family had emigrated from the Ukrainian city, then part of the Soviet Union, when Gertsberg was 4, so that her father wouldn't have to serve with the Soviet forces in Afghanistan. They settled in Howard Beach.

Gertsberg, 25, had graduated from the Mark Twain School for the Gifted and Talented in Brooklyn, Stuyvesant High School in Manhattan and SUNY Binghamton. She spoke Hebrew and had studied Russian so she could communicate with her grandparents. She also talked of studying in Israel, but her parents were leery of that, too. "We thought this is the safest country in the world," Anna Gertsberg said of her adopted country.

A thoughtful daughter, Gertsberg, who had her own apartment in Brooklyn, called her parents at 10 p.m. on September 10 to assure them that she was safe at home. It was the last they heard from her. Gertsberg had recently changed jobs because she had enrolled in a graduate program at Baruch College, her mother said, and her former employer, Morgan Stanley, wouldn't adjust her schedule so she could attend classes. So the next morning she was at work as a junior manager at Cantor Fitzgerald on the 101st floor of Tower One when the hijacked plane struck. She had been on the job only seven days.

MARK ELLIS
A Birth Put His Life in Fast Forward

Just a couple of weeks before the World Trade Center attacks, Mark Ellis was visiting another police officer and his wife at their Commack home on Long Island. He held their days-old baby girl in his arms and, moved by the tenderness of her new life, decided to put his plans in fast forward.

Ellis, 26, told his girlfriend of six years, Stephanie Porzio, that he wanted to marry her and have a family of his own. The next week, they went shopping for rings. They went to a jewelry store, but did not settle on anything because they wanted something that would properly symbolize what they felt for each other.

That same Sunday, Ellis rode for the first time on the fishing boat he had purchased from his uncle. Ellis was nervous about handling the 24-footer, but he drove it flawlessly on Long Island Sound. With marriage plans under sail and his law enforcement career on track, Ellis was about to create the life he wanted, surrounded by his friends and relatives.

But Ellis, a transit officer in downtown Manhattan, was on Delancey Street two days later with partner Ramon Suarez when they received frantic radio calls. They commandeered a taxicab and arrived in time to help terrified people out of the World Trade Center before it crashed down on both of them. Suarez was caught in a news photograph helping someone to an ambulance. Ellis' body was recovered before the Christmas Eve weekend, not too far from where his partner had fallen.

Mayor Rudolph Giuliani attended the standing-room-only funeral, praising Ellis' courage—he had received four medals for excellence. He was also the youngest New York City police officer killed in the attack. "He was very fair and kind, and he was always there for me," said Eric Semler, his partner for more than three years. "He was a good cop, a very good cop."

So good, in fact, that a few weeks after he was lost, the call he had been awaiting came from the Secret Service: He had been accepted as a candidate to the elite force. Relatives saw that as a posthumous recognition of his dedication and valor. "Mark was making his plans to climb the career ladder, sail the Seven Seas on the boat, and God called him," said his uncle, Kenneth Nilsen. "He answered God's call, and he answered that call while helping others."

AMY TOYEN
She Was Going to Wed Her College Sweetheart

The phone calls were frantic: The kind when fingers fly over the Touch-Tone buttons and someone picks up before a greeting is formulated. Martin and Dorine Toyen dialed Thomson Financial at almost the same moment, and heard the same words from two different people. "They told us, 'We are sorry to tell you, but Amy is supposed to be on the 106th floor of World Trade Center One,'" said Amy's father, Martin. "We both broke down."

Amy Toyen, 24, of Newton, Massachusetts, was a marketing specialist for Thomson and traveled only eight days a year. Her parents knew only that she was in New York on business. When they saw the blazing towers, they called her employer.

Just two weeks before the attacks, Toyen had purchased the dress for her wedding, scheduled for next Father's Day. It was one of her father's saddest thoughts. "I said to my wife, 'At least you got to see her in her wedding dress. I don't have those memories,'" Martin Toyen said.

Amy had selected a beaded A-line dress in which to wed her fiance, Jeffrey Gonski, whom she met when she was a freshman in college. Gonski was president of the business fraternity that Toyen pledged.

In April 2001, Gonski constructed a secret plan to propose. He told her that he was planning a weekend getaway instead of a weeklong trip to Ireland. Toyen bugged him for the itinerary for weeks. Finally, the day they left, he gave her a booklet: Do you like . . . things that are green? slow cars? . . . turn the page . . . and there she saw "depart Boston for Shannon airport."

When they arrived, it was raining. But as they drove through the valleys to a bed and breakfast in Killarney, the sun came out. They passed a tiny lake and Gonski stopped. It was time. "From that time on, she was absolutely radiant," said Toyen's father. "She was just absolutely in love."

As a child, Toyen played piano and drew pencil sketches. As an adult, she was outgoing, but quiet, Gonski said, and her demeanor belied her drive.

"I had seen her determination, but I don't think a lot of people saw that side of her," Gonski said. Today, he is comforted by Toyen's other sides. He has found a little treasure in her journals, a window into her world that gives him a lasting view of their life together.

NICOLE MILLER
A Last Kiss Goodbye

Nicole Miller, 21, a sophomore on the dean's list at West Valley College in Saratoga, California, was working her way through school as a waitress. She had been mulling over some decisions: whether to major in business or communications, and whether to transfer to Chico State or San Jose State universities.

She never got to choose: She was killed when United Airlines Flight 93 crashed in Pennsylvania.

An outdoor and exercise enthusiast, Miller played softball at Pioneer High School in San Jose. Later she taught body-sculpting classes for workers at IBM. "She was beautiful, like model beautiful," said her sister Tiffney, 23. "She had this reddish-brown hair and warm eyes and this beautiful smile and dimples."

The sisters were almost inseparable, working at the same place, attending the same school. "We were always looking out for each other." The daughter of a retired Xerox field engineer and a dental secretary, who had divorced and remarried, Miller had a large blended family, which included a stepmother, a stepfather, four brothers and two sisters.

Miller's boyfriend, Ryan Brown, was her high school sweetheart. She had flown to New York the week before September 11 to join him on his visit with relatives after he had called and said he missed her.

At the gate to Flight 93, they kissed goodbye.

PETER O'NEILL JR.
A Scion of Finance

On July 30, 2001, just two months after his college graduation, Peter O'Neill Jr. started training for a career in finance at his uncle's firm, Sandler O'Neill & Partners, on the 104th floor of Two World Trade Center.

When the first hijacked plane hit the north tower, the 21-year-old called both his parents at their respective workplaces in Amityville at about 8:50 a.m. to let them know he was OK and not to worry. "There's smoke and papers flying everywhere. I think we're going to evacuate," he told them, according to his mother, Jeanne.

Then the second hijacked plane plowed into Tower Two. O'Neill, who was also an Amityville volunteer firefighter, was among 67 employees of Sandler O'Neill who were lost.

It would not have been unusual for Peter O'Neill, who lived with his parents, Peter Sr. and Jeanne, to make two reassuring phone calls to them amid the confusion following the attack, according to his mother. "He always worried about us worrying about him," said his mother. He would call constantly, even when he was backpacking with four friends in Europe this summer, paragliding and taking part in other adventuresome sports.

He became a junior firefighter while in the sixth grade and an official Amityville firefighter at the age of 17. "He went to as many fires as he could make," his mother said. He graduated in May 2001 with a degree in finance from Bentley College, which had included a summer internship at Sandler O'Neill. He loved the work, his mother said.

"We are a very close family," Jeanne O'Neill said. Peter was especially supportive of his younger sister and brother, Bridie, 19, and Thomas, 17, who looked up to him, she said. "There is a constant hollowness and pain in our hearts, and I don't know if it will ever go away."

YVETTE C. ANDERSON
From Restaurant to Roller Coaster, She Aimed High

If Yvette Anderson's friends sometimes mistook her for the Energizer Bunny, a glance at her schedule would explain why.

By day, the 53-year-old was a keyboard specialist with the New York State Department of Taxation and Finance on the 87th floor of Tower Two. By night, she was chasing a bachelor's degree in hospitality management. On weekends, she worked at Charles' Southern Style Kitchen in Manhattan. On Sundays, she drove a van to pick up the elderly and infirm so they could pray at the White Rock Baptist Church in Harlem. And in between there was time for her son, Marvin Jr., and daughter, Rasha McMillon, both of Harlem.

"Yvette was the kind of person who put 48 hours in a 24-hour day," said friend and co-worker Wanda Simmons. "How she did all that with her school, church and family life was beyond us."

But Yvette Anderson had her eyes on a prize. After more than a decade of night classes at New York City Technical College, Anderson was just months away from getting her degree. Next step: open a soul food restaurant in Harlem. "She probably would have been the new Sylvia," said Terrell Silver, a friend, alluding to restaurateur Sylvia Woods, who went from waitress to soul food "queen."

And, somehow, Anderson also fit friends into her crowded life.

Rajwant Walia, known at the office as Raj, recalled a fearless woman quick to defend minority rights. "She grew up tough," Walia said of Anderson, who was orphaned as a youth and reared by relatives. "I asked her, 'Don't you feel lonesome in life with no parents?' She said, 'No, I don't have time.'" Walia also recalled her friend's playful side: "She always called me Jacqueline Kennedy because I like to wear nice clothes and jewelry."

Silver began his friendship with Anderson with a conversation about religion. "She always was talking about the Lord," he said. And there was one more thing about Anderson. When it came time to test her mettle on the most hair-raising amusement rides around, she stood her ground. A "gung ho" Anderson made a beeline for the roller coasters when they went to Great Adventure in July with two other friends, Silver recalled. "That's all we did—roller coasters the whole day. We got there early in the morning and didn't leave until the park closed."

MICHELE ANN NELSON
She Had Tasted the Future

Michele Ann Nelson truly lived by the adage "Seize the day." Even as she held down a demanding full-time job as a benefits specialist with Cantor Fitzgerald, she was busy putting the pieces into place for a future business

venture, her mother, Winsome Nelson, said. Michele Ann, who regularly put in 15-hour days, dreamed of becoming a pastry chef. She had just wrapped up a 200-hour internship with the New York Restaurant School and was scheduled to graduate September 25, 2001.

"She was very motivated," her mother said. "She worked very, very hard. Anything she did, she put her whole heart and spirit into it."

Nelson, 27, was excited about her job with Cantor, her mother said, where she had been for 15 months. A Penn State graduate with a degree in industrial organizational psychology and a student of human resources at Baruch College, she believed that the position was a step in the right direction. During her internship she often didn't make it home on weekdays until after midnight. But she refused to let it get in the way of the multitude of activities she was involved in with the Linden Seventh Day Adventist Church in Queens. She used her lone week of vacation to teach Bible school. That was in addition to her regular duties as clerk, usher and deaconess, and sundry other roles including her involvement on committees for the youth and new members.

Nelson often invited her mother to share lunch with her at her 104th-floor offices in Tower One. But Winsome Nelson said the idea of being so high up that she had to change elevators made her somewhat jittery. Her daughter, she said, never expressed any concern about working near the top of the skyscraper.

ADRIANA LEGRO
She Wanted to Make It Big

At first glance, it seems that the good things in life came easily to Adriana Legro. A successful young stockbroker with a degree from Boston University, Legro loved to travel and shop, and spent her weekends biking, skiing and training for marathons.

But the successes Legro achieved in her 32 years were hard-won and precious. The youngest of four siblings, Legro lost her mother to cancer when she was 15. Because her parents, Colombian immigrants from Queens, had divorced, Legro found herself taking on many of the challenges of school and adolescence on her own.

"She struggled," said her older sister, Maria Legro, 42. "It wasn't easy, because we didn't have a lot of money."

Still, Maria said, "She wanted to make it big, and she had a lot of determination to do that."

With the support of her brother and two sisters, Legro excelled in school and went on to Boston University, where she earned a business degree. She was the only one of her siblings to graduate from college. She worked to supplement her scholarship, taking jobs ranging from catering to working for a law firm.

Legro was hired straight out of college by the investment company Dean Witter and ended up in industrial sales at Carr Futures. She was in her office on the 92nd floor of Tower One when it was hit on September 11.

Maria called her kid sister the pride of the family and said it's a consolation that she achieved so much. "But it's kind of bittersweet," Maria said. "I feel that she had so much more to do, and so much more to accomplish, and I feel that she was robbed of that at such a young age."

Legro was determined to pass on her success to those around her, and was a tireless supporter of her two nephews and one niece. She arranged for them to attend summer school and found tutoring for them when they needed it, Maria said. "It really was a dream of hers that my nephews would go to school and achieve a lot, like she did."

LISA EHRLICH
In Her Life and Career, She Overcame the Odds

About 3½ years before the attack, Lisa Caren Ehrlich began toiling as a temporary secretary for Aon Corporation at Two World Trade Center. She latched on full time, becoming a technical assistant, shouldering chores for brokers who serve corporate insurance needs. Then she met Maria-Agnes "Annie" Chee, vice president at Aon rival Marsh Finpro. In their first conversation, Ehrlich wondered aloud whether she would ever rise to become a broker.

Chee steered Ehrlich—"Lee" to her friends—to a professional group, the National Association of Insurance Women International (NAIWI). Ehrlich began going to meetings, absorbing the culture—

and seeing her future. "I held her in my palm in the beginning," her mentor said. "All I had to do was open my palm and let her fly."

Ehrlich's career took wing. She became an assistant broker, then a full broker and was promoted to assistant vice president in March 2001. In June, she was inducted as a vice president of NAIWI-New York City. "She was up and coming," Chee said. "She was on a rocket going up."

The rapid rise of the Brooklyn resident was all the more remarkable considering that not long before, Ehrlich, 36, had endured an abusive relationship and her career was waiting tables. About the same time she began at Aon, her personal life was rebounding as well, with a new marriage to Johnathan Ehrlich. And always at the center of her life were her two sons, Ryan, 13, and Myles, 12.

Determined to expose the boys to all facets of life, she took them to her office on weekends and to conferences and often studied insurance literature while they did homework at the same table. Last spring, Ehrlich and the boys set a goal to raise $500 in the March of Dimes WalkAmerica, but finished with pledges well over $1,000. In her thank-you letter, she wrote: "You have helped show my sons that the sky's the limit, that goals are not necessarily set just to be reached, but to be exceeded, and that by working together, anything can be achieved."

JOHN MURRAY
A New Father Had a Zest for Life

John Murray was a week shy of his 33rd birthday the day the Twin Towers tumbled.

He'd been bathing in the newfound glow of fatherhood for the past six months. And he was beginning to see the toil and sweat of 12-hour days blossom into a fruitful career brokering derivatives for Cantor Fitzgerald on the 104th floor of Tower One.

"John had a certain zest for life, living each day to the fullest and seldom getting caught up in the small stuff," said his wife, Rory.

Murray, of Hoboken, New Jersey, had been with the company since 1995. Before the Boston College alumnus joined the firm, he spent his summers as a lifeguard for the town of Hempstead. He started his Wall Street career learning at several financial-district firms. "He was happy to go to work every day," his wife said.

He played golf just as hard. He was equally at home on the greens as he was on the dance floor, his wife said. It was his fun-loving spirit that first caught her attention when they met seven years ago through a mutual friend.

They exchanged wedding vows in 1999. And 18 months later, with some coaching from him during the delivery, Alyson was born. His wife said their daughter brought out yet another side of her husband: the devoted dad. Despite his long work days, he was happy to change and feed her in the middle of the night, she said. "He embraced fatherhood."

Now it's as if she's in a "Twilight Zone," Rory said. And not finding her husband's body makes it even more surreal. "Aly is my saving grace," she said. "In her, all of us still have a part of John."

GIOVANNA PORRAS
Her Family's First College Graduate

Adela Romero, of South Ozone Park, left her native Peru to escape terrorism there 10 years after her first daughter, Giovanna Porras, was born in Lima. Adela, Giovanna and Giovanna's sister, Roxanna, settled in Richmond Hill, Queens, and later moved to South Ozone Park.

It was in Queens that Giovanna, 24, excelled in school, and graduated with honors from John Adams High School in South Ozone Park in 1995, said her aunt, Ruth Romero. "She always tried to do her best," her mother added.

Giovanna graduated from Baruch College in Manhattan with a bachelor's degree in business administration and accounting in March 2001. "Giovanna was the first one in our family to graduate from college," said cousin Denisse Arrunategui. "Everyone was proud."

Arrunategui said Giovanna was a motivator, role model, confidante and friend. "I didn't have too many aspirations when I was in high school," she said. "Giovanna always told me that I had to get an education. No matter what." Giovanna also helped her cousin get over her shyness, which resulted from low self-esteem, said Arrunategui, of

South Ozone Park. "When I was a kid, I was pretty husky. I was scared I would get made fun of. Giovanna always protected me. She always made me feel safe."

An accountant for General Telecom on the 83rd floor of Tower One, Giovanna Porras was last heard from in a voice-mail message that she left for her boyfriend, James Xantopolous, in which she said she had felt the impact from the first plane hitting the building, and that she was trapped.

Her aunt said that along with destroying the Twin Towers, the attacks on September 11 destroyed her niece's hopes. "Giovanna was planning to go to graduate school to earn a master's degree in accounting," her aunt said. "It's sad because she never got to realize her dreams. She had so many plans. The buildings can be rebuilt, but you can never get back those lives."

CATHERINE FAIRFAX MACRAE
Chasing Away the Clouds

Catherine Fairfax MacRae, economist and athlete, loved many things about her life, but her favorite thing in the world was swimming in the ocean, most often at Southampton, where she spent summers with her family.

"Her face would light up when we walked over the beach," said her boyfriend, Andrew Caspersen of Manhattan. "It was the one place where she felt free and at peace with God."

To say that MacRae had everything going for her would be an understatement, friends said. At 23, she was on the fast track as a stock analyst with Fred Alger Management at One World Trade Center. She had graduated magna cum laude from Princeton University, where she earned a degree in economics and a special certificate in finance. She played varsity squash, and was equally accomplished at tennis and field hockey, Caspersen said.

Beginning her career in finance, she would arrive in her office at 7:30 every morning so she could get her work done in time to have dinner with her family and spend evenings with Andrew and friends. But on the morning of September 11, on the 93rd floor of Tower One, she was in the direct path of a hijacked plane. "She never had a chance," Caspersen said.

At a memorial service attended by 1,000 friends and relatives on October 6, 2001, at St. Andrew's Dune Church in Southampton, friends talked about MacRae's achievements but "mostly about her love," Caspersen said. Cat, as she was called, "exuded love wherever she went. She wanted to make everybody happy," especially her parents, Cameron and Annie MacRae of Manhattan and Southampton, her 20-year-old sister, Annie, and friends, Caspersen said.

The couple had been dating for four years. Though not officially engaged, "we talked about our future and we were getting impatient," said Caspersen, a law student at Harvard.

For all her accomplishments, he said, MacRae was also funny and self-deprecating. She talked on the phone to her mother at least three times a day, remembered her friends with small gifts and was always on time for an appointment. She grew up in Manhattan and Southampton and graduated from the Brearley School in Manhattan, where she first showed her proficiency in math and sports, Caspersen said.

The couple last swam together in Southampton over the Labor Day weekend.

So many friends wanted to come to the memorial service that her family had a tent set up outside the church. "It was amazing," Caspersen said. "There was a gusty storm with 40-mile winds in the morning. But then it stopped, and as people began talking about Cat, sunlight flooded the church."

The First into Heaven

DENNIS DUGGAN

Father Mychal Judge

Of course fire department chaplain Father Mychal Judge— "Father Mike"—was the first of thousands of victims of the World Trade Center horror. His death certificate bears witness to his eagerness to lead the men he loved into the crumbling towers. It has the number 00001.

No surprise there. Certainly not to the Reverend Michael Duffy of Philadelphia, Judge's hand-picked homilist at a moving, three-hour Mass of Christian Burial that I attended in September 2001, after the attack.

Duffy, a longtime pal of the dashing, impossibly handsome Franciscan friar, said that "I think he planned it so he could be the first to lead the other firefighters into heaven and I see him now standing before the pearly gates with that big, Irish smile of his welcoming the rest of the firefighters."

I first met Judge in the summer of 1991 when robbers stole money from St. Francis of Assisi, the West 31st Street home of the Franciscans. The friars are noticed in a town that celebrates the latest in fashions for their cloaks and cassocks and leather sandals.

He was then 58 and his hair was silvery, his face tanned and his look one of perpetual bemusement. A lot of people glow, but Judge glittered.

He was angry at the thieves, or "thugs," as he called them, because the money was raised to celebrate the feast of St. Anthony. It was to have been used to serve the 500 homeless people who showed up each morning for food or AIDS counseling. But Judge was still able to squeeze a bit of humor out of the robbery.

"I guess St. Anthony was tired from all the partying the day before and he wasn't able to guard the money," he quipped.

With the help of former governor Mario Cuomo, a fan of Judge's, the money was raised from friends all over the city.

From that first meeting on, I kept an eye on Judge because he seemed steeped in the drama of the city and of his own life, which began on Dean Street in Brooklyn, where he shined shoes to help his Irish immigrant family make ends meet.

He was intellectually gifted, loved sports— especially his Knicks, who played a few steps west of his church home—and he had friends in high and low places whom he treated with equal respect.

Some of them were at his burial mass. There was former president Bill Clinton and his wife, Senator Hillary Clinton, who had dined with Judge in the White House, and outside there was Henry, a homeless man who came to St. Francis for the food it served to the poor.

Judge took Henry under his wing. "Henry drinks a pint of Granddad in the morning and another in the afternoon," he explained, "but he shops at Gristedes and eats only the best of food."

It was fitting, if little noticed, that Judge's body, taken by firefighters from the World Trade Center to St. Peter's Church and placed on the altar, was found by Jimmy Boyle, a former firefighter and fire union president.

Boyle's 37-year-old firefighter son Michael also died that fateful day, and Jimmy had been desperately searching for him. When he heard that Judge was at St. Peter's, he rushed there.

"They had him lying under a sheet," said Boyle, who invited me all those years ago on my first ride on a fire truck to the scene of a fire. "I lifted up a corner and held his hand and said a prayer for him. He was an old friend of the family. He helped my son get into the fire department."

There wasn't a man, or woman, in that department who didn't know and love Judge.

When Judge was taken from St. Peter's in a body bag, he was brought back to Engine 1, Ladder 24, across the street from St. Francis Church, where shocked firefighters placed him on a cot at the back of the station.

There they formed a small shrine and got down on their knees to pray and to cry for Judge and for many of their comrades who died that day going into a building most people were fleeing from.

Judge most loved the firefighters. They were a kind of secular order, men who bonded. Many of them were Irish Catholics. He became their chaplain in 1992 and he once told them, "You do what God called you to do. You show up, you put one foot in front of the other and you do your job, which is a mystery and surprise. You have no idea, when you get in that rig, what God is calling you to."

His death made strong men weep, perhaps as much for their own vulnerability as for his. If the God that Judge worshiped couldn't protect him from being crushed in the lobby of one of the Twin Towers, what chance did they have?

One of his close friends was Representative Peter King, who broke down on the floor of Congress when he noted the passing of Judge. Peter Johnson, the lawyer, reminded me that Judge was a true Franciscan who gave away everything his well-meaning friends gave him. If you gave him a coat to ward off the winter cold, you'd be likely to see that coat being worn by a homeless man at the lunches served each day by St. Francis.

Judge once invited Johnson and me to see his spartan quarters on the third floor of the friary. On a chair there was a large photograph. It showed Judge leading a procession of pallbearers carrying a casket containing the body of a firefighter.

It was titled *The Last Roll Call*.

Dennis Duggan is a columnist for Newsday.

5
They Died Together

They were tied together by family and friendship. They were buddies and brothers, husbands and wives, aunts and nieces. Death came for them in twos.

Co-workers who died as one tried to save the other. Two men who met in a small storage room each morning to read the Bible and pray. A pair of brothers—one a firefighter and the other a cop—each doing his job as they disappeared into the destruction of a burning skyscraper.

They live in the memories of those who loved them. "We were supposed to grow old together," a young man says of his two lost friends. "We'd all have wives and play golf and then have a barbecue."

And a woman talks of a sister who stood by a trapped friend. "The goodness in people will go on," she says.

HOWARD KESTENBAUM and VIJAYASHANKAR PARAMSOTHY
A Friendship of Kindred Spirits

When a World Trade Center elevator fell several stories in 2000 with Vijayashankar Paramsothy aboard, it was his boss and mentor, Howard Kestenbaum, who went floor to floor, talking to him on a cell phone, to locate his friend. It was Kestenbaum who directed the rescuers to where the 23-year-old Malaysian was trapped with a fractured back. And it was Kestenbaum who visited him in the hospital afterward and bought him books to read while he was recovering at home.

On the morning that a plane hit the Aon Corporation office, on the 103rd floor of the south tower, Vijay, as he was known to all, had a chance to return the favor. Kestenbaum, a 56-year-old executive vice president at Aon, was knocked unconscious by the impact, witnesses told his wife. "They saw Vijay had gotten Howard up on his feet with his arms around him, and he put Howard's glasses in his pocket to keep them safe," said Granvilette Kestenbaum. Vijay refused to leave his side. When the building collapsed, both men were lost.

"He died trying to save my husband," said Granvilette.

The two men—divided by age, race and culture—had a friendship that was, nevertheless, "extraordinary," she said. "They were like two kindred spirits."

Paramsothy had his mentor to thank for hiring him, and for winning him a promotion to financial consultant. Granvilette didn't meet her husband's protege until they visited him in the hospital after the elevator accident but, she said, "I knew of him every day from Howard. He was just proud of him. He said Vijay's so brave, he'll go anywhere, do anything."

"The son I didn't have to buy diapers for," was how Kestenbaum jokingly referred to his young friend.

On the surface, the two men's lifestyles couldn't have been more different. Paramsothy juggled three different cell phones and used e-mail to stay in constant touch with his many friends. Kestenbaum was technologically backward, listening to his favorite blues on a record player amplified with vacuum tubes, and eschewing modern innovations such as the microwave.

Paramsothy, who lived in Astoria, fell in love with the big city when he moved from Malaysia in 1996 to attend college. "It's vibrant, fantastic," he told his parents in daily phone calls back home. "It's *the* place, *the* place in the world." Kestenbaum was enjoying peaceful domesticity—growing tomatoes and eggplants in the garden of the home he had made in Montclair, New Jersey, with his wife and daughter, Lauren, 24. "He was a Jersey boy who never in his life grew anything," said Granvilette. "When we moved here, he became Farmer Joe."

Paramsothy was a fervent fan of British soccer and British beer, preferably at the same time. "He never missed a Manchester United game," said his friend, Sedat Kunt. Kestenbaum, in recent years, had begun tapping a deep well of religious devotion, studying the Jewish mystical movement, the kabbalah, and serving as his congregation's interim leader until a new rabbi was found.

But the two shared a vast generosity of spirit. Kestenbaum sometimes slept at the homeless shelter he volunteered in, and when a friend had a stroke, he coached him to restore his speech. If Kestenbaum was in a group and anyone was gossiping or speaking ill of another person, he would walk away.

Paramsothy was the kind of person who went out of his way to help friends, even new ones. When Kunt arrived in New York from Turkey, not knowing anyone, "He showed me New York," Kunt said, recalling Paramsothy's advice on everything from bargain-hunting at Century 21 department stores to looking for housing in the outer boroughs.

And neither Paramsothy nor Kestenbaum was inhibited by convention. Paramsothy's father, Sivapkiam, remembers his son's singular response, at the age of 3, when asked whether he would be more like his mother or his father. "I don't think I want to be like any of you," replied the self-assured toddler. "I want to be myself."

Granvilette remembers Kestenbaum calling to ask her out when the two were students at Columbia, where he was doing a doctorate in astrophysics. "This is Howie," he said when she answered the phone. "Howie who?" she asked, confused. "I'm fine, Howie you?" he replied, not missing a beat. That goofy opening turned into a 31-year union of a white man and a black woman determined not to let society's taboos interfere with affairs of the heart.

"These men, they both thought they were ordinary men, but they were extraordinary because they were such good men," said Granvilette. "We know what the human spirit is capable of from their friendship."

"If Howard had been conscious, he would have said 'go on,'" she said. "He would have never said 'stay with me.'"

But the Paramsothys try to soothe her. "They said to me, 'Even if Howard had said that, Vijay never would have left him. Vijay couldn't have left.'"

DIANNE GLADSTONE and DIANE URBAN
"Like Buddies in the War"

For 31 years, Diane Urban and Dianne Gladstone were close friends as well as co-workers. For the past three years, they worked for New York State on the 86th floor of Tower Two. On September 11, one of them tried to save the other.

Urban nearly escaped down a staircase, when she changed course to help her friend, who had injured her leg. "I know my sister—she never could have lived with herself if she ran for those stairs," said Terry Corio of Manhasset. "It's like buddies in the war."

The story of how Diane Urban, 50, of Malverne tried to save Dianne Gladstone, 55, of Forest Hills was told to Corio and to Gladstone's husband, Herbert, by co-workers of the missing women.

Shortly after the first tower was hit, Urban and Gladstone ran hand in hand, following colleagues to a concourse area on the 78th floor. There, hundreds of people waited for elevators to take them down to safety. Then the second plane crashed into their tower, unleashing a tidal wave of reverberations.

Gladstone was hurled away.

From the staircase, Urban spotted her friend. Her leg seemed broken. "I think Diane could have gotten out," Corio said. "She was quick on her feet. I guess she thought she had time enough to carry her friend out."

"I'm going to help Dianne," Urban said to co-workers on the stairs. By the time she reached Gladstone, fireballs were spewing paralyzing smoke and heat. As they ran down the stairs, the co-workers saw Diane and Dianne huddling with two male colleagues—all of them shielding their faces with their hands.

"I don't think they ever made it to the stairs," Corio said. "And then the building collapsed. They probably suffocated very quickly."

If the blast hadn't broken his wife's leg, she might have survived, said Gladstone's husband. "She wasn't a typical 55-year-old woman," he said. "She could keep up with most people in aerobics class."

His wife loved the view from her 86th-floor office, he said. Both women worked for the state Department of Taxation and Finance. They were working in the same office in Queens three years ago when they accepted promotions that transferred them to the Twin Towers. Gladstone planned to retire in April 2002 after 37 years of service to the state.

Urban moved to Malverne early in 2001 after a lifetime in Queens. The house was "like her toy," said Corio's husband, Ray. She spent her free time "dolling it up" and planned to retire there in five years.

"My sister just felt that she had picked the most wonderful place for herself," Terry Corio said. "She was looking forward to the holiday season, the tree lighting in Malverne."

For Terry Corio, the co-workers' story is a gift, a "wonderful thing they can tell us," she said. "It gives me a picture." It is a picture, Corio said, that proves the terrorists did not prevail. "You can kill some of us, but you cannot conquer us. The goodness in people will go on."

JUDD CAVALIER and JOSEPH ANCHUNDIA
Inseparable Best Friends

Ian Crystal recalls how he and Joe Anchundia planned a surprise birthday party in 2000 for Judd Cavalier at the apartment the three 26-year-old best friends shared in midtown Manhattan. Fifty people came.

"Joe and I were so proud we pulled it off," Ian said. "Judd had no clue."

In September 2001, many of the same people got together again, though not to celebrate, but to mourn. Anchundia and Cavalier both were lost in the World Trade Center disaster, and their friends gathered at the apartment for an informal memorial.

"It kind of brought a smile to everyone's face, even though it was such a sad time," said Eytan Gutman, 26, a roommate. "These two guys really touched a lot of people's lives. They were two amazing people. Extraordinary people, I'd have to say."

Since Anchundia and Cavalier first met as junior high–schoolers in Huntington, Long Island, they were inseparable.

"Joe's former girlfriend said she felt like she was dating both of them," said Linda Cavalier, Judd's mother. "She said it was always Joe and Judd, Joe and Judd. They did everything together."

As teenagers they fished, skied, went to ball games and hung out in downtown Huntington together. And in recent years, they were colleagues—investment bankers at Sandler O'Neill—as well as roommates, enjoying the lights and delights of New York City together from their swanky midtown neighborhood.

On September 11, Anchundia and Cavalier were in their 104th-floor office in Tower Two. "It's comforting for me to feel that they were together at the end," said Christene Anchundia, Joe's mother.

It is but a small comfort, however, as families and friends process the loss of two young men just coming into their own. "He loved living in the city," Linda Cavalier said of her son. "He loved his work.

"Anytime you looked at a picture of Judd, he was smiling from ear to ear," she said. "He was so happy."

Anchundia recently was promoted at Sandler O'Neill, his mother said. "It was a very demanding, stressful job, but he enjoyed it. And he loved the city."

The two took full advantage of what New York City has to offer—bicycle-riding in Central Park, and tasting Manhattan's restaurants and nightlife.

But what they did was less important than doing it with friends, said Ian Crystal, who grew up with the pair.

"We used to go to a concert five hours early and just hang out, and we never got sick of each other,"

he said. "We used to kind of speak our own language. We had so many sayings and slogans that nobody knew what we were talking about."

It's hard for him to imagine the future without his best friends, Crystal said.

"We were supposed to grow old together," he said. "We'd all have wives and play golf and then have a barbecue. . . . That's what we were supposed to do when we got older."

SEAN BOOKER and RICHARD ALLEN
Death in a Place of Prayer

The little room on the 99th floor of the World Trade Center's north tower held great meaning to Richard Allen and Sean Booker. Every morning before work, the two friends would head to the storage room and read scriptures from the Bible and pray.

The two, who also served as Christian ministers at churches in New York and New Jersey, would sometimes prepare their sermons in the small space. It was quiet—a place for reflection.

It is in that room of peace and piety that family members believe the two men died when American Airlines Flight 11 crashed into the tower. The crash occurred shortly before 9 a.m.—minutes before the two usually left the room. Allen would go to work on the 98th floor for the mailroom at Marsh & McLennan, while Booker would go to the 93rd floor, fixing photocopying machines for the firm.

"Richie and Sean would always go into work early," said Allen's mother, Denise. "Every morning, without fail, they would read the Bible and pray. I think they were doing that when they died."

Allen, 30, of Brooklyn, was a minister at Rivers of Living Waters Ministries in Brooklyn, while Booker, 35, of Newark, was a pastor at Tabernacle Outreach Ministries in Newark.

They met while working in the American Express building across the street from the World Trade Center and then moved across the street to Marsh after Booker found a job there.

About a week before the terrorist attack, Allen invited his mother, a folk artist, to speak at Rivers of Living Waters Ministries. "Our destiny is already written, I've believed that for quite a long time," Denise Allen said. "There's a reason God allowed this to happen."

For Sharon Booker, though, questions linger. On the day of the terrorist attack, she had begun a new job in the Met Life building in midtown Manhattan—giving her a clear view of the airplane crashing into her husband's building.

"You can't question God," she said. "But now I feel that when I leave the house I won't come back. I just want to feel peace and comfort, but I can't."

DOLORES COSTA and DOROTHY CHIARCHIARO
An Inseparable Aunt and Niece

Dolores M. Costa, a vice president at Fred Alger Management, could not have been happier when she got her aunt, Dorothy Chiarchiaro, to join the firm.

The two women, nine years apart in age, were close friends who vacationed together with their husbands. Chiarchiaro was the youngest of Costa's mother's 12 siblings, and the women grew up together in Brooklyn's Cobble Hill section.

They died together on the 93rd floor of the north tower. Costa would have turned 53 on September 13. Chiarchiaro would have been 62 on October 4. But it wasn't their birthdays that occupied the women in the days before the attacks. They were planning an 80th-birthday party for Costa's mother, Marie Barbosa of Brooklyn, in October. The hall had been booked, and the invitations had been sent out.

"It's been a tough year," Costa had told her husband, Charles. "We'll get everybody together and have a good time and forget our troubles."

His wife, he said, "had a heart of gold. She would do anything for everyone." An avid birder, she fed the birds assiduously in the backyard of their Port Monmouth, New Jersey, home. "One day she called me to come see the big chicken in our backyard," he recalled. It turned out to be a wild turkey that had come to partake of Costa's treats. She also

enjoyed birding in Hawaii, where they owned a time-share.

Costa joined Fred Alger Management 15 years ago and moved with the investment firm to One World Trade Center two years ago. The Costas would rise at 5 a.m. to start their jobs early. On the morning of September 11, she asked her husband to make her a sandwich before she sped off to the train station.

Chiarchiaro, who joined the Fred Alger firm as "a glorified file clerk" eight years ago, was in demand for "reorganizing the offices of the stock analysts," said her husband, Nicholas Chiarchiaro of Vernon, New Jersey. Everyone wanted her services. She was "a very organized woman" who had previously run the school library at Our Lady of Czestochowa School in Brooklyn.

Though she normally worked part time on Mondays, Wednesdays and Fridays, she chose to stay home on Monday, September 10, with her granddaughters, Karen, 7, and Corinne, 5, and go to work Tuesday instead.

Chiarchiaro, who loved to read psychological thrillers, would try to analyze the behavior of mass murderers. It's spooky, her husband said, "that she should be killed by terrorists."

PETER and TOMMY LANGONE
Lifesaving Ran in Their Family

Tommy and Peter Langone grew up in a world where dealing with danger was a family tradition. It made sense that Tommy wanted to be a firefighter and Peter wanted to be a cop.

Along the way, they switched roles.

When they disappeared into the smoke and destruction of the World Trade Center, Tommy was the cop and Peter was the firefighter. But they were both following their essential dream—they were trying to save lives.

"This is what they do for a living," their sister, Joanne Ciborowski, said in the wake of the tragedy. "They live it, they breathe it, they love it. It's what they've always done, both of them."

The Langone family is no stranger to the perils of life-saving. They're all in professions where moments are measured by life and death.

The brothers' father, Paul, was a volunteer firefighter for more than 30 years in Roslyn, where the brothers grew up, as was Paul's uncle before him. Ciborowski and Tommy and Peter's other sister, Rosemarie Langone, are nurses and former ambulance-company volunteers in the same community. And Tommy and Peter were members of the Roslyn Rescue Fire Department.

Tommy, 39, was a police officer with New York City's Emergency Service Unit. Peter, 41, was a member of Engine Company 252 in Bushwick, Brooklyn.

Ciborowski described both her brothers as "very funny." She described Tommy as highly organized with a dry wit. "Peter always tells it like it is," she said. "He's always there to help people. If you needed something done, it would be done and you wouldn't know who did it, then you'd find out it was Peter. He did things without fanfare. You didn't have to ask twice."

Both brothers were familiar with disasters. Both responded to the 1990 crash of Avianca Flight 52 in Cove Neck, and both were at the World Trade Center bombing in 1993. Tommy was sent to Oklahoma City for a week after the bombing there.

The brothers Langone and their sisters grew up in Roslyn Heights, where Peter's home is around the corner from his mother's. Tommy lived two towns away in Williston Park. Both graduated from Roslyn High School and attended Nassau Community College. Neither one could wait until he was old enough to join Roslyn rescue with their father, who died in 1985. He had been a volunteer for the company for about 33 years, finally becoming chief.

Tommy followed in his father's footsteps by becoming, at 24, one of the youngest chiefs the department ever had. Tommy and his wife, JoAnn, have two children, Caitlin, 12, and Brian, 10. Peter and his wife, Terri, have two daughters, Nikki, 9, and Karli, 5.

Tommy was riding back to his unit on Queens Boulevard with a sergeant on September 11 when they heard the news. They turned right around and headed for the scene. They suited up, got equipment and went in to rescue survivors.

Peter had just finished his overnight tour and was on the phone with his wife. Then a call came over the radio and he told her that he had to go.

RICHARD POULOS and JAMES HOPPER
A Husband and a Brother Are Gone

So many husbands, wives, sisters, brothers, mothers, fathers and children face a world made unbearable by the loss of a loved one on September 11. For Margaret Poulos, that loss is double—her husband, Richard Poulos, and her brother, James Patrick Hopper, both died in the World Trade Center.

"It's devastating," said Margaret, 54, of Levittown. Though she finds some comfort in the thought that the two men may have been together, "it was still a horrible thing that happened."

Poulos was 55, Hopper was 52. Both were avid Yankees fans. They had been friends for almost 40 years—ever since Margaret met her husband on a blind date when they were teenagers. Hopper and his wife, Rita, and their two children, James, 23, and Lauren, 18, used to vacation with the Pouloses and their three children, Lisa Sarni, 32, Richard, 27, and Erin, 22. Lake George, Long Beach Island, New Jersey, the Poconos, Las Vegas—wherever the two men went with their families, Margaret said, "they always had a good time, joked, talked."

"My brother was always the nervous one," Margaret said. As for her husband, "Nothing ever bothered him. . . . He always had nicknames for everyone. He was always joking." One famous joke was the one he played on Hopper's wife when his niece, Lauren, was less than a year old. Poulos persuaded the infant to address her mother by name, much to Rita Hopper's exasperation. "Mommy!" Rita pleaded with her baby. "No, Rita!" Poulos insisted. It took a while before "Mommy" stuck. Hopper loved a good laugh too, Rita said, but "he had a strange sense of humor . . . very dry."

Both Poulos and Hopper had done two decades of law enforcement work, Poulos as a New York City detective and Hopper as a corrections officer. Both retired in 1993, and went to work as security guards at Cantor Fitzgerald—within months of each other and a floor apart. Poulos was on the 104th floor of Tower One, and Hopper on the 105th.

Hopper's son, James, worked just across from the World Trade Center, and on the morning of the attacks, saw the gaping hole in his father's building moments after the plane hit. "I saw people falling out," he said. "It looked like it hit right where my dad was located."

On the Cantor Fitzgerald tribute Web site, Lauren Hopper wrote of her father and uncle, "I know that together they are watching over all of us, and laughing as they watch us cry. Make sure you eat good," she told her Uncle Richie. "And don't let Daddy get any fatter!"

Since that terrible day, the cousins, who have always been close, have sought each other's support even more, Margaret said. The holidays were hard, but Poulos's two grandsons, Christopher, 5, and Joseph, 2, made it seem important to celebrate anyway. And Richard Poulos' son, Richard, was to be married in May 2002.

As the family's life went on, Margaret found herself still plagued by anxiety. Her brother's body was found January 16, but by mid-February there had been no sign of her husband. "I'm just hoping," she said. "Every time the phone rings, I'm hoping for something about my husband."

TIMOTHY and JOHN GRAZIOSO
They Knew What Was Important

They were brothers who worked in a world of sales and trading, but Timothy and John Grazioso put the most stock in family values.

Timothy Grazioso, 42, lived alone during the week in an apartment in Brooklyn. His 12-year-old daughter, Lauren, was diagnosed with diabetes when she was a baby, and Grazioso and his wife, Debbie, decided that the family should buy a house in Florida because the warm climate would be conducive to his daughter's health.

His job as chief operating officer for institutional sales and trading for Cantor Fitzgerald kept him away from his family on weekdays, but he flew back to his Gulf Stream, Florida, home every weekend to be with his family, his wife said. "We probably had it better than most people because when Tim came home on Friday nights, he was all ours."

She said the couple did "normal things together" whenever her husband came home: shopping at Target, eating at restaurants, organizing play dates

for Lauren and her twin sister, Briana, and playing bingo at the Boca Raton Hotel.

Tim's 41-year-old brother, John Grazioso, was a salesman for eSpeed, a division of Cantor Fitzgerald. He was equally caught up in his family and in everyday pursuits. His wife, Tina, of Middletown, New Jersey, said both she and John were fans of Bruce Springsteen, who as she put it "talks about everyday life. The good and the bad. Bruce is a regular guy, just like John."

Tina Grazioso said she and John met at Newark International Airport when they both worked for Piedmont Airlines. The two would unwind with co-workers on Thursday nights, after work, at local restaurants or bars. "One Thursday night happened to fall on Christmas Eve, and the only ones who showed up were John, my roommate and me," she said. The couple began dating and had been married for 10 years.

The couple and their three children, Kathryn, 7, Kristen, 5, and Michael, 1, attended the World Amateur Dupont Classic, a four-day golf tournament in Myrtle Beach, Florida, every August. John Grazioso, an avid golfer, used this time to perfect his short game and to spend quality time with his family. "John would get his golf in, but we'd also make it a family vacation," his wife said.

John and Tim had dinner with their mother, Sandra, of Clifton, New Jersey, at an Italian restaurant in New Jersey the night before the attack. She described her sons as "beautiful people," stressing their generosity and consideration for her. "If I asked them what kind of TV I should buy, they would tell me not to buy one at all," she said. "They'd end up buying it for me."

Both Tina and Debbie Grazioso said their children have helped them get through the days since September 11. "I can't even imagine not having children, because they are the reason you go on," Debbie Grazioso said. "A lot of times you don't have that bright and cheery face, but you put it on for them."

EDWARD BEYEA and ABE ZELMANOWITZ
No Greater Friend

As Sean Southard watched the attacks on the World Trade Center, his mind was on his uncle, Edward Beyea, a quadriplegic who worked on the 27th floor of Tower One.

"My biggest concern is that Ed would be left alone," he said. "I just had this vision of complete chaos, and everyone taking off and leaving him."

Chaotic it certainly was, but Southard needn't have worried that his uncle would be left. Not with his uncle's best friend, Abe Zelmanowitz, there. "He couldn't have left him," said Zelmanowitz's sister-in-law, Evelyn Zelmanowitz of Flatlands, New York. "That's what made Abe, Abe."

Both men were lost in the collapse of the north tower.

Based on the accounts of witnesses and loved ones' knowledge of the two men's characters, a bittersweet picture emerges—a picture that has inspired and saddened many, including President George W. Bush, who mentioned the two friends in a speech days after the attack.

When the first plane hit the building, Zelmanowitz, 55, and Beyea, 42, both systems analysts for Blue Cross/Blue Shield, fled the office with their co-workers. The elevators were not working, and Beyea, a 300-pound man in a heavy mechanized wheelchair, could not get down the stairs, which were choked with streams of panicked workers.

Beyea's home health aide, Irma Fuller, had gone to pick up breakfast on the 43rd floor when the plane struck the tower. She hurried back to the 27th floor and found the two friends waiting for help in the stairwell. Fuller, 69, was affected by smoke from the higher floors, so Zelmanowitz told her to go on ahead. It wasn't the first time she had left Beyea in Zelmanowitz's care. As well as working "hand in hand" for 12 years, the two regularly had a beer or a bite to eat together in the evenings.

"If Abe says go, then I knew he would stay with him, because he had always done that," said Fuller. "I didn't have to worry about it, because he was that type of person."

On outward appearances, the two best friends made an odd couple. Slim and reserved, with gray hair and a short gray beard, Zelmanowitz, an Orthodox Jew from Brooklyn, was the quiet one. Friends and acquaintances have written of the calm he exuded, the sense of peacefulness that surrounded him. "He just had a way of connecting with people," said his sister-in-law, "of finding a common bond."

Beyea, a Catholic, and paralyzed from the neck down in a diving accident when he was 22, was jovial and outgoing, always ready with a joke to put people at ease. "A lot of people meeting someone in his disabled condition are kind of standoffish, and nervous that they would say or do something wrong," said Southard. "He was able to disarm them.

"I think they probably shared somewhat of a common bond with each other in that neither of them had any children of their own," Southard said. "They were both the special uncle of the family." Zelmanowitz, who lived with his older brother's family, was very close with his six nephews and nieces, and Beyea had been a father figure to his two nephews after their father died.

Beyea needed 24-hour nursing assistance, but otherwise led as normal a life as possible, taking the subway to work from his apartment on Roosevelt Island, using a mouthpiece to tap the keys on his computer, and keeping himself busy with books, movies, TV and dinners with friends. His most regular dining companion was Zelmanowitz, said Fuller, his aide for the past 14 years. She recalled dinners with the two men as merry and immoderate three-course affairs with wine throughout and cigars afterward.

The different needs of the two men required some planning, said Evelyn Zelmanowitz, but "if Ed was going to make the arrangements, he'd make sure it was kosher, and if Abe was going to make the arrangements, he'd make sure it was wheelchair-accessible. They always had each other's best interests at heart."

In the days following the terrorist attacks, the story got out of the man who died standing by his disabled best friend. The response was overwhelming.

"We've got so many letters stating that it meant so much to people to hear about such compassion in a time of evil," Evelyn Zelmanowitz said. "People needed something positive to look to at that time.

"I say it's a story of two heroes," she said. "I really feel that way. Two inspiring people."

SYLVIA and JOHN RESTA
They Matched Like a Pair of Shoes

Halloween, with its orange candy, spooky costumes and family fun, is not generally considered a romantic holiday. But since John

Resta and Sylvia San Pio Resta met five years ago at an office costume party, Halloween had always been about romance for them.

Two Halloweens ago, on the third anniversary of their meeting, John, 40, stayed home from work and rented a tuxedo. He bought flowers, lit candles and set the table with a stone crab dinner specially flown in from Sylvia's favorite restaurant in Miami. When Sylvia, 27, got back to the couple's Bayside apartment, he got down on his knees and proposed.

"She said yes, of course," said Laura Perez, 20, Sylvia's sister.

They were married in 2000. On the morning of September 11, John and Sylvia were on the 92nd floor of Tower One, where both worked at Carr Futures, he as a project manager, she as a commodities broker. Sylvia was seven months pregnant, a week away from maternity leave. Both were lost in the terrorist attack.

Halloween without the fun-loving pair was difficult to face, say their relatives. Chris Mazzeo, John's older sister, recalled their yearly ritual of taking their five youngest nieces and nephews out pumpkin picking and on hayrides.

"They adored children," she said. "They were just so anxious for their baby to be born."

John's 10 nieces and nephews in New Jersey adored the couple right back, said Mazzeo, of Hazlet, New Jersey. The Restas spent almost every other weekend in New Jersey, taking the kids out on outings, to movies and for pizza. Sylvia even played Pokémon cards with the smallest ones.

"The kids used to fight over whose house they would stay at, mine or my sister's," said Mazzeo. "They would say, 'They stayed with you last time—they should stay with us this time.'"

John's younger sister, Dawn Angrisani, of Howell, New Jersey, was overcome when she recalled telling her daughter, Brittany, then 11, about John and Sylvia's engagement. "I said, 'Uncle John waited a long time to get engaged,'" she said through tears. "Brittany answered, 'I'm really happy he waited for Aunt Sylvia.'"

"They were like matching shoes," said Mazzeo. "They were like a right and a left. They just fit together so well." And, she said, "They were so excited to be parents—which is the sad thing now, that we won't get to experience that with them."

On Halloween, John's sisters tried to cheer up their children, taking them pumpkin picking even without their beloved aunt and uncle. "It wasn't the same," said Mazzeo. "We went on the hayride, but it just wasn't the same."

6
Rescuers

Among those who gave their lives trying to save lives were 37 members of the Port Authority and 23 New York City police officers. The ranks of fallen rescuers also included emergency medical technicians and an FBI agent who came hurrying into the inferno from eight blocks away.

They were bound together by their callings. A public safety director who was a "cop's cop," tough on the outside and gentle on the inside; a one-time operating room nurse who became one of only two women captains in the Port Authority Police and a decorated New York City officer who once told his devout mother, "Look, Mommy, you save souls and I'll save bodies."

He did that and more. They all did.

FERDINAND MORRONE
"A Cop's Cop" to the End

Ferdinand "Fred" Morrone lived two contrasting lives: The first, as the hard-nosed, take-charge superintendent of the Port Authority Police and director of public safety for the Port Authority; the second, as the romantic husband, devoted father and humble man who was horrible at golf.

"He was very athletic," Linda Morrone said of her husband, who ran in the Marine Corps Marathon in Washington, D.C., when he was 48. "But it was only in the last two years that he played golf. And he was terrible at it." She had caddied for her husband on a few occasions, and had been there to watch him wade through water hazards, looking for countless poorly hit balls. But it was still an achievement, she said. "I thought that it was great that he reached a point in his life that he was comfortable being bad at something he loved. It showed a real growth in him."

A doting husband, Morrone took his wife on a second honeymoon to Hawaii on their 25th wedding anniversary several years ago. It was a much-needed break for the couple since he had been in Australia as the head of security for a gaming corporation there, and she had just endured chemotherapy for a rare form of leukemia. "He pulled out all the stops," his wife said. "He always made sure we had our time together."

Early in 2001, Morrone surprised his wife with an overnight trip to Manhattan. Once again he didn't scrimp, springing for tickets to *The Full Monty*, dinner at Ben Benson's and a posh suite at the Plaza Hotel. "I never, ever took him for granted," she said.

Morrone, 63, phoned his wife on September 11 while en route to his Jersey City office. The "cop in him" came out, she said, when he heard about the first plane crashing into Tower One. He had delegated his responsibilities to others in his office while he headed across the Hudson to assist in the evacuation of the stricken skyscraper. "To this day, people don't understand why he went," she said.

But that was who "Fred" Morrone was: "a cop's cop," his wife said. "He would never send men to do a dangerous job if he wasn't willing to go in there himself."

Morrone was appointed to his position with the Port Authority in 1996. Within the last five years, he had established the Port Authority Police Academy in Sea Girt, New Jersey, used helicopters and motorcycles for greater mobility for officers in New York City and butted heads several times with Mayor Rudy Giuliani over the role and efficiency of the Port Authority Police. "He went in there with an attitude that if he was going to get something done, he had to appear strong," she said, "and there may have been some people who thought he was unyielding." His superiors saw him as "a force to be reckoned with. He expected a great deal from himself and probably from other people as well."

At home, though, Morrone was soft-spoken and humble, his wife said. Home was an arena where opinions were to be voiced and heard, she said. "His ear was always available." Linda said she can see her husband in their three children: Ferdinand, 31, Alyssa, 30, and Gregory, 23. "My oldest son is very organized, like his father. Alyssa, a detective for the Bergen County prosecutor's office, has her father's gusto for law enforcement," and their youngest son has his father's "spirituality."

Morrone's own spirituality was never clouded by his work, his wife said. He would sometimes attend the 6:30 a.m. mass at his local church, praying for his wife's health, and for "the wisdom to do his job well."

JEROME DOMÍNGUEZ
He Gave All He Had

Jerome Domínguez had gone diving off the coast of Long Island with some police pals who were also his friends outside the job.

After exploring the chambers of a shipwrecked boat, they glided to the surface and started popping up, one after another, to take their places on their boat.

But they noticed that one of them was missing. Without much hesitation, Domínguez was the one to jump right back in the water.

Domínguez found his friend lying unconscious inside the dilapidated ship with little air left. Pulling him up, Domínguez swam toward the light of the surface, sharing his own air supply with the unconscious man. His friend survived.

But the act of heroism more than two years ago was not the first time, and would not be the last, that the decorated New York City cop offered all he had for the sake of others. Domínguez did it regularly, whenever he encountered people in danger, or while on duty as a member of the department's elite emergency services unit.

Domínguez was at the World Trade Center on September 11. His colleagues told his family that he was making his way upward in the building when the north tower collapsed.

The 37-year-old West Islip resident grew up in the Pelham Bay section of the Bronx as one of two sons of devout Catholic parents who spend much of their time trying to spread the faith. Domínguez, though, had his own sense of mission. "I once told him, 'Jerome, don't strain yourself so much,'" recalled his mother, Gladys Domínguez of the Bronx. "And he said, 'Look, Mommy, you save souls and I'll save bodies.'"

After graduating from Mount St. Michael Academy in the Bronx, Domínguez entered the police academy in the mid-1980s and became a patrol officer for a local precinct in the Bronx. Two years later, Domínguez joined the highway division, and became committed to his job of helping people on the roads. Even when off duty, Domínguez carried power-cutting and other tools in his vehicle to help stalled drivers or to extricate victims at accident scenes.

Once, while heading to Texas for Air Force training in 1999—he was a member of the reserves—Domínguez encountered an overturned school bus with several children inside. He quickly took charge and rescued more than a dozen kids before the bus burst into flames. His feat earned praise, and he appeared on a television news show and was mentioned in the newspapers. The Air Force offered him a permanent job, but he took an offer from the NYPD to join the emergency unit.

"He enjoyed himself helping people in some way, morally or physically," said his father, Geronimo Domínguez, a physician who hosts a Bible-reading television program in Spanish. "He was very courageous."

In his last conversation with his father, some days before September 11, Domínguez discussed the idea of a heavenly place for souls to rest in happiness after death. His parents find comfort in their belief that Domínguez is already there. "He loved helping others," said his father, "and there isn't in the Bible or anywhere else a greater love than that, giving your life for others."

MOIRA SMITH
She Kept Going Back In

On two occasions during her police career, Moira Smith plunged into a major disaster scene, pulling out the maimed and wounded only to turn around and selflessly immerse herself in danger again.

She emerged from the first disaster—the August 27, 1991, subway crash in Union Square in which five were killed and more than 130 hurt—with the NYPD's Distinguished Duty Medal for saving dozens of lives.

Ten years later she would be awarded another medal for her heroic actions during another catastrophic disaster. This one, however, would come posthumously.

In a heartbreaking scene three months after the September 11 terrorist attack, Smith, of Bay Ridge, Brooklyn, and the other 22 NYPD officers who died were awarded the department's highest honor, the Medal of Honor, at a special ceremony at Carnegie Hall.

Patricia Smith, a tiny 2-year-old in a red velvet Christmas dress, accompanied her father, Jimmy Smith, onto the stage to accept the medal for a mother she would never see again. That sight—the wide-eyed, blonde-haired little girl who seemed oblivious to all the tragedy, tottering small-hand-in-big-hand with her grief-stricken father—was more than even some of the most grizzled cops in the audience that day could stand. The famous concert hall soon was filled with the sounds of sobbing.

"That was a tough day," recalled Lieutenant Charles Barbuti, who accompanied James Smith that day. "She's a doll, that kid, she's an angel. It's going to be hard, but Jimmy's a tough guy."

Barbuti, who serves in the 13th Precinct, where Moira was last stationed, described the 38-year-old as an active, dedicated, courageous cop. He said he wasn't surprised that she died trying to save others. "We had indications that on a number of occasions she had come out of the World Trade Center carrying people out, then had gone back in," he said. "She had the opportunity to leave, and she chose not to." Barbuti said that at least two pictures from newspaper photographers show Smith rescuing people trapped inside Tower Two.

Smith was the only woman NYPD cop to die in the rescue effort, a fact that didn't go unnoted around the city. The Policewomen's Endowment Association and *Glamour* and *Ms.* magazines all tabbed her their "Woman of the Year." In February 2002, a new East River ferry from Manhattan's Upper East Side to the Wall Street area was named after her. On what would have been her 39th birthday, a memorial service was held for her in the city's most prestigious church, St. Patrick's Cathedral.

A Valentine's Day baby, Moira was born and bred in Brooklyn. Advancing from P.S. 170 to Our Lady of Angels to St. Savior and Our Lady of Perpetual Help, she met the friends who would remain her lifetime confidants. After attending Niagara College upstate, she joined the NYPD in 1988. She met her husband, Jimmy Smith, also an officer, introducing herself in her usual outgoing way by snatching his Yankees cap off his head and flinging it across the squad room.

"She was a lot of fun," Barbuti said. "She was vivacious, she was fun-loving, she was a joy to be around. That may sound like a cliche, speaking well of people who have passed, but in her case it was true."

After years of dating, Jimmy and Moira, known as a fun couple who loved nothing better than taking road trips to New Orleans in their recreational vehicle, tied the knot in May 1998. And on July 20, 1999, Moira's dream came true, her friends said, when her daughter, Patricia Mary, was born. The devoted cop was now a doting mom.

"After that, Moira seemed happier, more fulfilled," Barbuti said. "Having Patricia was the happiest day of her life. She was devoted to Patricia."

CLAUDE RICHARDS
He Made His Colleagues Feel Safe

 Working on the New York City Police Department's bomb squad can be nerve-racking, to say the least. But there was something about Detective Claude Richards, known to his friends as Dan, that made his colleagues feel safe.

"It's a great comfort to be working with someone you can trust," said Detective Daniel McNally, a friend and colleague of Richards' since their

first day at the police academy in 1983. "Danny was the kind of guy that you'd want to introduce your loved ones to, to reassure them."

Richards, 46, was with McNally, searching for survivors in the World Trade Center's Building Six, when Tower One collapsed, killing him and two other officers, and injuring McNally.

"It would sound very cliched to say he died as he lived, helping people," said McNally. "The guy was a New York City detective who was on the bomb squad for 15 years. He had placed his life in harm's way many, many times. This is just another time that tempted fate."

Richards, who was unmarried and had no children, was utterly devoted to his job, said his brother Jim Richards. "He put 100 percent into it, to the point where it took over any personal life that he might have had," he said. "I think this is what he wanted to do. I don't think he was ever sorry about not having a family."

Richards grew up in Bethpage, the sixth of seven children. He served in the Army, enlisting at 22 and serving as an Airborne Ranger and as a member of the elite "Presidential Honor Guard" in Washington. After he left the Army, he earned a bachelor's degree at New York University and joined the police department in 1983.

His sister, Debbie Popadiuk, 44, of Tennessee, remembers Richards as a kind and protective older brother. "He was just so good to me," she said, adding, "He just wanted to help people." For example, she said, "If he saw someone who needed a coat, or shoes or something, he would just give it to them. That's the way he was."

In 1996, Richards spent a year helping people thousands of miles away—on an assignment few would volunteer for. He was part of a United Nations international police force in Bosnia, where he disarmed land mines and other bombs. While abroad, he indulged his love of travel, using his time off to visit countries across Europe.

Eventually, it was his quiet integrity that earned him the trust and admiration of his fellow bomb squad members. "Dan Richards was the kind of man who knew the difference between right and wrong, and he knew the difference between difficult and easy, but he would never let something difficult stand between him and doing something right," said McNally. "He was a man who was comfortable in his own skin."

ANTHONY SAVAS
He Always Was Retiring "In a Couple More Years"

At 72, Tony Savas was among the oldest victims of the terrorist attack on the World Trade Center, but for the Port Authority construction inspector September 11 was another day to live life the way he liked—by keeping busy.

He looked at least 10 years younger than he was, and retirement was nothing more than an abstract concept, said his wife of nearly 42 years, Phaedra Savas.

"He was the type of guy who always had to be busy," she said. "He always said that as long as he was able to work he was going to work. I sort of wanted him to retire and he always said, 'Well, maybe in a couple more years.' A couple more years always turned into a couple more years."

Tony Savas, of Astoria, served in the Korean War with the U.S. Army. He didn't speak much about the battlefront, but he did enjoy telling the story of how he falsely accused a fellow soldier of pilfering his Hershey bars, only to discover the thief was a rat. And only since September 11 has his wife learned from a friend that Tony Savas had saved his life during the war. Savas also downplayed the medal he received for helping escort people to safety in the aftermath of the 1993 bombing of the World Trade Center, in which six people died. "He said he was just doing his job," Phaedra Savas said.

Tony Savas, who had three children and two grandchildren, was fiercely patriotic. He reveled in a ritual with Jessica, his 2-year-old granddaughter, with whom he would march to plant an American flag at his weekend home on the North Shore. "It was a wonderful sight to see," Phaedra Savas said.

On the day the Twin Towers were struck, Savas last spoke to his son, John, who works for the Federal Reserve. Tony seemed unruffled, complaining only that he was wet from the sprinkler system and that he had left his house keys in his desk.

"They were stuck somewhere, or helping people, knowing Tony," his wife said. "When he didn't come home by 5 o'clock, which he always does, we knew something was wrong."

WALWYN STUART JR.
Waiting for His Baby to Walk

Port Authority Police Officer Walwyn Stuart Jr. savored each new wonder of his baby girl's life.

He got on the floor himself and showed Amanda Camille how to crawl, crowed when her first tooth came and pestered his wife, Thelma, about videotaping their daughter more often while he was at work.

"He was very anxious to have her walk," his wife said.

And despite his wife's teasing, he knew that when Amanda babbled something like "da-da," she was calling him by name.

Thelma Stuart last saw the 28-year-old on September 11 when he kissed her forehead before leaving their Valley Stream home for his post at the World Trade Center PATH station.

On September 28, his daughter's first birthday, "He wasn't there to celebrate with us," his wife said. On September 11, she called the front desk at his office. Someone told her, "Your husband is safe. We spoke to him at 8:50 a.m. He's evacuating people." She said, "That was the last I heard of him."

A Brooklyn native, Stuart was the youngest in a family of six children. He graduated from Westinghouse High School in Brooklyn in 1991 and studied for two years at SUNY Stony Brook, where he played baseball and chess and sang in a gospel choir.

In 1993, he decided to pursue his dream of becoming a police officer and joined the New York Police Department. As an officer in the 88th Precinct in Brooklyn, he earned commendations during his two years on patrol.

He then worked as an undercover police officer in the narcotics division of the organized crime control bureau for a year and a half. He became a detective and continued to work undercover for another year and a half.

In 1994, he met Thelma Lewis at Brooklyn Tabernacle after a Tuesday evening prayer service. The couple married in 1997 in Brooklyn. He impressed his wife as a strong man with an easy smile, and whose Christian faith was vital to his life. He loved to play chess, with friends or on the Internet, and tried to get his wife to learn the game. He wanted to save his chess books, he told her, for their daughter. Indeed, Stuart left the NYPD and began working for the Port Authority Police Department when he found out his wife was pregnant, she recalled: "He thought it would have been a safer job."

LEONARD HATTON
A G-Man at the Scene of the Crime

Leonard Hatton made a career of seeking out the perpetrators of crime and terror. On September 11, they found him first.

Agent Hatton worked on more than 800 bank-robbery cases during his 16 years with the FBI. He also investigated the bombing of the USS *Cole*. When a terrorist bomb tore a crater in the parking garage of the World Trade Center in 1993, he helped comb the rubble for evidence. And he spent weeks in the Suffolk County morgue in 1996, identifying victims of the downed TWA Flight 800.

Hatton, 45, was on his way to his Federal Plaza office when the World Trade Center was attacked. After rushing to the burning towers eight blocks away, he was seen by other agents assisting firefighters with the evacuation, said James Margolin, spokesman for the FBI's New York office. He helped an injured man to safety before heading back into the south tower. That was the last time he was seen. "Len Hatton would have done that whether he was an FBI agent or not," Margolin said. He was the only active agent to die in the attack.

His bureau career was just one facet of a life dedicated to public service. Following in the footsteps of his father, Leonard Sr., he was a volunteer fireman in his hometown of Ridgefield Park, New Jersey, where he grew up and lived with his wife, Joanne, and four children.

Hatton, who investigated kidnappings and extortion, collected evidence in the field as a bomb technician. He also was an instructor in forensic science and crime-scene investigation at the International Law Enforcement Academy in Budapest, Hungary. "He had a reputation for being a very skilled interviewer, one who could establish a rapport with anyone from any walk of life," said Margolin, who regularly worked with Hatton to publicize suspects and cases connected to them in hopes of getting tips from the public.

The soft-spoken Hatton, who was a Marine Corps captain before joining the FBI, often managed to get confessions from suspects, Margolin said. "He was very personable," Margolin said, "extremely kind."

JAMES ROMITO
Handling a Crisis Was a Familiar Role

Port Authority Police Chief James Romito was familiar with disasters. He was assigned to the World Trade Center when it was bombed in 1993, and was an integral part of the investigation of the crash of TWA Flight 800 in 1996.

Both times, said his friend and colleague Tom Farrell, Romito's training and calmness helped others through the crisis. "He was big on training, to be able to anticipate and respond to these types of incidents."

On September 11, Romito once again found himself in the middle of a disaster. As commander of the Port Authority headquarters support team, which oversaw emergency operations, he led a group of highly trained officers into Tower Two.

"The eyewitnesses talk about how commanding he was on the scene," said Farrell. "He was telling the officers, 'Don't worry. Follow me. We need to get people out.'" Romito and his group of officers probably were on the 27th floor when the building collapsed.

Prior to his most recent command, Romito served as chief of the Field Aviation Section, from 1998 to 2000, responsible for Port Authority police operations at Kennedy, LaGuardia and Newark airports. An inspector at the time of the TWA Flight 800 crash, Romito spent many exhausting days and nights at the scene of the disaster. He lived in Westwood, New Jersey, with his wife, Jody, and a daughter, Ellen.

In the 1990s, he was assigned to the Port Authority Bus Terminal and instituted a program that would be the cornerstone of his career. Now considered a national model, "Operation Alternative Program" offered safe housing, medical care and social services to the homeless who had made the terminal their home.

The effect was a dramatic drop in crime. "It's gotten praise from both law enforcement and homeless advocacy groups," said Port Authority spokesman Greg Trevor. Farrell agreed. "That was the visionary nature of Chief Romito," he said. "He could see a problem before it got out of control."

In 1993, Romito was among the first commanders on the scene of the World Trade Center bombing. He received a commendation for valor for his work in that attack. After placing subordinates in charge outside the building, he headed into the smoke. "He went right in there," said Farrell. "Just like he did this time."

During his precious downtime, Romito loved to fish and hunt. Last summer, Romito and Farrell took a fishing trip upstate that they had always postponed for one reason or another over the years. "It was in the planning for 21 years. We finally took it in June . . . Now I'm glad we had that time together."

MARK SCHWARTZ
A Family Man at Ground Zero

Five days a week, Mark Schwartz helped oversee operations at Hunter Ambulance in Inwood as assistant vice president. On weekends, the West Hempstead resident took calls as an emergency medical technician for the same company.

It seemed the only chance he had to relax was during annual family vacations he took with his wife, Patti, and their two children, Jennifer, 22, and Andrew, 20.

"My dad saved to take us away to Florida or on cruises," his daughter said. "He worked a lot, because he wanted to give my brother, my mom and myself everything that he possibly could. He

would get up at 4:30 in the morning and go to work and not come home until 7 at night. On weekends, he worked overnight shifts on the ambulance."

On their most recent vacation, in June, the Schwartzes boarded a cruise ship to the Caribbean, swimming with stingrays and taking a safari in Mexico.

Mark Schwartz, 50, served on a regional disaster task force organized by the city's Office of Emergency Management, and he responded to the World Trade Center on September 11 to help set up a triage center, his daughter said.

He called his wife at work on a two-way radio after arriving at the scene, describing the debris and bodies all around him. Soon after the couple said goodbye, Jennifer and her mother watched the towers collapse on television.

His body was found two days later. The following week, Mark and Patti Schwartz would have celebrated their 25th wedding anniversary.

Mark Schwartz was a large man, his daughter said, but "he wasn't as tough as he looked. I remember him crying at my sweet 16. He was a big mush."

With his children, Schwartz stressed the importance of education. He did not attend college and wanted them to have that privilege. Jennifer is working toward a master's degree in education at Adelphi University, and Andrew Schwartz is studying to become a paramedic.

Since her father's death, his daughter said, her mother has repeated a line about him: "On September 11, he became America's hero, but he was always our hero."

JOSEPH LOVERO
A Rescuer Who Wouldn't Be Stopped

Growing up in Jersey City, New Jersey, Joseph Lovero spent every minute he could hanging out at the firehouse across the street, daydreaming that he was latched to each truck that raced out onto Bergen Avenue to douse a blaze somewhere, relatives said.

Lovero even formed a fire company with his neighborhood pals and built his own fire truck. The baby carriage he used had a 20-gallon water jar on each side, a garden hose and a toolbox from his basement.

A heart condition robbed Lovero of his dream to fight fires when he became a man. Still, he wouldn't be denied his thirst for public service. He racked up commendations over 10 years of serving as an emergency medical technician for the Jersey City Medical Center.

He volunteered for more than four decades, driving a canteen truck to keep emergency workers and firefighters supplied with food and beverages at multiple-alarm fires. And he worked for the past seven years as a dispatcher for the Jersey City Fire Department.

Along the way, Lovero worked for a glass company and then in construction and indulged in his passion for photography, amassing a sizable library of pictures he took of hundreds of fire scenes.

Lovero, who had turned 60 on September 8, 2001, arrived at the World Trade Center soon after the first jetliner swooped into the north tower. As he and others from the Jersey City Fire Department approached the FDNY command post to check in, one of the blazing towers caved in. The group split up in a desperate dash to dodge raining debris. Lovero never made it.

He was the type of man who felt compelled to shoulder the burden and take control no matter the situation, said a daughter, Maxine McCormack. Deep down, she said, he was a softie with an extremely caring nature, who would take the leftover supplies from the canteen to St. Lucy's shelter in Jersey City.

McCormack said her dad—who had another daughter, Joanne, and a son, James—was also warmly embraced as a mentor. It was a side of him she never knew until after he died. More than a thousand mourners attended his funeral, including an honor guard of firefighters from Engine Company 19 and Ladder Company 8, where Lovero hung out as a kid. There, at least half a dozen relatives of the volunteer canteen group, the Gong Club, reminisced about how her father took them under his wing after they lost their own fathers.

There wasn't anything Lovero wouldn't do to help out, said Tom Murphy, deputy of fire and emergency services for the Jersey City Fire Department. "In our minds, he was a firefighter. He did everything but fight fires, and there were times when he even did that in a way, loading a truck or maneuvering hoses around."

KEITH FAIRBEN
At the Scene Within Minutes

 As firefighters were praised and mourned for their work during the terrorist attack at the World Trade Center, Kenneth Fairben, a volunteer firefighter for 32 years, quietly and painfully was saying prayers for the emergency medical technicians who also played an important role in the search and recovery effort.

One of them was his own son, Keith, who responded to the call minutes after the first plane hit.

Ken and Diane Fairben have lost their 24-year-old son, their only child, who wanted to save lives. In May 2001, he completed an 11-month EMT program at North Shore University Hospital in Manhasset. He had been working for four years as a medic at New York Presbyterian Hospital in upper Manhattan.

Days after the tragedy, the Fairbens and Presbyterian Hospital's chief operating officer, Dr. Herbert Pardes, rang the 9:30 a.m. opening bell at NASDAQ as a symbol of the hard work and lost lives of the hospital's EMT workers. "These were the greatest guys," Pardes said. "They were committed to saving people."

"It was Keith's love and passion," said his father, who called his son on his cell phone at 9:10, minutes after he heard about the plane crash. "I knew he would be there," he said. The 6-foot-3, 240-pound medic loved helping people, so his father wasn't surprised when his son answered the phone and said, "Dad, I'm really busy. I'm at the World Trade Center. I can't talk now." Be safe, his father said. "Call us later."

By 5 o'clock that evening, Fairben called his son's dispatcher and asked how everything was going. "Keith and Mario are missing," he was told. "They found their ambulance. But they were not there." Mario Santoro, of Manhattan, father of a 2-year-old daughter, was Fairben's partner. They had been riding together for four months.

Keith, who lived with his parents in Floral Park, was also a volunteer firefighter. Two weeks earlier, Keith arrived home to find his uncle in the throes of a ruptured aorta. He recognized the signs and immediately began life-saving treatment. Unfortunately, his uncle didn't make it through. Keith was devastated, his father recalls. "It's God's hand," he told his son. Now, he takes those words to heart. "We are realistic. I know that he wouldn't have wanted to be anywhere else."

KATHY MAZZA-DELOSH
A Woman Captain in a Man's World

 Kathy Mazza had been saving people at the Port Authority long before she charged into the blazing towers on September 11.

Mazza, 46, was a captain in the Port Authority police department and the first female commanding officer of its police academy. Two years earlier, she had stood in the Oval Room on the 43rd floor of One World Trade Center, being honored for setting up a 1997 program that trained 600 officers to use defibrillators. The Port Authority credited the program with saving 14 to 16 lives. What's more, Mazza used her background as a former operating-room nurse to supervise and tweak a broad array of Port Authority emergency medical services, and she taught emergency medicine at the academy. "She was the person that breathed life into the Port Authority training program," said Marie Diglio, executive director of operations at the New York City Emergency Medical Services Council.

Officer Eugene Fasano was the last one to see Mazza alive at the trade center while she was attempting to reroute victims who were unknowingly walking into a blaze. "She was very proud to attain her rank," Fasano said, "very proud to be part of the Port Authority."

Mazza—whose husband, Christopher Delosh, is an officer in the New York City Police Department—enrolled in the Port Authority Police Academy herself more than 14 years ago. She had been an operating-room nurse at St. Francis Hospital in Roslyn, but she told *Newsday* in an interview in 2000 that she was looking for a "more secure retirement."

After patrolling Kennedy Airport for a year, Mazza was quickly promoted to sergeant. She rose to lieutenant in 1998, and in April 2001 became one of only two female captains in the Port Authority. There are 12 male captains. "She advanced so quickly in the police department, before you knew it she was something else," said her mother, Rose Mazza. "She said, 'I'll retire as police chief.'"

"She's a woman in a man's world," Diglio said. "And she was tough as nails. She had to be so hard on the exterior. There was a suit of armor around her, because there had to be. But when you got to know her, she could be so funny, so lighthearted."

The tough facade was the result of having to contend with three rambunctious brothers while growing up in Massapequa, said her mother. Kathy Mazza was the prankster of the bunch, and her lighthearted side was most evident in how she treated her nephew and five nieces, and her dog, Petey, whom friends and family called her child. "She spoiled all of them," said Rose, who credits her daughter with saving her life, too. One day the elder Mazza was complaining of chest pains, and Kathy recognized that her mother's arteries were blocked. "She saved my life," Rose Mazza said. "If it wasn't for her, I wouldn't be here today."

7
Mothers, Fathers, Sisters, Brothers

They leave empty places in the families that knew them best.

Identical twins worked in the same tower—but only one escaped. A wife undergoing treatment for cancer replays her husband's words: "He said, 'You can't die.' And then he died."

The bereaved cling to memories. Three sisters remember the soft-spoken father who loved eating home-grown tomatoes and singing "La Bamba" in his native Spanish. And who loved them. "If there was a male voice calling for one of the girls, he'd get chest pains," said his wife.

And an entire family misses the young woman who phoned each of them every day— who was "at the happiest point of her life."

She was pregnant with her first child.

RICHARD PALAZZOLO
Twins in the Towers: One Smile Lives On

Maria Alfano will never again see her kid brother Richard Palazzolo's blue eyes and "little sly smile." That is, except when she looks into the face of her other kid brother, Ronald— Richard's identical twin.

It's always been that way, she said. "If I looked at one, I thought of the other."

The 39-year-old twins had done everything together since the day they were born—fishing, stargazing and raising six Easter chicks to full-grown roosters as children in Corona, and, as adults, mountain-climbing, running marathons, biking, shark-fishing and flying kites.

Both single, they shared an apartment on Broadway just five blocks from the World Trade Center. And they both worked as securities and bond brokers in Tower One, Ronald at Garban-Intercapital on the 26th floor, and Richard at Cantor Fitzgerald on the 105th floor.

On September 11, only Ronald escaped the destruction.

Even as the skyscraper shuddered from the impact of the first plane that morning, almost throwing Ronald from his chair, "his other hand was on the phone, calling Richard," said Alfano, of New Hyde Park.

Ronald couldn't get through to his brother, but was assured by a co-worker that the office was being evacuated. Then, his sister said, "He just dropped the phone and ran out." Once outside, he wanted to stay and wait for his brother but was shoved away from the building by rescue workers.

In the nightmare that followed, Ronald somehow made his way to the South Street Seaport, where he ran into two friends and clients of his brother's, also identical twins, named Peter and Paul.

"They were like the apostles," Alfano said. "They took my brother Ronald around to see if [Richard] was in any of the hospitals. They searched all night."

Though brother and sister alike were hoping against the odds, she said, "Reality was there, and it was staring you in the face. It was hard to think that a miracle would have happened."

There's some comfort in thinking of Richard at peace, Alfano said. "Where he is now is in a better place." But, she said, "We're left with a great loss."

As for Ronald, she said, "I think he's in the worst place right now, because half his soul is in heaven, and the other half is suffering through this here on earth."

BRIAN CANNIZZARO
A Family of Firefighters

When he became a firefighter three years ago, taking the badge number of his retired firefighter father was the fulfillment of a life's dream for Brian Cannizzaro.

"His dad was his hero, his idol," said Cannizzaro's wife, Jacqueline. "He wanted to make him proud every day." But to Cannizzaro's father, Sam, of Staten Island, Brian was the hero—even before he became a martyr, lost in the terrorist attacks. "Everyone says, 'He always wanted to be like you,'" his father said. "I told him, 'Brian, I wish I could be half the firefighter that you are now.'"

In the months that followed the attack, Cannizzaro's younger brother started the process of becoming a firefighter. Craig, 27, hoped to start classes by spring. He had always planned to be a firefighter, he said, but his brother's loss "just makes more motivation to actually finish what he started." Meanwhile, family members have honored the fallen firefighter with tattoos. His badge number, 11126, is on his father plus both brothers, Craig and Charles, and Charles' wife, Tami.

Cannizzaro, 30, of Staten Island, seemed an ideal firefighter to his younger brother. "He was built like an ox," his brother said. "He had the perfect build, the perfect mentality for the job. Almost like a Sylvester Stallone in *Rambo* type of person." But to his wife, Cannizzaro's strength was his balance— his ability to handle anything he took on. "He was very confident in everything he did, and really excelled in everything he did," Jacqueline said.

That was clearly evident in his marriage proposal. In 1996, Cannizzaro surprised her before a packed Broadway show, *Beauty and the Beast*. During the curtain call, the actor playing the prince asked the audience to sit down. Then he asked Cannizzaro and Jacqueline to stand. "He said, 'Brian has given me the honor of asking you if you will marry him,'" she recalled. "I turned to Brian, and he was on his knee with the most beautiful ring I had ever seen."

In October 2000, Cannizzaro used his firefighter training to deliver the couple's first child, Christopher. He handled fatherhood with his usual grace, rearranging his schedule to stay home with Christopher during the day when his wife returned to work as a schoolteacher in September. "You have just never seen a more proud father," she said. "He cooked. He took care of the baby. . . . He'd walk my son around the neighborhood."

On the morning of September 11, Cannizzaro left for work early, as usual, his wife said. "I kissed him and said, 'Be careful. I love you,' as usual." He was last seen evacuating workers in the lobby of Tower Two. Seven people from Ladder Company 101 in Red Hook were lost that morning. "He was never one to back down or be the shy one. He was always the one leading the charge," said Charles, his older brother. "His fate was probably inevitable with that kind of drive that he had.

"At least, that's the way you try to look at it."

KEVIN MURPHY
A Medal for St. Kevin

Whenever Beth Murphy had to travel to Manhattan for cancer treatments, her husband, Kevin, always made sure she spent the day in style. "He always made a day of it," she said. They would go to lunch with colleagues at Marsh & McLennan, or gaze out at his coveted view of the Statue of Liberty from his desk on the 100th floor of Tower One. At other times they just wandered around the trade center's shopping mall before she returned home to Northport.

But sometimes her melanoma got the better of him, Beth Murphy said. Just a few months ago, "he was crying. He said, 'You can't die.' And then he died."

Murphy, who turned 40 the weekend before September 11, was an assistant vice president at Marsh and was due to be promoted to vice president in October.

He was proud of his job, and loved to give tours of the Twin Towers, but Murphy's true passion was reserved for his family. Every evening, his two children—Connor, 7, and Caitlyn, 4, would collapse into his arms as he came through the door, his wife said. On weekends, "He did it all," she said, adding that friends joked she should rent him out. He

took the kids to the dry cleaner, to the grocery store, on dozens of other errands. In fact, the children identified the car with him so much that she sold it to eliminate the painful reminder.

Murphy was so well known for his generosity that some friends had nicknamed him St. Kevin. "He was one of those people that at three in the morning would help you out," his wife said. So about a week after he died in the terrorist attacks, his wife was amused to find a St. Kevin medal at the bottom of one of his drawers. A friend must have given it to him as a joke, she guesses.

She now wears it on a chain around her neck.

DEANNA GALANTE
Missing the Call That Doesn't Come

Deanna Galante was always checking in with the people she loved.

"She would call everybody a couple of times a day," said her husband, Anthony Galante. "She would call her brother, her mother, her father, me, my parents, at least two or three times a day." Anthony's voice cracked slightly as he added, "That's why it's so hard now. She doesn't call."

Deanna, 32, a personal assistant at Cantor Fitzgerald, was on the 106th floor of One World Trade Center. "She was at the happiest point of her life," Anthony said. "So was I, until September 11." The couple had lived together for two years, and Deanna was seven months pregnant with their first child. "She loved kids," Anthony said. "She just basically had two goals—to be with me forever and to have the baby and be a loving mother."

Anthony only knew his son-to-be—already named Matthew Giacomo Galante—from the doctor's office and from the movements in Deanna's belly. "From going to the doctor every other week, the sonograms, we'd see him suck his thumb," he said. "Just the night before, we were looking at her stomach and he was moving around." The couple had already bought diapers and baby clothes, and started renovating their house. Deanna's mother had planned a baby shower for October 28.

There was some small consolation for Anthony in the memory of the couple's wedding several weeks before, which fulfilled a dream for Deanna. About 40 family members and guests took a cruise ship from Manhattan to Bermuda and the marriage took place on board. "She was pregnant and all, and she was dancing every night," Anthony said. "She was the only one that didn't get seasick."

Athletic and outgoing, Deanna loved skiing, Rollerblading and going to the gym. She had been an aerobics instructor at one point. After high school, she went on to beauty school, and she still cut hair for a few private clients. And, Anthony said, "She had a million friends. She'd meet you one time, and then the next time she'd speak to you, she'd talk like she'd known you for a long time," he said. "She was that type of person."

"It's not what I was planning for," he said while arranging a memorial service. "I was planning for a baby, not a funeral. She always said, 'That's it.' I was stuck with her forever.

"I can't believe it ended this way."

LARS QUALBEN
He Had All the Time in the World

 Inside Lars Qualben's kitchen, his wife walks across the wide wooden boards he finished by hand. Martha Qualben skirted the gaping hole he left in their floor for several years before he finally covered it. There would be time, too, to paint the flaking facade of the townhouse where the couple lived together for a quarter of a century, time to renovate the weathered window frame looking out on their lush green backyard. He cleared the yard of rubble day by day when Carroll Gardens, Brooklyn, was becoming a gentrified neighborhood, planting 75 trees there, pruning them, mowing the lawn, laying paths of red brick, building a place where he could smoke his cigars.

This was the way Qualben nurtured the things and the people he loved as he approached his 50th birthday: slow and steady. Morning after morning, he walked his younger son Kai, 14, to the school bus stop on Court Street, testing him on prime numbers or square roots. What's the square root of this? What's the square root of that? He did that the morning of September 11, then took the subway to his job at Marsh & McLennan, on the 100th floor of Tower One.

"He was the kind of person who expected to live a long life," said Martha, his wife of 28 years. "He looked forward to seeing his children going

through all of those passages and celebrating all those milestones. And we celebrated the milestones not in an ostentatious way, but just an ordinary way. We had a really pretty plain life, but it was solid, and he was just a solid guy."

They met during college in 1970 at a Lutheran summer camp in the Catskills. She came from Nebraska, and he was a boy from Bay Ridge, who went full of energy and optimism to St. Olaf's College in Northfield, Minnesota. In his freshman year, he was arrested as one of "The Minnesota 9" in protests against the Vietnam War. "Of course, his parents were horrified," his wife said.

They married his senior year, and moved to Bay Ridge, while continuing to travel to Washington to rally for former president Richard Nixon's impeachment. A few years later, they went to Carroll Gardens, bought up a handful of vacant lots along with their building on half an acre, and began to carve out a suburban existence in the city. Fifteen years before the attack, they had their first son, Paul, the first test-tube baby in the metropolitan area born in an outpatient facility. Martha, who could not become pregnant for nine years, conceived Kai a year later.

They stayed in Carroll Gardens. Qualben was the president of the congregation of Trinity Lutheran in Sunset Park, Brooklyn, where his parents and a brother attend. Kai went to Polytechnic Country Day School in Bay Ridge, where Qualben studied as a boy. The children were just beginning to transfer their loyalties from mother to father. Now their mother is all they have, and the house where he left his fingerprints, and his expectations for the future. It is hard for her, with his clothing, his office and his clutter everywhere around. For now, this is where they are.

"I think my children will insist that we stay here," she said, "because they absolutely love it."

EDELMIRO ABAD
He Joined His Family in the Dance of Life

 Being the father of three daughters and living in a house full of women was not always easy for Edelmiro Abad, whom everyone called Ed. It meant the unavoidable issue of boyfriends. "If there was a male voice calling for

one of the girls, he'd get chest pains," his wife, Lorraine Abad, remembered with a laugh. "The boyfriend issue was big."

Abad, 54, who worked on the 90th floor of Tower Two at Fiduciary Trust Company International for 26 years, was senior vice president at the time of the attack. But his daughters were his treasures. Rebecca, 26, Jennifer, 23, and Serena, 19, all still lived at home, and the family always took vacations together. The close Brooklyn family also includes Abad's parents, Ascension and Jacinto Abad, who also lived in the house. What first attracted her to Abad, said his wife, was "his charming ways, his sense of family."

For his daughters, life revolved around dance. And since his life revolved around them, Abad was always a part of the dance-circuit scene. He attended countless recitals and competitions over the past 22 years. "Even some of our vacations had to do with competitions," his wife said.

Twice, Abad even performed at the recitals. The normally soft-spoken and reserved man sported a white shirt and black pants and slung on a guitar to sing "La Bamba" in his native tongue. It was a big deal for the girls, which is why he did it. "It's not the thing for him to do," his wife said. "He's not showy like that."

Born in Spain, Abad came to the United States when he was 7. His wife described him as a simple man with simple pleasures. He loved war- and religious-themed movies, took long walks along Shore Road in Bath Beach and was happiest just to nosh on his parents' homegrown tomatoes, lovingly grown in the backyard. Abad said he didn't feel well if he had to go a few days in the summer without the tomatoes, and waited anxiously through the winter months until they grew again. Even while on summer vacations, said his wife, he would take some along in a paper bag.

The Abads traveled to Spain twice with their daughters to visit family. The last trip was a month before the September attack, when they went to Abad's hometown of Moncayo Dela Sierra in northern Spain. His wife said she felt a sense of comfort knowing he spent time with many of his relatives just before the attack, including some he hadn't seen in 14 years. On those trips to Spain, he would take his wife to places he remembered from his childhood—a hilltop to eye a certain vista, even a drinking well where he almost drowned as a child. "He loved going up to the highest point in the mountains," his wife said. "There he felt at one with the earth."

JOSEPH ZACCOLI
Circling the Words: Devotion, Perseverance

Hoping to precisely describe his best friend, Christopher Griffin sat down in a quiet corner of his brother-in-law's Valley Stream home and began putting words on paper.

"I circled these words: devoted father, wonderful husband to my sister, extraordinary sense of humor, a man who persevered," Griffin said, his emotions quickly swallowing his soft voice.

Workers pulled the body of Joseph Zaccoli, 39—father to Joseph, 13, Regina, 11, and James, 7, husband of Helen, 39—from the wreckage of One World Trade Center in the first week of recovery efforts. Since 1993, Zaccoli had been a trader at Cantor Fitzgerald on the 104th floor, where he was usually chatting with clients and colleagues by 7:30 a.m. "Joe would get up early to catch the train to Manhattan for work, but get home by 7 in the evening to be with his family," Griffin said. "He loved his job, but he wanted to be home."

Born and raised in Valley Stream, Zaccoli graduated from Nassau County Community College with an associate's degree in liberal arts, but quickly headed to Wall Street to pursue his career. He worked at several brokerage houses before settling in 1993 at Cantor Fitzgerald. Soon, he was telling his family he loved the job, the company and the people he worked with. He said they were more like a big, extended family than the denizens of a billion-dollars-a-year company with worldwide business.

His career on a fast track, Zaccoli and his wife, Helen, moved into a Tudor-style home. Like so many others who live on Long Island and commute on trains to jobs in New York City, Zaccoli carved out a busy life at home, coaching his kids' softball and basketball teams. "His commitment to his family was extraordinary," said Griffin. "The word I circled, perseverance, was Joe to a T. He was so committed and loving to his wife and children. As evidence for how much he wanted to be with his kids, he coached their teams. He coached his daughter's softball team, the Rockies, and the kids' basketball teams. He loved basketball. He would set up rims every time there was a family gathering. He had the best shot in the family. His nickname was Shooter. You had to cover him all the time."

Griffin wanted to repeat several of the words he had circled on the sheet of paper, making sure his brother-in-law would be remembered as he was. "Devoted father and husband," Griffin said. "That was Joe."

MUKUL AGARWALA
The Loss of a Son Is Too Much for His Father

One day in October, Karta Agarwala lost the will to live. The Kendall Park, New Jersey, resident simply could not deal with the loss of his son, Mukul, 37, a research analyst who had been working at the World Trade Center for less than a month.

"My father said God's gift to him was that he had four sons that would one day be his coffin bearers," Atul, Mukul's older brother, said.

But in the days after the tragedy, their father was unable to find solace. "He wanted to ask God why his son was taken from him. . . . He finally came to the realization that Mukul was gone, and it broke his will," another son, Ajay, said. Their father died from heart failure at the age of 71. His sons said their father was never quite the same after the South Brunswick, New Jersey, police arrived at his home a few weeks after the attack on the Twin Towers and told him Mukul had likely perished there.

The second of four brothers, Mukul Agarwala was hired by Fiduciary Trust Company International in Manhattan in September as a research analyst. "He was very excited about starting a new job at Fiduciary," said Ajay, Mukul's younger brother.

Born in New Delhi in 1963, he came to the United States with his family in 1972 and later became an American citizen. "We didn't have too many friends when we first came to this country. But we had one another," Atul said. Agarwala attended the University of Pennsylvania, where he received a bachelor's degree in computer science and an MBA from the prestigious Wharton School. He did investment banking in the United States and abroad, and later headed an Internet-based company in San Diego that dealt with stock research, Ajay said. He was courted by Fiduciary Trust, which offered a position in early September.

Mukul, who was married to Rhea Shome, took the job at Fiduciary because he wanted to get back to the East Coast, and because he wanted to be able to help his family. Atul said his younger brother was ill-suited to be an investment banker because of the fiercely competitive nature of the work and his brother's passive disposition. "He could not cut somebody's throat in the market he worked in," Atul said. "He was what a gentle businessman was in the 1940s and 1950s."

The night before the attack, his mother, Daya, and Ajay dropped him off at the Tribeca Hotel in Manhattan, where Mukul stayed on nights when he worked late. "Mukul was proud to work in the World Trade Center," said Atul. Before she bid her son farewell, his mother asked what would happen if there were a fire in the towers. Mukul reassured his mother that the buildings were safe.

In the weeks that followed, she struggled with her Hindu faith. Although she found solace in it at times, she also dealt with the realization that no amount of praying could bring back her son. "My mother goes through this cycle where she prays for peace," Atul said. "Then she'll get angry and break all of her religious statues. Then she'll pray again."

FRANCO LALAMA
An Engineer Who Built on Tradition

Franco Lalama was an engineer for the Port Authority, ensuring the structural integrity of all the bridges and tunnels across the Hudson River. But when it came to projects at his Nutley, New Jersey, home, his wife, Linda, said, he would never have any luck with anything.

"Sometimes I would wonder if Murphy's Law was in effect with him," she said. "You know, if something can go wrong, it will. And it did to him." Lalama would find drops of water on the floor and dismantle the whole kitchen sink, pipes and all. "He'd always have to run out to Home Depot to get another piece," Linda recalled with a laugh. "He'd say, 'It won't take long,' and then it would take all day."

But nothing seemed to faze Lalama, 45, she said. "It would all get fixed in the long run, everything would work out. That's the type of guy he was. He just kept going, kept plugging along."

The oldest son of seven children, Lalama was born in Pacentro, Italy, and moved with his family to Paterson, New Jersey, when he was 7. His parents, Attilio and Maria Lalama, have retired and moved back to Italy. Lalama retained many of his family's Italian traditions, listening to Italian music on the radio every week, gardening and even making barrels of red wine with his sisters, using their father's equipment. It tasted good, his wife said, but "I could only drink like one glass. It was potent stuff." Lalama would give bottles to family and friends every year.

Lalama loved his work, whether it was directing projects from his office on the 64th floor of Tower One or going out into the field, up the towers of the bridges or deep down into the tunnels. "He liked heights," his wife said. "He liked being out there, you know?" He would have stayed on at the Port Authority for as long as he could, she said. "He loved his job. He never missed a day."

Without her husband, she is following his example, taking comfort in their three daughters, Marianne, 17, Patricia, 15, and Katharine, 7, and in her closeness to his family. "I have moments when I think I'm just going to fall apart," she said, but then added, "There are a lot of good things to remember. . . . That's how I look at it, in a way, to try to get through the days. It's hard."

SALVATORE PEPE
He Brought Two Families Together

Every August, Salvatore Pepe would gather his family, buy 8 to 10 bushels of tomatoes and continue the canning tradition his mother started decades ago. "This is a good way to remember our parents and the tradition," he would tell his family, recalls his sister, Leonida Pepe. There was more: He'd spend hours creating a custom calendar on which every family birthday, anniversary or notable date was recognized with a picture. All told, Pepe would make three calendars: one for his own 45-member family, one for his wife's 16-member family and one for both families. "He enjoyed doing things that would bring family together," said his wife, Cathy Ng-Pepe of Elmhurst.

Working on the 97th floor of the north tower, Pepe, 45, was an assistant vice president in the global technology unit of Marsh & McLennan. "We kept watching the news," said his wife, who kept vigil with her father and her 18-month-old son, Salvatore Loong Pepe. "We kept looking for him as part of the group making their way home." They never saw him, and they never heard from him again.

Born six months after his family arrived in New York from Italy, Pepe was the youngest of seven and the only one born in the United States. In 1997, he married Cathy Ng, who had emigrated from Malaysia. Although Pepe was an Italian Catholic and Ng-Pepe was a Chinese Buddhist, both respected each other's culture, Ng-Pepe said, noting that her husband built a Buddhist altar table for her family to honor their dead relatives.

But Pepe's family said they will remember him most for his unselfish love. "He never thought of himself," Ng-Pepe said. "He would never ask help for himself." When his mother couldn't take care of herself anymore because of cancer, he devoted time to her before she died in 1992. "He would bathe her, feed her," said Leonida Pepe. "That's so rare."

SUSAN GETZENDANNER
Her Circle of Friends Encompassed the World

Two years and 59 floors. That was the separation between Susan M. Getzendanner, 57, and her brother, Tom, 55. He was temporarily working on the 38th floor of Tower Two. She held a longtime job on the 97th floor of Tower Two, working as a vice president at Fiduciary Trust Company International. They spoke briefly on September 11, moments after the first plane slammed into Tower One. "We agreed to stay put," her brother said. When the second plane struck, he walked the 38 flights down to the ground. His sister never got out.

Getzendanner, a Manhattan resident, was the oldest of Joseph W. and Betty Anne Getzendanner's four children, in a tight-knit family that grew up in Shaker Heights, Ohio. Getzendanner was independent and adventurous, trekking through the Himalayas many times, a pastime that landed her on the pages of *Sports Illustrated for Women*. She lived a life of contrasts. She was a successful businesswoman who loved the city she lived in but an outdoors enthusiast who fled to Salisbury, Connecticut, on weekends, hiking up Mount Riga and gardening at the house she bought there.

Her siblings remember her most for her compassion and loyalty, a woman whose circle of friends encompassed the world—from Tibetan monks to friends she met on treks through Peru. "The trekking she did was incredible," said her sister Martha Lingen, 48, of Nevada City, California. "We all lived, or traveled, vicariously through her." Getzendanner was also a beloved aunt to 11 nieces and nephews, whom she adored. "She would come here every Christmas," recalled her sister Lydia Kriso, 50, of Great Falls, Virginia. "She was always really interested in my children. She supported them emotionally and financially."

The Getzendanner family had gone through her two homes, the house in Salisbury and her Upper East Side apartment. It's a painful but healing task, yielding things like a note Getzendanner wrote to herself. "It said 'Take piano lessons,'" recalled Lydia, a piano teacher. She has been compiling a memory book for other people to learn about her sister's spirit. It will include notes like the one in Getzendanner's house that was either a letter to her former classmates at Wells College in New York or an attachment from a Christmas card. Getzendanner wrote it after the 1993 bombing of the World Trade Center. She called the towers safer than they were before and safer than a lot of other places. And she said she'd always stay in Manhattan, her home, a place she loved, where living was an adventure in itself.

GARY HAAG
A Pied Piper to the Neighborhood Kids

If it weren't for her three kids, their three children, it would be a lot harder for Mary Haag to move on. To move on from a wonderful life where her husband, Gary R. Haag, would be sure to get home on time to pass the evenings with his three children.

There were evenings of coaching his 7-year-old son Michael's T-ball team, or reading to the younger ones, Kevin, 4, and Molly, 2. And it wasn't just his own kids who flocked to Haag, 36, a vice president of claims for Marsh & McLennan on the 100th floor of Tower One. He was a Pied Piper of sorts on their tree-lined street in Ossining, New York. "Everyone in the neighborhood called him the Pied Piper," his wife said. "Our yard was the yard that everyone played in. He was always pitching the ball, kicking the soccer ball, organizing a game. When he came home from work, the kids would all dump their bikes or scooters wherever they were and run on over."

The Haag family held a memorial service a little more than two weeks after the attacks. It was easier, his wife said, to have some kind of closure rather than prolong the inevitable, stretching the pain.

She and her husband met in Spring Lake on the Jersey shore in 1989. He and his friends had a summer house there. She was down for the weekend. She saw him playing beach volleyball. They married three years later.

The children were everything to him, are everything to her. There were summers by the pool and at Mary's parents' place in Florida. There were winters bundling up the kids and going sledding. There were family outings to Mets and Yankees games, though the Yankees are their team of choice.

Now there is a gap, an empty space, a sadness mixed in with the ins and outs of daily life. His absence at Michael's seventh birthday highlighted it. So does his wife's inability to share the children's daily developments with him. "If I had no kids, I could crawl into bed and not get up," she said. "But with the kids, you can't fall apart. You have to keep things as normal as possible, if there is a normal, for their sake. . . . Life goes on, and it will go on, and we'll always miss their father, and he'll always be a part of their lives. But he would want us to go on."

LINDA RIVERA
Immortalized in Her Brother's Comic Book

A regular guy from Brooklyn goes to the crop circles of Peru searching for signs of extraterrestrial life. His quest starts shortly after his sister, Lynda Raven, has been killed in the World Trade Center attack. He establishes contact with some otherworldly creatures and, through some mysterious processes, they turn him into a mutant superhero known as Knightmetal. With his superhuman powers, and dressed in the impervious shining armor that protects him from most injuries, Knightmetal goes back in time. His goal: to stop the terrorist plot and, somehow, bring his sister back from the dead.

In real life, though, Knightmetal is the alter ego of Rafael Alex Rivera, 28, a sci-fi devotee who wants to make it as a comic-book storyteller. Lynda Raven, the heroine he created for his latest story project, is named after his sister Linda Ivelisse Rivera, a human-resources employee lost on September 11. Rivera, 26, worked for the insurance brokerage firm Marsh & McLennan on the 100th floor of the north tower.

"When I saw that plane crash, in my heart I kind of knew the floor she was working in must have been incinerated," her brother said. "That story expresses the pain that I feel, the severe depression that comes from this, so this is how I deal with it."

Born in Puerto Rico, Rivera grew up in Brooklyn. After high school, she held jobs during the week to pay for her studies at Berkeley College in Manhattan, graduating in 1998 with a business administration degree. She was a jovial person who liked going to the movies, listening to alternative music, playing video games and reading romance novels. She had moved with her boyfriend, Daniel Rojas, to a Rockaway apartment that she had turned into her weekend paradise. She hooked up her portable laptop and audio equipment and the PlayStation 2, Sega Dreamcast and Nintendo GameCube entertainment systems.

Rivera could spend hours scouring the virtual landscape, trying to rid the world of evil and discovering new levels of video gaming, as music from Sarah McLachlan or Dido played softly in the background. Her hobby was rooted in her appreciation of technology and animated art, her brother said. But she still made time to keep in touch with friends from college and high school and to visit her parents, Carmen Alvarado and José Rivera. She paid particular attention to her 11-year-old brother's education—Rivera had already set aside funds for Rafael Joey's college tuition.

The week before the attacks, while helping her mother paint her bathroom, Rivera struck up what her mother thought was an unusual conversation. Her daughter asked her to care for her American Eskimo dog, Suki, and her cat, Sony, if anything happened to her.

Rivera also made her mother commit to a promise. "She said, 'When I die, you are going to cremate my body and then take my ashes and plant a tree, whatever tree you like, because I want to live forever.' . . . She said that trees die in the winter, but are reborn in the summer," Alvarado recalled.

To fulfill that promise, Alvarado was waiting to see if her daughter's body was found, but she remains missing. So her mother is now planning to cremate the umbilical cord she had saved from Rivera's birth and plant a tree in her daughter's memory.

KAREN KLITZMAN
Twin Sister "Was Pretty Special"

The identical twins shared a room until they were teenagers. They were co-captains of the Half Hollow Hills High School tennis team and spoke with each other on the phone every day. That is, until September 11, the day that Donna Klitzman lost her best friend, her other half, the twin sister that she nicknamed "Rennie" when they were growing up in Dix Hills.

Karen Joyce Klitzman, a 38-year-old who worked at Cantor Fitzgerald, was among those lost in the terrorist attack.

"She was pretty special," said Donna, a physician in Princeton, New Jersey. "She was very bright, very witty and clever. She had nicknames for everyone."

The Klitzman family knew Karen was gone when they saw the media images splashed across the television, the plane crashing through the World Trade Center, below the 105th floor where she worked.

Five days after the towers collapsed, the Klitzmans held a memorial service. But that wasn't enough. The family—which includes Joan Klitzman, Karen's mother, and three siblings, Donna, Robert and Susan—wanted to do something more. So they decided to keep Karen's memory alive by endowing the Karen J. Klitzman Memorial Fellowship for the Elimination of Terrorism and the Resolution of Conflict at Columbia University's School of International Studies and Public Affairs, where she received her master's degree in 1988. "It's one small thing we can do so, hopefully, her death will not have been in vain," said Robert, 43, a psychiatrist at Columbia University.

Their mother, a widow, moved a year ago from Dix Hills to the Upper West Side, 13 blocks from her adventurous, quick-on-her-feet daughter, who was an avid tennis player and traveler.

Karen was a woman with a zest for life, teaching English for two years in Macao, near Hong Kong, and Beijing upon graduating from Princeton University. After getting her master's degree, she worked at the New York Mercantile Exchange and, about a year ago, she began a job at eSpeed, a division of Cantor Fitzgerald.

Joan Klitzman was supposed to have dinner with her daughter on September 10 but left a message saying they'd have to reschedule it. That night, Donna did speak to her twin sister. "I asked her who she was going to vote for for mayor," said Donna, whom Karen nicknamed "Babinga," a rare African wood. "I don't know if she actually ever went to vote."

The Klitzman family is contributing money to the fellowship fund and is asking friends and other family members to donate money as well. "Something more worthwhile has to come out of this horrible tragedy," Donna said.

LEE ADLER
A Brilliant Big Brother

Randi Adler couldn't get her big brother on the phone. She knew that wasn't good. Seconds earlier, she had heard on the car radio that a plane struck the World Trade Center, where Lee Alan Adler worked on the 103rd floor. Lee had always taken care of her since they were little. Now all Randi wanted was the comfort of his voice. "I called him immediately, but there was no answer," she said. "My heart sank. I don't even remember how I got to work."

A grief counselor at Jewish Community Services in Aventura, Florida, Randi also can't remember what she told other people to ease their pain. Her brother can't comfort her now, but she sought strength in the rest of her family, including her mother and two younger brothers.

Lee was two years older, smart and protective of his little sister. Lee was the one who, when he was

only 5, thought he could make the two of them feel better when they were home sick one day. So he pulled a chair to the kitchen counter, hoisted himself up and grabbed the bottle of baby Tylenol, which he shared with his sister, half and half. Despite his good intentions, they ended up in the hospital having their stomachs pumped.

In school, Lee was always brilliant in math and science, blazing a trail Randi could never follow—she was a music major. ("But then, he wasn't a very good singer," she said.) Lee would eventually get his doctorate in nuclear chemistry at Texas A&M University, where he met Alice. They were married for 15 years and had one daughter, who was 12 at the time of the attack.

Lee worked as a computer programmer at Cantor Fitzgerald, one of the hardest-hit companies in the World Trade Center. Though he worked on the 103rd floor, Lee was scared of heights and always asked for an inside office. Randi loved to tease him about that.

The last time Randi saw her brother was two weeks before the attack, when the family got together for her grandmother's funeral. "When someone who's 92 years old passes away, there's a sense that they've had a full life," she said. "When someone who's 48 passes away, it's hard to understand."

TIMOTHY BYRNE
His Mother's Right Arm

Timothy Byrne was a wide receiver for Syracuse University in the 1980s. He never got much playing time, but in 1984, he gave his father, Patrick, the pleasure of seeing him play against the top-ranked University of Nebraska in a game that is regarded by some people as one of the greatest in college football history.

Patrick, the family patriarch, died in his sleep after a seizure in 1986. Timothy, then in his final year of college, stepped into his father's role as best he could. "Timmy was instantly my right arm," said his mother, Charlene. "He used to have fireside meetings with the kids. He was always there whenever we needed him."

The third of 10 children, Byrne was always eager to take on as much as he could. "Tim set the example for all of us," said his brother Jim. "He would fly back to his Manhattan apartment after a business trip to San Francisco, and drive out to Huntington to check up on my mom. That was just the kind of person he was."

Timothy Byrne, 36, was last heard from when he phoned his mother and brother to tell them he had just seen the first plane crash into Tower One of the World Trade Center. He was watching from the 104th floor of Tower Two, where he was an investment banker for Sandler O'Neill. He was single and sincere, relatives said, and successful: He was able to take on his mother's mortgage, much of his younger brother's tuition at Cornell University and "always picked up the check," Charlene Byrne said. He never got married, according to his mother, because he knew that the travel demands of his job would keep him from being the husband and father he envisioned himself being. "When people asked him why he wasn't married," his mother recounted, "Tim would always say, 'I love being me.'"

ANDREW FRIEDMAN
At His Best in Toughest of Times

 Andrew Friedman just might have been the most laid-back man on Long Island. Instead of fretting when a corporate takeover left the 44-year-old institutional trader between jobs in April 2001, he spent the spring and summer coaching his twin sons' sports teams and whittling his golf handicap to 9. He went back to work when he found a job that felt right: vice president in charge of equity trading at Carr Futures.

Friedman began work at Carr's 92nd-floor offices in Tower One just a few weeks before the September 11 attacks. After the two planes hit the Twin Towers, he made a last call to his wife, Lisa Steinberg Friedman, telling her that despite the smoke, "we have plenty of air, we're going to be fine." It was "typical Andy," his wife said. He never wanted others to worry on his account.

Friedman's approach to life was infectious, brightening even the toughest of times for those around him. Friedman had been dating Steinberg for three years when she was diagnosed with ovarian cancer. She felt extremely self-conscious that

her hair had fallen out afterward, so Friedman visited the hospital every day with a rose and gave her a playful new nickname.

"He would lean down and kiss her, and her red hair would be all over the pillow," said Esther Tanenbaum, a longtime family friend. "And he would say, 'I love you, Kojak,'" a playful reference to the bald TV detective. And when Steinberg felt self-conscious about wearing her wig in public, Friedman would tell her to forget the wig, saying, "'Let's bag it. Let's just go out to dinner,'" his wife remembered. And he would mean it.

Friends said the two made a good match. Stature aside—Friedman was 6 foot 4 and Lisa is 6 foot 1—the two were a study in opposites. A type-A high achiever, his wife is a self-described "neurotic" who jokes that she worries so much "I take out insurance on my insurance policies." Her husband's lighthearted attitude tempered her anxious tendencies—he used to joke, "All I worry about is you."

His temperament made him a favorite among his clan of friends, some from his childhood in Valley Stream, others whom he met through David Goldman, a Great Neck native with his own extensive buddy network, who was Friedman's roommate at George Washington University. Some 2,000 people showed up at Friedman's memorial service to mourn the man Goldman called "a big teddy bear."

"We used to tease him, saying we only wished he had a mean streak," said Goldman, whose 26-year friendship with Friedman was founded on their mutual passion for sports and their hometown teams, the Yankees and the Giants. In college, the two went to Bruce Springsteen shows at the Stone Pony in Asbury Park, New Jersey, and saw the Grateful Dead.

"Since the '70s we always went to the playoffs and the World Series together," Goldman said. On the way home from late games at Yankee Stadium, Friedman would invariably fall asleep on Goldman's shoulder. They stayed close with each other through the years, calling each other as many as "25 times a day" on the weekends, said Tanenbaum.

The Friedmans prospered as they matured—he was a successful trader, and she became a vice president at Fleet Bank—and they bought a house in Woodbury. Friedman remained down-to-earth despite his posh surroundings. He preferred simple food—he once teased Tanenbaum for making crème brûlée, asking her, "Where's the Hostess cupcakes? Where's the soda?"

The Friedmans doted on their sons, Michael and Daniel, 11-year-old sports enthusiasts whose favorite coach was their father. To Andrew and Lisa, the twins' birth was a kind of miracle, since Lisa had lost an ovary to cancer and it wasn't clear if she could bear children. Still, they tried to instill simple values in the boys; this year they had pooled savings from their allowances and donated $104 to a charitable foundation headed by Yankees shortstop Derek Jeter. Jeter returned the favor after hearing that his young benefactors' father had perished in the terrorist attacks, inviting them to his Christmas party and promising to take them to a game.

The weekend after the attacks, Friedman's golf foursome, now a threesome, convened as usual, on the course of the Tam O'Shanter Club at Glen Head. They hung his bag of clubs on the back of a golf cart and played a round, swinging his clubs when it would have been his turn. Noted Tanenbaum, "They said he had a great round."

DANIEL PATRICK TRANT
A Coach Who Brought Out Kids' Potential

 Dan Trant was an All-American basketball player in college and was drafted by the Boston Celtics. But rivaling his finest moments as a player are the times he spent in elementary school gymnasiums teaching grade-school boys basketball, or on nondescript Long Island fields teaching teenage girls soccer.

At a memorial service for Trant, lost in the World Trade Center attacks, boys in uniforms from the teams that Trant, 40, had recently been coaching—and former teammates from the Clark University team that played in the 1984 Division III finals—sat among the thousands in attendance.

Some of the boys were around 10 years old, like Trant's son Alex. This group included a boy whose mother said that two winters ago Trant showed her son the best basketball season of his life. Trant kept pushy parents out of the way of the children's having fun, she said, and always made sure her son scored at least one basket each game. Some of the boys were about 12 years old, like Trant's son Daniel. Among them was a boy from the travel basketball team that Trant coached whose parents credited Trant with inspiring their son to take school seriously.

Not in uniform, but equally dedicated to their old coach, was a group of college-age girls, friends and teammates of Trant's daughter, Jessica, 19, who now plays soccer at Pace University. Trant had coached Jessica since she was 5, and in the process earned the respect and admiration of many girls, including one who remembered in a recent letter that Trant "brought out the best in me," and made her "want to play soccer."

It was Trant's confidence and cool manner, his wife, Kathy, said, that made him such an effective and well-liked coach. It was this commanding yet unassuming way that made adults like him just as much. "Danny knew how to handle every person, every situation in life," said Kathy Trant, his wife of 14 years. "He had this presence that you could never explain."

Trant, a bond broker at Cantor Fitzgerald, was in his office on the 104th floor of Tower One on September 11. After the plane hit below him that morning, he called his wife to tell her he loved her and to take care of their kids. Then he said he had to go because his office was filling with smoke.

Trant went to high school in Westfield, Massachusetts, and was a two-time All-American basketball player at Clark, in Worcester. He is a bit of a legend there, where he scored 1,663 points, the third-highest in school history, before being picked by the Celtics in the fourth round of the 1984 NBA draft. While Trant was a great shooter, at 6 foot 2 he didn't have enough size for the team and was cut before the season, his wife said.

He played pro basketball in Ireland after college, then returned to Massachusetts, where he worked as a witness advocate in the Hampden County prosecutor's office from 1986 to 1991. He met his future wife in 1987 and married her three months later, and the couple moved to Long Island in 1991. He adopted her daughter, Jessica, as his own.

In recent years, Trant got up at 4:15 every morning for work, but that didn't stop him from spending every night and weekend day coaching. He led so many teams that Kathy Trant couldn't keep track of them all. There was the Long Island Lightning, a travel basketball team out of Hempstead, and the Northport Bandits, his daughter's old junior soccer team. He even helped found the St. Philip Neri Catholic Youth Organization travel basketball program at the church.

"My husband should have probably been a college coach. He had a basketball mind that you would not believe," Kathy Trant said. "But he had this way with the kids. They would look at him and not say a word, they just listened and learned . . . Every child wanted to play for him. He never had to raise his voice, he just had this ability to gain respect."

LORISA TAYLOR
She Had a Lot to Celebrate, So She Did

Lorisa Taylor and her husband, Frank, celebrated their seventh anniversary on September 10. It was a quiet, homey affair, in contrast with the previous Saturday, when they got a babysitter for their three daughters and went dancing to mark the occasion. Taylor, 31, loved dancing to R&B. She danced so much that night that she had to take her shoes off to walk back to the car.

So on the day of their anniversary proper, Lorisa picked up a DVD to watch, and Frank came home with cake and champagne. They passed out sparkling cider to the girls—Tatiana, 11, Imani, 4, and Cyann, 3—so they could join in the party. "We toasted to seven years, and we toasted to just having our little family," her husband said.

From her children to her burgeoning career, Taylor had a lot to celebrate. An aggressive businesswoman, she enjoyed the challenges of her job at Marsh & McLennan, where she tailored personal insurance plans to the needs of a high-end clientele of wealthy individuals and families. "She didn't like getting stagnant," said her mother, Geneva Dunbar. "She was a woman who knew what she wanted to do."

Taylor's determined nature manifested itself early. She was a tomboy who loved baseball and played it with the boys, both in the streets of Flatbush and as a slugger with the Marine Park Little League. "As a teenager she was headstrong," said Dunbar. "My husband would tell her to do one thing, and she would do the opposite."

After attending the State University College of Agriculture and Technology at Morrisville, she returned to Flatbush and took a job as a broker in Manhattan. But money wasn't what drove Taylor. She treasured her relationships. "I bent over backwards to make my wife happy," said her husband, "and the gift she gave me back was unconditional love. There was nothing left undone between me and her."

Outgoing and affectionate, she was always reaching out to people, he said. Where other adults would cross the street to avoid the groups of teenagers hanging on the corner, Taylor would just walk on by and say hello. "She got a kick out of it," said her husband. "The kids on the block loved her." At home, Taylor enjoyed spending time with her daughters and made frequent visits to her mother, who lived just eight blocks away. "She would come in the door with that big smile and greet me with a kiss," Dunbar said.

The family was running late on September 11, so Taylor insisted on walking to the subway while her husband dropped the girls off at school. Taylor leaned into the family van to distribute hugs and kisses, giving her husband a peck on the cheek. "Get back over here and give me a real kiss," he told her, and she did.

Taylor rode the subway into Manhattan with her mother that day. Dunbar had been out of town on vacation for a week, so her daughter filled her in on all the anniversary festivities before getting off at the World Trade Center to head up to her job on the 94th floor of the north tower. Less than an hour later, the first plane slammed into the building.

The family initially tried to shield Taylor's three daughters from the truth, a difficult job given the ubiquity of footage from the attacks. "My little 4-year-old . . . saw on TV," Frank Taylor told ABC News the day after the attacks. "She knows something happened to Mommy's building."

ALBERT JOSEPH
He Lived to See the New Year, and His Son

Thousands flocked to New York hospitals after September 11 in the fervent hope that injury, not death, had prevented their loved ones from coming home.

For most, the hunt was futile. But two days after the attack, Cicely Cornelius of the Bronx actually found the person she sought: her father.

A fit, fiercely independent 79-year-old maintenance man at Morgan Stanley, Albert Joseph was in bad shape when she first saw him. He was in a coma. Struck by falling debris after he evacuated from the south tower, the Manhattan resident had sustained multiple head injuries and fractured several bones in his face. Doctors told his daughter that brain damage was likely.

Despite the massive assault on his body, Joseph clung stubbornly to life. A few days after the attack, he woke up. Soon afterward he began to recognize family members and was able to sit up in a chair for a few hours at a time. Sometimes he had to be physically restrained—there were days when he felt particularly spry and kept trying to get up and walk around.

The doctors were surprised by his tenacity. His daughter, the eldest of his eight living children, wasn't. As a young man in Antigua, Joseph once paddled four miles back to the coast after a fishing boat he was on capsized. "If you have 11 children to support, you better be strong," Cornelius said.

Joseph, a carpenter and cabinetmaker, and his wife, Ruby, raised their large family in Antigua, a small Caribbean island east of Puerto Rico. Joseph spent what time off he had with his children. "He wasn't the type to be roaming the streets," said Devon Joseph of Statesville, North Carolina, his youngest child.

Joseph reveled in family history. He told the children long stories about his parents and grandparents, who had been slaves, always ending with, "You're a Joseph, and be proud of it."

Other times he taught the children to strategize with checkers and card games. Every time Devon was about to make a move, Joseph would fix him with an implacable eye. "Think about what you're doing," he would say.

Joseph's house was a block from the beach, but that didn't mean that the Joseph kids could go for a dip any old time. "We went when we were told," Devon Joseph said. His father, a strict disciplinarian, used to "actually taste our skins" and hair for traces of salt, he said. Those who flouted the rules "got a whupping. After a while you knew not to pull certain things on him."

Following the lead of their adult children, Joseph and his wife immigrated to the United States in 1977 and settled in Harlem. Each year a family reunion at a state park on Long Island pulled the Joseph kids, who had scattered from Canada to the Virgin Islands, back to their parents. Joseph, who had 22 grandchildren and seven great-grandchildren, cherished those times. "He was really a family person," Cornelius said.

He got the job at Morgan Stanley 22 years ago and worked long past the age of retirement. "We used to tell him, 'Pops, why don't you hang it up and relax?'" Devon Joseph said. But it was lonely at home without his wife, who had died 15 years earlier, and Joseph couldn't abide sitting still.

That vigor sustained him in the months after the attacks. While he never made a full recovery, he eventually was transferred to a rehabilitation hospital in Edison, New Jersey, where he received physical therapy. Over Christmas, his doctors "even suggested . . . that I bring some warm clothes and some sturdier shoes, because he wanted to walk," Cornelius said. "They said he was ready."

Devon Joseph visited his father the weekend before New Year's Eve. It was the first time Joseph had seen his adored youngest son since September 11. "His face lit up like a Christmas tree," Cornelius said.

Later the two talked. "You OK?" he asked his son.

"I'm all right," replied his son.

"You sure?"

"Yes, I'm fine," he said. Looking back, Devon Joseph said, "He heard what he wanted to hear. His youngest child was OK . . . the fight was over now."

Joseph went into cardiac arrest stemming from his injuries and died on New Year's Day.

8
On the Planes

The jetliners had been cleared for takeoff and they swooped into the sky. The passengers sat back for their journeys—perhaps glancing at the window or opening the newspaper. And then, suddenly and terribly, terror took human shape and their lives ended in fury.

Forty-four people died on the plane that crashed in Pennsylvania, 64 on the jet that hit the Pentagon, 157 on the flights that smashed into the Twin Towers. Those aboard were as diverse as the world they traveled—a salesman who knew most of the gate and flight attendants at Newark International Airport by name, a television producer responsible for one of the medium's funniest shows, a *National Geographic* director flying to a marine research project with a group of teachers and students, a pilot who faced the possibility of catastrophe but never thought about a hijacking.

And a wife whose husband was on the ground tracking her flight on a Web site. As he watched the screen, the image disappeared.

MARK ROTHENBERG
A Super Salesman with a Gift of Gab

Mark "Mickey" Rothenberg was a mover and a shaker.

Whether it was traveling the country, visiting department stores to sell glassware for the Brooklyn company he took over from his father, or traveling the world for the import business he started a few years ago, Rothenberg was always on the move.

He never forgot a name, his wife said, and knew the phone numbers of most people he dealt with by heart.

"He could sell anyone anything," Meredith Rothenberg said. "He had a way with people. He was extremely outgoing and charming."

Rothenberg, 52, of Scotch Plains, New Jersey, regularly flew on United out of Newark International Airport, and he knew most of the gate and flight attendants there by name, too. That's how he was, his wife said.

Rothenberg was on his way to Taiwan aboard United Flight 93 on September 11 when the plane crashed just outside Pittsburgh. He always used his frequent-flier miles to upgrade his tickets to first class, and his wife thinks that he probably talked to the men who hijacked the plane, two of whom were reported to be sitting near him. "If they were up there, which I think they were, he would have talked to them," she said. "He talked to everyone."

Rothenberg met his wife at Franklin & Marshall College in Lancaster, Pennsylvania, in 1969, when he was a senior and she was a freshman. They married in 1971. After college, Rothenberg joined his father's company, Culver Glassware. He started as chief salesman and eventually took over the business.

Finding it hard to make money manufacturing goods in the United States, Rothenberg sold the business in the mid-1990s. A few years ago he started MDR Global Resources, where he served as a middleman between manufacturers in Asia and buyers in the United States. When Rothenberg wasn't working, he spent time with his wife and two daughters, Rachel, 27, and Sara, 23. "He adored them, and it went both ways," his wife said.

Even though Rothenberg traveled often, he called his wife every day, "even if he was halfway around the world," she said. For the year before the crash, his daughter Rachel was studying in Lisbon, but she talked to her father two or three times a week. "We were AT&T's best customer," his wife said. "It doesn't explain why I didn't speak to him on September 11. . . . I have to assume that his cell phone didn't work."

BARBARA OLSON
She Shone Even Outside the Spotlight

Barbara Olson's fine features, sleek blonde hair and conservative politics are remembered by television viewers across the country.

But to her husband, U.S. Solicitor General Theodore B. Olson, the memories that stick are of the dinners she cooked for the two of them at home in Great Falls, Virginia; the bike rides in the countryside near their place in Wisconsin; the deep sleep she would fall into after days spent constantly on the go; the way his three small granddaughters would follow her around "like little ducks."

"She was a fantastic cook, she dressed beautifully, my granddaughters thought she was the best thing in the world," he said. "She was always full of energy, sparkling all the time."

Olson was scheduled to fly to Los Angeles on the night of September 10 to be part of a panel on telecommunications and appear on the television show *Politically Incorrect* the next day. She changed her schedule, however, to be with her husband on the morning of his 61st birthday, September 11. Olson was on American Airlines Flight 77, the plane that crashed into the Pentagon.

As a voice from the Republican right, Olson was in great demand on shows such as *Crossfire*, *Hardball*, and *Meet the Press*. And, her husband said, she appeared on *Larry King Live* more than any other guest but Bob Dole. "She was so good, because she was very direct and she was very pleasant," he said. "The more people saw her, the more they wanted her to be on television."

Olson's first book, *Hell to Pay*, was highly critical of Hillary Rodham Clinton and became a bestseller. *Final Days*, her follow-up on President Bill Clinton's last weeks in the White House, was released posthumously and also made the *New York Times* bestseller list.

Author and commentator are only the most recent hats Olson wore, however. At 45, she had been a ballet dancer, a Hollywood producer, a lawyer, and a lobbyist.

Born and raised in Houston, Texas, Olson graduated from college in her hometown and became a professional dancer, performing with the San Francisco Ballet and the Harkness Ballet in New York City. She had always wanted to go to law school, her husband said, but knew she would have to raise the money to do so herself. So she switched careers and went to Hollywood to work as an assistant producer for television and movies. As a newcomer, she achieved a surprising measure of success, working for HBO and Stacy Keach Productions. When she had raised enough money, she quit to pursue her dream.

After graduating from the Benjamin N. Cardozo School of Law at Yeshiva University in New York, she went to Washington, where she did civil litigation for several years before becoming an assistant U.S. attorney. In 1994 she left to work for the House of Representatives, becoming chief investigative counsel for the House Government Reform and Oversight Committee. In that position, she led the "Travelgate" and "Filegate" investigations into the Clinton administration.

"She believed she could do anything, and she really allowed no one to put any limitations on that," said her husband. "I've gotten so many letters, especially from women, who say, 'She was an inspiration. Because she could do anything, she made me believe I could too.'"

In the moments before the crash, Olson called her husband twice from the plane. "She said, 'What can I tell the pilot to do?'" he recalled. "She was a fighter. She was never the kind of person to sit back and watch something happen and not do something about it. So she was struggling with the idea of what to do."

In those frantic moments, he said, "We talked about personal things. We assured one another that everything was going to be OK.

"Then the connection was broken."

JOSEPH DELUCA and LINDA GRONLUND
Strong People Found the Perfect Balance

  He was a computer expert, an antique car collector, an astronomy buff, a certified junior high school teacher, a devoted stepfather, a cartoonist and an artist.

She was a lawyer, an environmentalist, a sailor, a scuba diver, a brown belt in karate, a car mechanic, a gardener, a photographer, a gourmet cook, a guitarist, an emergency medical technician and a volunteer with autistic children.

Between the two of them, Joe DeLuca and Linda Gronlund pretty much had it covered.

The couple had been friends for almost two decades before they began dating in 2001, and "they were crazy about each other," said DeLuca's sister, Carol Hughes, of Middletown, New Jersey. Her brother had been telling her about his wonderful new girlfriend for months. "He always liked strong women, and Linda was very strong."

That's an understatement, said Gronlund's sister, Elsa Strong, of Amherst, New Hampshire. Despite growing up with asthma, eczema, and various allergies, Gronlund possessed an intense energy that made her friends marvel. "She was always someone who would dive in wholeheartedly."

In DeLuca, she seemed to have found the perfect balance.

"It took someone really unique to fit in with her life," Strong said. "Although he was very kind, and seemed to be very gentle towards her, he definitely had his own opinions and knew what he wanted to do.

"I think that for a lot of her adult life, she had been kind of searching for a relationship that she felt that she could stick with," Strong said. "In the last three or four months of her life, she was as happy as I had ever known her."

DeLuca, 52, and Gronlund, 46, were on United Airlines Flight 93, flying to San Francisco to tour the vineyards in Napa Valley for her 47th birthday. Both divorced, the two had met through a shared passion for amateur car racing. Gronlund, who worked for BMW, was chief of flagging and communications for the New Jersey chapter of the Sports Car Club of America, and DeLuca was a board member. He edited the group's newsletter, which included his comic strip, "Raymond the Cat"—about a cat who loved cars. His yellow Morgan roadster was handmade in England.

Despite his job as a computer-systems consultant at the pharmaceutical company Pfizer, DeLuca, of Ledgewood, New Jersey, still found time for his family. He visited his mother, who suffered a stroke a year and a half ago, every second day, and had trained her nursing aides to take care of her. Knowing how close his younger sister was to their mother, he tried his best to comfort her, she said. "He would call me and talk to me, because he knew I was having a hard time."

This protectiveness was something he shared with Gronlund, said her sister, recalling an incident from their childhood. "I remember getting teased and called 'four-eyes' by one of the boys," Strong said. "She promptly ran and grabbed him and beat him up, like 'don't mess with my little sister.'"

On September 11, Strong returned home to see the light on her answering machine flashing. She pressed the button and heard her sister's voice, calling from the air before her plane crashed in Pennsylvania. Gronlund explained the situation, sent love to everyone in the family and told Strong her safe combination and where to find her will. "She sounded mad and scared and calm, all at the same time."

"She said, 'I really hope I get to tell you in person how much I love you,'" Strong said. "And then she said goodbye."

ANN JUDGE
She Lived (and Loved) to Travel

It was Ann Judge's job—even her mission—to somehow get National Geographic Society photographers to some of the most remote places in the world.

"They can't do what they do if they can't get there," said Kent Kobersteen, director of photography at *National Geographic* magazine, describing complicated itineraries to backwater destinations from Africa to China. "She took all of this in stride. And she made it happen. She is a pro, a real pro."

For the Hempstead native, traveling was a passion she turned into a career. Friends are sure Judge was excited about September 11's field trip to California with three teachers and three 11-year-old students. They were on a field trip sponsored by *National Geographic* to Santa Barbara, where they were to participate in a marine research project.

It was Judge's last mission. She was traveling on American Airlines Flight 77, which crashed into the Pentagon.

In the aftermath of the tragedy, bouquets of flowers, some from strangers, streamed into *National Geographic*'s offices. At the entrance sat a bouquet of yellow roses between pictures of a smiling Judge and another of her co-worker, Joe Ferguson, director of the Geography Education Outreach program. Scores of people had signed books offering their condolences to Judge's friends and family, including her husband, Geoffrey James.

"She was a good one, that's for sure," said friend and co-worker Susan Smith. She described Judge as funny and full of vigor, someone who loved to party and dance. Judge prided herself on her garden of wildflowers and impatiens.

But it was her love of travel that she turned into a career at *National Geographic*, moving up the ranks over 22 years to eventually head the society's travel department.

"It's so ironic she should go this way—traveling," said Kobersteen.

CORA HOLLAND
Her Husband Watched Her Disappear

When his wife left from Boston for Los Angeles, Dr. Stephen Holland watched the plane's flight path on the American Airlines Web site, tracking the altitude, speed and even images of the plane turning on a map.

Stephen enjoyed tracking the flight paths of loved ones while they were traveling and noticed nothing unusual about the flight pattern. But suddenly, the image disappeared.

"It had been taken down, and it said, 'Please contact American,'" Stephen Holland recalled.

But Holland, 50, still wasn't unnerved. Then he turned to local Web site Boston.com, where he saw a message about a plane accident. Soon after, a colleague called him, notifying him that a plane from Boston to Los Angeles had crashed. "And I knew," he said.

His wife, 52-year-old Cora Hidalgo Holland, was a passenger on Flight 11, which crashed into the World Trade Center's Tower One. She left behind three children, Stephanie, 25, Jessica, 22, and Nate, 18. Jessica was in SoHo when she witnessed United Airlines Flight 175 crash into the World Trade Center's Tower Two. Nate was attending class uptown at Fordham University.

Five minutes before the flight departed, Holland had spoken to his wife on the cell phone he recently bought her. She mentioned she had a pleasant seatmate. Just weeks before, the couple became empty nesters when Nate became a college freshman. "We were going to be alone together," Stephen Holland said. "We had a lot of plans. She was in the midst of planning the second half of her life."

Holland recalled Cora as a wonderful wife, mother and grandmother. Until five years ago, she helped teach single mothers how to raise their children. "This woman was the center," he said. "She was the glue."

The Hollands' 25th anniversary was to be December 21. But they celebrated it early in Paris. "The joke was, did she want to spend another 25 years with me?" he said. "And I passed the test."

CHARLES F. BURLINGAME III
He Was Ready to Root

For Charles F. Burlingame III, September 12 would have been a day to cheer. It was his birthday, and he planned to mark it by going to a baseball game.

But Burlingame was at the controls of American Airlines Flight 77 when hijackers commandeered the plane and plowed it into the Pentagon. The next day, he would have turned 52.

The veteran pilot, who was known as "Chick," planned to cheer for his one-time home team at a Los Angeles Angels baseball game. In fact, he'd hoped his wife, Sheri, would accompany him on the flight from Washington, D.C., to L.A., so they could go to the game together. But she stayed behind at their Herndon, Virginia, home when he couldn't muster up two good seats, according to the pilot's brother, Brad.

Burlingame was a former Navy pilot and officer who served in the Navy Reserve and had once worked in the same area of the Pentagon where the airliner crashed. A 1971 graduate of the U.S. Naval Academy, he was organizing the 30th reunion of his class.

Burlingame had a daughter and a grandson and enjoyed boating, inline skating, golf and weightlifting.

"He was aware that when he went to work there was always a possibility of some kind of catastrophe," said his sister, Debra Burlingame. "But it was very, very remote. I don't think he thought about hijacking."

LESLIE WHITTINGTON and CHARLES, ZOE and DANA FALKENBERG
Off to See Kangaroos and Koalas

Georgetown University professor Colin Campbell thought he was helping a bright and well-liked colleague get a great opportunity to do scholarly research in an exotic setting. But when a Los Angeles–bound plane crashed into the Pentagon on September 11, Campbell realized his efforts had helped put Leslie Whittington and her family in harm's way.

Whittington, 45, her husband, Charles Falkenberg, and their two daughters, Zoe, 8, and Dana, 3, all died in the crash. The Hyattsville, Maryland, family had been passengers on the flight from Washington, D.C., to Los Angeles that was to have been the first leg on a 2½-month trip to Australia.

An economist and associate professor at Georgetown's Public Policy Institute, Whittington was a specialist on the impact of taxation on families, particularly poor families. She was the co-author of several papers with James Alm on the effects of taxation on marital decisions, including a 1998 study that found that the federal government would gain substantial revenue if same-sex couples were permitted to marry.

Campbell said he hired Whittington six years ago when he was head of the institute. He also was instrumental in getting her a fellowship to do research at the Australian National University in Canberra, where she and her family were headed at the time.

"This is terrible," Campbell said. "This is the first time in my life that I was complicit in a tragedy—that I actually played a role in someone being in the wrong place at the wrong time."

He described Whittington as one of the best teachers he had ever met. "She was loved by the students . . . she could never give them enough time. If you rated our faculty on a scale of 1 to 10, she would probably be the only one that was up there at 10."

He said that many faculty members burst into tears when they heard of Whittington's death. If she were alive, he said, "she'd be chiding us for being a bunch of babies."

But Whittington was deeply involved with her own children, Campbell said. "The last six months she would tell us what Zoe had said about going to Australia, and kangaroos and koala bears."

Whittington's co-author, Alm, a Georgia State University professor and a family friend, described her as "funny, quick-witted and loyal and warm." He said she was a skilled skier and an enthusiastic cook.

Alm described Falkenberg as "very cerebral in an engaging way." He said Falkenberg left college to found a computer business but later earned undergraduate and graduate degrees from the University of Maryland.

Falkenberg, 45, who worked for the ECOlogic Corporation in Lanham, Maryland, worked on data-delivery systems involving oceanography, ecology and space science. He also had worked in Alaska, studying the long-term aspects of the Exxon Valdez oil spill.

Ray Simanowith, president of the firm, described Falkenberg as "the conscience of our company. Most of his work dealt with things that would make a difference."

MYRA JOY ARONSON
A Woman on the Verge

She seemed a woman in perpetual motion, networking and strategizing at seminars or weeknight dinners, running out to catch a late jazz show, outworking men at the gym to keep her petite body in impeccable shape.

Her friends said Myra Joy Aronson, a marketing analyst for Compuware of Michigan and a resident of Charleston, Massachusetts, led a perfectly put-together life. Often clad in black, with large brown eyes, she cut a sharp figure at the age of 50. "She was, as I put it, maddeningly organized," said a friend, Pamela Waite. "For those of us who have hit middle age, she was one of those people who never found her coffee cup in the refrigerator or her car keys in the microwave."

On September 11, as Aronson waited for American Airlines Flight 11 to take off, she called Waite because she wanted to buy Harley-Davidson T-shirts for some mutual friends on her trip to a software conference in California and needed their

sizes. When not flying off on business, Aronson wrote press releases for her friend Felice Pomeranz's musical company, the Gilded Harps, or did publicity for the Handel & Haydn Society in Boston.

The second of four children, Aronson was raised in Elgin, Illinois, with two sisters and a brother. She spent her junior year of college in France and fell in love with the culture. Every year, she attended a French-themed, seven-course meal, where guests spoke the language and sipped cognac—but ate American cuisine and drank California wines. That was the type of tradition she kept. The last Monday in August was Martha's Vineyard Day with her girlfriends. Only she and Pomeranz went this year, and they bicycled around the entire island together.

She never married, and had been focused in her 40s on finding a husband. But that had not bothered her lately. "I think she had worked things out in her life," Pomeranz said. "That's why I think she was probably on the cusp of meeting someone. She had a great job, and she had wonderful friends, and she had good health, and she looked terrific, and she had a darling apartment. And she got on the wrong plane."

WALESKA MARTINEZ
She Loved Travel and Technology

Waleska Martinez, 37, loved just about everything about New York City: the music, the plays, the restaurants, the sports teams, the diversity of its people.

"She was such a positive, happy person," said her friend and co-worker Ligia Jaquez. "She'd chuck her head back and laugh. She'd irradiate everything around her."

Martinez, a native of Santurce, Puerto Rico, moved to Jersey City—just across the river from lower Manhattan—in 1987. A year later she found a job as a clerk with the U.S. Census Bureau, but she didn't stay a clerk long. Armed with a college degree in computer science, she rose quickly through the ranks. She won many performance awards during her 13-year career, including the Bronze Medal in 1998, the highest honorary award granted by the Census Bureau.

For the 2000 Census, Martinez was responsible for automation hardware, software and support for the Census Bureau's New York regional office.

"She was very good at training her staff. Not all managers can do that," said Tony Farthing, director of the regional office. Her talents weren't just directed at those who worked under her.

"What I loved about her was that she would give constructive feedback," Farthing said. "She used to tease me about not keeping up with computer software. She'd call me 'Mr. No-Tech.' As I started getting better she changed it to 'Mr. Low-Tech.'"

Martinez's high-tech proclivities weren't confined to her job. At home she had an elaborate stereo system, a state-of-the-art laptop computer and two TV sets. Whenever she traveled—which was often—she would take along three cameras, Jaquez reported.

"She had photos all over her apartment," said Jaquez, who often traveled with Martinez on business trips. Although she loved the wide-open vistas of the West, Martinez's favorite travel destination was New Orleans.

But New Orleans lacks New York's variety of pro sports, and Martinez loved sports. She was a Mets fan during the regular baseball season, turning her loyalties to the Yankees during the playoffs. She closely followed the Giants in pro football and was also a boxing fan. Felix Trinidad was her favorite fighter.

Madonna and Tina Turner were among the many entertainers Martinez admired and had seen perform, although she had a special affection for legendary Cuban-born singer La Lupe.

Quiet and shy by nature, Martinez "was really intense when she liked something," Jaquez said. But she wasn't always shy. Jaquez recalled a Halloween party in which Martinez dressed up like a hippie. "Nobody knew who she was," Jaquez said. Two months before Halloween 2001, Martinez already had her costume picked out. She was going to be a geisha girl.

But on September 11 Martinez boarded United Airlines Flight 93 in Newark.

LISA RAINES
A Health-Care Advocate Behind the Scenes

Getting the best new medicines to the patients who needed them was a mission for Lisa Raines. With Senator Ted Kennedy of Massachusetts, she worked to enact legislation to fast-track drugs for life-threatening illnesses. "When you think of AIDS and cancer drugs that were

approved more quickly under the provision, you really have Lisa Raines to thank," said her friend Nick Littlefield, a former chief of staff for Kennedy.

The 42-year-old Raines was a passenger on American Airlines Flight 77—the plane that crashed into the Pentagon.

As senior vice president of government relations for Genzyme Corporation, a biotech company based in Cambridge, Massachusetts, Raines was responsible for federal legislation and regulatory policy issues regarding pharmaceutical drugs.

But perhaps her most influential achievement was as a behind-the-scenes broker for the FDA Modernization Act in 1997. Working with Kennedy, she pushed for language that streamlined the process of drug approval.

Raines also worked to enact the FDA Export Reform and Enhancement Act of 1996, and the Biotechnology Patent Protection Act of 1995. And she played a prominent role in FDA policy development for cellular therapies in the mid-1990s. "She was truly exceptional, and intellectually really remarkable," said David Nexon, senior health policy staff member on the Senate Health, Education, Labor and Pensions subcommittee.

Raines, who was also a lawyer, loved to travel and had recently returned from a vacation to Santa Barbara, California, with her husband, Stephen Push, a former vice president of corporate communications at Genzyme. She enjoyed decorating the house she shared with Push in Great Falls, Virginia, and delighted in classical music concerts.

KAREN MARTIN
She Tried to Block the Cockpit

When she was 6 years old, Karen Martin's father died, leaving four small children and a mother who had to work full time as a traveling saleswoman to support them.

"Karen pretty much brought us up," said her older brother, John Martin. The second-oldest child, "Karen was the one who cooked dinner. Karen was the one that did the laundry, cleaned the house. Karen was like the mother figure. She sacrificed quite a lot."

And when their younger brother, Paul, was burned over 65 percent of his body about a year later, Karen helped John and their mother care for him when he returned from the hospital, bathing his wounds and changing his dressings. "She was the type that when she had to step up to the plate, she did," John said.

As the head flight attendant on American Airlines Flight 11, which crashed into the World Trade Center's Tower One, the 40-year-old Martin stepped up to the plate again. When the plane was overtaken by hijackers, investigators told her family, she and another flight attendant blocked the door to the cockpit. She was stabbed as she tried to prevent the disaster. "They did what they could do," said her brother, "but they just got overpowered."

"To tell you the truth, I wasn't surprised," he said. Athletic and street-smart, his sister was "the type to get in your face if you were being a loser." At the same time, he said, "If you met her, you would go, 'Wow, what a nice girl!'"

Though she never married or had children of her own, Martin stayed in her hometown of Amherst, Massachusetts, and became "Auntie Karen" to all her friends' children. "She always took certain kids skiing or kayaking," John said. "It was 'Oh, Karen's coming up!' and all the kids would get excited."

She was always gregarious and had been a bartender before she became a flight attendant 12 years ago. And Martin was known for her distinctive and infectious laugh. "It was almost like a machine-gun laugh," said her brother. "It was her trademark."

It was she whom the other flight attendants would call during layovers on the "trans-con" flight routes that she favored. "When she was on a layover, there was always something she did," John said. "Bike riding, Rollerblading, golf, maybe a couple of cold ones."

When it came to sports, he said, "She was a better golfer than most guys and she was a much better skier than most guys." She wouldn't play from the women's tee, instead joining her brother at the men's tee. "She was just very competitive."

Martin's work often brought her to Los Angeles, where her brother lives, and she would stay with him in Redondo Beach. The two had a golf date for the afternoon of September 11.

Losing his sister has been a huge blow for John. But he's grateful for one thing. The night before Martin was killed, he spoke to her on the phone. The call was brief. "She was like, 'Hey, Johnny, I gotta go,'" he said. "And the last thing she ever said to me was 'Johnny, I love you.'"

ROBERT and ZANDRA PLOGER
A Late-Blooming Love Affair

  With their children grown and their careers established, Robert Ploger III and Zandra Flores Ploger were hardly expecting to find themselves in love again. But after they met, in love is exactly where they found themselves—"totally and completely," in the words of Zandra's daughter, Erin Cooper.

In May 2001, the Plogers tied the knot in a low-key, romantic ceremony—just the two of them and two friends in a little pontoon boat on a lake in Virginia. They had a reception for close friends and family a few weeks later. But it wasn't until September that the busy pair—she a marketing brand manager at IBM and he an engineer at Lockheed Martin—found time to take their dream honeymoon in Hawaii.

The couple, who lived in Annandale, Virginia, were on American Airlines Flight 77—the first leg of their trip—when the plane was hijacked and slammed into the Pentagon.

Robert's death came at what had been a joyous time in his life, said his daughter, Wendy Chamberlain. The 59-year-old "definitely was very happy. He was ready to start his new life with his new wife." And it was obvious that the feeling was mutual, said Cooper of her 48-year-old mother. "It was the way he would look at her and the way she would look at him. She was just so relaxed and calm and happy. It was amazing."

Robert, who had previously been married for 34 years to Sheila Ploger, had two children, Chamberlain and Robert Ploger IV. Zandra's two daughters, Cooper and Zena Tedesco, stayed in frequent touch with their mother, and both spoke with her on the evening before the attacks.

As the news came in the next morning, Cooper said, "I was hoping she was just stranded somewhere." But no such luck. Zandra's daughters are left with just memories of their mother, and the example she set for them. "I think I was lucky," said Cooper. "Because most people don't have as good of a mom as I did."

An "entertainer" who loved to throw dinner parties, Zandra had a "take-charge attitude about life," said her daughter. "She was the kind of person who

ldn't sit around and wait for things to happen."
ted as an example the way her mother took
f to take care of her sister when her brother-
ed a couple of months before September
big fan of *Star Trek*, Zandra once ventured to
a "Trekkie" convention, coming back somewhat
bewildered by the characters she encountered.

Chamberlain described her father as a man with
"a serious intellect combined with a childlike sense
of humor." He had two engineering hardware
patents to his name for "something I could never
understand," Chamberlain said, and his days were
spent happily immersed in science. But he was just
as happy watching *The Three Stooges*.

In the 1960s, Robert was involved in developing
the ARPANET, the precursor to the Internet, at the
University of California. "I know he was very
proud of being there during that exciting time,"
said his daughter.

He remained close with his children, playing tennis regularly with them on the weekends. "I think as a
father, he brought us up being honest and having fun.
We did a lot of playing games and tossing the football
around. He was very much a part of our lives."

To describe losing her father, Chamberlain said, "I
sometimes make the comparison with watching the
Twin Towers fall. Where once there was something
strong and familiar, now there's a big hole . . . I guess
the skyline is completely changed, as our lives are."

TODD BEAMER
The Man Who Said, "Let's Roll"

He had asked the phone operator to tell his pregnant wife and
two sons that he loved them.
He had passed along everything he knew about the hijackers aboard his flight. He had
recited the Lord's Prayer and the 23rd Psalm. Then
the operator, Lisa Jefferson, heard him ask, "Are you
guys ready?" The last words she heard from him
have since become a rallying cry—"Let's roll."

When Beamer picked up a seat-back phone and
hit "0" at 9:45 a.m., the situation already looked
desperate. During the 13-minute call, he told Jefferson that the pilot and co-pilot were injured or
dead. Hijackers were flying the plane. And one
hijacker guarded the passengers with a bomb tied
around his waist with a red belt.

"Some of the passengers on the flight had decided to 'jump on' the hijacker with the bomb and try
to get him down," said Jefferson in a memo she
wrote to the Beamer family. "I know we're not
going to make it out of here," Beamer told her.

Beamer, 32, an account manager for Oracle Corporation, has been hailed as one of the heroes of
United Airlines Flight 93. He was on his way to a
business meeting when the Newark–to–San Francisco flight crashed in Pennsylvania. A group of
passengers apparently prevented the plane from
hitting another terrorist target by rushing the cockpit and overpowering the hijackers. All 44 people
on board were killed. U.S. officials believe the Boeing 757 was heading for the U.S. Capitol or some
other target in Washington when it came down.

The words Beamer has become famous for—
"Let's roll"—are painfully familiar to his wife, Lisa,
of Cranbury, New Jersey. "When I heard that part
of the conversation, I knew that was Todd," she
said. "He uses that with our little boys all the time."

Someday, Lisa Beamer said, she will tell the story to
her sons David, 3, and Andrew, 1, and to Morgan Kay,
the daughter she gave birth to on January 9, 2002.

"This doesn't change the future of my family,
but it sure gives credence to the person I know
Todd was," Lisa Beamer said. "Certainly when the
chips were down, his character, his faith, his love
for his family and his love for his fellow man
showed through."

At a memorial near the crash site, Lisa left a
Chicago Bulls hat to represent her husband's devotion to the basketball team, a pack of M&Ms, an
Oracle pen for the job he loved and other items to
represent his spiritual and family life.

David Beamer, 59, called his son a "freedom fighter."
"Obviously there was a struggle, but I can tell you who
lost," he said. "That plane was headed for a target, and
it wasn't a field with nobody there in Pennsylvania."

COLLEEN FRASER
An Advocate for Little People

Born with a form of dwarfism,
Colleen Fraser stood less than
4 feet tall. But that didn't stop
her from making a big impression on people.

She walked with a cane,
which she would shake wildly to make a point.

Often that point was making the world friendlier to people with disabilities. Fraser clearly had a flair for it.

"She was a firebrand," said longtime friend Ethan Ellis, executive director of the New Jersey Developmental Disabilities Council. Fraser, 51, of Elizabeth, New Jersey, was vice chair of the council and served in other organizations for the disabled. She was aboard United Airlines Flight 93, which crashed in Pennsylvania.

In 1989, when she heard that New Jersey's U.S. senators were undecided about supporting the Americans with Disabilities Act, she loaded about a dozen disabled individuals aboard a bus and rode to both senators' offices to win their support.

Fraser knew how to make a personal statement. She fashioned her flaming red hair into spikes like a punk rocker and wore numerous earrings. She wore open-toed sandals with orthopedic lifts. Her interests were eclectic. She liked gothic novels and horror movies. She was a wood carver and loved to bake.

She was also a passionate and tireless advocate. In fact, Fraser was flying to a grant-writing seminar when she died. "I think there's a certain delicious irony that a small person like Colleen has given a small state such a big voice," Ellis said.

DAVID and LYNN ANGELL
"Good People, Aptly Named"

Frasier Crane to brother Niles: It doesn't look like anybody's leaving. Shall we take a table outside?
Niles: Why not. I'm feeling al fresco.
Frasier: How does Mrs. Fresco feel about that?
From the Frasier *episode "My Coffee with Niles" by David Angell and Peter Casey*

Frasier co-creator David Angell and his wife, Lynn, were passengers aboard the American Airlines jet that terrorists hijacked just out of Boston and that crashed into the north tower of the World Trade Center. The Angells, who had a home in Chatham, Massachusetts, were headed to Los Angeles for an Emmy Awards ceremony that would twice be postponed out of respect for the victims of the September 11 attacks and concern about security for the event.

Frasier didn't claim any statuettes when the Emmys finally were held, but Angell, 54, already had enough of the winged trophies to start his own academy. The series has won 24 since its debut on NBC in 1993, including five for best comedy. He also won awards and acclaim for his contributions to two other NBC comedy hits, *Cheers* and *Wings.*

His creative partners, Peter Casey and David Lee, in a joint statement called him "a kind and gentle man with a quiet exterior that masked one of the sharpest comedy minds ever to write for television." At a September 16 memorial service, *Cheers* co-creator Les Charles recalled watching Angell "in a writer's room, surrounded by some of the best pure joke-writers in the business, all pitching at a white-hot heat. And he would sit back and listen and think, and then when things got quiet, he would, almost inaudibly, give you the perfect joke—one that was funny, character-specific, tasteful, totally unexpected, and usually one that defined the scene."

"And lest we forget," Charles added, "if he had never done another thing in his career, David Angell would have earned immortality as the man who added *boink* to the English language."

Success in TV didn't come easily to Angell, a Rhode Island native who joined the Army after he graduated from Providence College with a degree in English literature. He worked at the Pentagon and in the insurance business before he moved to Los Angeles in 1977 to try his luck as a writer. He quickly sold a script to the producers of a forgotten sitcom called *Annie Flynn*, then struggled for five years to sell a second. During that stretch, he once told an interviewer, he did "virtually every temporary job known to mankind."

His career-making break was being hired in 1983 as a staff writer for *Cheers.* And he was one of the writers asked to shepherd one of its supporting characters, the erudite, easily flustered psychiatrist Frasier Crane, into his own series.

Lynn Edwards Angell, 52, grew up in Birmingham, Alabama, and attended Auburn University. She met her future husband when she was a waitress one summer on Cape Cod. She converted to Catholicism when they married in 1971. With her husband being quite religious—his brother, Kenneth, is a Catholic bishop in Vermont—they were regular churchgoers.

In the years her husband struggled to establish himself, she supported them with her wages as a librarian at Campbell Hall, a school in Studio City, California. Later, she was volunteer head librarian at Hillsides, a Pasadena residential facility and school for abused children. She and her husband never had children, but friends say they helped hundreds over the years.

To Les Charles, the Angells were good people, aptly named. "They were gracious and courteous in an old-fashioned, substantial way," he said at that September 16 service. "They were kind and thoughtful and enormously generous. They were totally unpretentious and never lost their sense of proportion. They were incredibly well matched and seemed almost supernaturally attuned to one another.

"When Peter Casey asked me to do this, he said they wanted it to be a celebration of their lives. And I thought, 'Of course.' It's easy to celebrate the lives of two people for whom life itself was a kind of celebration."

A Husband Is Missing No More

JIMMY BRESLIN

Vincent Danz

The line of men in red, white or blue hard hats went up the path through the wreckage of the old World Trade Center to the smoke at the top of the gray hill. It was one of four clouds of smoke coming from deep in the guts of the ground. This smoke rose to the top of a 40-story financial building.

There were about 200 men on the hill in white, blue or red hard hats and they were passing down five-gallon buckets. At the bottom of the hill, two men stood with a four-by-three-foot screen and the buckets were emptied onto the screen and they shook the screen as if they were trying to find coins at the beach. They were looking for any trace, any identification of the dead in the gray wreckage. Often they would shake the screen and get a hand, a piece of a heel.

At 1:30 in the afternoon they were digging in the smoke at the top, and somebody came up with a credit card for Officer Vincent Danz. He was in the wreckage right under them, they all agreed. The hands reached into the gray rubble.

By 3 o'clock a truck from Emergency Service Unit 3 in the Bronx pulled into the lot and parked at the foot of the hill. If it was Danz's body, it was theirs to carry. He had been part of a high-rise rescue team.

"That's the widow," a sergeant, Ricky Kemmler, said.

A few steps away, a light-haired young woman who wore a short tan coat and a white hard hat stood with her hand being held by Joseph Dunne, who is the deputy police commissioner.

"She lives on the Island. They called her," somebody said.

"She already had a memorial service for him. I was there," Andrew McGinnis, a sergeant, said.

"In Farmingdale," another one said. "It was the first one for an officer."

"I think she's from Ireland. She had the guts to get up and speak at the memorial. She has three kids. I know she said something funny about meeting him in a bar."

"I met my two wives in bars," I said.

The widow, Angela Danz, was silent and there was no talking around her. Her eyes were red-rimmed, but she was not close to weeping. This is the toughest breed of them, a young woman who now raises three kids, with the oldest 8, while living in loneliness.

She stood in the mud and before her was the coliseum where her husband fought his last fight for her. The wreckage strewn everywhere looked exactly like it was, buildings dropped from the sky. A few high thick stubborn metal teeth of the south tower were still rooted in the gray mud.

The remains of a wall of the north tower leaned backward, as if resting against a fence.

Off to the right, yellow smoke came up in billows. Water from a hose attached to a hydrant that somehow had lasted was played with great force at the yellow smoke. It did not stop.

A large machine, a grappler, dug into the earth around the yellow smoke. As the grappler came up with its jaws clamped on pieces of steel and mud, the yellow smoke subsided for a few moments. Then it burst angrily out of the spot.

A dozen cranes waved angrily high in the smoke. Everywhere in the mud, generators barked and dozens of backhoes and grapplers chewed on the disaster.

She watched with strength stronger than the buildings that killed her husband. She was out of the old coal mine disasters, with women waiting at the top of the elevator for news of their husbands in a fire below.

Except this time, Angela Danz knew that her husband was dead. She had already eulogized him in a church. Right now, the least they could do was get her the body.

On the hill in front of her, twin lines of men went up the hill that is several stories high. Then at the top it hooked to the right. The head of the line was lost in the smoke.

Now a police commander in white uniform shirt climbed to the turn in the line, kept going and disappeared into the smoke.

"Esposito," somebody said. He is Joseph Esposito, the chief of the department.

"I never saw a guy that big get down and work with the men," one of the cops said.

Up on the hill, the white, red or blue hard hats bobbed and at the top they formed a little circle around something and then burst like a soap bubble. Some hard hats went to one line and the rest to the other. Now they took off their hard hats and saluted.

"It looks like they got him," the sergeant, Kemmler, said.

The cranes and ground machinery stopped. The generators were turned off.

"It looks like we had a good day," another enthused. They dig all day, day after day, and do not find many bodies.

"If that's what you call it," somebody said.

Dunne and the widow walked a few steps to the emergency service truck parked at the bottom of the hill.

At the top, Esposito's white shirt appeared. He was in front of a gurney that was cloaked with an American flag.

Somebody called, "They want police officers up on the line."

McGinnis and Kemmler walked up the hill and got on a line.

Now Esposito walked first down the slope. Walked slowly, for they could not slip with the gurney. Men in the lines on either side saluted.

At the bottom of the slope, Esposito had the pallbearers step at an even slower funeral pace.

Dunne and the widow went to the back of the truck.

Esposito led the men with the gurney to the back of the truck.

Now there was no motion or sound for several seconds. They prayed over the body. Then Dunne and Angela Danz came from the back of the truck and walked away. The hard hats filed along the truck and formed an honor guard for many yards from the front of the truck. A patrol car moved in front.

All saluted. The patrol car's roof light went on and the big emergency truck followed through the mud. It went past the great hole that looked down on what had been a subway station. Then they went out onto the streets and headed for the morgue on First Avenue with the body the widow and his emergency outfit had wanted so much.

Jimmy Breslin is a columnist for Newsday.

9
High Finance

They were on the fast track, working under pressure in a world of investments and banking and insurance. More than half were in finance. Most of them worked on the higher floors—at the point of impact or above. Many enjoyed the good life of luxury apartments and high-priced vacations; others coached their kids' ball teams and loved the beach and lived quietly in the suburbs.

Some were experts in their field, like the market analyst who made frequent television appearances but "couldn't change a light bulb" and spent summer Saturdays outside reading in a folding chair, wearing purple shorts and a Grateful Dead T-shirt. Others were just beginning to savor the rewards, like the energy analyst who "was literally on top of the world, 104 floors above the city he loved and one floor below a five-star restaurant."

And there was an investment banker who had lifted his life out of the morass of drugs and alcohol and was rediscovering life and himself when the jetliner hit his tower. He called his parents and seemed at peace. "It's out of my control," he told them.

BETTINA BROWNE-RADBURN
A Pilot Who Soared Through Life

It began with an ad in *New York* magazine: divorced male seeking soul mate. Never in his wildest dreams did he think he would find her. Then Bettina Browne answered the call.

"Do you know how wonderful that is? When you can just spend hours walking on the beach holding hands, and you don't even have to utter a word," said Edward Radburn, Browne's husband of 10 years. "Even before I met her, I fell in love with her. She just had a grace and a beauty about her."

Browne, also previously divorced, was an accomplished businesswoman, attorney and pilot who possessed limitless energy along with unconditional love. That was all taken away when Browne, 49, of Atlantic Beach, was trapped in her 105th-floor office in Tower Two on September 11. The senior vice president of mergers and acquisitions for Aon Corporation had held the position for only six months, and she usually spent her time on the road.

She had called her husband from her cell phone to tell him she was trapped and running out of oxygen. Radburn hung up and called 911. Five minutes later, the building collapsed.

Browne left behind a legacy of accomplishments ranging from owning one of the largest facility-maintenance companies in the country to operating a flight school with a fleet of three planes.

"She was brilliant. I would have to read something 10 times and she would scan it, and a year later she would remember every word. I would have to go back and look it up," said Radburn.

Browne had a unique ability to turn her hobbies into businesses. Gourmet cooking led to an international-cuisine restaurant in Dorset, Vermont. Weekend antiquing resulted in an antiques store in New Hyde Park, selling jade figurines and Remington statues.

Earlier in life, she had aspired to be a commercial pilot, but at 5 foot 1 Browne couldn't reach the rudder pedals, and industry height restrictions blocked her efforts. So she earned an FAA license, later opened a flight school at Stormville airport in Dutchess County and, eight years ago, taught her husband to fly.

"She didn't believe that you couldn't achieve something because you were a female," said Radburn.

With a juris doctor degree from Pace University, Browne used her legal expertise mostly in business. She did a stint as prosecutor for the Village of Atlantic Beach in 1997. Radburn was a trustee at the time. A bid for village justice followed, but Browne lost to her opponent.

For 13 years, she worked at ISS, a Danish facility-maintenance company. When the company splintered, Browne formed her own. As chief executive of Omni Facility Resources, a special facilities-maintenance group, Browne initially raised $125 million in capital and acquired three businesses. Within two years, Omni, launched in 1997, had grown to nine companies and 5,500 employees.

Browne received several honors for her business accomplishments. She was even invited to the White House—more than once. But if her success could have gone to her head, it never did. "My wife . . . always thought that it did you no good to puff out your chest at somebody else's expense," Radburn said.

The couple had planned to retire in a year or two—head for their home in Vermont and spend the days skiing and traveling. "I guess not now," choked Radburn. "We should have retired, but we never did."

WILLIAM MEEHAN JR.
It Was the Thought That Counted

William J. Meehan Jr. never minded when his family laughed at him and his ineptitude for household chores. His wife says he couldn't change a light bulb without breaking the lamp, and his kids would yell for their mom whenever they saw him with a screwdriver. Meehan would always play along, the goofball in their Darien, Connecticut, home.

One of the family's best times was Christmas Eve, when they'd force Meehan to go upstairs alone and wrap the presents he'd bought that year for his wife, Maureen.

Years ago, Meehan cajoled his oldest son or somebody at work into wrapping his gifts. But that was too easy, and soon his family realized the entertainment they could glean from making him do it himself. "It was hysterical. He would go up there and you would hear cursing and scissors dropping on the floor," Maureen Meehan said. "We would laugh and he would laugh. He didn't care."

Meehan would come back downstairs with packages "horrendously wrapped," his wife said. "I could wrap the entire tree with the amount of paper he used for a jewelry box. And there was just so much tape all over the place."

The picture that Meehan's family paints of him at home is a sharp contrast to the image Meehan presented in the financial world. Cantor Fitzgerald's chief market analyst, Meehan spoke with an authoritative voice about Wall Street trends during frequent appearances on network television financial news shows, and in a column for Cantor's online magazine, *The Cantor Morning News*. Meehan, 49, had just started working regularly at Cantor Fitzgerald's Manhattan offices, rather than in the ones near his home, in Connecticut.

Meehan was born in the Bronx and met his wife, who is from Westchester, in 1975. They were married in 1980. He began his career in advertising in 1969 in Manhattan. In 1977, he began working for Jericho Inc., which produced ads for Long John Silver's restaurants, and the couple moved to Lexington, Kentucky. It was the first of three different stays—which later included their children—in that city. Meehan enjoyed the neighborly attitude in Lexington and especially the horse racing at Keeneland. They also lived in Sacramento, California, and Severna Park, Maryland. Meehan decided he wanted to be a broker in 1987, and the couple moved back to Lexington for the final time. In 1993, they moved to Darien, and in 1997 Meehan took a job with Cantor Fitzgerald.

While his opinion was highly respected on Wall Street, neighbors in Darien knew him as "just Bill," his wife said. He coached youth sports teams for each of his three children—Billy, 20, Danny, 17, and Katie, 10—and was a fixture at their games when he wasn't coaching.

A voracious reader, Meehan would spend each summer Saturday in the same way—in a folding chair outside his house, listening to music and reading. His routine started about midmorning, his wife said, when he would fetch the business and financial weekly magazine *Barron's* from the mailbox. Meehan would inevitably be dressed in what his son Billy called his "summer outfit"—purple shorts, a Grateful Dead tie-dyed T-shirt, and red, white and blue Chuck Taylor All-Star sneakers.

He'd turn on music such as the Grateful Dead or Lucinda Williams on the stereo that he kept in the garage and settle into the chair on the driveway,

because that is where the sun shined the brightest in the morning. "Half the time I'd be mowing the lawn," his wife said. "In the afternoon when the sun would shift, he'd move to the back of the house." Meehan would proceed to novels and biographies and anything else he could get his hands on, taking breaks to throw the ball with his kids or talk to his neighbors in the cul-de-sac.

"He could sit for hours and just read and listen to music, just soaking in the sun," his wife said. "I have to say that Bill enjoyed his life."

BART RUGGIERE
He Lived Well on Top of the World

Bart Ruggiere and his wife, Claudia, were to leave September 21 for Paris and Monte Carlo. In March 2002, they would be off again for a ski vacation in Switzerland. In between, they planned to do the holidays in grand style: an 8-foot tree exquisitely decorated, a big Christmas party with 200 guests.

It's not that the Ruggieres were rich. It's just that Bart Ruggiere, 32, believed in enjoying life to the fullest. "Bart celebrated each day. He loved good food, good wine, good company," his wife said. In fact, she said, in the Ruggiere circle of family and friends, his name had become a synonym for living well.

"People would say, 'That's so Bart,' when they were talking about things like wearing a custom-made suit or having a great barbecue or just doing things without hesitation," she said. "Bart never hesitated. He was always confident, even when he was between jobs. He knew he would land on his feet." Six months ago he landed a job as an energy broker with Cantor Fitzgerald on the 104th floor of Tower One.

"Bart was literally on top of the world, 104 floors above the city he loved and one floor below a five-star restaurant," his brother-in-law, Lawrence deParis, said in a eulogy.

Ruggiere was still confident and calm, though a bit annoyed, when he called his wife a moment after a hijacked plane struck the tower on the morning of September 11. "He said something like, 'Can you believe this place? A plane has just hit our building. They're getting us out of here.'" That was the last she heard.

She gave the red vest that had become his signature for the holidays to his brother, Frank Ruggiere of Massapequa Park.

Bart Ruggiere grew up in Port Washington, where he spent much of his time on his father's wooden boat. "He dreamed of having a wooden boat like his father's. That was another of our plans," Claudia recalled. Her husband graduated from LaSalle Military Academy in 1987, attended the University of Wisconsin in Oshkosh and ran his own seafood-packaging business for five years. "Bart didn't live to work; he worked to live," she said.

The couple had been married for only a year and a half. Claudia says Ruggiere proposed on a spring day in Central Park. They were wed at St. Patrick's Cathedral in Manhattan, honeymooned in Bali and Malaysia and moved into an Upper East Side apartment, where they entertained frequently. "He taught me how to live life," his wife said. "I have no regrets."

BALEWA BLACKMAN
Music Lover Listened Also with His Heart

Balewa Blackman heard music in the most prosaic of noises.

One time, the 26-year-old hip-hop enthusiast from East Flatbush, Brooklyn, even recorded the sound of a pan dripping water into a sink. He used it to create a beat, the rhythmic basis for a rap song.

"His beats were just original, unique," said Nisan Lessane, a friend who met Blackman when they were students at Cornell University. "It was his art form. His ear was always listening, and his brain was always working."

Blackman, a junior accountant at Cantor Fitzgerald who worked on the 101st floor of Tower One, threw himself into life with the same zeal. Once he hit upon a decision, he stuck to it—whether it was getting into business school or learning the secret to preparing his Jamaican-born mother's rice and beans properly.

"He was one of those who was always elevating himself," said his mother, Hyacinth Blackman, speaking from the family home in East Flatbush, where Balewa and his older sister, Susan McMillian, grew up. "I always told him, 'Reach for the sky if that's what you want. Go out and get it.'"

He took her advice to heart early. After his first day of kindergarten, Blackman informed his

father, Albert, that he had had enough of sitting around playing.

"I want to go into the class where the kids do work," announced Balewa, who was named after a Nigerian leader. Soon afterward, his mother said, the precocious 5-year-old asked his father to bring home a copy of the *Wall Street Journal*.

Blackman worked hard over the years to get where he was, graduating from Cornell in 1996 with a bachelor of science degree in biochemistry. "All that stuff didn't necessarily come easy to him, but he never felt intimidated," said Amanda Williams, another friend from college. "He was always setting new goals."

It was the challenge that was important to him, not just getting into the right school or landing the right job. "He was definitely not a conventional person," said Ed Robes, also a Cornell classmate. "He didn't go against the grain, he made his own."

If Blackman didn't try to fit in, it may have been because he was constitutionally incapable of doing so. "Balewa was himself," said Lessane, with a laugh. "He was no other."

His frank, offbeat sense of humor had a way of setting people at ease. At his boss' wedding last August, Blackman was seated across from a notoriously shy cousin of the groom's. Within minutes, the two were chatting like old friends—much to the amazement of the other relatives.

Asked who he was, Blackman, who was black, pointed to the groom, who was white. "I'm his illegitimate brother," he said with a straight face. "You must be Mom!" he exclaimed, upon meeting the groom's mother.

By the end of the reception, everyone was asking when he was going to come back and visit. "It really was his personality," Lessane said. "Jokes that would be pointed coming from anyone else would be funny coming from him."

LOUIS MINERVINO
Terror's Third Strike Was Fatal

Twice before, Louis Minervino escaped death at the hands of terrorists.

In 1988, returning from a business trip to London, he was booked on Pan Am Flight 103, which exploded over Lockerbie, Scotland, killing everyone aboard. He was saved by a seeming misfortune—his daughter, then in the fifth grade, had broken her ankle, and he had rushed home to her a day early.

"When we went to church that Sunday, I thanked God for giving me more time with Lou," said his wife, Barbara.

The second scare was in 1993. Minervino, of Middletown, New Jersey, was at a meeting on the 52nd floor of the World Trade Center's Tower Two when a bomb went off in the underground parking garage. "I didn't hear about him for about four hours," Barbara said. "But he was OK, just shaken up and covered in soot."

On the morning of September 11, Minervino, 54, a senior vice president at Marsh USA, called his wife from his office on the 98th floor of Tower One. For them, it was a routine call. "I told him I loved him and he told me he loved me," Barbara said. She hung up the phone and turned on the television, just in time to hear the news that a plane had hit the building he was in. "When I saw the first visual on TV, I knew he was dead," she said. "And I was right."

The couple had never considered the possibility that he would be the first to die. Barbara suffers from chronic pancreatitis, diabetes, thyroid disease, high blood pressure and high cholesterol. "Because of these things, we've had to face my mortality many times," she said. "In our lives together, we never discussed his mortality . . . I knew that one of us would be alive after the other. We never gave a thought to the fact that it would be me. We always thought it would be him."

Without him, she said, "Every morning I wake up—and I'm a person of great faith—so I thank God for letting me get up . . . But then I ask, 'Now what am I going to do? What is the direction of my life?'"

Still, Barbara calls herself lucky. "We were able to share 26 years of a beautiful, loving marriage. . . . I felt he was the greatest gift that God could have given me. And that it was only God's right to take that gift away."

An only child who grew up in an Italian neighborhood on Staten Island, her husband was "a quiet, selfless, giving man," Barbara said. "He was not a man to go out and have a few drinks with the boys. He came home when his day was finished . . . He would come home and eat whatever the family meal was for the evening."

Among the things she finds herself grateful for now is the fact that her husband saw both his daughters, Laina, 25, and Marisa, 23, graduate with "a great Jesuit education" from Loyola University.

And Barbara is grateful for her memories.

The way he used to hold her hand while they slept. "I still reach out and look for that hand."

The second honeymoon in Hawaii the couple took in 1998, after she was diagnosed with a fast-moving cancer and they decided against treatment. "We looked at nature. We spoke in great detail about our love for each other and our children. We renewed our friendship. If it could be renewed—it never died."

The cancer diagnosis turned out to be mistaken, Barbara said. "It was not for me to die at that point."

When it comes to understanding the loss of her husband, she has turned again to her faith. "Someone said to me, 'That was his third strike.' You could look at it that way. I'd rather look at it as each time—each event that he survived—was God giving me a little more time with him. And I can't question God."

CHRISTOPHER QUACKENBUSH
The Definition of a Close Friend

 A poster was Scotch-taped to Jimmy Dunne's new office window for months. It read: "Missing: Christopher Quackenbush: born January 5, 1957, 195 pounds, 6 foot, 4 inches" with a head shot attached.

Quackenbush was one of 66 employees at Sandler O'Neill & Partners killed in the World Trade Center collapse. But for Dunne, the managing partner at the closely knit investment banking firm, "Quack" was extra special. Dunne had met his lifelong buddy at a driving range in Bay Shore when both were in their early teens. Both were swinging their clubs when a golfing pro told Quackenbush, "If you practice hard, you can be like him," Dunne boasted. Quackenbush turned around to Dunne and said, "I'm going to beat you." Eventually, he did—"a mortifying experience," Dunne recalled—at a local junior club championship.

Instead of a rivalry, the result was a close friendship that lasted 30 years. They went on to tend bar together at night in downtown Bay Shore, and formed a whimsically named company called Tuition Paying Painters that painted houses to pay for college. (Quackenbush went to the University of North Carolina at Chapel Hill, while Dunne went to Notre Dame). Later, their relationship helped lead to the establishment of Sandler O'Neill.

But it was more than just business. Their families have spent holidays together, and their children are close, too. Dunne's voice softened as he reminisced about the times he and his wife, Susan, and his kids sat around and discussed Charles Dickens' *A Christmas Carol* with Quackenbush's family, including his wife, Traci, and their three young children. They were so close that the Dunnes named their second-born son Christopher, and both men were godparents to one another's children. Dunne told mourners at a memorial service about how he often sought Quackenbush's advice about life in general. "Hey Quack, what do you think about marrying Susan?" he said. "Hey Quack, do I party too hard?"

The loss was also keenly felt by charitable groups. Quackenbush was the president of the board of directors for Adventures in Learning, a cultural-enrichment and after-school program for children, and served on the advisory board for Mercy Haven, a nonprofit housing corporation for individuals with mental illnesses. And he created the Jacob Marley Foundation, a nonprofit organization that funds educational, literacy and religious programs for underprivileged children. "Chris wanted to help everybody in the world who didn't have what he had," said administrator Diana Holden.

What Quackenbush had was a blue-chip career. He worked as an attorney with Skadden, Arps, Slate Meagher & Flom, a prestigious mergers and acquisitions law firm, then joined Merrill Lynch Capital Markets' mergers and acquisitions group before becoming one of the seven founding partners of Sandler O'Neill in 1989. He established the firm's investment banking arm, and was credited with bringing in many clients. "You can't replace people like Chris Quackenbush," said Tom O'Neill, the firm's namesake. Fortunately for the firm's future, O'Neill points out, "he helped train the people who survived."

That's small consolation to Dunne. "It's not going to be as good here," he says. "Not as much fun."

KIRSTEN CHRISTOPHE
A Devotion to Family, Law and Life

Kirsten Christophe's daughter, Gretchen, was only 4 weeks old when she attended her first American Bar Association meeting. Christophe, an attorney and vice president at Aon Risk Ser-

vices, still had a couple of months left in maternity leave at the time. But she wasn't the type to shirk her responsibilities, be they professional or personal.

An energetic, organized woman who volunteered with the Junior League and spent time on the board of the New York Audubon Society, Christophe was used to juggling demands on her time. Rather than skip the bar association meeting, she simply packed her daughter, now 1, and husband up in the car and took them with her on the 275-mile journey from their home in Maplewood, New Jersey, to the meeting in Sagamore, in upstate New York.

"Kirsten was an extremely devoted mother, a loving wife," said her husband of six years, Charles Christophe. "But she was also very good in her profession."

At 39, Christophe was a recognized expert in risk management and had published numerous law articles. She had been involved with the bar association since the late 1980s, serving most recently as counsel in tort and insurance practice.

Her husband, an attorney from Düsseldorf, Germany, was equally committed to his career, and shared Kirsten's devotion to family. The two spent most holidays either at her parents' home in Peoria, Illinois, or hosting the whole clan at their own house in Maplewood.

The couple loved to travel. After their daughter was born, they took her along on cross-country trips or for walks through the park near their house. "We would have a diaper bag, a stroller . . . so much stuff!" he said. But it was worth it, he said, so the family could be together.

The Christophes' union began in 1993, when they met at a bar review course in Manhattan. They forged a friendship during long hours of intense study, he said. When the exam was over, he asked her out. Friendship quickly turned to love in a courtship conducted to the sounds of the many classical and chamber music concerts they attended. "Even when we were away on business, we would call each other and talk for hours," he said. "We couldn't separate from each other for very long."

They were married in April 1995, and three years later moved from Manhattan to New Jersey in search of good schools and ample play space for the children they hoped to have. "We bought a house, and everything was so good," he said. Their daughter's birth completed the picture.

She returned to work three months after giving birth. The Christophes, ever close, crossed the

Hudson River together each morning on the ferry that took them to their jobs in lower Manhattan. It was part of their routine; they would walk to the World Trade Center, where she worked on the 104th floor of Tower Two, and then he would continue on to his law offices one block away.

On the morning of September 11, Charles kissed his wife goodbye at the foot of the towers and rushed off, late for a 9 a.m. hearing. In hours, terrorists had destroyed the building where his wife worked.

At first he refused to give up hope that his wife, who was still breast-feeding Gretchen, had survived. His office building had been shut down after the tragedies, so he spent almost all of his time combing local hospitals. "I was looking for her for three weeks," he said.

Her family, more resigned, decided to hold a memorial service on September 30. Her body was found two weeks later.

Her husband visits her gravesite each week to bring fresh flowers to the woman who loved him like no one else. "I had never experienced so much love," he said, "even from my family." One November pilgrimage was particularly hard. It would have been her 40th birthday.

DAVID RICE
Clean, Sober and Calm at the End

It had not been an easy life that brought David Rice, 31, to his job as an investment banker with an office on the 104th floor of the World Trade Center.

He was a C-minus high school student whose classmates elected him "most likely to succeed" because of the illegal warehouse parties he threw, profited from and was arrested for. He was a drug and alcohol addict who flunked out of the University of Oklahoma, but who sobered up two years later, enrolled at Loyola University in Chicago, finished first in his class, won a Fulbright scholarship, and got a master's degree from the prestigious London School of Economics. Rice had lived in Lake Forest until February, when his firm, Sandler O'Neill & Partners, transferred him to its New York office. Before he died—his body was one of the first to be found—Rice had been sober for nine years and was still rediscovering himself.

"David was very human," said his brother, Andrew, 28. "You'd be having a lot of problems with him and he'd be driving you crazy, but you loved him to death."

Rice had been in another recent brush with death just before the World Trade Center was attacked. Two weeks earlier, he had been on an airplane that nearly crashed. Rice later told family members he felt an incredible calm on that plane, because he knew he had no control over events. "David told them he'd learned that in tough times, get down on your knees and pray to God," said the Reverend Joseph Ross, the priest at his family church, Christ the King Catholic Church of Oklahoma City. "His family believes that's what he did at his desk at the World Trade Center just before he died."

Indeed, David managed to call his parents after a jetliner struck the north tower. He told them he'd been instructed to stay put in the south tower for now and added, "It's really out of my control." Said his father, Hugh, "He seemed at peace with himself."

KAREN HAGERTY
Humor Never Deserted Her

Karen Hagerty was so organized, she lined up cans of cat food in her pantry in alphabetical order with the "beef" first, the "chicken" next, and so on. Cans and bottles in her refrigerator were lined up with similar precision in neat lines and labels facing outward.

That dedication to organization and detail helped propel her up the ladder at the huge Aon Corporation insurance brokerage to become a senior vice president at the age of 34, her family said. That's where she was, on the 78th floor of Two World Trade Center, when it was hit by a hijacked plane.

Survivors told the family that Hagerty and her co-workers were fleeing the building after the first plane hit Tower One. A message came over the public announcement system saying there was no danger in Tower Two, and they could go back to work.

But they still wanted to leave, and Hagerty sat down on a bench on the 78th floor to wait for the elevator, according to relatives. Someone suggested a man should be allowed on a full car because he had two children. Hagerty, known for her outrageous sense of humor and her love of animals, joked to one colleague, "Wait a minute, I've a horse and two cats."

Then the second jetliner hit. Her colleagues found that Hagerty was unconscious and had no pulse, said her stepfather, Linzee Whittaker. The survivors climbed through the debris and carnage and escaped down the stairwells.

Hagerty's body hadn't been recovered, but her family decided to accept her death and proceed with the grieving process. "The uncertainty can just eat you alive," Whittaker said. So the family held a memorial service and a reception afterward that included a special invited guest—Hagerty's horse, Ricardo, a German warmblood that she adored, along with her two cats, Kitty and Buddy.

Hagerty was no stranger to insurance. She spent her early years on Long Island, but by the age of 12, she went abroad with her mother, Lena, and her stepfather, who was an overseas manager for another insurance company.

She moved up the ladder quickly at Aon and ended up handling major accounts, including AOL Time Warner and General Dynamics, until the day of the attack. "We are convinced she did not suffer," said Whittaker. "She never knew what hit her."

JOHN WALLICE JR.
A 40-Year-Old Rookie on Wall Street

At the age of 40, John Wallice Jr. was an old man to be entering the competitive world of Wall Street. But tough times at the family real estate company he had been part of for 20 years in Huntington made the change seem necessary three years ago.

"He said, 'If I need to do this to better support my family, I'm going to make it a success,'" said Chris Rohrecker, 40, Wallice's brother-in-law. "He was willing to try something different and make it happen. He was willing to fail and wasn't afraid of that, and that says something about him as well."

But Wallice did not fail. As an international equities broker at Cantor Fitzgerald, he built up the company's "cross-book" business, bringing in new customers. He was in his office, on the 104th floor of Tower One, when the building was attacked on September 11.

It was no surprise to his wife of 10 years, Allison, that he pulled off his career change. "He just kind of made things come to fruition," she said. "Almost every time the challenge got tougher, he rose higher. And he was really on top when the fall happened."

Everything looked rosy in Wallice's life, said his wife. "He was in a tremendous growing phase," she said. "He was happy, satisfied with his career."

But even more than his career success, it was family life that sustained Wallice. The couple had three sons—Jack, 9, Christian, 7, and Patrick, 4—and a house in Huntington, where Wallice grew up. "He would do whatever he could to get home as early as he could every day," Allison said. "He felt like his work was really more at home, raising the kids. He had a lot of pride in being able to be home and part of their lives."

And, Rohrecker said, "His boys revered him. He was a hero to his sons. When he came home from work, they would light up when they saw him." An active outdoorsman, he would take them to the beach, on bike rides or for a jog, and he coached their baseball team. He loved living near the beach and made it his practice to swim in the sea every day when it was warm enough.

"He'd still be swimming in the Sound right now," said Rohrecker in early autumn. "He had mandated that he'd swim at least until Halloween and, given this Indian summer we're having, he'd consider himself fortunate to have a couple more weeks."

As far as future hopes, his wife said, Wallice looked forward to watching his sons grow into men. "I think he just wanted to live a simple life," she said. "Probably retire early, and just spend quality time raising the children. And just enjoy life vicariously through them."

GRACE GALANTE
She Was the Youngest, but She Had Strength

Grace Galante may have been the youngest daughter in a traditional Italian family, but she was no helpless little sister.

"She was a fireball," said her older brother, Frank Susca. The charismatic 29-year-old broker assistant at Cantor Fitzgerald had a sharp wit and made friends easily. But her bubbly exterior cloaked a steely inner core.

"We used to call her Leona Helmsley," Susca said with a laugh. "When it came to family, she didn't mess around. She didn't take any guff from us."

He still remembers the day when they were kids and he and Grace decided to play office. Frank, then 9, set up a little work space in a corner of their parents' home in South Brooklyn. He was going to be the boss, he told 6-year-old Grace, and she was going to be his secretary.

Settling into place, Frank made the appropriate noises simulating a ringing telephone. Grace, all 6-year-old secretarial efficiency, answered, "Boss' office."

So far, so good.

Then he asked to speak to the boss. "Speaking," Grace said.

Her strong personality notwithstanding, Galante shared the traditional family-focused values that her parents, Francesco and Lucrezia Susca, brought over from their coastal hometown of Mola di Bari in southern Italy. She spoke Italian and lived at home until 1994, when she married John Galante, a Sicilian-born boy from Bensonhurst.

They met when she was 17 and he was 20. She was a smart girl, and beautiful, with long dark hair and hazel eyes, said her husband. "Her parents were strict, so we started slowly," he said. "I knew being with her had to be a serious thing."

After their marriage, the pair settled in Staten Island, where both of their parents had moved from Brooklyn. With family so close, they rarely ate dinner at home. "We'd take turns," said her husband. "One time hers, another mine. We both worked, and our parents loved having us over."

As a child, Galante used to tutor older children in the neighborhood. Her aptitude for math won her a job at Cantor Fitzgerald straight out of high school. She enjoyed her work, but the main point of it, said her brother, was to save money to start her own family.

Those plans were dashed when Galante perished in the World Trade Center, where she worked on the 105th floor of the north tower. Her husband, who worked nearby on 14th Street, searched fruitlessly for her outside the towers after the planes hit. Police forced him from the scene after the first tower collapsed; he watched his wife's building crumble as he trudged home, covered in ash, across the Brooklyn Bridge.

Trouble came in threes that day for Grace's family. Her husband's cousin, Anthony, lost his wife, Deanna Galante, who was seven months pregnant with the couple's first child. A close friend of her brother's was also killed. "We knew a lot of Cantor people," Susca said softly.

"She is the youngest, but the strongest," said her husband. In life, Galante took charge of everything from wedding arrangements for her older sister, Cathy, to deciding what kind of furniture to buy for her parents' new house.

"She was the perfect Susca," her brother said.

"She had my mom's devotion to the family and my father's work ethic. She had Cathy's huge heart. I like to think that I'm the security in my family, the strength. But she had all my strength, and then some."

LAURENCE NEDELL
He Stayed to Check On an Elderly Colleague

He could have gotten out.

But Laurence Nedell, last seen on the 92nd floor of Tower Two, felt compelled to go back up one floor to check on his employees at Aon Corporation, where he was a risk-management specialist.

"He was somewhere on the 92nd floor when one of his other directors said, 'Let's get out of here,'" said Lorraine Nedell of Lindenhurst, his wife of 30 years.

Nedell had just hired an elderly man whom, among others, he wanted to check on. He turned around.

The other man escaped. Nedell didn't. He is among the missing and presumed dead from the terrorist attacks.

"Everyone I tell that story to says, 'That's Larry,'" his wife said.

He was a dedicated worker. Even at the age of 52, Nedell worked long hours, leaving on the 4:43 a.m. train out of Lindenhurst and returning home at 8 or 9 p.m.

Nedell loved nothing more than kicking back after a long day of work and watching a science fiction movie or television show—"the bloodier the better," his wife said—with his two dogs. Clint Eastwood flicks like *The Wild Bunch* and shows like *The X-Files* were among his favorites.

"We did everything together," his wife said. "From grocery shopping to regular shopping to going to Atlantic City to going to the beach . . . Whatever we did, we did together," even if it meant trekking to Pennsylvania to an obscure flea market or craft fair to buy a pocketknife or fossilized shark teeth, two unusual things that Nedell collected.

The couple grew up just one mile down the street from each other in Kew Gardens Hills. He was in the first graduating class of John Bowne High School; she, the second.

They didn't know much of each other in high school, but they reconnected at a reunion dance in 1968, just a few months after she graduated.

A few years later, they married, living in East Northport and Massapequa before settling in Lindenhurst 24 years ago, where they raised their two daughters, Laura, 28, and Jennie, 23.

Now, Lorraine feels her husband's absence everywhere, whether she's doing the grocery shopping or preparing for the holidays. And knowing he could have made it out makes it all the more difficult.

"There was one point I had a dream," she said. "I said, 'Why, why did you do that, Larry?' He just shrugged his shoulders and said, 'I just had to do it.'"

STEVE POLLICINO
No One Could Resist His Fun-Loving Nature

When Steve Pollicino would take his family to his wife's uncle's house in New Jersey for a summer barbecue, he would put on an old suit before arriving and light a cigar. Then Pollicino would burst into the backyard and start apologizing for being late. He'd say he was held up at a meeting, and then, suit on and cigar in hand, he'd jump into the pool.

"He had this happy-go-lucky attitude and the ability to make people around him enjoy themselves," said Pollicino's wife, Jane. "When he was at a party he'd always make the DJ play 'Shout' . . . He just loved to throw his hands in the air and shout."

Pollicino, 48, a corporate bond trader and vice president at Cantor Fitzgerald, worked on the 104th floor of Tower One. He lived in Plainview with his wife and 12-year-old daughter, Celeste. His 19-year-old son, Steven, is a sophomore at the University of Delaware. About 800 people came to Our Lady of Mercy Church in Hicksville on September 28 to honor Pollicino, and about 10 family members spoke at that memorial service, remembering Pollicino's easygoing personality and enthusiasm.

But it has been the unexpected contact from people she didn't know that has surprised and touched Jane Pollicino the most.

There was his third-grade teacher from Dutch Lane School in Hicksville who sent a note remembering Pollicino's intelligence, his thick, brown eyebrows and his smile—attributes Jane Pollicino said he never lost.

There was an old friend who worked with Pollicino at his first job in high school, unloading skids in the basement of Pathmark, who wanted to tell Pollicino's kids about their dad's sense of humor that got a group of guys through their shifts with "nonstop laughter."

And then there was the group of commuters that Pollicino knew from his usual 6:11 a.m. train out of Hicksville who sent a card to tell his family about what a good friend he was to them.

Pollicino met Jane Elefante in biology class at Nassau Community College in 1971. They continued to date through his years at Long Island University's C.W. Post Campus and hers at Buffalo State College, and were married on April Fool's Day in 1978. For five years after college, Pollicino owned a club in St. James called Flaggers, a wine and cheese cafe that eventually became a disco. He also owned a coffee shop in a Melville office building, Broad Hollow Cafe.

His personality translated perfectly to being a small-business owner, his wife said. But after a year of staying home after his son, Steven, was born in 1982, Pollicino looked for more stability and used his people skills to become a successful securities trader. He joined Cantor Fitzgerald in 1986.

Jane Pollicino remembers how her husband loved to go out to dinner and always wanted a round table so everyone could converse easily, and how Pollicino was as comfortable with a group of his daughter Celeste's friends as he was in the financial district. "My daughter had a bunch of girls over at a sleepover, and they were playing basketball," his wife said. "Steve was shining his laser light on the backboard, and the girls asked what that was. Celeste said, 'Oh, that's my dad, he's like having another kid around.'"

ELIZABETH LOGLER
She Was Driven to Have Fun

Owning a car can be more of a hassle than a convenience in Manhattan, with its gridlock and alternate-side parking rules.

But to Beth Logler, her car was worth the trouble. It gave her the freedom to see the people she loved at a moment's notice. Once behind the wheel of her hunter-green Saab, she could visit her fiance in Scarsdale, shoot out to her parents' home in Rockville Centre or drive up to her grandparents' place in Yonkers. And with characteristic efficiency, the investment relations professional had the parking situation in her neighborhood east of midtown "down to a science," said her mother, Claire Logler.

After her grandmother passed away in 1999, Logler made a special effort to swoop up her grandfather and take him out for lunches and long walks in the city. "She would pick up her grandfather, roll back the sunroof, turn the radio up full blast and drive off with her 87-year-old grandfather laughing like mad," her mother said. "Or she would buzz him out to Rockville Centre and we would all go to the beach."

That flexibility was important to Logler, 31. A vice president at Cantor Fitzgerald who traveled often for work, she had a jam-packed professional schedule and an equally busy personal life. She had recently bought an apartment, which she was busy decorating, and she was in the thick of planning her wedding to Doug Cleary, her boyfriend of six years.

"She was a wonderful person—driven, smart, successful and, at the same time, fun," said Cleary, a mortgage broker. The two met by chance at a restaurant in Manhattan. Taken by her quick wit and willowy, blonde good looks, Cleary asked her out for lunch the very next day.

Since then, "We were joined at the hip," he said. "We did everything together, even just going to get the newspaper."

The two balanced each other out, Logler's mother said. "He knew how to make her have fun and relax, to put away the books," she said.

The couple traveled to Europe and all over the United States. Eschewing guidebooks, they relied on their own outgoing personalities to get a sense of a new place by asking locals where to go and what to do. "They had an incredible amount of fun together," said her older brother, Brian.

Back at home, Cleary and Logler made regular trips out to Long Island to visit her family, especially after her brother's daughter, Carolyn, Logler's goddaughter, was born. Much to the amusement of Brian, who hardly considered his wisecracking sister the maternal type, Carolyn and Beth formed a sort of mutual admiration society. "It was fun to see," he said.

Born just 22 months apart, the Logler siblings were always together. Logler, athletic and lively, tagged along with her brother and his friends and

gave "all those boys quite a run for their money," said her mother. Although they attended separate high schools—she went to Sacred Heart, he to Chaminade—they shared friends throughout high school, forming a close-knit group that remains so to this day.

Brian Logler turned to that circle of friends for comfort after the attacks on the World Trade Center reduced his sister's office on the 101st floor of the north tower to a heap of dust and crumpled steel. "Everybody knows what everybody's going through," he said.

FRANK MOCCIA
She Wouldn't Let Him Go Alone

In 1976, Frank Moccia skipped an overnight work shift to spend his daughter's 10th birthday at home in Brooklyn.

That night an explosion rocked the American Chicle chewing gum plant in Long Island City where Moccia worked, killing six people, including, his wife said, the man working at Moccia's usual machine.

Twenty-five years later, Moccia, 57, of Hauppauge, couldn't cheat death a second time. He was killed September 11 at the World Trade Center, where he worked as a facility planner for Washington Group International.

"For all the years I had with him, I am very lucky," said his wife, Elaine. "I was with him over half my life, and those were the best years."

He made days at work at the Washington Group easier by telling jokes that broke up long work days in their offices on the 91st floor of Tower Two. Friends say that while the building was being evacuated on September 11, Moccia went back to their offices to make sure everyone got word to leave.

Away from work, Moccia made his daughter, Donna Marie Velazquez, happy when he would stop by unannounced at her Port Jefferson Station house to play with his three grandchildren: Brianna Marie, 7, Toni Ann, 3, and Vincent, 2.

"He was just a silly guy," she said. "He could always put a smile on your face."

Moccia was very close with his son, Frank Jr., 26, and the two played golf frequently in the summer and watched football in the fall, especially the Giants.

"We liked to hang out together," said his son, a New York City police officer. "He always saw the best in every situation. I don't think he ever yelled at me my whole life."

And Moccia meant the world to Elaine, whom he married in 1970. She was from Long Island City, and he was living in Williamsburg. "We went bowling one night, and I had so much fun, and he made me laugh," she said. "I said, 'This guy isn't too bad. He makes me laugh.' . . . He was a big old teddy bear. Cute and cuddly."

The couple moved in 1980 from Williamsburg to Hauppauge. Moccia commuted to his job with the Washington Group, where he had worked since just after the explosion at the American Chicle plant.

The weekend before he died, Moccia and his family went to Six Flags Great Adventure in New Jersey for his granddaughter Brianna Marie's seventh birthday.

Elaine Moccia said she usually doesn't like roller coasters but went with her husband on the Medusa ride after he had asked. "I said, 'Sure, hon, as long as I'm with you, I'll try.'" Moccia spent the whole time laughing, his wife said, while she prayed and squeezed his hand hard enough to leave fingernail marks.

After the ride, Moccia asked his wife why she went. She said, "I told him, 'All I could see was that ride going off the track, and I didn't want you to go without me.' Unfortunately," she continued after a deep sigh, "he went without me."

TARA DEBEK
Her Family Outings Were a Treat for All

Tara Debek was like a one-woman social committee for her family, tirelessly coordinating vacations or outings to Yankees games or the theater.

A running joke in the family is how Debek's 5-year-old niece, Shannon Reahl, never sat farther back than the third row at a Broadway show because of her aunt.

Debek, 35, had just started her own family. She and her husband, Derek Debek, married three years ago after meeting on the 98th floor of Tower One, where both worked for Marsh USA; she was an assistant vice president in the treasury department there. Their only child, Paige, was just a few months old.

Her husband had started a new job at a different office about five months ago, and he and Tara went their separate ways the morning of September 11.

"When she left that day, I was running a little late, and I was changing our daughter in the other room, and I never got to say goodbye to her," Derek said. "From the other room I shouted, 'See you later,' and she said, 'See you later.'"

In his eulogy at a memorial service on October 8, her husband said, "I'm not going to say goodbye here, either. I'm just going to say, 'See you later.'"

She grew up in Lindenhurst as Tara Moore. As adults, she and her siblings settled near their parents on the South Shore. She and her sister Lisa Reahl, born on the same day one year apart, bought a house together in Babylon. Reahl lives upstairs with her husband and two daughters; Tara lived downstairs with her husband and baby Paige.

"We were so happy when she finally had her own child, and now she doesn't even get to see her grow up," Reahl said. "It's just horrible."

In August, the entire family—the Debeks, the Reahls, brother Robert Moore and his wife, and mother Maureen Moore—traveled to Disney World.

As usual, Tara planned the entire trip and acted as tour guide, showing her family around the various theme parks and attractions.

"That was like her dream vacation," Reahl said.

Derek described his wife as a kind, honest, energetic woman with an optimistic attitude.

"Her favorite phrase was 'It doesn't matter,' as in, don't let it get to you, or the clouds will pass and the sun will come out," he said.

After their father, Robert Moore, died last year, Tara comforted her family by telling them that "everything happens for a reason," Reahl said.

Since September 11, Reahl has tried to find solace in her sister's words, but "we don't know what the reason could be," she said. "We still don't know what the reason is."

MICHAEL ARMSTRONG
A New York Native Who Loved His Town

Despite being a Manhattan native, Michael J. Armstrong never tired of learning more about the place where he was born and raised and loved that he was able to work atop the World Trade Center, with its stunning views of the city.

"He always fought me for a window seat on planes, because he loved to look at the city as we flew in or out," said his fiancee, Catherine Nolan, whom he was to marry in October 2001. Despite the enormity of the tragedy, there was something fitting about how Armstrong died, "just because it was on top of the city he loved," she said.

Armstrong, 34, was a vice president at Cantor Fitzgerald who grew up in Manhattan and lived on the Upper East Side. He told Nolan that he wanted their children to attend the same schools he did as a boy. He enjoyed riding his bike in Central Park and reading up on his hometown, which he already seemed to know everything about.

"You could say you went to a building on 14th Street, and he would know exactly what building it was and what it looked like," Nolan said. "He had one of those antique maps of old New York on his wall, and he would get books on the history of New York and the history of Central Park."

MICHAEL JACOBS
A Cool Army Vet Who Helped Evacuate Others

During a winter Salvation Army coat drive inside Grand Central Terminal, Michael Jacobs decided that he would buy a new coat and donate the one he was wearing as he headed home that night. But in a rare moment of absent-mindedness, he gave up his brand-new coat instead. He never retrieved it because he felt someone needed it more than he did.

That's the kind of person he was, said his son Michael Brady, who remembers his father as generous, level-headed—and very busy. With the demands of his job as vice president of tax operations at Fiduciary Trust Company International combined with 2$^{1}/_{2}$-hour commutes each way, Michael Jacobs chalked up 15-hour days most weeks, said Brady. Jacobs worked from offices on the 90th floor of Tower Two and had been with Fiduciary Trust for almost 20 years. Despite the grind, Jacobs was a true professional, Brady said. "He enjoyed what he did."

Jacobs, 54, was an Army veteran and the type of person who kept a cool head when most folks would tend to lose theirs, his son said. People who

escaped from the towers told Brady his father helped others evacuate and herded them onto elevators ahead of himself. "It was like the captain on a sinking ship. He wouldn't have been the one to panic. He was just a take-charge type."

Despite leaving home in Danbury, Connecticut, at about 5 a.m. each day and not returning until 8 or later, Jacobs made the most of what little spare time he had. He was restoring a 1969 Volkswagen Beetle and teaching himself to play the bagpipes. "He called me one day," Brady recalled, "and said, 'Guess what I'm learning to do?' I said, 'Why the bagpipes? Why not guitar or piano?'" Jacobs responded, "Why not the bagpipes?"

Divorced, Jacobs had three other children, Peter, Jenny and Mary. Brady remembers that he had a way of seeing the humorous side of even the most serious situations. Jacobs was stationed in Germany after enlisting in the Army during the Vietnam War, his son said. He always joked that none of the pubs he guarded had ever been attacked by the Vietnamese.

RAJESH MIRPURI
Dutiful Son Always Had His Parents in Mind

Some days, Arjan Mirpuri has flashes. Perhaps Rajesh, his only child, is in his bedroom, sleeping. Or watching television.

Or maybe he's on his way to their Englewood Cliffs, New Jersey, home, about to knock on the door. Just like that time in 1996 when he surprised his parents on their 30th wedding anniversary, telling them from Tokyo, where he was on business, that he was taking a jaunt to visit them in Honolulu.

"The evening of our anniversary he called me in the evening, and he said he reached Honolulu and he's in the car and he's going to a hotel," recalled Arjan Mirpuri, 61. "After half an hour the doorbell rang . . . I opened the door and he was there. He was there at the door."

He pauses.

"He wanted to give us a surprise," he adds, choking back sobs. "He didn't care about Honolulu. He loved us so much."

Arjan and Indra Mirpuri lost their only son in September 11's terrorist attacks. He was on the

106th floor of Tower One for a three-day conference. Mirpuri, 30, was vice president of sales and business development at Data Synapse in Manhattan, and he lived with his parents in New Jersey.

Aside from when he attended college, first at the University of Vermont and then at New York University, Mirpuri always lived at home with his parents, a dutiful son who remembered his parents' birthdays and anniversaries when they forgot.

Born in Hong Kong and raised in New Jersey, he was friendly and entertaining, the type of guy who made those around him smile and laugh.

He liked playing and watching sports, traveling all over the world and tasting the culinary delights of the city's restaurant scene.

Now his parents are taking solace in their religion. Devout Hindus, they held 12 days of puja ceremonies, in their home, followed by a large memorial service on October 5 at the Sadhu Vaswani Center, a temple in Closter, New Jersey.

For the next year they will have a puja in his memory on the 11th of every month. They will also soon go to their native India and visit holy sites, such as the Ganges River, to pray for their son's spirit and those of all the other victims.

"The shock won't go away until we die," his father said. "We also have to accept the will of God. We cannot fight it. We will accept God's will."

CHRISTOPHER LUNDER
The Young Man and the Sea

On this summer day, the panorama of the East River appeared especially gratifying. Christopher Edmund Lunder's view from his office on the 104th floor of Tower One homed in on the 38-foot cruiser that he had just bought in July. His mom, visiting from Florida, savored the joy on her youngest son's face.

"He was just proud as proud could be," Maureen Lunder said. "It was like a dream come true."

Chris Lunder's love affair with the sea began as an infant 34 years earlier in Northport Harbor, and now he had become captain of his own boat. His father, Ed, the captain who had taken his wife and five children cruising every summer weekend, would be his first mate. As an adult, he reveled in bluefishing and waterskiing.

On land, too, Lunder had a zest for life, as a wine connoisseur, a cigar aficionado and a barbecue "grillmaster," as his buddies called him. His popularity at Cantor Fitzgerald, where he traded bonds for five years, was an extension of the leadership Lunder exhibited as a teenager in Centerport. After becoming a Suffolk County all-star pole vaulter at Holy Family High School in Huntington, also lettering in wrestling and football, Lunder transferred to The Knox School in St. James. There he captained the wrestling and cross-country teams and played lacrosse, capping off his senior year by being elected student body president.

In 1997, a year after his parents moved to Stuart, Florida, Lunder married Karen Dittenbinder, whom he had met at Stetson University in DeLand, Florida, where he majored in finance. "They were so perfect together," Maureen Lunder said. "Karen was really devoted to him. When he was running, she would follow him in the car to make sure he was OK."

Her concern stemmed from his fifth knee surgery by Dr. James Parkes, the Mets' longtime team physician. Lunder was told to rehab his knee with a machine until he couldn't stand the pain. "Chris stayed up all night and did not stop the machine," said his oldest brother, Bobby, 41, of Manhattan.

Dedicated at home, too, Lunder rented a backhoe to excavate his backyard for a pool. And how he loved entertaining: He would decorate his house in green and white when friends came over to watch the Jets. His passion reached the ski slopes of Colorado, Utah and New Hampshire.

On the morning of September 11, after a hijacked plane hit five stories below his office, Lunder e-mailed his wife about the crash and wrote, "I love you." From their sixth-floor apartment on Chambers Street, Karen Lunder peered through binoculars at the day's unfolding events. "She watched the whole thing," Maureen Lunder said.

"They murdered my brother," said Dave Lunder, 36, of Port St. Lucie, Florida. "The media calls it a tragedy, like an earthquake or a tornado. You can sugarcoat it like a natural disaster, but it was cold-blooded mass murder."

In his eulogy, Bobby Lunder recalled the search for his brother: "The detective asked for his height and weight. I replied, 'He was 10 feet tall and weighed 900 pounds. And you should look for an especially big heart.'"

RONALD CARL FAZIO
A Hero with a Weakness for Reese's

Ronald Carl Fazio wasn't a fireman or a policeman or a paramedic. But like those who gave their lives to help others on September 11, he was just as much a hero.

Fazio, 57, of Closter, New Jersey, was an accountant for Aon Corporation who worked on the 99th floor of Two World Trade Center. After the neighboring tower was struck by a hijacked jetliner, he called his wife, then started to evacuate. When he realized employees on the other end of his floor were still at their desks, he went back to help. He yelled at them to evacuate, and held open the door as they made their way to the exit. On the way down the stairs, he cracked jokes, trying to keep people calm.

At some point, Fazio diverted from the stairs to the elevator. A co-worker remembers leaving the building with him. Ronald Fazio was last seen in front of the Sam Goody store at Four World Trade Center.

"My children think their father was a hero, too," said Janet Fazio, his wife of 33 years. "You don't hear about the corporate workers who risked their lives to get others out. And I think that should be said. They went to work that day like everyone else and they didn't come back."

His son Robert added, "His colleagues told us, 'Your dad is the reason I'm home with my family right now.'"

Helping others was typical of Fazio, who loved to ride his bike on the Jersey shore, shop the outlet stores with his wife and feast on the Reese's peanut butter cups that his doctors forbade. Sunday afternoons, he made a famous marinara sauce for family dinners.

His family always came first. "I've known him since I was 19 years old and I'm 54," Janet said. "He was the love of my life. He always took care of me and my children. We all depended on him totally. His mother was a widow and he took care of her."

Fazio was equally devoted to his three children: Ronald Jr., 30, Robert, 28, and Lauren, 22, whom Fazio always called his princess.

Despite exhausting work days, Fazio always had time for Boy Scouts, Little League and family camping trips. "He was the type of dad that after work he'd show up in his suit and watch the boys play Little League," Janet said. "He lost his dad when he was 8 years old. Now my sons are trying to fill their father's shoes."

"The truth is, my dad was my hero before he went to work that day," said Robert. "He was just such a positive role model. The metaphor of him holding the door for others that day . . . that's what he did for each of us kids. He held the door open for us throughout our lives, for our careers, our social lives, and our emotional well-being."

In the weeks before September 11, Fazio had been helping his oldest son and his fiancee plan their wedding. He helped the couple pick out their new furniture. Ronald Jr. and Diane Fazio were married on October 14, 2001, as they had planned. "We had a family discussion, and we knew he would have wanted us to do that," Janet said. "Everyone supported us totally. I cried, they cried, and we had a wonderful time. It was a beautiful wedding. It was the hardest thing I've ever had to do. But we got through it." Robert gave the toast with a tribute to his father.

In the days after September 11, Robert had distributed fliers with a picture of his missing father, and a bit of his trademark humor. "We put on the bottom, 'If found, please feed Reese's peanut butter cups,'" Robert Fazio said. "We always gave him a hard time. With his heart condition, he wasn't allowed to eat them. But he cheated a lot."

Soon after, Hershey sent the family three cases of the candy, which they handed out at the memorial service.

KRISTIN IRVINE-RYAN
A Gift for Listening and a Lifetime of Helping

Brendan and Kristy Ryan knew each other most of their lives. They were best friends, soul mates and, for 94 days, husband and wife.

"We knew each other when we were 12 years old, and we always knew we would end up together," said Brendan Ryan, who married Kristy on June 9. "My heart goes out to the fiancees affected by this tragedy. When I talk about it, I can say, 'Kristy is my wife.' At least we had our day. I'll always have that to hold on to."

Kristy Irvine-Ryan was an equities trader for Sandler O'Neill & Partners and worked on the 104th floor of Two World Trade Center. On the morning of September 11, she spoke to Brendan three times.

"She was very calm and very poised," said Brendan, 30. "She said they made an announcement that the fire was contained and the building was safe. When the second plane hit, the phone went dead. She called right back and said, 'We're going down now.'

"I said, 'I love you' and 'Call me when you get down.' The more I kept seeing the replay of the second plane, I knew."

Kristy, 30, grew up in Huntington and graduated from St. Anthony's High School and the University of Dayton in Ohio. She enjoyed reading novels, writing, listening to music and taking walks in the couple's Greenwich Village neighborhood. The things most dear to her were her husband and family and the idea of helping others.

"I always looked up to her in so many ways," said her sister Michelle, 27, who lives in Tucson, Arizona. "Because we were close in age, I could tell her anything. She was a great listener, and she was such a great friend."

Kristy's gift for listening often made her the sister each sibling confided in. "She was my anchor," said her sister Wendy Toomey, 35, of Cary, North Carolina. "She was always there for you. She had time for everybody whether her day was busy or not. She was very involved in my children's lives. I named my daughter Kristin after her, and she's godmother to my son, Dean."

In 1999, she and friends Meredith O'Neal and Louise Rexer started a charity called Secret Smiles. They would anonymously provide families with gifts or other basic necessities during the holidays. One year, they delivered a stove to a family.

"The funny thing about Secret Smiles is that she never talked about it," Michelle said. "It really was a secret. She never wanted to show it off. It started as something small and just grew and grew."

Brendan Ryan, a keyboard player for the rock group the Bogmen, will carry on her mission with Secret Smiles. The Bogmen, who broke up in 1999, planned to reunite for a benefit concert in Kristy's honor.

"My therapy," Brendan said, "is to help other people through this."

THOMAS STRADA
Life Was an Ocean of Possibilities

Find a fish, any fish, the biggest fish you can dream, and Thomas Strada could charm it like no one else. "He had an uncanny ability to communicate with the fish," said his father, Ernest Strada, mayor of the Incorporated Village of Westbury. "If there was one fish to be caught, he could catch it."

In fact, Thomas Strada, 41, a devoted family man and successful bond broker for Cantor Fitzgerald, looked forward to retiring, if only to pursue a new career as a bass fisherman. For the present, though, he was hooked on his family. "He was very excited about what the future held for him . . . as a father and a husband," said Ernest Strada. Just four days before the World Trade Center disaster, Thomas Strada's youngest son was born. Strada, of Chatham, New Jersey, had spent most of his spare time prepping the nursery.

"There wasn't a night that he walked through these doors that he didn't play with the children, read to them . . . or ride bikes with them," said his wife, Terry Strada. They even purchased a time-share so they could take the kids to Disney World for the next 40 years. And Strada protested when his wife tried to enroll their son in golf lessons, because he, the former golf pro, wanted to teach his son to play.

It was golf that brought Strada and his wife together 18 years ago. Terry Strada waited tables at Meadowbrook Country Club, where Strada was assistant golf pro. But Strada soon abandoned golf when he realized his earning potential was limited. Instead, he embarked on a more lucrative Wall Street career.

He loved the Twin Towers, said his father, and would bring his family to visit sometimes. But be it harness racing, deer hunting, golf or fishing, Strada was an outdoorsman to the core. "He had a zest for life," said Ernest Strada, and "was an extremely exceptional human being."

EAMON MCENEANEY
A Poet and an Athlete

Eight and a half years ago, in the first terrorist attack on the World Trade Center, Eamon J. McEneaney led 63 people down 105 flights of stairs to safety. This time, McEneaney didn't make it.

McEneaney, 46, of New Canaan, Connecticut, was a senior vice president and limited partner with the brokerage firm Cantor Fitzgerald. As soon as the first hijacked plane hit Tower One, he tried to call his wife, Bonnie, at her office in Westchester County. She had not yet arrived. "He talked to my assistant . . . and he said, 'Is Bonnie there?' He said, 'I love her, and I love the kids, and tell her I'm all right,'" his wife recalled.

Friends remember him as a hearty Irishman, athlete and poet. His wife recalled him as "the life of the party. He had that leprechaun spirit—that spark. And he was able to make a bad situation better. He didn't care about material things. He cared about people." Among them: his children, Brendan, 12, Jennifer, 8, and twins Kyle and Kevin, 6.

McEneaney also "had this way with words," his wife recalled. "I intend to publish a book of poems that he had written. Eamon was so humble. He had always wanted to publish." A poem he wrote to his wife ends:

> . . . the end
> is a bend in the road
> that we'll never find
> a death I will always
> defend
> you from.

Bonnie met her husband when they were both students at Cornell University, where he was an All-American in lacrosse and All–Ivy League in football. He was also a member of the Cornell University Athletic Hall of Fame. "There was a streaking," she said, referring to the fad of running naked through public places. "I met him in a bar. He was wearing a towel and I said, 'I like your outfit.'"

LAURENCE CURIA
A Broker Who Shunned the High Life

He worked in one of the city's premier brokerages and lived in upscale Garden City, but Laurence Curia never did put much stock in wealth and its trappings.

While his neighbors displayed their collections of expensive antique cars, the 41-year-old Cantor Fitzgerald bond broker shared the family's Jeep with his wife until last year, and arrived at the train station every morning on foot.

In their neighborhood, filled with Wall Street executives, "That's kind of unheard of," said Curia's wife, Linda.

But it never bothered him, she said. "We didn't live a very lavish life," she said. "He wasn't one to always get me cards for my birthday, or flowers."

Curia had his own way of showing love, his wife explained. "He worked hard," she said. "We have a beautiful home. We live in a very nice area."

Working in the financial world, where lavish parties and everyday extravagance are the norm, maintaining a modest lifestyle was sometimes a struggle, his wife said.

"When you work in a brokerage, you're around a lot of money, and your whole outlook on life is affected," she said. "Some people became very materialistic." Her husband, on the other hand, was "very laid back," she said. "Stuff like that, it didn't matter to him."

What did matter to him was simple, she said—his family, and especially his two children, Cherilyn, 8, and Mitchell, 4.

That's why the house has no precious furnishings or fragile antiques. "He never wanted to have such expensive furniture or anything to the point that the house would become a museum and the kids wouldn't feel comfortable," his wife said.

Besides, she said, "Sometimes we did crazy things—the kids would sometimes ride bikes in the house or do Rollerblading."

The gifts Curia bought his children were always thoughtful and well chosen: for example, the telephone with a flashing neon light, which he gave his daughter when she learned to dial 911. This year, he dreamed up Cherilyn's Christmas gift when he noticed how much she hated being woken up in the morning.

"My husband was going to buy her an AM-FM alarm clock," his wife said. "Not an expensive gift, but that way she could wake up with music."

Curia outfitted the house with gadgets and entertainment the family could enjoy together—a big-screen TV and cinema-style lighting in the basement, motion-sensitive lights in the kitchen, and a stereo system wired throughout the house.

And he loved to take his family on holidays. Last year, the couple surprised their children with a trip to Disneyland. After surreptitiously packing the children's clothes while they were at school, they woke them at 5 a.m. to go to the airport.

"We both went into the room because we wanted to see the looks on their faces," his wife recalled. This year, they surprised the kids again, this time with a trip to Puerto Rico.

Every weekend, the family had a "special day" together—a trip to the beach, to an amusement park or to a video arcade. On Sunday, they ate dinner early and the whole family bicycled into town for ice cream.

On the Sunday before the attack on the World Trade Center, which claimed Curia's life, the family drove to Jones Beach, where they planned to stay in the park. The day was hotter than they had expected, and none had brought bathing suits. The children wandered off to look for seashells with their father, his wife said, and returned soaked from head to toe. The three had gone swimming with their clothes on.

It was typical of her husband, she said. "He didn't get frazzled by stuff like that," she said.

Curia, however, was becoming tired of his work, she said, with its high-stress atmosphere and the pressure of working on commission. He seemed to long for a simpler life.

"He always said he would just do this for two more years," she said. After that, "He used to tell me he was going to pump gas."

10
New Americans

They came from all over the globe—from Uzbekistan and Cuba and Bangladesh and England. From El Salvador and China and India and Poland. And they all came with the dreams that have inspired immigrants to America over the centuries—to raise families, to escape oppression, to carve out better lives.

They came searching for opportunity in the city that has always teemed with newcomers, and found jobs in the tall towers that symbolized heights to be reached, promises to be realized. They worked as waiters and stockbrokers and security guards and lawyers' assistants. One of them was a machine operator who became an accountant and was only credits away from a college degree, another played the Beatles and the Bee Gees on his guitar but proudly championed his Filipino culture. A third was preparing to take the state bar examination to become a lawyer, as he had been in his homeland.

They were all part of what makes America special.

ARCELIA CASTILLO
"The Epitome of the American Dream"

In the difficult days, when she found herself raising two children on her own, Arcelia "Chela" Castillo rented a rat- and roach-infested apartment in Elizabeth, New Jersey. To get enough heat during winter nights, Castillo would place a bag of ice on top of a small cage the landlord had put around the thermostat, blocking it from tenants. The ice would affect the thermostat's reading, giving the family a little more heat.

The run-down apartment was the type of place that a single mother with no skills, limited English and a factory job could afford. But the bleak surroundings did not stop Castillo, 50, from working toward her dreams. Not only did she move from the place, but the Colombia native learned English, developed new skills that eventually landed her a job with a prestigious financial firm in the World Trade Center and bought a house of her own.

"To me, my mom is the epitome of the American Dream," said her son, Silvio "Alex" Román, 31. "She is to me a role model who showed that there is opportunity in this country if you work for it."

Castillo was born in Palmira, a mountainous village in Colombia. She grew up there and in the city of Cali, where she attended only elementary school. She immigrated to the United States in 1972, following her husband, who came looking for work. But her husband soon left her and the two children and returned to Colombia.

Through the '80s, Castillo lived in the small apartment with her children while working as a machine operator for Sterling Plastics. At night, she learned English at a community school. When the plastics factory closed in 1986, Castillo received a plaque of recognition for her 10 years of service.

She then got work as a temporary clerical worker through an agency. That year her hard-earned savings became enough for the down payment on a two-family home in the same community where she had been renting. It was not exactly a dream house, but Castillo decided to take on the repairs herself. Her sons have photos of her at home, usually doing homework for the accelerated bookkeeping and data processing courses she enrolled in, or wearing goggles because she was fixing something around the house. Castillo and her boyfriend, Edward Skyrpa, were planning to move into a new home in Clifton, New Jersey.

Castillo was such a hard worker, her relatives say, that it was no surprise that the insurance company Johnson and Higgins hired her full time for their offices on Manhattan's Broad Street. Marsh & McLennan, another insurance company based in the World Trade Center, bought that company in 1997, and Castillo moved to the north tower's 98th floor three years later. A junior accountant, Castillo had only a few credits left to attain her associate's degree from Union County College. She had gone to work early on September 11 so she could leave early for classes.

Castillo's sons said they never saw her complain about their economic situation. "She admitted she made sure she did not cry in front of us," said Román, an auto mechanic. "She would cry in her bed at night . . . We were never aware of any hardships." Her other son, Anthony, 27, is a Marine. He says he wants to be deployed abroad to fight terrorism.

HECTOR TAMAYO
A Love for His Filipino Roots

Hector Tamayo arrived in New York City from the Philippines 21 years ago, but in a sense, he never left home.

The 51-year-old construction project manager's house in Holliswood, Queens, was decorated with traditional parol lanterns every Christmas. The family's daily table bore Filipino dishes cooked by his wife, Evelyn, such as sinigang soup and Tamayo's favorite, pinangat—fish steamed with vegetables. And the couple's two children, Ian, 20, and Pamela, 16, were brought up to respect their heritage, learning Filipino dance and traditions such as respect for elders.

"The family always sticks to the Filipino culture and the values," Evelyn said. "That was his priority also for his children."

Tamayo worked tirelessly to promote Filipino culture in America, and to improve the quality of life back in the Philippines. As past president of the Aklan Association, a Filipino social and philanthropic club named for his home province, he was the driving force behind the club's famous "Ati-Atihan" tribal costume parade. He also supported civic, social, educational and medical projects back home, dipping into his own resources and building networks of expatriate Filipinos to donate money.

His niece, Gail Prado, 28, remembers happy, hectic Christmas Eves at his house, crowded with family and friends, with Tamayo in a Santa Claus hat passing out gifts to the children and teasing them. "One year he was passing out gifts with one hand while holding a bottle of beer in the other," she said.

Almost every weekend, the Tamayo house was filled with Filipinos—friends, relatives and neighbors, including four of Tamayo's siblings and their children, all of whom live within a few blocks. They gathered to play chess, mah-jongg and card games, to eat a potluck meal and to gossip. Often, the guitar would come out and the gatherings would turn into sing-along sessions. In this regard, Tamayo had Western tastes, and loved to perform songs by the Bee Gees, the Beatles and Engelbert Humperdinck.

Tamayo was lost on the 86th floor of the World Trade Center's Tower Two, where he was overseeing the renovation of a law office. In the days that followed, his house was full again with close friends and family, though the singing was replaced with praying and mourning. A mass was held in the family's driveway and garage for a week after the tragedy, with 150 to 200 people coming every night to pray for Tamayo's safe return. The family received hundreds of phone calls from across the country and the Philippines. "We really felt blessed by it," Prado said. "It was wonderful. It was incredible."

In the wake of the attacks, the family tried to avoid anger by looking to the Roman Catholic faith that Tamayo himself held so dear. A written plea from Ian Tamayo urged America "not to indulge in the trauma of this experience or turn to hatred, but instead dwell on the positive aspects and love that was illustrated so vividly by my father's life."

GODWIN AJALA
A Guard with an Eye on the Law

There were no evenings of playing basketball with the kids, watching television with his wife or rocking his 1-year-old to sleep. For Godwin Ajala, 33, life meant rising at 5 a.m. to get to the World Trade Center, where he worked as a security guard, returning to the cramped studio apartment he shared with a friend in Jamaica, studying for the New York State bar exam and falling asleep again.

In between, there were phone calls to his family in his homeland of Nigeria. There, in the city of Enugu, lived his wife, Victoria; his three children, Onyinyechi, 8, Uchechukwu, 6, and Ugochi, 1; his parents, Mabel and Godwin Ajala, and three siblings, Alaeze, Samuel and Chukwunta. All relied on him for the weekly checks that he sent home, the home he returned to for a month just once a year.

He should have been there September 11. He had planned to take his annual trip to Nigeria on September 9, but postponed the trip because he needed to earn more money, his roommate, Christopher Onuoha, said. "It was kind of stressful for him because it was only him here," Onuoha said. "Every morning, he has to get up in the morning to make sure he gets money for them and for him. It's not been easy."

It was a frugal lifestyle that began six years ago, when Ajala gave up the comforts of Nigeria, where he was a lawyer, in an effort to provide his family with more. "He was a wonderful husband," said Victoria, his wife. "I don't think there was any other husband like him . . . He was so special to me. He did everything that a husband is supposed to do, a husband who takes care of his wife, his children and his family."

Ajala had hoped to apply for visas to bring his family to the United States after he passed the bar exam and could practice law here. That dream was shattered September 11 when Ajala, who worked for Summit Security Services, was seriously injured in the terrorist attacks. For days, his roommate and other friends searched for him, finding him at New York University Hospitals Center on September 15. "He was lying there," Onuoha recalled. "He was unconscious, on the ventilation. The doctor said he was unconscious the whole time. He hadn't spoken to anyone."

The following day, he died. Victoria Ajala, 27, wouldn't believe it. She called her husband repeatedly. He didn't respond. The reality settled in only after Ajala's body arrived in Nigeria on October 19. "I can't even accept that my husband was dead until the day he came to Africa," said his wife, who attends Oau University in Nigeria. "It's really rough. I don't know what to do."

IRINA KOLPAKOVA
She Left Uzbekistan to Make a Better Life

Arsen Kolpakova was prepared for a long day on September 11. It was Primary Day. Aware of his need to get up early, Irina Kolpakova, his mother, woke him up at 4 a.m. "I didn't want to get up," he said.

Irina went back to sleep, and her son went to a nearby polling place to be an inspector. It was the last time he saw his mother.

A Brooklyn resident, she worked as a lawyer's assistant with Harris, Beach & Wilcox on the 85th floor of the World Trade Center's south tower. "I know that she was there," said her son, 19, who spoke with her colleagues. "They just told me that they saw her there in the morning. And that she was evacuating."

Kolpakova, 37, arrived in New York from Uzbekistan five years ago. "She was very determined and she sacrificed a lot to come here," her son said. "She had a lot of problems with immigration, and she came with no English, no money." She also had no family in the United States when she arrived, but within a year and a half she had helped her son and husband move to New York.

In Tashkent, the capital of Uzbekistan, Kolpakova taught math for 10 years, from the basics to calculus. She wanted to teach again, her son said, and was a few classes away from getting her master's degree and becoming a math teacher in New York City. Before joining the law firm at the beginning of 2001, she checked program code for a Connecticut software company. She had earned an associate's degree in computer programming at a technical school in New York. And last year, Kolpakova studied English at the Brooklyn campus of Long Island University.

"She didn't have much time for hobbies," her son said. But she did like to travel. The family drove to vacation spots in many northeastern states.

Her son returned to do his job at the rescheduled primaries later that month. "It was like a repeat, you know. The same situation," he said. "And I thought I would come back home and see her, but she wasn't here."

But her voice on the answering machine was still greeting callers.

VÍCTOR PAZ-GUTIERREZ
He Wanted His Family to Be Safe

Before most people got up in the morning, Víctor Paz Gutierrez was out in the dark neighborhoods of Long Island City, Astoria, Ditmars and Steinway, delivering the morning newspapers. Paz, 43, then rushed downtown and up to the top floors of the World Trade Center's north tower to prepare the desserts patrons enjoyed at the Windows on the World

restaurant. Eight hours later he would return to his Long Island City apartment and rest, until the next day.

Back in his native Colombia, his mother, younger brother and two sisters knew little of Paz's daily struggle. They watched as the Twin Towers collapsed, not knowing that the son and brother who called them every week and sent them money for food and gifts for their birthdays was one of the victims. They knew, though, that he had been making sacrifices for the sake of his family and his dream of bringing them out of Colombia.

It was no idle dream. Paz's relatives say they face death threats in their homeland because Paz's brother, José Cipriano, worked as an investigator of official corruption. Paz's other brother, Juan Manuel, was killed 10 years ago in what relatives believe was retribution from a warring street gang. Since then, Paz had been trying to persuade relatives to leave Cali, the city where they live, and reunite in the United States or Canada.

Paz, who was undocumented, had not seen his family for 16 years, when he traded his life as a furniture store manager in Cali to come to New York. He ended up at Windows on the World about two years ago, relatives said, after working his way up to a chef's position at the Plácido Domingo Restaurant and Tapas Bar.

The week before September 11, a relieved Paz learned that his brother José had a chance of gaining political asylum in Canada for himself and the entire family. The Friday before the attacks, Paz spoke excitedly over the phone about how he and his girlfriend, Liliana Ospina, would cross the Canadian border to meet José, his mother, Blanca, and his sisters, Julia and Patricia, so they could all start a new life together.

"Life is completely different now," said Julia, who stayed in Paz's Long Island City apartment with her mother after coming to New York in search of Paz's body. They hoped other relatives could eventually join them in Canada. "We don't have any idea now of what the future will be like, of where we are going to end up. We always thought he was safe here."

SHABBIR AHMED
He Lived His Dreams Through His Children

Upon hearing of the terrorist attacks on the World Trade Center, Shabbir Ahmed's family prayed he'd been running late that day and didn't make it to his job as a banquet waiter at

Windows on the World. But they knew Shabbir too well. "He was punctual, never missed a day of work," said his brother, Abdul Mosobbir. "He was always early at work. He left at 4 a.m. to be there at 6."

It was a job Ahmed loved but hoped his children would never have to do. "He wanted me to be a lawyer," said Nadia, 12, one of Ahmed's three children. "He wanted us to do the things he wasn't able to do. He came to America for this reason."

Ahmed, 45, one of six children, emigrated from Bangladesh in 1982 to join his brother Abdul, who was a cook at Windows on the World. The elder brother secured Ahmed a job as a waiter. After the 1993 bombing at the World Trade Center, Mosobbir quit to work at an uptown hotel, but Ahmed stayed.

The family says Ahmed especially wanted his children to earn good grades and attend college because he had dropped out of college to come to the United States. It was, his family said, as if he lived his dreams through his children, who included his daughter Salma, 19, and son Thanbir, 16. In fifth grade, Nadia brought home straight A's, received a commendation letter from Brooklyn Borough President Howard Golden and graduated as valedictorian. "He was overwhelmed by that," Nadia said. "He was so proud."

In the backyard of his house in Marine Park, Brooklyn, Ahmed grew tomatoes, squash and the "hottest chilis in the world," Mosobbir said. Ahmed's wife, Jeba, often used those chilis and other spices to cook the trout and catfish he caught on weekends, an activity that reminded him of his native Bangladesh.

Right before his death, Ahmed, Thanbir and Mosobbir made a fishing excursion to Long Beach. "We had fun. He carried a bucket of tackle a quarter of a mile and kept saying, 'I'll take it. I'll take it,'" Mosobbir said. "We are fun people. We enjoyed life. Somebody put a stop to it for the meantime."

JENNY LOW WONG
A Hard-Working Social Spark Plug

At 25, one of the youngest in the group she worked in, Jenny Low Wong had just been promoted to assistant vice president at Marsh & McLennan. Her sister wasn't surprised. "She was a hard-working person," said Mary Low Wong, who lived in California. "She stayed late at

work and most of the time went in on the weekend as well, or brought work home."

Wong had always worked hard, her sister said. Born in Venezuela to Chinese parents who ran a restaurant, she came to the United States at the age of 12 to continue her schooling. She stayed with an aunt in Bensonhurst. Her mixed cultural background enriched but did not confuse Wong, her sister said. She spoke Cantonese and Spanish, and cooked Chinese and Venezuelan dishes at home.

She was a good student, earning A's throughout high school, and went on to New York University, where she majored in finance and information systems. Marsh & McLennan snapped her up straight out of college and put her to work in the World Trade Center. She excelled there as an information analyst in the market information group, keeping track of Latin American insurance companies.

But Wong brought more to her company than her work ethic. "Before she came to the group, people were just working, they weren't socializing," her sister said. Wong changed that, organizing trips to nearby Chinatown for dim sum, and taking charge of starting a company newsletter. When she wasn't working, Wong spent her evenings and weekends with friends exploring the city's restaurants and indulging her love of fine wine.

Nothing seemed to scare her big sister, Mary Low Wong said. "Every time we went to Six Flags Great Adventure, she would try every ride," she said. And Wong recently went sky-diving for the first time. "It's probably a new thing that she hadn't done, so she wanted to try that," her sister said. "One thing that she always said . . . was that one has to enjoy life, because you never know what's going to happen tomorrow. So I think if she said that, she must have enjoyed her life."

CESAR MURILLO
Dedicated to Diversity, and Dancing

When the electric company threatened to cut off the power at his family's home in Connecticut, 7-year-old Cesar Augusto Murillo had to do the negotiating. He was the only one in his Colombian family who spoke English. "So he took on a real role in the family, being the oldest child," said his wife, Alyson Becker.

Though they were newcomers to America, arriving when Murillo was 2, his parents, Nilvia and Dario, instilled in him and his sister, Karolyn, the idea that education was the key to success here. Murillo won a partial scholarship to the University of Vermont.

"When he got to UVM, he realized he was in the whitest school in all of North America, probably," Becker said. Murillo dedicated himself to increasing the diversity, going to high schools to recruit students of color.

After college, Murillo, 32, got into equities, working for the Mexican bank Valores Finamex. Only three weeks before the attack, he went to work at the World Trade Center as an equities trader at Cantor Fitzgerald. His office was on the 104th floor of Tower One.

"I think he did have a sense that he came from nothing, and I think he was very proud that he was able to help his mother buy a condominium," said Becker.

And the field suited his personality.

"He actually loved it," Becker said. "He loved trading, he loved talking to people—it was very high-energy. He'd be at work all day, screaming at people down the phone, talking to 20 people . . . Then he came home, and he was an absolute champion napper."

Yet he seemed to find time for many other activities and hobbies, too. From their TriBeCa apartment, he and Becker took full advantage of their proximity to the West Side Highway and its bike paths, Rollerblading, running and biking, playing volleyball at Pier 25 and kayaking on the Hudson.

Murillo's favorite activity, however, was dancing. He loved hip-hop and Latin music, and the couple took salsa lessons together. As a teenager, he even break-danced. After September 11, when a group of his friends got together to tell stories about Murillo, "everybody seemed to have a Cesar-dancing story," said Becker. "This guy, he danced in his sleep," she said. "His mother told stories of him dancing in his crib."

The couple had bought land in Vermont, a state both had fallen in love with when they went to college there. The plan was for Becker to practice law and Murillo to be a high school teacher, probably teaching history or Spanish.

"He was amazing with kids," Becker said, recalling the crowd of children that would always surround him at birthday parties. "He used to do this thing called 'the human beatbox,'" she said. "People would call up and say, 'My kids are crying' . . . and they would say, 'Do you think Cesar could leave the beatbox on the answering machine?' The kids were fascinated by it."

She and Murillo had looked forward to having children together, Becker said. "He would have been an amazing father."

LUKASZ MILEWSKI
"He Loved New York, He Loved America"

She bought him his first bicycle, filed papers to bring him to this country, gloried in his scholastic achievements. He was the kind of grandson that any grandmother would give the family treasures for. He was the family treasure, his grandmother says. But when Lukasz Milewski died at 21 in the ashes and rubble of the World Trade Center, pieces of her heart died with him, says Wanda Milewski.

Lukasz, a graduate student living in Kew Gardens, had been on the job for five weeks as a food server at Windows on the World on the 106th floor of Tower One and expected to work one more week when disaster struck on September 11. He had a ticket to return to Poland on September 23 to pick up his master's diploma in business and marketing at Bialystok University. He expected to come back December 10 to spend the holidays with his parents, Frederick and Anna, in Queens, and take steps to become a permanent resident.

"He loved New York. He loved America. And he was so proud to be working in the World Trade Center," his grandmother said.

A quick study, Lukasz learned to speak English fluently. He also was a whiz at the computer, according to his grandmother, a former Polish language teacher. And he was a devoted and appreciative grandson. "I hoped that he would love me and be a comfort in my old age," Milewski said. He spent his summer vacations with his grandmother in Queens while completing his studies in Poland, but she sent Lukasz on a trip to Washington last summer. "He wanted to know everything about this country," she said.

BARBARA GUZZARDO
A Sunny Personality from Cuba

Barbara Guzzardo was no stranger to turmoil. Amid Fidel Castro's revolution in Cuba, she and her parents were stripped of their sugar plantation in Camagüey province and expelled from the country.

"They put them on a boat and said, 'Get out,'" said her husband, Anthony Guzzardo. "She was about 5 years old, and they left with two pieces of luggage." The family settled in Brooklyn, where they struggled to carve out a niche in their new country. Guzzardo began studying English by watching movies, eavesdropping on conversations on the street and decoding newspapers. Her determination led her to a job at insurance underwriter Aon Corporation in the south tower of the World Trade Center.

When she was 31, she went on a blind date. The couple went dancing, syncing to the salsa beat. "I'm an American boy, but I knew how to dance salsa, too," her husband said. There was an instant connection off the dance floor, as well. "It was a blind date, but it wasn't so blind, because it was love at first sight," he added. "I said, 'I'm going to marry you'—and we did."

The couple settled in Glendale and had a son, also named Anthony. A few years ago, Anthony, now 17 and a senior at the Academy of American Studies in Long Island City, wanted to dye his hair red. Rather than lay down the law and risk a teenage backlash, Guzzardo compromised. She helped her son dye his hair—but the color was blue.

Around the office, Guzzardo, 49, was legendary for her devotion to work. She often could be found at her desk until 7:30 p.m. and hadn't tapped her vacation time in several years, except to take care of her son when he was ill. Yet she still would come home and shop, clean and cook. "She sounds like the perfect woman," her husband said. "And she was for me."

Equally remarkable was her sunny disposition. "I was the grumpy one," her husband said. "She had a smile for everybody and a great deal of respect for everyone." Her colleagues at Aon agreed. Maria Crespo recalled a woman whose charm only enhanced her good looks. Former co-worker Maryann Petti remembered Guzzardo arriving at the office in dark glasses, leather coat and perfectly coiffed. "I always remember smelling her perfume," Petti said. "It would linger after she was gone." When colleagues needed counseling, they often could be found huddling in Guzzardo's cubicle.

There was laughter at the office as well. Picture a bunch of women getting together at lunch. Someone says something startling. Then comes Guzzardo's rejoinder: "For real? Get outta town!"

WINSTON GRANT
A Man of Faith from Grenada

Winston Grant was a man you could rely on, 24 hours a day, seven days a week.

If a relative was going on a trip, he would always call the night before the flight so the two could pray together for a safe journey. On weekdays, Grant, 60, rose at 4 a.m. to make sure his wife, Joyce—who suffers from Lou Gehrig's disease and has limited mobility—had finely chopped food and everything else she needed for the day set out within easy reach. Only then would he leave to catch the 6:56 a.m. train from Lakeview to Manhattan, where he worked at Empire Blue Cross/Blue Shield's offices in the World Trade Center.

Before the September 11 attacks, she said, "I could depend on him to be in the house at a certain time each day. Now when 6 o'clock rolls around, my heart just gets really heavy, because I know he's not coming home."

Born in Trinidad, Grant was educated in Grenada, where he played bass drum in a steel band before coming to the United States. He and his wife-to-be met in 1965 at Harlem's Renaissance Ballroom at a dance sponsored by the Grenada Mutual Association (her parents were also from the Caribbean). "Boy, is he good-looking," his wife recalled thinking. The two danced that night and married one year later, on Grant's birthday, October 2.

He was a hard-working husband and father who raised his wife's two sons from a previous marriage, Adrian and Jerome Duran, as his own. She gave birth to two children with Grant, a daughter, Joya, in 1971, and Winston Arthur Grant II—known as Artie—in 1974. "There was no distinction between the four," said his wife.

Grant taught all the children computer skills, which he picked up while working at RCA and IBM. He enjoyed the work and further honed his knowledge at night school, eventually receiving a bachelor's degree from New York University.

A striver, Grant still made time for those around him. He had the sort of equal-opportunity kindness that benefited not only his family, but any acquaintances or strangers who struck him as needing help. When a commuter in his train car became ill one morning, he stayed with her until the paramedics arrived. Co-workers knew they could turn to him for advice on tricky technical problems at any time. If that meant the Grants' home phone sometimes rang at 2 or 3 in the morning, well, that was OK. "He was always ready to help," said his wife.

That's exactly what she thinks Grant was doing on the morning of September 11. Grant worked on the 30th floor of the north tower, and she believes he should have had plenty of time to get out in the 1½ hours before it collapsed. But her husband was the sort of man who put others' safety above his own. "That's his M.O., to stay and help someone," she said.

"Never left you helpless," read one inscription on the program for his memorial service. "Always fixed my car better than the mechanic." "Role model." "Quite frankly," wrote his stepson, Jerome Duran, "a prince among men."

AVNISH PATEL
A Fan of the Twin Towers

Avnish Patel's Web site—www.avnish.com—unfurls page after page of a digital catalog of his thoughts, travels and passions. The home page shows Patel, 28, hiking in New Zealand. A few clicks away are two photos that Patel, an amateur photographer, snapped of the World Trade Center, where he worked as a financial analyst for Fred Alger Management. Online, the Twin Towers still dominate the skyline, shimmering tall in the bright sunlight of a clear day.

"I work in the one on the left," he wrote in the accompanying text. "I am only a few floors from the top. The view is amazing!"

He loved his adopted city. Born in England to Indian parents, Patel went to high school in Connecticut and attended New York University. He stayed in the city for the next nine years, thrilled by the cultural mix and financial opportunities the city offered. "His love for New York City was so immense," said his brother Yogish. "When we used to drive into Manhattan, my kids would look at the skyscrapers and say, 'That's where my Uncle Avnish is.'"

Manhattan's pace fit Patel just fine. Disciplined and energetic, he regularly worked 10-hour days and quickly became a certified financial analyst. But he found a way to balance his professional and

personal life, squeezing in sailing and photography lessons and calling his parents in England at the same time each Wednesday, whether he was at home or abroad. He loved to read, particularly the novels of Ken Follett and J. D. Salinger. "I don't know where he found the time," said his brother.

To the friends from school and work, these things summed up his personality. So did his "million-dollar smile," a flash of white teeth and a warmth that set people at ease. "He was always helping people," said his brother, and he got along well with all generations of his family. Avnish hoped to get married and start a family—as soon as he found a partner who could keep up with him, his brother said.

"Happiness isn't driven by setting and achieving goals," Patel wrote on his Web site. "It comes from knowing your passions and understanding what it takes to live life through those passions."

IGNATIUS ADANGA
From Cabbie to Transportation Planner

He lived the sort of existence that wears most people down, driving a cab for 20 years—first while attending school, then as a second job to support his wife and daughters. But Ignatius Adanga's spirit never sank. While money was not abundant, he didn't crave it. Though he spent a decade as a New York City case worker for troubled families, his heart didn't harden to children in search of an open ear.

"Nothing really gave him any sleepless nights," said Adanga's wife, Affiong. "He took life very easy. ... He would go out of his way to do things for people. Even though he wasn't a rich man, he would spend his last money to do something for a friend."

Adanga, 62, who came to the United States from Nigeria in 1968, changed careers two years ago and joined the New York Metropolitan Transportation Council, located on the 82nd floor of Tower One in the World Trade Center. He was one of three people in the office who did not escape.

Adanga had been excited in February 2001 as he moved into the first home of his own, in the Williamsbridge section of the Bronx, with his wife, 43, and their three daughters, Nene, 15, Emem, 14, and Esang, 6. Adanga's wife said that after occupying a string of city apartments, they had spent two years preparing to buy that house. "They both worked hard and scrimped and saved," said Gerry Bogacz, Adanga's supervisor at work. "At least he had a little bit of time there. But he should have had the rest of his time there."

After emigrating from the state of Akwa Ibom in southeastern Nigeria, Adanga studied anthropology in college. He then earned a master of public administration degree from John Jay College in Manhattan, all the while driving a taxi. He remained a cab driver while working for the city's Human Resources Administration so his wife, whom he married in the mid-1980s, could go to school to become a nurse.

But Adanga wanted a change, and two years ago became a transportation planner, helping different government agencies around the region coordinate their activities. Nassau and Suffolk Counties were in his domain. "He had a high learning curve, and he was patiently working through that, and was getting better and better," Bogacz said.

Adanga doted on his daughters, including Inyene, who died two weeks before her sixth birthday. And he kept a watchful eye out for other children, such as his co-worker Judith Wilson's 10-year-old son, Kareem. "He was my son's mentor," Wilson said. "He just showed an interest. He wanted to turn him into a real man."

His wife said that typified Adanga. He had helped many young people in their neighborhood with legal problems or the simple difficulties of growing up. "Some of them I didn't even know until this thing happened," she said. "And they started calling me to tell me what he did for them."

KUM-KUM GIROLAMO
Devout Hindu Sought Acceptance as American

Kum-Kum Girolamo was barely 5 feet tall, a tiny woman with huge brown eyes and a streak of generosity a mile wide. One winter, she bought a Christmas present—a brand-new shirt—for a homeless man she passed each day on her way to her job as an administrative assistant at Aon Corporation, where she worked on the 99th floor of Tower Two. The gesture was typical, her friends said.

Girolamo, 41, who married before she was 20, devoted much of her life to taking care of others—her husband, her 13-year-old son, her elderly Indian parents. "She was a good mother, very sweet, very giving," said her friend Diane Moreno.

But when Girolamo hit her mid-30s, a new desire bubbled up inside. "There was a whole other side of her that needed to emerge," said Leslie Chin, a close friend. Defined for years through her relationships as a wife and a mother, Girolamo wanted "to discover her own self as a person," Chin said. "She was longing for something that she never got a chance to have."

Born in Bombay, India, Girolamo came with her family to Kew Gardens. Here she went by the name of Kim instead of Kum-Kum, one of many navigations she would make between the ways of the country she came from and the one she called home. A devout Hindu and lifelong vegetarian, "she did chant and practice her belief," Chin said. "But she also wanted to be accepted as an American and to enjoy that life."

Finding that middle ground wasn't always easy. Girolamo's parents were initially dismayed when she married a non-Indian, a meat-eater and Catholic named James Girolamo. But they eventually came around. After her marriage, Girolamo came up with her own cultural compromises. She enrolled her son, Krishan, in all-American activities such as the Boy Scouts, took him to Yankees games and accompanied him to the sci-fi movies he loved. As far as food was concerned, she would cook meat, but not taste it. "Kim was a very good cook," Chin said. "At Thanksgiving, she would make a big turkey for 'the boys,' but never put a spoon to her lips."

Chin said she met Girolamo seven years ago, when the two were out dancing at Club G in Garden City. Chin was a recently divorced single mother. Girolamo was just starting to develop her own social life outside of marriage. "Our friendship was based on two girls coming into themselves," Chin said.

The things they had in common grew over time. Girolamo was growing increasingly independent, and filed for divorce soon after her father's death in 1998. She dated and enjoyed going out. When the transition to single life proved difficult, she turned to her new friends for counsel and laughter about relationship woes. But Girolamo thrived on the new discoveries she made about herself along the way. "She liked to dance, she liked white wine, chocolate-covered strawberries," Chin said. Shortly before Girolamo's death in the World Trade Center attacks, she rode on the back of a motorcycle for the first time.

"She loved life," Chin said. "She looked forward to each day coming."

11
In the Pentagon

Ironies abounded. A Naval intelligence officer who worked in the Pentagon made a time capsule as a schoolboy. His parents opened it after September 11 and found a drawing of two dragons clawing at the World Trade Center. Or the graphic illustrator in the great complex that houses the military's nerve center. His wife called after the World Trade Center was hit. "Don't worry," he told her. "I'm in the safest place in the world."

Inside the Pentagon, the death toll was 125. It included a Defense Department analyst who had escaped from a fiery bomber crash near Hanoi 20 years before. And a veteran who made history. In 1973, the world watched on television as he accepted a painted mat from a North Korean colonel and became the last American soldier to leave Vietnamese soil at the end of that war.

He was visiting the Pentagon to help obtain benefits for survivors of soldiers killed in the line of duty.

On September 11, no place was safe.

PATRICIA MICKLEY
Filling the Gap

Joseph Mickley would wake sometimes in the dark, late in the night, alone in the bed. He'd go downstairs to find his wife, Patricia, balancing her checkbook or doing some other task around the house. Between the activities she organized for their daughter, Marie, and Patricia's full-time job as a financial manager at the Department of Defense, there was simply no time during the day.

Since she's been gone, killed when a plane crashed through her office at the Pentagon, Joseph has been trying his best to keep up the house in suburban Springfield, Virginia, to take Marie to gymnastics, to ballet, to swimming, to karate, to tap dancing and Sunday school.

"'Admiration' was the term I've thought of many times," he said. "The way she could juggle that and still be a professional—I see it now, because I have to do it."

But Marie has provided a reason to go on. "She depends on me, and I depend on her. We're kind of filling that big gap in our lives that was Patty. And we're filling it with each other."

Two days after the attacks, Joseph took his daughter by the hand and the two of them went for a walk. "I told her Mommy might not be coming home," he said. "I said, 'Marie, I'm going to tell you everything that I know, and I'm going to answer your questions if you have them.'"

Marie asked if she could see the pictures of "Mommy's building." When he showed her the photos, "She would point to something and say . . . why did it collapse? Where were the people?" Though she's only in grade school, he said, "She asked me all the questions, basically, that the adults were asking me."

Not all her questions are easy to answer. "We talk about why did the bad people kill Mommy? Why did they choose the Pentagon to fly the airplane into? And she tells me that she misses Mommy."

Joseph does too. He thinks back to the first time he met Patricia, when he, also a financial manager, first arrived at the Department of Defense. How attractive she was, and how, at that moment, he thought, "We're going to be good friends." He thinks of coaxing her off the bunny slope so they could ski together. He thinks of that time he took her flying over Washington, how clear the night was, how beautiful the city looked, how smooth his take-off and landing. And how Patricia still had white knuckles the whole time.

There's so much he's learned about his 41-year-old wife since she died—from her friends and her family, and from the 800-odd cards still piled on the dining room table. That she used to call her mother every single day. That even though she was the youngest of four, she was the one who kept her immediate family together. That she touched the lives of casual acquaintances and co-workers in ways they now struggle to express.

And just looking at his daughter stirs thoughts of his wife. The artistic talent that Patricia nurtured has become a way for the little girl to comfort her father.

"She's all the time making me little cards to tell me she loves me," Joseph said. "She's drawing pictures all the time of me and her holding hands. I always look to see if there's smiles on the faces, and I have yet to see a frown on any of them."

ROBERT HYMEL
Death Called Once Before

In the wake of the tragedy that took her husband's life, Beatriz Hymel thinks of his first face-to-face encounter with death.

Robert J. Hymel was a young Air Force pilot when his B-52 was shot down by a North Vietnamese surface-to-air missile during an 11-day offensive in December 1972. Another American pilot cut Hymel from the wreckage after the bomber crash-landed near Hanoi. They escaped before it burst into flames. Only two members of the five-man crew survived, said his wife.

"He was administered last rites, and the doctors said they didn't even know why he lived," Beatriz "Pat" Hymel said. "They thought maybe it was because he had never met his daughter," then only 2 months old.

"I feel like God gave us another 29 years," she added, noting that some of her friends lost their husbands in Vietnam. She said their daughter, Natalie Conner, "got to know her father and his granddaughter got to know her grandfather. When I really needed him in my life, he was there."

Robert Hymel was awarded the Distinguished Flying Cross, the Air Medal and the Purple Heart for his Vietnam service.

His wife, an elementary school principal, said she served as a foil to her husband, whom she called "a bad little boy." In his younger days, she said he partied with military buddies on Friday and Saturday evenings, though still managed to attend church on Sundays.

Hymel, 55, of Woodbridge, Virginia, received a bachelor's degree in 1969 in industrial engineering from Southwestern Louisiana University and later obtained a master's degree in business administration from New England College. He retired in the early 1990s as a lieutenant colonel after more than 20 years in the Air Force. He was working as a management analyst for the Defense Intelligence Agency at the Pentagon when it was attacked.

He was in the basement of the building and was preparing to move to a new workstation when the building was struck, his wife said. The new desk, which he was to occupy the following day, was in an area spared from destruction.

MAX BEILKE and GARY SMITH
They Soldiered On for Their Fellow Vets

 They are moments that have an eternal quality, moments that replay constantly in the personal and collective memory:

Gary F. Smith, a 24-year-old soldier, running into the wreckage of a crashed helicopter in Vietnam in 1970. Pulling his fellow soldiers out to safety.

Master Sergeant Max Beilke, the last American soldier to leave Vietnamese soil at the end of the war in 1973, turning to accept a gift—a painted straw mat—from a North Vietnamese colonel. Then walking up the ramp to the waiting airplane as his family in Minnesota watched him on TV.

Their moments of glory had become history and their medals and uniforms were long packed away, but neither Smith nor Beilke ever truly left the Army behind. As civilian employees, Smith, 55, the chief of Army Retirement Services, and Beilke,

69, his deputy, arranged benefits for veterans and military retirees.

On the morning of September 11, the two were at the Pentagon to gather support for legislation to provide retirement benefits for survivors of military personnel killed in the line of duty. Both men were killed when a hijacked airliner smashed into the section of the building they were in.

They died doing what they loved, say their families. "He really enjoyed working with the retirees, making sure they got what they had coming and needed," said Beilke's sister, Lucille Johnson of Evansville, Minnesota.

Smith "liked talking with the old soldiers," said his wife, Ann Smagacz Smith. "He used to go visit a World War I veteran at the Army-Navy retirement home . . . He really worked hard for the people. He really cared about it."

Despite his military history, Beilke was "a very soft person," said his sister. "A very low-key person." Beilke's neighbors in suburban Laurel, Maryland, remember him as a quiet, friendly man who never talked about his military experience. The kind of man who loved his flower beds and flourishing crape myrtles, who audited the books of the homeowners association for free, saving his working-class neighbors $1,000 or so a year. The kind who kept doing so even after the association turned down his request to put a flagpole by his driveway.

Beilke, who grew up on a farm in Minnesota, was drafted in 1952 and later shipped out to Korea. He served his hitch and returned to civilian life. But something was missing. In 1956, he reenlisted, this time prepared to stay. Beilke was approaching his 40th birthday and already a master sergeant with nearly 20 years of service when he got to Vietnam. He retired in 1974, only to return 10 years later as a civilian employee. He and his wife, Lisa, raised two daughters.

Smith received the soldier's medal for heroism for his action in the helicopter crash. He also was awarded the Bronze Star, Legion of Merit, Meritorious Service Medal and Army Commendation Medal. The son of a World War II veteran, Smith grew up in France, Hawaii and Wisconsin. He joined the ROTC in college and, over his Army career, worked in Italy, Maryland, Kansas and the Netherlands, as well as Vietnam, before settling in Washington, D.C. He was a lieutenant colonel when he retired in 1991, and he returned to the Army as a civilian employee soon afterward.

The couple had three daughters, and the family recalls Smith as a soft-spoken man who liked to read history and coach sports in his spare time.

"He basically had a happy life," his wife said. "He was proud of his military career and his family. That's what gives me comfort. He gladly would have suffered for his country to become a better place, and I think since September 11, the country has become a better place."

STEPHEN LONG
He Could Have Escaped, but Stayed

Army Major Stephen V. Long survived the initial impact at the Pentagon. He could have left, officials told his mother, Susan Weaver—he wasn't even stationed there, he was just attending a meeting that day. But Long stayed in the building to help others and died from breathing too much carbon monoxide.

Long, a 39-year-old career soldier, had faced death once before. During a raid in Grenada in 1983, when he was serving with the 2nd Battalion, 75th Ranger Regiment, he was in a crash that destroyed three helicopters, including the one he was riding in, and many of his fellow soldiers died. He was pinned under a tail section and broke his back.

He thought he might die there, but when the section shifted, he was able to free himself. He decided not only to carry out his mission that day but to stay in the Army for life. According to his mother, he decided, "I will serve God and I will serve my country."

Long grew up in Martinsville, Indiana, where he was the middle child of five children. His father, George Long, still lives in Martinsville, but Stephen moved with his mother to Clayton, Indiana, as a teenager. When he joined the Army straight out of high school, "Somebody told him to keep a low profile," said his mother. "We had a good laugh." He knew how to take charge, she said. "He made good decisions, he was a good leader."

He attended Augusta State University in Georgia on a Green to Gold scholarship and became an officer. While stationed in Georgia, a couple at his church invited him to dinner. He hit it off with the couple's daughter, Tina, and married her in 1986.

He also became a father to two stepsons, David Hopkins, now 27, and Tryon Hopkins, now 22.

His military career next took Long to Saudi Arabia, where he was one of the first soldiers to arrive for Operation Desert Shield. He stayed throughout the Persian Gulf War.

As Tina and Stephen continued to travel with his Army assignments, including one at Fort Bragg, North Carolina, and a three-year stay in Germany, they made an effort to learn about their surroundings and visit local sights every weekend they could. In his free time, Long was a history buff who studied the Civil War and World War II. He was an avid reader, liked animals and enjoyed gardening.

"He lived a full life for his 39 years," says Weaver. "He lived every minute."

SANDRA WHITE
The Boss of Everybody

Her mother misses Sandra Letitia White's regular phone calls the most. "We talked all the time," said Gloria Murray. "We would talk in the afternoons, and every Saturday, and she'd always ask, 'Mama, what are you going to do today?'"

As the eldest of four siblings, White had a take-charge attitude that typically resulted in her spearheading family projects—such as organizing a family trip to Disney World for Christmas. "She was the boss of everybody," said her mother.

At least twice a month, White would travel with her family two hours each way to her parents' house in Hampton, Virginia, where she grew up. There, Candy, as her family liked to call her, would marinate steaks in a secret sauce and go shopping with her mother. "She could shop until she dropped," said Murray. "If there was a sale, she couldn't buy just the one pair or one blouse." Then they'd return home, where they would enjoy "steaks you could cut with a fork," said Murray.

On September 11, Murray thinks her daughter, an accountant in the Army's budget office, was working hard to "pay the Army's bills" and trying to finish year-end work. Her remains were found on September 24. It gave the family the closure they needed to deal with their loss.

A graduate of Hampton High School and Virginia State University, White met her husband, Lieutenant Colonel Oscar White Jr., through her sister, Gloria, who was under his instruction at the local base. Six months after they first set eyes on one another, they were married. With one baby born, they left for Germany for a few years, bringing back a second son to the States when they returned. She raised her boys, Oscar III, 17, and Jonathan, 14, to be mindful of their chores and their manners. "She was very strict with them," her mother said, "protective in a good way."

JONAS PANIK
His Time Capsule Opens to Irony

When Jonas Panik was in eighth grade, he made a time capsule for school. He filled the jar with sports clippings and his favorite Gary Larsen "Far Side" cartoon. Days after Naval intelligence officer Jonas Martin Panik was killed at the Pentagon, his parents opened their son's 1989 time capsule.

The "Far Side" cartoon showed two Godzilla-like dragons clawing at the World Trade Center towers. "Hey! Is that you, Dave? Small world!" one dragon says to the other. An airplane aimed at the World Trade Center is also pictured.

"How ironic can it be?" said Panik's mother, Linda Panik.

In the Navy Command Center on September 11, Lieutenant Panik had briefed his superiors on the World Trade Center attack when hijacked American Airlines Flight 77 crashed into the Pentagon. Panik was identified by his fingerprints.

Raised in Mingoville, Pennsylvania, Panik fulfilled his dream of attending a military school when he entered the U.S. Naval Academy. Nicknamed "Big Joe," Panik was a weightlifter and a reserve lineman on the Navy football team. Panik graduated in 1997 with a degree in history. In his military career, Panik, 26, toured the world before beginning work at the Pentagon two weeks before the attack. His sister, Martina, named her son, Andrew Jonas, now 2, after him. Panik lived with his wife, Jennifer, in Odenton, Maryland.

"Our son called every week, no matter where he was," said his mother. "What you miss the most is when that phone rings now and it's not him."

DEAN MATTSON
Retirement Was at Hand

Lieutenant Colonel Dean E. Mattson, 57, was less than three months away from retiring, after more than 35 years in the Army, when he was killed in the Pentagon.

"I was always informed he was going to retire at the end of December, but as it was, he was going to be retired in November," his mother, Bernice Mattson, said from the family home in Luck, Wisconsin, where she recently celebrated her 85th birthday. "He had planned an 85th-birthday party here, with his brothers. He was going to walk in and surprise me at my birthday party."

Mattson was born and raised in Luck, about 65 miles northeast of Minneapolis, and his three brothers, Glenn, Dwain and Dale, still live in or near the town where they grew up. He was living in Alexandria, Virginia, at the time of the attack, and was serving as the executive officer for the Army Information Management Support Center in the Office of the Administrative Assistant to the Secretary of the Army. He had been in the military since being drafted in 1964.

Before committing to the Army, his mother said, he had plans of becoming a Lutheran pastor. "He was a single man, but he was very family-oriented," his mom said, noting that Uncle Dean was always a big hit among his many nieces and nephews. "He was a very good housekeeper, and a very good cook. He was always a cheerful man."

Her son also enjoyed the outdoors, Mattson said, and the two of them traveled together frequently. "We had the same likes," she said. "He would take me to the Smithsonian. He took me to Florida and we toured all the way down to south of Orlando. We loved going to the mountains."

DAVID SCALES
With a Song in His Heart

David M. Scales was a Broadway composer trapped in the body of a brilliant Army administrator.

From the age of 8, when he began playing on the family's new piano, Scales viewed himself as a music composer. He wrote piece after piece, including, as a gift to his younger sister, 67 compositions to the poems of Robert Louis Stevenson's *A Child's Garden of Verses*. Someday he hoped to see his work performed on the Broadway stage.

Scales grew up in Berea, Ohio, and graduated from the conservatory at the University of Cincinnati. But, as his wife, Patricia, said, Scales realized "it would be hard to be a starving musician and provide for a family at the same time."

So the copper-haired, ever-smiling Scales, who attended college on an ROTC scholarship and earned an MBA, decided to make a career in the Army, where he proved to be a gifted administrator. At the time of his death, Scales, 44, was a lieutenant colonel in the Army's Office of the Deputy Chief of Staff for Personnel in the Pentagon.

His family life was unusual. Because his 12-year-old son, Ashton, suffers from asthma, his parents decided it would be best for Patricia and Ashton to live in Arizona, while Scales kept a home in Arlington, Virginia. But Scales carried on an intense e-mail and telephone relationship with them. "He and Ashton had games they made up and played literally over years," Patricia said.

And he still had his music. In Washington, he played piano with a trio in bookstores, fairs and nursing homes. He was also a runner and bicyclist.

Patricia said Scales planned to retire from the military in May 2002, reunite with his family in Arizona and concentrate full time on his lifelong passion—music composition.

KRIS BISHUNDAT
A Good Son Left His Mark on the Navy

Scores of officers and enlisted sailors crowded onto the busy deck of the USS *Shreveport* on September 20 to honor a fallen comrade and officially open a facility named for him.

The Media Resource Center—which provides about 700 sailors and Marines access to computer-aided learning opportunities, as well as e-mail and Internet service—was named for Petty Officer 2nd Class Kris Romeo Bishundat, who served on the *Shreveport* before being transferred to the Pentagon four months before the terrorist attacks.

Bishundat, who would have turned 24 on September 14, was assigned in May to the communications division of the Chief of Naval Operations Center at the Pentagon. An information-systems technician, Bishundat had moved to newly renovated offices three weeks before the attacks. He had enlisted in the Navy six years to the day before the terrorists struck.

The Guyana native was a sensitive, humble son, said his mother, Basmattie Bishundat. He did not talk much about the awards he won, she said, and it wasn't until his death that she learned about his accomplishments. Bishundat had received the Navy and Marine Corps Achievement Medal, a Navy Unit Commendation, the National Defense Service Medal, the Sea Service Deployment Ribbon, the Armed Forces Expeditionary Medal and the Good Conduct Medal. He was awarded the Purple Heart posthumously on October 18 at his funeral in Arlington National Cemetery.

Bishundat came to the United States in 1980 and settled in Waldorf, Maryland, with his mother and his father, Bhola. He was the oldest of three children, including sisters Danita, 21, and Devita, 18. As manager of the *Shreveport*'s automated information-systems department, Bishundat was responsible for a multitude of complex computer and data-processing equipment, operating as the ship's Webmaster.

He was an adventurous, fun-loving soul who was into surfing, golf and tennis, his mother said.

"He loved life and lived every day to its fullest." She recalled that in a conversation with him about an hour before the attack, he expressed how touched he was that his sister, Danita, not only took the time to pack his lunch but also wrote a note telling him to enjoy it. He also told his girlfriend, Lisa Kenney, about the note in a phone call to her before the attack.

"He was very sensitive," his mother said. "I couldn't have asked for a better son."

CRAIG AMUNDSON
He Was Committed to Peace

When Amber Amundson heard that the World Trade Center had been hit, she called her husband, Craig, at the Pentagon. "Honey, don't worry," he told her. "I'm in the safest place in the world."

The fact that he was there at all in the U.S. military's nerve center was something of a paradox. Amundson was a graphic illustrator committed to helping other people, and his Toyota Corolla bore a bumper sticker that said "Visualize World Peace."

Amundson, who grew up in Iowa, truly was committed to world peace, according to the Reverend Linda Olson Peebles of the Universal Unitarian Church in Arlington, Virginia, who presided over his memorial service, and he saw his enlistment as a way of preserving that peace. Amber Amundson wrote in the *Chicago Tribune* that her husband believed that "by working from within the military system he could help to maintain the military focus on peacekeeping."

Amundson, 28, discovered in Iowa that he had a facility for both computers and video work. He took those skills to the University of Iowa, where he honed them on his way to a bachelor's degree in film studies. He and Amber lived in Dubuque until two years ago, when they moved with their two children, Elliot, 5, and Charlotte, 2, to the Washington, D.C., area. He took a position at the Pentagon as a multimedia illustrator for the Army's deputy chief of staff for personnel. But Amundson turned down a promotion because he didn't want to be away from his family. He planned to be an elementary school teacher after leaving the Army.

As for his goal of keeping the military focused on peace, Amber Amundson tried to keep that alive. She wrote that she hoped her country would resist the temptation to exact violent revenge. "Because I have lost Craig as part of this historic tragedy," she said, "my anguish is compounded exponentially by the fear that his death will be used to justify new violence against other innocent victims. . . . I call on our national leaders to find the courage to respond . . . by breaking the cycle of violence."

JERRY DICKERSON
A Man of Discipline, a Man of Caring

When Jerry Dickerson went to engineering school at Mississippi State University, he had a grueling schedule. He'd wake up at 3:30 a.m. and deliver newspapers. He'd take a whole day of difficult classes. After that, he'd work for a fence-construction crew. And when it got dark, he'd go to a fast-food place, operate it and lock it up at closing time. At college, his grade-point average was 3.8.

No one, not even his father, Jeffry Dickerson, could quite figure it out. The boy had no military role models, but for some reason, even during his childhood, Jerry knew he wanted to be a soldier. He never wavered. He went into the Army National Guard in high school—at the first opportunity. He spent 10 years in the National Guard, not to mention 18 in the regular Army.

It proved disciplined work for a disciplined man. He was blessed by rarely needing as much as four hours' sleep a night, which left him time to pursue family life, hobbies, an active spiritual life and a career. "I don't know how he did it," said Jeffry Dickerson. "All I know is, he got more living in his 41 years than most people do in their whole lifetimes."

So structured was his existence that he could tell you where he'd be "on the third of August three years from now," said Dickerson. "And you know what? He'd be there. You could set your watch to it."

Dickerson cut his teeth in the military in planning and logistics, and he always wanted to be where the action was. "It was in his nature to want to engage," said his father. "He would have wanted to be on the ground in Afghanistan." To Dickerson, his work at the Pentagon was part of a paper-pushing bureaucracy. "He'd always say, 'This isn't what I trained for,'" said his father. He was slated for a transfer to Germany no later than the summer of 2002.

Dickerson was also a loving and caring family man. He made sure to give his children—Beth, 15, and Will, 11—the quality time they needed, not to mention his wife, Page. He played a little golf with his dad and still found time to share an interest in NASCAR racing with his son. "He was a planner," said the elder Dickerson. "He was strong mentally and strong physically. If he believed in doing something, he did it. His word was his bond."

"He brought our family together a lot," said the elder Dickerson, a Durant, Mississippi, native. "We didn't get to see him much. But when he'd come to town, they'd all gather around him. Those were the good times."

JOSEPH PYCIOR JR.
A Second Career Was a Few Months Away

The Saturday before he died, Joseph Pycior Jr. took his Cub Scout troop to the Baltimore & Ohio Railroad Museum. His wife was taking her den, too, and he arranged the trip so the whole family, including sons Joey, 10, and Robbie, 8, could be together.

Pycior, 39, who worked in the Navy command center at the Pentagon, was a few months from retirement after a 20-year career in the Navy when he was killed.

When he wasn't working, Pycior was a full-time father. Every weekend he would lead the family on day trips, taking them hiking, to museums, to parks. He loved history, and touring places that bring it alive: Jamestown, Williamsburg, Gettysburg. "He was very good at navigating our way, in the car or in the woods," said his wife, Terri, 38.

Sometimes the destination was a surprise. One day when Terri was driving, he directed her to the end of a lonely road. To her delight, a lighthouse loomed. Lighthouses are her favorite thing. "He liked to make people happy," she said.

Pycior enlisted in the Navy after graduating from high school in his native Carlstadt, New Jersey, in 1980. His career began on a ship. He spent five years recruiting for the Navy in Philadelphia so he could be near home when the Pyciors' first son was born. He then worked on airplanes, where he tracked submarines with sonar. At the Pentagon, he worked for the chief of naval operations. "He knew where all the ships were," Terri said. He was also the guy to go to with a question, his wife said. "He always knew, or he knew where to go to find out," she said.

Pycior earned a degree in history in May 2001 and hoped to become a middle school history teacher after leaving the Navy. The first week of September, the family viewed houses with a real estate agent in New Jersey, where they expected to move. Pycior had one requirement: He wanted a large basement, so he could build a whole town made out of Legos, his wife said. He loved toys, and bought his wife the pink and white "girl" Lego set.

"He was a big kid at heart," said Terry Pycior.

A Man of Unusual Disposition

PAUL VITELLO

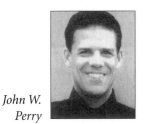

John W. Perry

At any gathering of more than a dozen people these days, it seems someone is missing; either first-hand or second-hand or by some other link in the chain to which everybody and everything turns out to be connected, just as we always suspected.

At the annual fund-raiser for the Nassau County Civil Liberties Union, the missing one was John W. Perry, a 38-year-old board member and son of the chapter president, Patricia, and her husband, James, of Seaford. Perry was a New York City police officer, a lawyer in the department's legal office for many years.

On September 11, as it happened, Perry was at headquarters submitting his resignation papers—he had decided after 10 years on the job to join a private law firm—when the first of two planes struck the World Trade Center. He went to the scene to help. He did not come back.

He was by all accounts a man of unusual disposition—a police officer who served on the Civil Liberties Union's board, a cop who privately opposed the war on drugs; a man who grew up in the suburbs but who chose to live in a public housing project in Manhattan.

Of the thousands of people who were lost in the attack that day, Perry is just one. Every one of them was that contradiction wrapped in an enigma that we refer to as a human. His contradictions and enigmas just happened to be numerous, and in plain view, and in some ways parallel to those in the fabric of the American character.

That he submitted his resignation and gave his life on the same day just seems to sum it all up.

"John was a figure of authority who questioned authority—a free spirit in a cop's uni-form," said Barbara Bernstein, executive director of the Nassau chapter, one of several people to address the 150 people at the fund-raiser in Sands Point shortly after the attack. "He didn't think it a paradox that he was a police officer and a libertarian." He opposed all infringements on people's personal choices, whether it was sexual orientation, or use of drugs, or free speech.

His mother laughs and says he became a cop because "he had a mother who wouldn't let him have toy guns." He showed her.

A lawyer admitted to the bar of the highest courts in the land, he lived on the seventh floor of an Eighth Avenue building of the Amsterdam Houses, a fairly grubby public housing project near Lincoln Center. (The city housing authority offers a limited number of apartments to police officers, as a security measure.) "He marched to a different drummer," said his mother, "and he also liked to save money."

In a job that almost fetishizes the bond of brotherhood, he was often at odds with fellow officers in his role as department advocate in disciplinary proceedings. Going after cops who broke the rules did not make him a very popular cop, though his supervisor, Captain Tim Pearson, said Perry's identification with the underdog often put him at odds with being at odds. "He could see the other guy's point of view," said Pearson.

To some extent, being the child of a mixed-race marriage was probably a factor in Perry's attraction to the paradoxes of life. His mother is white, his father black. The family settled in Seaford 40 years ago; and though there was never much of a racial problem, Perry's mother remembers a few instances when the young man had to defend himself against taunters. "He grew to six feet, four inches, which solved a lot of problems," she added.

It doesn't explain why he joined the police department, or became a lawyer, or why he learned to speak Swedish and Russian, French and Spanish and a little Portuguese; or why at NYU Law School he chose to live in the foreign students' dormitory, or what made him pursue a parallel career in the National Guard. He had just made captain.

Nothing explains anything, least of all why hijackers crashed those planes into America, killing so many people.

But Perry's life raised the questions that the American character has always raised: Where is the line between the personal and the public spheres of life? How do we integrate personal freedoms and collective responsibilities?

What do we do when fellow human beings need us?

"I met John at the scene, at Church and Vesey Streets, when people were already jumping out of windows," said Pearson. "We decided to keep people from the concourse, where people were getting killed by falling debris and bodies. John and I were showing people where to go, when a woman suddenly was having an asthma attack, and we decided to take her out on the street to triage her . . ."

They were taking her out when the building started to shake and everything grew dark.

Paul Vitello is a columnist for Newsday.

12
Free Spirits

Every lost life was precious—every one mattered and left an emptiness in its wake. They all belonged to the madding crowd that fills the city streets and the days of all our years. They were leaders and followers, young and old, struggling and successful. Among them were some who stood out by virtue of their very natures, by their thirst for life and their desire to dance to their own music.

One of them was a red-haired jazz singer who thrived on commotion and turned down a contract with Duke Ellington. "I love you," she told the man who could have made her famous, "but when you work with such a large band . . . there is no room for creation." Another was an insurance executive who had a doctorate in mathematics but whose idea of a really good meal was a giant burrito and who kept a moped in his living room and stored his crab traps all over the kitchen. Yet another was a managing partner in a large firm who sneaked into big-time golf tournaments and crashed mob funerals.

They were among the very young at heart. They were free spirits.

ELIZABETH FARMER
This Jazz Singer Lived Life on a High Note

Years ago, when the red-headed firebrand would walk into a room, a buzz would course through the crowd. "Oh, Lord, what's going to happen tonight?" they would say. Sometimes drinks were thrown, sometimes egos were bruised and sometimes there were tears, but Betty Farmer always gave a great show.

Her voice had good pitch, her looks were easy on the eye and her style, in song and in life, was vinegar-spiked matter-of-fact. "She was a very complex and diverse woman," said her daughter, Kathryn Nesbit of St. Simons Island, Georgia. "She would never win the mother of the year award, but as a human being, she was right up there in the top 10 percent."

For most of her life, Farmer, 62, remained an underappreciated jazz singer, associates said. She bounced back and forth between clerical jobs and attempts at full-time singing. When the World Trade Center attack occurred, she was a temporary executive assistant at Cantor Fitzgerald.

Nesbit had no idea her mother was working in the towers. They hadn't spoken in almost three weeks. When Farmer did not return to her Manhattan apartment, it was the landlord who informed Nesbit.

Farmer, a New Orleans native, did not have a happy childhood, but by the age of 17, she had gotten her first singing gig with a Dixieland band in the French Quarter, Nesbit said. With her long legs, hazel eyes and striking red hair, Farmer quickly attracted attention. She met New Orleans–based jazz pianist Fred Nesbit in 1960. He was 24 years her senior, talented and working regularly. "She used to follow him around. . . . She was a babe in the woods," her daughter said.

The two married and as a duo traveled the East Coast, grabbing gigs in venues across Florida, Alabama and the Carolinas. Heading home alone from a stint in Biloxi, Mississippi, Farmer, pregnant with her daughter (she had a son, Shawn, from a previous relationship), went into labor. She stopped at a hotel instead of a hospital. Farmer wanted to dye her red roots blond before she gave birth. After Nesbit was born, Farmer and her husband went back on the road. A laundry hamper in the back seat of the car served as a crib. But soon, shady managers and slim paychecks drove the couple apart and in 1966, Farmer took the baby back to New Orleans.

In her days as a singer at The Bistro, perhaps the most notable time of her career, Farmer fused late-night drinking with early-morning jam sessions. "She wasn't really out to make a lot of money," said Ronnie DuPont, a pianist who hired Farmer to sing with his quartet from 1966 to 1969. "She was out to enjoy herself." Indeed, Duke Ellington spotted Farmer at the club and asked her to tour with his band. After two months and a performance at Carnegie Hall in 1972, Sir Duke offered Farmer a five-year contract, Nesbit said. "Mom said, 'Duke, I love you and I respect you. Please don't take this the wrong way, but when you work with such a large band . . . there is no room for creation,'" Nesbit said.

Instead, Farmer moved to Las Vegas, married again, performed occasionally and wrote often. In a journal, she put down her thoughts, prose and poetry. She won a contest for the only work she ever submitted, but fear of rejection kept her from trying again, said Nesbit. When that marriage ended, mother and daughter moved to Denver, where they opened a nightclub and started a magazine. The magazine lasted a year; the club closed within six months. With their business ventures all dried up, Denver lost its lure and Farmer moved around until she landed in Manhattan four years ago, her daughter said.

Weeks before the World Trade Center tragedy, Farmer had discussed moving again. "Betty sometimes created situations, and I believe she would run after a while," DuPont said. But this time she stayed. By day, she played it straight, taking her place among the throngs of workers on Wall Street. And at night, in the smoky venues of Greenwich Village, she mustered her intense emotion, belted out song and received, as she once described to her daughter, the "unconditional love from afar" that kept dragging her back for more.

PHILIP GUZA
Living Day to Day, Always with a Smile

He was an insurance executive with a doctorate in mathematics. But Philip Guza's formula for living life was very simple: no fuss, no muss, no airs. He was a man who thumbed his nose at convention and did things his way, despite the occasional raised eyebrows, his brother Robert said.

A client specialist for Aon Corporation in Tower Two, Guza wasn't the sartorial type. For him, a JC Penney suit, accessorized by his trademark suspenders, worked just fine, day in and day out until it was threadbare, said his brother. His digs on business trips were a Motel 6, and his wheels were reminiscent of a Rent-a-Wreck. His home in Sea Bright, New Jersey, was unmistakably him. Furnished with a hodgepodge of pieces, much of it from two previous marriages, the house boasted a living room with a surefire conversation starter: a moped parked center stage. Crab traps all over the kitchen gave clues of his favorite pastime.

Guza, 54, didn't seem to care that his habits often made him the butt of jokes, his brother said. "If you met him on the weekend when he was crabbing, he had on these big overalls like a pig farmer or something, and he'd be in his element throwing fish heads around in these salt creeks on the Shrewsbury River," his brother said. He was a workaholic, his brother said, but he thought nothing of commuting two hours each way, five or six days a week, just so he could be closer to his sons, Thomas, of Boston, and Peter, at Lehigh University in Pennsylvania.

As a youngster, Guza had "odd" hobbies, his brother said: He collected bus transfers. And his odd taste in collectibles didn't wane with adulthood. Going through his belongings, family members happened upon jugs of steel pennies, U.S. coins that were minted during World War II when copper was in short supply.

Sometimes it appeared that Guza was obsessed with watching his pennies, his brother said. But that wasn't the case. He was simply an unpretentious guy, and no deed was too much when it came to those he cared for. "If he was on, say, a business trip to Los Angeles, he thought nothing of driving down to San Diego to see me," Robert said. But he'd get there in the most primitive rental cars you could imagine: cars that had crank windows, no CD player, no air conditioning. And he refused to carry a cell phone. Or dine in fancy restaurants. "His idea of a really good meal was a giant burrito," his brother said.

Guza wasn't much into planning, either, family members said. On the frequent vacations he took with his sons, the only thing he bothered to do beforehand was purchase plane tickets. On one trip to Alaska with his sons and nephew, they showed up with no plans in place for accommodations or transportation. After renting a car, his brother said, they started driving around until they ended up at what probably was the northernmost Motel 6 in the world.

BROOKE JACKMAN
There Was More to Life Than Money

In kindergarten, when all the little boys would try to kiss her, Brooke Jackman would spit at them. Years later, when classmates voted her "most beautiful" and "best-dressed," Jackman tried to divert the attention from her appearance. "Those weren't important things to her," said her mother, Barbara Jackman; what was important was "what she could do to help people." And while she eventually came to enjoy kisses from boys, she remained fiercely independent, determined and compassionate.

The night before she was lost in the September 11 attack, Jackman, 23, told her mother she was applying to the University of California at Berkeley School of Social Welfare. Jackman had already enrolled in a review course to prepare for the Graduate Record Examination. "She said, 'There is more to life than making money,'" Barbara Jackman recalled. The irony is that Jackman had just started working as an assistant bond trader at Cantor Fitzgerald, one of two positions for which 70 candidates had applied. It was a departure for a young woman who had spent her high school and college career volunteering in soup kitchens and working as a teacher's assistant. But after a disappointing stint in publishing, Jackman, a graduate of Columbia University, decided to give Wall Street a try.

Even Wall Street couldn't break her independent spirit. Co-workers remembered Jackman's distinctive earrings—a barbell shape in one ear and three tiny hoops in the other ear. "Brooke was totally independent and she had her own mind," said her mother. "You could talk until you were blue in the face. She would listen," and then she would do her own thing, and it was usually the right decision, Barbara Jackman said.

Doing her own thing included making daily visits to a bookstore near her Manhattan apartment on the way home from work. She would read almost a book a day, said her mother, and she'd jot down passages or quotations she particularly enjoyed.

Jackman also loved to walk, covering miles at a time with her water bottle, backpack and sneakers.

But mostly she enjoyed helping people. At her memorial service in September, a crowd of 1,500 attended. Strangers told stories of how Jackman had befriended them when everyone else had ignored them. "Brooke sought everybody out," said Barbara Jackman. "She measured people by the size of their hearts."

LAURENCE POLATSCH
A Star in His Own Right

Larry Polatsch liked to hang out with the stars. So last fall, he donned a tuxedo and crashed the wedding of Catherine Zeta-Jones and Michael Douglas at the swanky Plaza Hotel in Manhattan. He even ate with Jack Nicholson before security guards caught on and forced him to leave. As the paparazzi waited outside, Polatsch left the hotel beside Anthony Hopkins. He sneaked in again and left beside Dennis Miller. Then again with Quincy Jones.

Formerly a lawyer, Polatsch, 32, changed careers six years ago so he wouldn't have to "fight with people the rest of his life," said his father, Bernard. The Upper East Side resident worked as a partner in equities sales at Cantor Fitzgerald on the 104th floor of One World Trade Center.

Though he once asked Julia Roberts on a date and even appeared on *Entertainment Tonight* reenacting the proposition, his true love was Marni Wasserman, 32, whom he knew since seventh grade. Just months ago, they rekindled their romance and, by all accounts, expected to marry. "He was the one," Wasserman said. "I felt 100 percent secure, 100 percent happy. I've never felt that way." In one discussion, he told her: "Marni, I don't get down. I don't get sad. I don't get depressed. . . . You can count on me to always make you in a good mood."

Polatsch had a personal Web site, www.larrypolatsch.com, which the family converted into a memorial where people could post their memories of him. "There are hundreds of stories because he was a character," said his brother Danny. "He lived his entire life as if each day was really his last day. It's as if he knew that his life was going to end early because he packed in so much in 32 years."

EMILIO ORTIZ JR.
"DJ Pete" Kept the Family Laughing

Emilio Ortiz's mother-in-law had bought a step-climbing machine to shed some pounds, and she was frustrated because it wouldn't help her sweat. So Ortiz jumped on it to show her how it was done, and when she was not looking, he sprayed his face, chest and back with water to create a fake sweat. She got on the machine again and again, and he repeated the ruse, pretending he was out of breath because of the strong workout. When she realized what was happening, it was too late, because she was already sweating from the extra effort he had coaxed from her.

"He was such a prankster," recalled his wife of three years, Wanda. "He was always making my mother and brothers laugh." Ortiz, 38, also had a serious and responsible side to him, which led to his job as clearing supervisor for Carr Futures, a brokerage firm at the World Trade Center. He was lost there on September 11, leaving his wife and their infant twin daughters, Emily and Amanda, whom he adored. Ortiz had prayed for a girl when he learned his wife was pregnant, and he played with his daughters every night when he came home to Corona, Queens—always careful to carry them one at a time because he was afraid he might drop one.

Ortiz grew up in the Williamsburg and South Side sections of Brooklyn. After one year of college, he got his first job at the World Trade Center at Klein and Company, a family-owned medical insurance firm. There he learned the day-to-day work of the company's accounting office, positioning himself for the job he held at Carr. When his wife met him more than a decade ago, Ortiz was saving his nights for his other passion, popular music. He was a DJ—he had christened himself "DJ Pete"—at Teddy's Bar in the North Side section of Brooklyn. They became friends and started dating.

The wedding proposal came on Valentine's Day 1995 in the form of another joke.

A nervous Ortiz gave his love speech in front of friends and relatives and handed Wanda a box containing a fake diamond ring. But the joke was on him—she was so overwhelmed by her emotions that the prank did not register. She thought the ring was beautiful and said yes. Then he pulled out the real thing, a ring with a marquise stone that she had wanted. The wedding followed in 1998. "I should probably have married him sooner," his wife said.

LAURA ROCKEFELLER
Music, Dance and a Dog Named J.T.

Laura Rockefeller was a familiar face—and voice—at the 92nd Street Y in Manhattan. Audiences of children and adults remember her singing, dancing and emoting in performances of the Traveling Playhouse, a children's theater run by her parents, Ken and Kay Rockefeller.

Some of the same audiences who had seen her onstage joined friends and relatives at a celebration of her life on October 13 at the Y. Laura also played at the Westbury Music Fair and other sites around Long Island with the Traveling Playhouse. She loved musicals, played in summer stock productions and served on the staff of the Jewish Repertory Theatre, her father said. The family is distantly related to former New York governor Nelson Rockefeller and other famous Rockefellers, he said.

To help pay the rent, the White Plains native would coordinate delegates for financial technology conferences for the Risk Waters Group, a London-based company. She was on the job at Windows on the World September 11, greeting guests for the opening of a conference when the hijacked planes struck.

Rockefeller, who would have celebrated her 42nd birthday October 13, was devoted to her two cats and her dog, whom she named J.T. after the singer James Taylor. Despite her famous surname, Rockefeller was known as "J.T.'s mom" among the other pet owners who walk their dogs in Riverside Park, near her Manhattan apartment, where a plaque was to be placed on a bench in her memory. "Typically, the dog owners didn't know each other's names; they just knew the dog's name," her father said.

Weeks after the tragedy, J.T. still rushed to the window looking for Laura whenever he heard a car.

MICHAEL SELVES
A Strip Show at the Pentagon

Michael Selves was no buttoned-down Pentagon bureaucrat. His wife, Gayle, said that about two years ago Selves, director of information management for the U.S. Army, was to deliver a speech before an audience of government contractors at the Pentagon. The briefings were known to be a bit staid. So to break with tradition, he walked up to the podium and started to loosen his necktie. He then took it off and began to strip.

Gayle said the audience was aghast as the portly man stood before them in his underwear. But "after that meeting, he got standing-room-only crowds," said Gayle, who had been married to her 53-year-old husband for six years. "Everybody loved him. He really knew how to boost morale."

The couple, who lived in Fairfax, Virginia, were both avid golfers. They had planned to retire the following year and "laugh and play golf forever."

MARIANNE SIMONE
She Brought Laughter and Comfort

With her crystal fox coat and hat, closets full of designer suits, 60-odd pairs of shoes and movie-star looks, Marianne Simone, 62, was sometimes compared with Elizabeth Taylor. But her daughter, Teresa Hargrave, said she always seemed more like Lucille Ball. "She was comical," said Hargrave. "When she was in a room, everyone was laughing."

Simone was the one discoing with co-workers half her age at company functions, singing Italian songs about "love or mama" at barbecues, and entertaining her grandchildren with her own silly sayings, such as "molli-colli-folli," meaning "smelly."

But Simone was also known for her more serious sayings—when someone lost a job or had a disappointment, it was "One door closes, another door opens," and when a friend needed encouragement, her daughter recalled, "She would say, 'Whatever you feel you can do, you can do.'"

Her advice had the weight of first-hand experience. An Italian-American girl from Bensonhurst, Simone was married at 23 and looked set for a life as a housewife and mother. She had three children—Lisa Cardinali, 36, Stephen Simone, 32, and Hargrave. For more than 20 years, she cooked and cleaned and her husband doled her a weekly allowance.

Their separation in her mid-40s proved a catalyst in Simone's life, Hargrave said. "She just looked at herself and said, 'I'm not going to fall apart.'"

And she didn't.

She entered the working world with vigor, starting as a receptionist at Cantor Fitzgerald 18 years ago, and working her way up to the position of communications specialist. She worked on the 101st floor of Tower One.

"She got a job, she got a career," her daughter said. "She showered herself with things, she loved herself, she taught us to love ourselves."

A memorial site set up by Cantor is full of reminiscences from co-workers and family. "I miss drinks with the girls and how crazy you were," wrote one colleague.

"I talk to you all the time, and I do hear you answer me," wrote another friend, "but Marianne, I can't tell anybody this. They'd think I was crazy. Only you would understand . . ."

To her six grandchildren, Hargrave said, "She was their friend." They looked forward to her arriving for the weekend with a bag of gifts, sometimes selected from her own substantial closets—old costume jewelry or makeup. She would join in the kids' games or goof around with them.

"The only person I would dance with at parties was you," wrote her granddaughter, Krystal, 11.

Simone would cook delicious meals even when the fridge seemed empty. And she would start card games that went late into the night.

Often she would go "house-hopping," her daughter said—she was so popular that she had six invitations to Labor Day barbecues. But at the end of the weekend, Hargrave said, she would happily go back to the single life and her house in Staten Island. "She didn't mind being alone," Hargrave said. "She'd say, 'You have a lot of patience with these kids and this husband.'"

Her children, grandchildren, relatives and friends now find themselves missing her laugh, her jokes and the voice of reason she provided. "We all learned a lot from her," her daughter said. "How not to fall apart during bad times, and pull yourself together by your bootstraps, and try to move forward.

"And that's what I know I'm trying to do now."

MYRNA YASKULKA
Mom Was Always in Fashion

Maybe it was the sweaters stuffed into hatboxes, the costume jewelry spilling from dresser drawers, and the sunglasses—more than 100 pairs in all—that gave it away, because everyone knew that Myrna Yaskulka was a clotheshorse.

"We called her 'the bag lady' because she always had her Century 21 and Strawberry bags," said her son, Jay Yaskulka. Her family even hoped that she had made her usual morning visit to Century 21, a clothing store, and escaped the tragedy at the World Trade Center. September 11 marked her 11-year anniversary as an executive assistant at Fred Alger Management on the 93rd floor of Tower One.

When Yaskulka, 59, did not return home, it brought back painful memories for her three sons, whose father was murdered 20 years ago in a robbery, Jay Yaskulka said. "Both of them went to work and they didn't come home," he said. "They both died in tragedies."

Yaskulka, a native of Borough Park, stood out in a crowd, said her son. But it wasn't her pink rhinestone sunglasses, leopard-print clothes or even her FUBU sweatshirt that made her special to her family. "She would do anything to help us out," Yaskulka said. She lent money when her sons were out of work or having trouble in their business. She regularly visited and took meals to her mother, who lived in the same building complex. And she would sit for hours on end as her granddaughters styled her hair and applied her makeup.

Jay Yaskulka said his mother's fascination with fashion began years ago when she worked in women's retail. She also enjoyed attending parties for singles, where she would dance to her favorite 1950s doo-wop tunes. She loved to dance and encouraged her granddaughters, who are both avid dance students. After each recital, "Grandma

Myrna" would be there with candy or a bouquet of roses or carnations to show her support.

Yaskulka would have turned 60 on November 11. Jay Yaskulka, at the suggestion of his daughters, got a strawberry cake, and they sang "Happy Birthday." "My mother wasn't just my mother," he said. "She was my friend."

CATHERINE FAGAN
Grandma's Yen for Yoga and Tofu

Catherine Fagan's five grandchildren sometimes called her "The Fun Grandma." "She didn't bake cookies or read stories," said her daughter Sarah. "She took them to yoga classes and fed them tofu."

Fagan was good at her job and loved working at the World Trade Center. She'd started after her husband died 17 years ago, leaving her in her early 40s with four children to support—Sarah and her three brothers, Christopher, James and Jeffrey. Fagan first headed back to school and then to Manhattan. Within two years, she settled at Marsh & McLennan in the north tower, rising from secretary to an executive position in its computer department.

But by September 2001, at the age of 58, she was ready to retire and take on a new career as a yoga instructor. "She was very into yoga, all that alternative stuff," said her daughter, who added that her mother's interest in the ancient art of healing came after she hurt her back. "She went to a yoga school and became certified to teach." She was also a vegetarian and interested in art history.

Fagan's other love was her dog, Hercules, who was rescued from the ASPCA in Manhattan. A mixed breed that had a lot of pit bull in him, Hercules was his owner's pride and joy. "He was her baby," her daughter said. Fagan and Hercules would spend time at her country home in Pennsylvania, where she could get away from her harried work in Manhattan and her home in Greenpoint in Brooklyn, spending her time outdoors walking and hiking.

Her daughter said that when some family members recently took the dog to the country home, he ran from room to room looking for Fagan. When he didn't find her, Hercules lay on the floor with his tail down and sad eyes. A veterinarian told the family the dog was depressed. "I don't think it hit him at first that she was gone," said her daughter, who lived with her mother in Brooklyn. "But I think we've finally got him out of mourning."

DARREN BOHAN
His Melody Lingers On

A banjo, a mandolin, three guitars and little else filled the Kew Gardens apartment where Darren Bohan lived. The handwritten lyrics and song sheets scattered about chronicled his transformation from harmonica-playing teenager to locally touted guitarist.

"He was very committed, and he had quite an aptitude, especially since he was largely self-taught," said his brother Gary, who was once a professional trumpet player. Bohan's early love of the Beatles, Woody Guthrie and other folk music melded in the bluegrass tunes he wrote and performed at jam sessions in Greenwich Village. But although he had decided to forgo life as a starving artist, each day Bohan and his mandolin held a lunchtime serenade for his co-workers at the World Trade Center.

Bohan, 34, had recently accepted a temporary assignment at Aon Corporation to help with budgets. It was an irony his family could not have imagined. For much of his adult life, they had encouraged Bohan to get a traditional job. "He was a free spirit from A to Z," said his brother. "He finally gets a job in accounting. And he gets there early . . ."

Bohan was raised in Hurley, New York, but he lived in Yosemite for almost 10 years, eventually becoming a tour guide for visitors and campers. Encouraged by the waterfalls and giant sequoias, a 20-year-old Bohan picked up a guitar and taught himself to play. His talent bloomed, leading him to experiment with several other instruments and, for a short time, to play in a band. "The environment was really important to him," said his cousin, Beth Udoma, who used to stay awake all night with Bohan, writing and singing funny songs. "He believed in the power of nature to heal. That was his religion."

In his late 20s, Bohan returned to college, obtaining a bachelor's degree in accounting from Sonoma

State University. "I think he did want to become a professional musician eventually, but he was practical in the sense of realizing that you have to eat and you have to pay your bills," said his aunt, Noreen Kahlftorf. Bohan wanted to have a family, and he knew that he needed to be more self-sufficient, Udoma said. "We called him a happy-go-lucky free spirit, but he was in touch with his source," she said. "I don't think that people knew how connected he was with his own inner wisdom."

Even while easing his way into corporate America, Bohan's music never stopped. "For him, the art was 24/7," said Udoma. So it seemed fitting that 350 people gathered in Hurley to memorialize him under an oversized tent smack in the middle of an apple orchard. From the 2-foot-high stage, friends and relatives gave testimonials, read tributes, and played music—Bohan's music—all day and all night long.

EDWARD C. MURPHY
A Strait-Laced Eccentric

On paper, Edward Murphy led the conventional life of a prosperous businessman.

He was a managing partner at Cantor Fitzgerald with a comfortable home in Clifton, New Jersey. At 42, he was the youngest Knight of Columbus in his local chapter and had served as the chairman of the local traffic safety board for several years. He telephoned his widowed mother each morning from his offices at the World Trade Center.

At least, that's what he did when he wasn't hunting down dead celebrities, crashing mob funerals or sneaking into golf tournaments. "He was an eccentric," said Maryann Flego, his longtime girlfriend.

An avid reader, Murphy fed his voracious appetite for information and trivia with a steady stream of books on Hollywood, the mob, modern art, the military and his two Republican heroes, Richard Nixon and Ronald Reagan. He refused, however, to read fiction. Murphy considered it "a waste of time," she said.

Flego met Murphy while jogging in a New Jersey park—he had taken up marathon running as an adult. The pair often vacationed in Los Angeles,

where Murphy enjoyed taking tours of celebrity-studded cemeteries like Forest Lawn and once tried to rent the hotel room where comedian John Belushi died. "In 17½ years," she said, "I was never bored."

Murphy "would do anything to save a buck," said his older brother, the Reverend Dan Murphy. But it wasn't the money so much as the kick he got out of getting a deal. "It was a game to him," his brother said. Once, Flego recalled, Murphy even hopped the fence at a women's golf tournament the two attended so he wouldn't have to pay.

Another time he tried to persuade Flego to brave a blustery snowstorm in order to attend the funeral of a mob figure. Murphy was fascinated by mobsters, she said. He loved how they managed to outwit the authorities, and their loyalty to "the family" struck a chord in a man who was fiercely loyal to his own family and friends.

"The attribute I loved most about Eddie was his devotion to my mom and my dad," said Dan, who remembers that Ed alone stayed in the town where he was raised, nursing his father through illness in the 1980s and then tending to his widowed mother. Now Dan takes comfort in learning about the sides of his brother he knew less well—the practical joker, the witty conversationalist. "In the family he was very quiet and reserved," Dan said. "We see family one way, and friends see it another way. That's a lesson of life."

ERICA VAN ACKER
Fearless in Pursuit of Change

Trauma can break people. In Erica Van Acker's case, it made her stronger.

As a young woman, in 1970, Van Acker was raped in the hallway of her Manhattan apartment building. Back then, many victims never came forth to charge their assailants, silenced by a stigma attached to rape and the burden of proof under New York state law, which at the time required corroborating testimony from a third-party witness. Instead of staying quiet, Van Acker found her voice. She told her story in a groundbreaking documentary by Bill Moyers called *No Tears for Rachel*, which aired on WNET/13 in 1971.

"She was just so outraged," said Susan Thompson, a longtime friend. "She just didn't want that to happen to anybody else." So Van Acker channeled her anger into activism, speaking out on behalf of rape victims and lobbying for changes in state law.

Van Acker, a 62-year-old consultant at Aon Corporation, was accustomed to finding strength from within. A child actor who worked in radio and onstage in New York, Van Acker was shipped off to postwar London at the age of 8 to live with her grandparents after her parents divorced. The move changed her life drastically. "Erica was very much on her own," Thompson said, first at boarding school and later at the prestigious Guildhall School of Music & Drama in London. "She really never had the support system that most of us do—input from parents, goals," said her friend. "She had to find that all out for herself."

Returning to New York at the age of 20, Van Acker switched her focus from acting to business. A warm, friendly woman with a knack for teaching, she developed a specialty during her years working for companies such as Ticketron and the New York City Off-Track Betting Corporation: training people to use automated machines in the workplace.

Van Acker had been in New York for 10 years when she was attacked. "The experience kind of galvanized her," Thompson said. Soon after, Van Acker joined forces with a business partner, Gail Soltisyk, and started her own company, a human resources consulting firm. They also invested in real estate, a sideline that unexpectedly opened the door on the next chapter in her career. In the early '90s, one of their tenants, a restaurateur in Water Mill in the Hamptons, defaulted on her lease. So Van Acker, a deft cook with no experience in the restaurant business, and her partner decided to reopen the place as the Station Bistro.

Van Acker was a hands-on owner. On any night, she could be found cooking in the kitchen, tending bar or charming customers and staff with droll stories, delivered with just a hint of a British accent. "She always wanted to make it a pleasure for everyone working there," said Marianne Toy, a former waitress. She said that Van Acker, who came in at midday, prepared dinner for her staff and often worked through midnight, and "really took an interest in everyone's life." She ultimately sold the restaurant a year and a half before her death and returned to consulting work in Manhattan, but she remained a fixture in Sag Harbor, near the beach that she loved. "Erica was not afraid to try anything," said Matthew Ryan, who tended bar at the restaurant. "She kept reinventing herself."

13
Tower People

They worked at a variety of jobs—some of them integral to the very operation of the Twin Towers. A father of five with the imposing title of Director of Vertical Transportation for the World Trade Center. He was in charge of its 350 elevators and escalators, and after the crash he stayed in the heart of danger, directing the evacuation. A fire safety director who helped save 30 children trapped in a day-care center and then rushed to his command center. He could have walked 10 feet to safety but was still helping to evacuate others when the tower collapsed. A window washer who loved a job that allowed him to look down on the city with his head in the clouds.

Then there was a pastry chef known for adding fanciful touches to traditional desserts that made even food critics smile. And a 66-year-old cook whose family wanted him to retire, but he, too, loved his job and the city he had adopted years before. His 4-year-old grandson asks for him. "If I pray," he asks, "will Papi come home?"

ROKO CAMAJ
The Clouds Were His Home

There were days when rain fell on lower Manhattan, but it snowed on Roko Camaj. And there were days when Camaj's job meant having his head in the clouds.

The 60-year-old Albanian immigrant was a window washer for American Building Maintenance, a company contracted by the World Trade Center, where he had worked for 27 years, his daughter Tereza Camaj said.

Roko Camaj was killed in the September 11 terrorist attacks on the towers. He phoned his wife sometime after the second plane hit and said he was on the 105th floor of Tower Two with a few hundred people who were waiting to be evacuated, his daughter said. "He told us not to worry," Tereza said. "He said, 'We're all in God's hands.'"

Camaj immigrated to the United States from Montenegro with his wife, Katrina, in 1969. The couple's first daughter, Angelina, was born a day after Camaj and his wife arrived, Tereza said. The culture shock, added to the limited support systems the couple had, and the language barrier, made their new lives in the United States intimidating at first, Tereza said. But Camaj kept many of the specifics from his children. "He never wanted us to know the extent of the hardships he went through," Tereza said.

The couple had shared housing with friends and family until 1970, Tereza said. The couple lived in Manhattan until 1991, when they moved to Manhasset. Tereza had gained admission to the C.W. Post Campus of Long Island University, so the move to Long Island seemed logical. "After they saw the house, and they knew where I was going to college, everything just fell into place," she said.

Two years later, Camaj phoned his family one day and told them that he wasn't fit to come home. A truck bomb had exploded in the trade center's garage and he had been trapped on the 107th floor for 2 1/2 hours. Camaj had made his way down the stairs with a dampened cloth over his mouth to protect him from suffocation. Except for the area around his nose and mouth that was covered by cloth, his body was blackened from the smoke and ashes that filled the stairway. "He didn't want us to see him," Tereza said.

After cleaning himself off, Camaj went home, several hours before he was expected. But there would be no personal or sick time. Camaj returned to work the next day. Camaj's dedication was something that he learned from the long days and hard work on his family's farm. "My parents have a huge amount of work ethic," Tereza said. "He said he wasn't worried, at all, about going back to work, because he thought security was so tight."

Two years later, his work was the subject of a children's book by Keith Elliot Greenberg called *Window Washer: At Work Above the Clouds*, part of a series about dangerous professions. "His picture was practically on every single page," his daughter said. But by then, he was used to the attention: Camaj had been interviewed by newspaper and television reporters and was featured on international news programs. "It was almost part of the job at that point," his daughter said.

The fact is, Roko Camaj didn't tell his wife the full truth about his job at the World Trade Center. He did tell her he was washing windows, which was true enough. He didn't mention that he spent some of that time dangling outside the towers. She finally found out by reading a newspaper article.

Most of the time, he simply ran an automated cleaner that did the washing mechanically. But at the top floor, odd-size windows meant he had to suspend himself from the roof to scrub them clear personally.

Camaj liked the solitude of the work. He wasn't scared of heights, or of much of anything else. He had a deep trust in the strength of the buildings and believed nothing could topple them.

When Camaj wasn't suspended hundreds of feet above the streets of Manhattan or giving interviews about it, he would sometimes take Angelina's son, Luke, his grandson, for walks along Northern Boulevard near his home. "He loved being a grandfather in a time of his life where he could enjoy being a grandfather," Tereza said.

EDWARD CALDERON
Spicing Up Night Life in the Towers

When Ilene Calderon, 23, went to the salsa and hip-hop events organized by her dad, Edward Calderon, it was hard for some of her peers to swallow.

"My friends were like, 'How

do you go clubbing with your father?' " said Ilene Calderon. "I was like, 'My dad is cool . . . ' I was loving it. I was there with my dad, hanging out, having a good time."

Eddie Calderon, 44, of Jersey City, New Jersey, was always cool. Growing up in East Harlem—El Barrio—music and performance were central in his life. Since he was in junior high school, he'd been acting in shows like *West Side Story* and *Bye Bye Birdie.* "He always liked to be in the light of things," said his sister, Caroline. He even attended the famed High School of Performing Arts in Manhattan for a time.

In the 1980s, Calderon was instrumental in bringing salsa to the New York scene, promoting club nights, parties and concerts. With his business partner, Tony Ortiz, he turned the World Trade Center into more than just a place for work. By day, he worked for the Port Authority, ultimately spending 22 years there. But at night, he and Ortiz put together wildly popular salsa and R&B nights at the various clubs and restaurants in the complex. "We created what we called the after-work parties," Ortiz said. "Instead of people going home, on certain days they would stay around until about 11 o'clock." The lines of office workers waiting to get in soon ran down to the next floor, Ortiz said. "We created a monster."

Calderon had to stop promoting events at the Twin Towers when he became the supervisor of the security division because it presented a conflict of interest, Ortiz said. But he still handled security for the salsa nights that Ortiz put on in the main plaza every Friday and Saturday in the summer. He also had a side business promoting music events elsewhere in the city.

Seeing the World Trade Center grow and change during the two decades he worked there left Calderon with a special attachment to the buildings, Ortiz said. " 'You're in my house now'—he would always say that . . . That's the reason he loved it so much that he gave his life for it."

On the morning of September 11, witnesses have told Calderon's family, he was seen running back into Tower One, where his office was on the second floor, to help free people trapped in the elevators. "I'm very proud of him," said his mother, Ida Bruno. "I'm proud to be his mother. He died happy, because he died doing what he liked to do—helping people."

Ilene Calderon, who credits her father with inspiring her to make her own music, sang "Hero" by Mariah Carey at a memorial service in October to an overflow crowd that included Edward Calderon's 15-year-old son, Jeremy. A Marine honor guard gave a folded American flag to his wife, Debbie. "I know, deep in my heart, that our dad is a hero," Ilene said. "He stood there to make sure that everybody was OK and his house was protected."

HEATHER HO
This Chef Had Plenty Cooking in Her Life

Heather Ho dreamed of opening her own pastry shop, and she was gaining the experience and acclaim she needed to do so.

A pastry chef at Windows on the World, Ho was named dessert chef of the year in 2000 by *San Francisco* magazine. She had made a name for herself at Boulevard, a popular and elegant restaurant on the San Francisco waterfront, where she was known for dazzling pastries that gave fanciful twists to traditional desserts. They included a lineup of three scoops of assorted sorbets with specialty cones on top, which one reviewer described as "three bad boys wearing dunce caps. You can't help but smile."

Ho, 32, grew up in Honolulu and later attended the Culinary Institute of America, a prestigious restaurant school in upstate New York. She began her career at high-profile New York restaurants including Gramercy Tavern, Bouley, Clementine and the Screening Room.

Her childhood friend, Malia Mattoch, said Ho's design sense reached from her pastries to the way she decorated her Manhattan apartment to her clothes, which were very simple and had a European sense of style.

"She had told me for a couple of years she wanted her own pastry shop," said Mattoch, who remembered Ho had an early interest in the field. "When we were in seventh grade, for Valentine's Day, she brought in Rice Krispies squares with perfect semi-sweet chocolate hearts on them. She would read cookbooks like they were novels. Food was her passion."

MON GJONBALAJ
He Wouldn't Retire from His "Second Home"

About two weeks before September 11, Mon Gjonbalaj and his wife discussed retirement. The Albanian immigrant was 65 and had worked in Tower Two for three decades. And he had plenty to keep him busy: three sons and a daughter, along with seven grandchildren. But Gjonbalaj balked. "He said, 'I can't do it. I can't turn my back,'" said his son, Sal. The trade center was more than a workplace for Gjonbalaj. "It was like a second home," his son said.

Gjonbalaj, a janitor for American Building Maintenance who cleaned the offices of the state Department of Taxation and Finance, was on the 86th floor of his second home when terrorists attacked. The Throgs Neck family was not unfamiliar with international conflict. Gjonbalaj, one of 13 children, regularly called his family in the Balkans during the 1999 war in Kosovo. He had one brother and two sisters in Kosovo and two brothers in Montenegro, all of whom survived the war. His daughter, Shkurta Nikaj, 36, serves as a translator with the NATO forces in Kosovo.

Gjonbalaj and his wife, Hanifa, left Montenegro in 1971 and came to the United States, where Gjonbalaj got a job as a busboy. "But he didn't like the restaurant business, so one of his friends got him a job at the World Trade Center," his son said. "He was so excited . . . He hardly ever called in sick."

He would go to work an hour early to see his friends at Tower Two, his son said. "When he came home, he would get on the phone and call them. 'Hey, Tony, what are we going to do tomorrow? Where are we going to meet?'"

Sal said Gjonbalaj was in good health and refused to consider quitting. "He was supposed to retire, but he wasn't interested," he said. "He'd say, 'What am I going to do? I want to work.'" So father and son continued to ride the bus into Manhattan every morning. Sal said he had a premonition something terrible would happen that day. "I definitely felt it, something was going on," he said. Later that morning, a co-worker told Sal about an accident at the World Trade Center. They watched on television as the second plane hit Tower Two.

Gjonbalaj called home after the first tower was struck and again at 9:08 a.m., five minutes after his building was hit, to say he was trapped. "I don't think I'm getting out," he said. "Take care of the family."

LAWRENCE BOISSEAU
A Fire Safety Director Who Wouldn't Leave

Larry Boisseau's job was to prepare for the worst-case scenario, the nightmare too terrible to come true. As a fire safety director at the World Trade Center, a position created after the 1993 bombing, he knew every nook and cranny of the center's seven buildings, every evacuation route, every emergency procedure.

On September 11, when that nightmare did come true, he was as ready as he could be. As Tower One was hit and showered debris, he rushed to the day-care center in Five World Trade Center, where 30 children were trapped. "Larry and the other fellas, they were up the hall, and they were breaking windows and they were getting the kids out," said Bernie Baldinger, a fire safety director who was not working that morning. "Everyone got out."

Baldinger heard from colleagues who survived the attacks that Boisseau, 36, made his way to the fire command station in Tower Two. There, he navigated firefighter crews through the building by radio and directed people to evacuation routes over the PA system. Boisseau was still trying to evacuate people in the ground-floor station an hour later when Tower Two collapsed.

"Larry had a lot of guts staying there, because they could have gone outside, they could have gone right out," Baldinger said. "They were 10 feet away from walking right out and away from it, but they didn't." Baldinger said he wasn't surprised. "I would have been surprised if he had gone out, if he had left," he said. "He was that kind of guy."

He was the kind of guy who was always eager to help out, Boisseau's family said, whether it was teaching a friend to drive, finding someone a job or standing by a loved one with cancer. "Whatever you wanted him to do, he would do it," said his sister, Donna LaBella.

After a somewhat troubled adolescence, Boisseau found his equilibrium when he met his wife, Maria Teresa, in 1985. "She was like his angel," LaBella said. "She came at the right time. . . . I think he was lost for some time, searching for something but not really sure what." Boisseau was then a security guard at Kennedy Airport, and Maria Teresa was dropping off her mother for a flight to her native Philippines. "He kind of whispered, 'Hello,' and I kind of whispered, 'Hi,'" his wife said. "I smiled, and he smiled, and that was it." The two were married a year later and, in 1994, fulfilled a dream when they bought a town house in Freehold, New Jersey. "My husband never believed dreams could happen," his wife said. "I proved him wrong."

For some time, though, she had a premonition that she would lose her husband in some kind of accident. "I thought, if God would take him away, I would like to be with him that day. But it didn't happen that way."

The couple, however, did have a moment together just before the attack. That morning, they huddled close for their regular 1½-hour bus ride from Freehold. Maria Teresa works in accounting two blocks from the World Trade Center.

As the morning sun streamed through the bus windows, the two joined hands and fell asleep.

PABLO ORTIZ
A Navy SEAL Lived and Died with Honor

As a child in the 1950s and 1960s, living in the projects of Manhattan's Lower East Side, Pablo Ortiz was, in the words of his wife, "a brat."

"He was mischievous," said Edna Ortiz, with a laugh. "He would cut out of class, run around with his friends." But by the time he finished high school, Ortiz was ready for a change. "The Lower East Side at the time was a lot of gangs, a lot of trouble," his wife said. "The environment he was in, he was not sure he was going to be the man that he wanted to be."

So, at the height of the Vietnam War, Ortiz enlisted, became a Navy SEAL and was shipped overseas. "How they deployed him, he never told me," she said. What she does know, however, is that those experiences left him suffering flashbacks for the rest of his life. Painful as it was, Ortiz's military service "made him the man he was," his wife said.

"He always said, if he survived Vietnam . . . what could be worse?" she said. "That gave him the strength to tackle a lot of obstacles." And the Navy's ideals became a source of strength for Ortiz, she said. "That honor code that the military has amongst itself, he definitely carried that throughout his life . . . being able to do things the stand-up way."

After finishing his tour, Ortiz became a construction worker. He never left the field, but gradually worked his way into management, eventually becoming the superintendent of construction for all seven buildings of the World Trade Center. "He was very good at what he did," Edna said. "He led by example."

Ortiz, 49, brought the same attitude to his family life. As a second-generation Puerto Rican, "He wanted to keep the Latin culture alive in his family," his wife said. "He felt the responsible person. He felt the leader of the family." When it came to his two children from a previous marriage, Justina, 17, and Ja-Shing, 11, Ortiz was, "Oh my God, so proud," she said. He was also in regular contact with his 86-year-old mother, visiting her in the project he grew up in. "He wanted to take his mom out of the projects, but she really didn't want to leave," she said.

Ortiz and his wife had bought a town house in Staten Island. "He was a homebody," Edna said. "He would come home, and this is where he wanted to be." Ortiz was the cook, his wife washed the dishes. And when she was stricken by one of her three-day migraine headaches, she said, "He would take all my calls, he would have me lie down, he would take care of everything that needed to be done in the house."

Indeed, Ortiz was so protective of his wife that this summer he asked her to quit her job, working in the projects for the New York City Housing Authority, because he was concerned for her safety. "We agreed," she said. "And a couple months later, look at what happened."

Still, his wife said, she takes some comfort in accounts of her husband's actions on the morning of September 11. E-mails and letters from co-workers on the 88th floor of Tower One describe him calming people down and helping them find escape routes, then staying behind to help a man trapped in an elevator.

"He always said he wanted his life to mean something, and it did, more than he'll ever know," she said. "During the last moments of his life, he died like he wanted to die—a hero."

FRANCIS RICCARDELLI
The Elevator Man Who Stayed at His Post

Most families pray they will have some trace of their loved ones to bury, that the recovery crews will find something, anything, in the rubble of the World Trade Center. "I'm praying they don't," said Theresa Riccardelli, who lost her husband, Francis. "He always said about dying that he didn't want to be embalmed, he didn't want a wake. Especially for the children, he wanted them to remember him alive."

So on October 6, the weekend the couple had planned to take their five children to Lake George, she organized a get-together for friends and family to remember Riccardelli at St. Andrew's Church in Westwood, New Jersey. "I wanted to just celebrate what a wonderful gift he was," she said. "He was a gift to me." And, she added, also to their children, Christiana, 10, Meghan, 8, Genevieve, 5, Zachary, 3, and Marielle, 1. Now, she said, "We'll just remember him as he was when he went to work September 11."

Riccardelli, 40, the manager of vertical transportation for the World Trade Center, played a vital role in the rescue of thousands that morning. As the caretaker of the 350-odd elevators and escalators throughout the center's buildings, his knowledge of the towers' systems was indispensable to firefighters and rescue crews, Riccardelli's co-workers told his wife.

From his office on the 35th floor of Tower Two, Riccardelli and his co-workers felt the impact when the first plane hit Tower One, his wife said. "They immediately grabbed the radios and flashlights and headed down to the operation control center to see if they could figure out the extent of the damage," she said. They set up base in Tower One, directing firefighters to people trapped in elevators and indicating which elevators could be used for evacuation.

"They were clearly in a very dangerous place, yet they all stayed because they knew they were the best chance for people. Without them, I don't think they would have got 20,000 people out of there in an hour," his wife said. When the operation seemed to be running as smoothly as possible, Riccardelli went with a group of firefighters to help out at Tower Two, she said. "It was probably within five minutes that the building came down."

Three months later, she said, she was sitting with 3-year-old Zachary in the family's home in Westwood. "Zachary said, 'You know what, Mommy? Do you miss Daddy still?' I said, 'I sure do miss Daddy.' And he said, 'Me, too.'"

Riccardelli hadn't imagined having such a large family when the couple married in 1989, she said. "Every time one was born, he'd say, 'Hey, what's another one?' . . . People would say, 'Are you ever going to stop?' and he'd say, 'I never say never.'" The size of the family didn't keep them from traveling. They visited Italy and New Mexico, took a yearly trip to Lake Placid and, in February 2001, had started the tradition of an annual ski trip to the Poconos. Every Friday night was "movie night," and Saturday was "family game night." And whenever Riccardelli was painting or doing renovations around the house, "He had all the helpers he needed," his wife said.

Without him, his wife tries to stay upbeat. "It's hard, without a doubt," she said. "The kids and I miss him with every beat of our hearts. But I know we'll see him one day. . . . Francis was a worrier, and I think about that, and I figure this way he can watch over us from heaven. I think about that often."

VERONIQUE BOWERS
Her Son Was Her Window on the World

Veronique "Ronnie" Bowers was full of love.

She loved shoes so much that she wanted to start a magazine devoted to them.

She loved being with her family and childhood friends from Crown Heights, where she still lived.

And even though she feared heights, she loved her accounting job at Windows on the World on the 106th floor of the World Trade Center.

Most of all, Bowers, 28, loved her 9-year-old son, Dior. So much so that she took him nearly everywhere with her, even on "Girls' Night Out."

Bowers was hysterical when she called her grandmother soon after reporting to work on September 11. "I was under the impression that she didn't know what had hit the building, but she knew something had hit the building," said Carrie Tillman. "I was trying to calm her down and then the phone went dead."

Dior was her pride and joy. "Every day she would speak about him," said Jennifer Gill, a co-worker from Windows on the World who was running late that fateful morning. "She would say it seemed like he was the parent, that he would ask about her day while she was asking about his. Whenever she came to my house, Dior was with her."

Bowers dropped out of high school when she became pregnant with her son in her senior year, said her childhood friend Tasha Sealy. After earning a graduate equivalency diploma, Bowers worked as a bookkeeper for a liquor wholesale manufacturer before learning on the Internet about a job at Windows on the World. She started working there in the fall of 2000, and friends and relatives said Bowers loved the camaraderie she shared with co-workers during and after work. "I feel that Ronnie is still close by, no matter where she's at," said Sealy. "I feel her presence around me."

JESUS CABEZAS
He Worked His Way to the Top of the World

Jesus Cabezas wouldn't quit.

His family told him to sell the house in Brooklyn, buy a place in Jersey or Staten Island, and learn to relax. But the 66-year-old line cook at Windows on the World said no thanks. He loved his job, and found New York as electrifying as when he arrived from Ecuador 33 years ago. "I'm a city boy," he told his wife, Victoria, and their four adult daughters. He wasn't going anywhere except off to work.

On the morning of September 11, Cabezas did just that. But he was running late for the breakfast shift, so he forgot to ask his wife's blessing and give her a kiss, as he usually did.

Cabezas was among 79 employees of Windows on the World lost in the World Trade Center disaster. They ranged from top management to unionized food-service staff, but they nevertheless formed an unusually close-knit and compatible group—one that truly became a community. "I lost my family," said Jules Roinnel, one of the managers. Located on the 106th and 107th floors of Tower One, Windows on the World was a magical place, a restaurant that boasted a celestial view and a global staff that came from places like India, Bangladesh, Mexico, Morocco, Poland, Ghana, Taiwan, the Philippines, Hong Kong, the Dominican Republic, Peru and Cuba. There was a feeling that Windows on the World was a small world of its own.

Cabezas himself was a native of Riobamba, Ecuador. In 1968 he left his family behind and came alone to New York to earn money to raise his children. Living by himself in rented rooms, he held down three jobs at a time, eventually landing one in South Brooklyn at a local Italian place called Felix's. He started as a dishwasher but soon showed that he could do more. He'd been a cook since he was very young, and before long, he was boiling pasta and twirling pizzas in Felix's kitchen. Meanwhile, Cabezas gradually brought his family over. First his wife and oldest daughter, then the three other girls.

For the 15 years he worked at Felix's, Cabezas developed a relationship with the owners. One helped him buy a house on St. Nicholas Avenue in Bushwick and, when his bosses retired, Cabezas thought about buying the restaurant. But his wife was not enthusiastic. So he found other restaurant jobs, and eight years ago, he started at Windows.

Nothing could stop her father, Blanca Bowers said. Even an operation for colon cancer didn't slow him down. "My dad thought he would be around forever."

Bowers said her son, David, 8, was expecting his grandfather to attend a soccer game on the weekend after the World Trade Center attack. "Don't worry, Chico, I'll be there," Cabezas had said. Now her kids ask about their beloved Papi. "If I pray," asked 4-year-old John, "will Papi come home?"

FRANCIS DE MARTINI
He Saved His Wife, but Not Himself

Frank De Martini was sharing a cup of coffee with his wife, Nicole, on the 88th floor of the north tower when the first plane hit. A Port Authority architect and manager of construction projects within the towers, De Martini urged his wife to leave. She refused. He insisted. His wife made it out of the building safely. De Martini, who stayed behind to help evacuate his colleagues, died in the collapse.

"That would be just like him," said his older sister, Nina De Martini-Day. De Martini, 49, always threw himself into everything he did, his sister said. On September 11, despite the damage and the smoke, reports show that he succeeded in getting almost everyone on his floor to the stairwell. Later, he freed people in an elevator by prying the door open with a coat rack. "It wasn't in his nature to not try to help," his sister said.

He had a way about him, and communicated easily, even with strangers, his sister said. "He had a gleam in his eye and engaged you and made you want to talk back," she said. "He brought all his different friends together and always created something bigger and better by his energy and love of life."

The loves of his life were his wife, originally from Switzerland, and his two children, Sabrina, 10, and Dominic, 8. "They were his greatest source of joy," his sister said, adding, "He always made simple things into adventures."

Sometimes the results were dramatic. When De Martini was working on a 100-year-old Upper West Side apartment building that his sister lives in, he took an innovative approach: He tore down internal walls and rebuilt them only halfway, using columns for the other half. The result: a dark hallway was made into a sunlit walkway. He was a true enthusiast, his sister said—a man "who brought the old and the new together and created something better."

ANGELO AMARANTO
He Was There from Beginning to End

Maria Amaranto was a 19-year-old bride arriving in Brooklyn from Salerno, Italy, with her new husband, Angelo. She remembers him being a perfect gentleman and a true romantic. "He took me everyplace the first time I came," she said. "We would go to the movies, the Statue of Liberty . . . We went to the theater, the Rockettes, the circus."

From their 40 years of married life together, Maria has many more happy memories—Angelo in his beloved garden, growing tomatoes, basil and eggplants; Angelo cooking his favorite marinara sauce; Angelo taking the couple's oldest son, Armando, to see *The Ten Commandments*; Angelo's joy in his three young grandchildren.

But the life of Angelo Amaranto, 60, was also one filled with long, hard hours of work. Amaranto had been a janitor at the World Trade Center since the Twin Towers first opened. He woke at 3 o'clock each morning and took the subway from Borough Park, Brooklyn, into the city. "He loved his work," Maria said. "He would go to work one hour or two hours before it started. Sometimes he would work Saturday and Sunday." Angelo had planned to retire in two years, Maria said. "He said, 'I work all my life, and I need to rest, and we need to go places, you and me together.'"

The couple had planned to return to Salerno, said their daughter, Emily Amaranto. "He never got to enjoy himself," she said. "Now he was finally going to enjoy a little bit of life, a little bit of what he earned. And then this happened."

Still, she recalled, her father was always a happy man. "He used to say to us, 'You know, a lot of people have money,'" she said. "'I have something better than money. I have grandchildren.'"

STEPHEN GEORGE ADAMS
He Ruled the Cellar on the 107th Floor

Everything about Stephen Adams smacked of a finer, a more elegant time—his love of British folk dancing and medieval musical instruments, the leisurely five-course dinners he prepared for friends, followed by fine ports, Stilton, dancing and conversation—even his tweed jackets and hats and his thick moustache. "He didn't belong in this century," said his wife, Jessica Murrow. "He was like a strange sort of aristocrat . . . An aristocrat out of place."

Murrow first met Adams, 51, in the early 1980s, at a Morris-dancing convention at Marlboro College in Vermont. He was a student there at the time, and danced with a group called Marlboro Morris and Sword. She played the pipe and tabor, a kind of drum, for another troupe, the Bouwerie Boys. "I had forgotten my drumstick, and he lent me one of his," recalled Murrow, 51. But it was another 10 years before the couple fell in love. They were married in 1994.

In some ways, it was a strange match, Murrow said. She, a musician and sound designer for the theater and TV, describes herself as "a modern girl, very aggressive, career-oriented." "I forget to smell the roses all the time," she said. "He had to remind me constantly . . . He appreciated life in a way I'm still trying to learn."

But life was not always easy for Adams. "In many ways, he struggled in our time," she said. "He wasn't a go-getter, he wasn't a New Yorker in that way." Originally from Cape Cod, Adams moved to Manhattan in 1992. A talented cook, he enrolled at the French Culinary Institute in SoHo at Murrow's urging. He went on to work in the kitchens of several New York restaurants but, his wife said, hated every minute of it. He couldn't stand the pressure, she said, the "getting screamed at by chefs," the "madly chopping all day long."

In this strained time, he and Murrow split and Adams returned to Massachusetts for three years. Only in April 2001 did he come back to New York, and the couple reunited. Adams had finally found his calling—fine wine. He was hired as assistant cellar master at Windows on the World. This time, his wife said, "He loved New York, he loved his job. They recognized his talent right away." The week before the attacks, Adams was promoted to beverage manager, Murrow said. "He had it. He'd found what he should be doing."

Adams was working on the 107th floor of the World Trade Center's Tower One on the morning of September 11. For his memorial service, Murrow returned with his friends to his college alma mater. She served a lavish five-course meal and, with two sommeliers from Windows, chose 10 cases of wine, as well as port and Stilton. Stories were told about Adams, eulogies were given, Murrow sang and then the guests got up from the table and danced.

"Everyone got sufficiently drunk and had a good time," Murrow said with a small laugh. "It was very much as Steve would have done. I'm sure he was smiling at us all."

SAMUEL FIELDS
Money Was Tight, Faith Was Abundant

Samuel Fields was born with a small hole in the cartilage at the top of his right ear. His family saw it as a sign.

"They said he was blessed because of it," said his wife, Angela Fields. "I believe it, because nobody ever really got angry with him . . . He was easygoing. Very easygoing."

That's how he was when Angela told him, about a week before September 11, that she was pregnant again. The couple already had four children—Samuel Jr., 11, Stefan, 7, Demetrius, 5, and Sharaia, 3—and providing for them all on Fields' salary as a security guard at the World Trade Center was a constant struggle.

"He just worried about where's all the money coming from to take care of the kids," Angela said. He worked as hard as he could, she said, but eventually faced the situation with his characteristic calm. "He accepted it," she said. "He just left everything in God's hands."

Fields loved being a dad above all else, which makes the fact that he never saw his youngest son even harder. Sharif Fields, a 6-pound baby boy, was born on February 11, 2002. Since his birth, she said, friends and family have helped her cope.

Shortly before he was killed in the terrorist attacks, Fields took a few days off from work to be with his children, taking them to the Bronx Zoo, the park, museums and on walks. Though money was tight, he loved to buy gifts for them, especially on Hanukkah. "He would do anything for his kids, anything to please his family," Angela said.

Growing up, she said, "He was one of those quiet kids, and then a quiet teenager and a quiet adult. He didn't party. He just went to school, came home, went to work, came home."

She met Fields when they were both music students at Bronx Community College and was attracted to his "big, beautiful eyes and lovely smile . . . He always had a smile on his face."

Fields' heart had been broken before, his wife said, and "he never thought he would ever get married and have children." When the two met, however, "He said I was the only woman he ever needed." They were married in 1991 and moved from the Bronx to Harlem. Fields was born again in the Hebrew Pentecostal faith in 1992, joining his wife's church, The House of God, on 119th Street and Fifth Avenue.

Six years ago, Fields got a job as a security guard at Summit Security Services in Tower One. "He liked working with the tenants," his wife said. "He just loved helping . . . That's him." On the morning of September 11, Fields helped many. He stayed at his post on the ground floor of the tower, his wife said, directing those evacuating the building. His body was recovered from the rubble in December.

Since then, his wife said, she has received many phone calls from people her husband evacuated that morning. They say that "he was a hero, that he helped them out, that he helped them try to be calm. That they always will remember him."

RICHARD PENNY
Gone Twice but Not Forgotten

Richard Penny Jr. hadn't seen or talked to his father in 14 years. In fact, his most vivid memory is the day his father went away. Penny, then 5, was walking to school when an older kid yelled, "Ha ha, your dad is in jail." Penny ran home, where his grandmother told him that the older boy's taunt was true. When his father was released from prison 14 months later, the elder Penny was depressed and unemployed, his son said, and then just disappeared.

In mid-October 2001, after years spent searching, Richard Penny Jr., 33, found his father—only to learn that he had lost him for good.

Richard A. Penny, 53, had been homeless and poor for more than a decade, but he had finally found an apartment and a steady job. On September 11, he was somewhere above the 90th floor of Tower One collecting recyclable trash for Project Renewal, an organization that helps people move from the streets to work.

That information, the first news that the younger Penny had heard of his father in years, was relayed by a reporter who wanted to interview the family. "I just couldn't believe it . . . after all of these years," said Richard Penny Jr., who has a wife of 12 years, four children and years of accomplishments he had planned to share with his father. "I had imagined me and my dad taking my children to the movies, having him sit down at my dining table and having dinner. Just realizing all of that was never going to happen and that he had died so terribly . . . it was just too much." The only thing the younger Penny could think of to do was to go to New York. "I wanted to talk to anybody that had been a part of my dad's life for the last 15 years," Richard Jr. said.

The early history, he knew well enough. His father was born in Brooklyn to an African-American mother and a Jewish father, who were not married. "Back in that time period, that was pretty scandalous," the younger Penny said. Scandalous enough for the birth mother to give her baby to a childless family down the block. Inez and Allie Penny eventually adopted the baby and raised him as their own.

His father was an only child and a good student, said the younger Penny, and the Pennys gave him everything. "He was the prototype of what should have been a successful person," said Richard Penny Jr. He became the Metropolitan High School valedictorian, married his sweetheart and was working as a technician at AT&T. But in 1975, he took a wrong turn. Richard Penny Sr., then 26, and his friends were accused of robbing a token booth. "That instance, right there, took his life and flipped it upside down," Richard Jr. said.

While his father struggled to get control of his life, Richard Jr. and his mother moved to Hampton, Virginia, where he still lives. Occasionally the younger Penny would visit his father in Brooklyn. "We would go to the movies and go to the park to play handball," Richard Jr. said. It seemed to him to be the only time that his father, by then a recluse, would venture out of the house and enjoy life.

When Inez Penny died in 1987, soon after Allie Penny died, new owners claimed the brownstone that had been Richard Penny Sr.'s stability. "At that moment, I lost contact with him," Richard Jr. said. "It's like he just dropped off of the planet."

So he began to search for his father. He called every Richard Penny in the phone book. He started in New York, then moved to surrounding areas. He got a computer and searched online. Eventually, he just started calling anyone with the last name "Penny." Oblivious to the son's desperate search for him, the elder Penny floated from one shelter to another, trying to keep a job and get back on his feet. He lived in shelters and worked for nonprofit groups designed to help the poor and homeless get a fresh start.

His son visited many of those places during his trip to New York in October, and with each stop he picked up pieces of his father's life. "Everybody gave me one little tidbit of information that I didn't know," Richard Penny Jr. said. One of his father's co-workers said his father had recently confided that he was ready to go find his son. "That was huge for me. It made me feel as though his feelings for me never changed," Richard Jr. said.

After so many years, he was encouraged. He said he will continue to look for his father's birth family, he will talk to all of the people who knew his father and he will keep hoping that even though his father is gone . . . he will find him once again.

14
Legacies

The legacies of the lost are frozen in snapshots and scrapbooks and videotapes. They are preserved in the photos we treasure in our minds—in recollections of the way a human being went through life, remembrances of a certain smile, a favorite saying, a tender hug, a special song. For more than 50 women left widowed by September 11, there is something more to help them hold the memories of the men they loved—to hold them in their arms as well as in their hearts. They are new mothers, and for them the miracle of life is doubly poignant.

It is intensely so for a young woman whose husband was working overtime on that sky-blue morning so that he could help save for the child he would never see. At a memorial service as his fellow firefighters marched past, she was timing contractions. Three hours later, she gave birth to a daughter. "This is a lifeline to Pete, and I'll always have that," she says.

The theme of life renewed is a constant for all of them. "She has a cleft chin like my husband did, and she has his nose, too," says one. "I have a part of him forever."

Another looks at her son's deep, brown eyes and sees her husband's face. "Inside my heart," she says, "I talk to him every single moment."

The gurgles of the newly born, and the crying too, soften the night. In a time of utter sadness, life goes on.

PETER NELSON
A Son Is Born As His Father Is Mourned

A fire official kept time for 1,500 firefighters as they filed in rigid groups of eight past the widow of firefighter Peter Nelson during a memorial service. But Gigi Nelson's mind was on another clock. She was timing contractions.

Three hours after the service at the Huntington Station firehouse and 25 days after her husband was lost in the collapse of the World Trade Center, Gigi Nelson gave birth to 6-pound, 1-ounce Lyndsi Ann. The next morning, she left the hospital by ambulance for an hour to attend a church service on his behalf before returning to care for their first child.

Peter Nelson, 42, a 15-year firefighter with the city, was a third assistant chief at Huntington Manor, where he had been a volunteer from the age of 18, and much loved as a fearless firefighter and skilled teacher. In the city, Nelson had spent most of his career in the pleasant Tudor-style quarters of Ladder Company 151 in Forest Hills, when he was selected for the faster-paced, elite Queens rescue company in July 2001. He was working overtime on September 11 to help save for his new baby.

The last time that Huntington Manor chief Charles Hoffman saw Nelson was the night of September 10. Nelson had attended a Lamaze class with his wife before going to a department meeting. "We all made fun of him, panting," recalled Hoffman, imitating the huff-puff breathing Lamaze students are taught to ease labor. "He was one of the best of the best."

Gigi Nelson spent her final weeks of pregnancy in a vigil by the phone, with a never-ending stream of firefighters and neighbors sharing the wait with her.

Twice a day, Huntington Manor firefighters sent over meals for up to 50 people, along with sodas and ice. Childhood friends came by to tell stories from Nelson's younger days, when he earned the nickname "Petley" because he was charming enough to "peddle" anything to anyone. Over and over, she said, friends described Nelson as a man who always put other people first.

"You're scared," she admitted just after getting home from the hospital with her newborn, as usual to a houseful of helpful people. "You think you're going to have the father there. I miss him.

"But I also know that I'm compiling a scrapbook for his daughter. I can safely tell her that her father is a hero and he gave his life to save others. That's a comfort. And I have her. She's kept me going. This is a lifeline to Pete, and I'll always have that."

STANLEY SMAGALA
A Mother Will Always Have Faith

Her middle name is Faith, because they never gave up hope they would bring a child into the world.

Not after Dena Smagala didn't conceive after one year of trying to get pregnant. Not after she had a miscarriage when she was six weeks pregnant. And not after being on fertility drugs for more than a year.

At 4:35 a.m. on January 9, 2002, Alexa Faith Smagala entered the world, all of 21 inches and 7 pounds, 7 ounces.

After seven hours in labor, Dena Smagala could do nothing but cry. Tears shed for the joy of finally having the baby she long sought. Tears shed because she did it alone. Her husband, Stanley, 36, a city firefighter, was killed at the World Trade Center.

Now, she is one of dozens of September 11 widows who have brought fatherless children into the world. "It was very emotional," Smagala, 31, of Holbrook, said from her hospital bed at Good Samaritan Hospital Medical Center.

Nine months ago, theirs was a life right out of a Norman Rockwell painting. She was a fourth-grade teacher in Seaford; he, a firefighter for Engine Company 226 in Brooklyn. They met at his fire academy graduation in April 1996 and were married two years later. "There were 400 firefighters there and he was one who stood out," she said.

They both wanted to have children soon. He was one of seven children; she, one of five. After years of trying to get pregnant, news arrived the day after Mother's Day. Dena's doctor called her at school to tell her the good news. She waited to tell Stanley in person, buying baby bibs and "I Love Daddy" shirts and setting an extra place at the dinner table. "He was thrilled," she recalled. "He cried."

They were cautious at first, telling few people. It wasn't until June 19, at their three-year anniversary dinner, that they started planning. "He talked about it all the time," said Jack Halaby, a firefighter in Engine Company 226. "He constantly kept us up-to-date with doctor reports."

Stanley never missed a doctor's appointment, reveling in every detail—sonogram pictures, the baby's heartbeat, the baby's movements. "I had a doctor's appointment September 13," Dena said. "He switched his schedule to work September 11 and not miss it."

After September 11, Dena stopped eating, stopped sleeping, but was surrounded by friends and family who forced her to drink lots of liquids and escorted her to biweekly doctor's appointments. She stuck to all the details she and Stanley had talked about. Alexa Faith if it was a girl. Nicholas Steven for a boy. Teddy bears decorating the nursery room. Baby Looney Tunes for the baby's playroom. "The fact that I was carrying the baby is what really kept me going," Dena said.

Raising their baby without him won't be easy. She'll feel his absence with every "first" she can't share with him, all those things he looked forward to. Giving her baths. Feeding her. Videotaping her first steps.

"I would have nothing but memories," she said, looking down at the baby. "Now, I have a life."

KIP TAYLOR
A Blessing That Once Seemed Impossible

The joys and trials of new fatherhood were on Kip Taylor's mind. At 8:26 a.m., he e-mailed friends from his office in the Pentagon about how his life had changed since the birth of his son, Dean, almost two years earlier. He was happily anticipating the birth of his second son in a month.

"After kids, there are days that just get going when you say, 'Hi honey, I'm home,'" wrote the Army major. "My conclusion is that what we do until that moment pales in comparison to what we do after that point in the day."

Forty-one minutes later, Taylor was killed when American Airlines Flight 77 hit the Pentagon.

"We were very happy, about as happy as we had ever been in our married life," said his wife, Nancy. "I guess it's better to be taken when you're happy than when you're not. But it doesn't make it any easier."

The Taylors were happy because they had achieved something that had earlier seemed impossible. After their attempts to conceive had failed, the couple turned to medical science to help them have children. Dean was the result of a successful in vitro fertilization, as was Luke, the baby born to Nancy on October 25, 2001.

That she has Taylor's babies is a great source of comfort, Nancy said. "I can't imagine if I had gone through the IVF two times and it had not been successful, and then lost my husband."

So, when her husband's friends and admirers started asking where they could donate money in his memory, the answer seemed obvious. Nancy started a charity for infertile military couples and called it the Kip P. Taylor Fund. There are only two military treatment facilities worldwide where in vitro fertilizations are performed, one in Washington, D.C., and one in Texas, Nancy explained, making it difficult for military couples stationed abroad or elsewhere in the country to receive the subsidized treatment.

The fund will help couples offset the cost of traveling to the clinics and paying for lodging and food. Its Web site, www.kiptaylorfund.com, estimates that couples pay up to $5,100 out of pocket for their treatments. Donations from family, friends and neighbors have brought the fund to $40,000 to date.

"It's a lot," said Nancy. "But it's not enough to sustain this."

Having children is a challenge for military couples, Nancy acknowledged, what with being stationed in various places, long absences and the combat service. But, she said, children play just as important a role in military families as they do in any other community. "The military community does really rally around its children," she said.

To Taylor, balancing his work with a home life was essential. Though the 6-foot, 5-inch major cut an imposing figure in uniform, he was just as happy in jeans, cooking on his outdoor grill, building a deck on the couple's McLean, Virginia, home, or tending the lawn. But most of all, Nancy said, he loved fatherhood and couldn't wait to coach his sons' Little League teams and attend their music recitals.

Without him, Nancy said, she tries to enjoy the "blessing" of her sons. But it's hard. She has not yet felt ready to return to her job as the editor of a medical newsletter.

"At first I was getting by hour to hour," she said. "Then it was day to day. Now it's week to week. I hope someday it will be month to month. But it will be a while."

MOHAMMAD CHOWDHURY
A New Star Is Born

For months, Mohammad Sallahuddin Chowdhury had prayed five times a day for a son, his wife said. The two already had a 6-year-old daughter, Fahina, and felt a son would complete their family.

Farqad Chowdhury was born on September 13, but the father who wished so fervently for him was not at the hospital. Mohammad Chowdhury was lost in the terrorist attacks of September 11. He was last seen by his wife, Baraheen Ashrafi, that morning at 5, when the two sat down for their morning prayer. Although Chowdhury and his wife never discussed the specifics of their prayers, Ashrafi said her husband had said that he prayed for "good health for himself and his family, and for a son." Chowdhury skipped breakfast that morning and left his Woodside home for work at Windows on the World, where he was a banquet server.

Born in Bangladesh, Chowdhury came to New York in 1988. Ashrafi said her 38-year-old husband believed in the spirit of New York City and could never see himself living elsewhere. "He said he liked New York because it never sleeps." The couple moved to Baltimore in 1994 at the insistence of Ashrafi, who was overwhelmed by the hustle and bustle of the streets of New York City. Three years later, they returned to New York City and moved to Woodside. Ashrafi said the serenity of Baltimore didn't appeal to her husband.

She said her husband embraced many American ideals, such as freedom of expression, and the opportunities that were available. "He loved to be an American," Ashrafi said of her husband, who became a citizen in 1997. "He loved the right of expression that America provided for him. He loved the freedom."

For the most part, Ashrafi is thankful for the support she has felt in this country since she lost her husband. But there have been painful incidents, too. Like the time she was yelled at by a group of girls on her way to the doctor's office in Manhattan. "They were saying, 'Let's go for jihad,' because my head was covered." Ashrafi's 6-year-old was with her at the time. "She didn't realize what they were saying. I don't want her to grow up with racial problems. I want them to grow up in a broad-minded way."

Now, whenever Ashrafi looks at the deep brown eyes of her son, whose name means "star," she sees her husband's face. "I see him everywhere," she said. "Inside my heart, I talk to him every single moment."

JONATHAN RYAN
They're Collecting Memories of Dad

Colin Jonathan Ryan was born in the early evening of October 2, 2001. He will go through life having never met his father, but family and friends will make sure that Colin and his 3-year-old sister, Autumn, know about the life he lived.

Their father, Jon Ryan, died during the attack on the World Trade Center. Ryan, 32, the youngest of four brothers from New Hyde Park, was captain of the lacrosse team at SUNY Stony Brook and graduated cum laude with a degree in economics in 1990. He worked at Eurobrokers, on the 84th floor of Tower Two, for five years.

"He enjoyed every minute of life," said his brother Scott, 37. "He got the most out of each day. He was looking forward to being a father again. He was so proud that he was having a son."

Ryan left a previous brokerage to work as a corporate bond broker with Tony Cabrera, a teammate at Stony Brook. They worked on the emerging-markets desk and often capped a day's work by playing in recreational lacrosse leagues.

Ryan and Cabrera saw the explosion in Tower One and planned to leave. According to Cabrera, when they learned a plane had crashed into the building, "We thought it was an accident, we thought we were safe." But the sight of people jumping from Tower One changed Cabrera's mind.

"I had seen enough," he said. "The smoke was thick and the flames were out of control."

"I yelled, 'We have to get out of here!' I thought J.R. was right behind me. I saw him standing at his desk, his bag was packed."

The following weeks were filled with agony and joy for Ryan's wife, Maria. On September 21 she celebrated Autumn's third birthday, and 11 days later she gave birth to Colin. "Everything didn't hit me until I came home from the hospital with Colin," Maria said. "It was definitely bittersweet. When I came home, the reality set in. But I got through it for Jon."

The Ryans live in Bayville and rented a home in the summer on Fire Island. "He loved the beach," said another brother, James, 35. "At night, he would just sometimes sit on the beach and have a cigar by himself. He loved the peacefulness of it."

His brothers, Scott, James and Michael, as well as other family members, have been soliciting e-mails and letters from friends detailing stories about Ryan that they can pass along to his children. "I want them to be proud," Maria said. "I want them to realize how much I loved him and how much he loved them. I'd want them not to be afraid to say, 'This is my dad, and this is what happened to him.' He set goals and he achieved them. He never did anything halfway. He always had to do his best with everything. That's what keeps me going."

NOELL MAERZ
A Son's Face in a Granddaughter's Eyes

The loss of his son in the World Trade Center was still raw seven weeks later when Ralph Maerz first saw his newborn granddaughter.

"Funny how things come back to you," he said. "When she opened her eyes and looked at me, the first thing I saw was Noell, his little face as a baby. God took my son, but he left me with a granddaughter. He didn't just take and leave a gap, he took and left me something in return."

Noell Maerz's only child was born on Halloween and named, to honor her father, Noelle Briana Maerz. A bond broker with Eurobrokers, a firm on the 84th floor of the south tower, Maerz's last communication with his family was a 9 a.m. phone call to his brother. "Erich, people are jumping out of the building. I don't know what to do," he said.

In the couple's home in Long Beach, Maerz's wife, Jennifer, was eight months pregnant and pacing the floor with worry. As the hours turned into days, she held out hope that her husband, a triathlete and former football star at Lansdale Catholic High School, had found a way to survive. She delivered Noelle—a healthy 8 pounds and 10 ounces—without complication. Her mother took her husband's place in the delivery room.

Ralph Maerz has started a hope chest for Noelle, filling it with letters from family and friends about her father and memorabilia such as Noell Maerz's

football shoes and the model Jeeps he played with as a child. "She'll never meet her dad," Ralph Maerz said. "But she'll know everything she needs to know about him."

CALVIN GOODING
A Chattering 7-Pound Comfort

Calvin J. Gooding was mesmerized by the photograph on the barbershop wall of the beautiful Broadway and TV actress LaChanze, and used to beg the barber to introduce him. The barber refused, but one night Gooding spotted the actress at a nightclub in Manhattan and made his move. Two years later, in August 1998, he and the *Ragtime* star were married.

On September 11, at about 5 a.m., he kissed her goodbye while she lay in bed in their apartment in Riverdale, nearly eight months pregnant with their second child. By 6 a.m., he was in his office near the top of Tower One in the World Trade Center, checking on the stock exchanges in Europe for his financial securities firm, Cantor Fitzgerald. Nearly three hours later, the first airplane struck the tower. Gooding couldn't even call his wife. He had left his cell phone at home, something the punctilious executive almost never did.

On October 23, LaChanze gave birth to a 7-pound, 6-ounce daughter, Zaya Gooding. The baby chatters happily away, as her father did when he was an infant, said Gooding's mother, Marjorie Gooding, of the Springfield Gardens section of Queens.

"It's sad that she never got to know her dad, but she's certainly been a comfort," she said. "While it can never compensate for such a terrible loss, it certainly enlivens our hearts. Seeing the new baby, to me it signifies new life versus the taking of a life."

Still, there is no answer to give when 2-year-old Celia asks, "Daddy, where are you?"

"That's the most heart-wrenching thing, I think," said Marjorie.

Gooding's father, Calvin R. Gooding, said his 38-year-old son was all a father could ask for. The younger Gooding grew up in Queens and attended Packer Collegiate Institute in Brooklyn, where he was a top student and a basketball star who made the all-city team for private schools. He went to Haverford College, where he also played basketball and graduated with a bachelor's degree in political science. In the early 1990s, he joined Cantor Fitzgerald and handled its international desk. He was still in charge of that desk at the time of the disaster, and was a partner in the firm.

Even as he climbed the ladder on Wall Street, Gooding kept his roots in the old neighborhood, his father said. Every August, he would organize a basketball camp in Springfield Gardens that would bring back former residents who had moved all over the country. Each year, Gooding awarded a $1,500 scholarship out of his own pocket to a promising neighborhood youngster.

Something Edward Cardinal Egan said in a ceremony at Ground Zero resonated for the family. "He mentioned in his talk 'God, we have no more tears,'" Marjorie Gooding said.

"I know what he meant. But we cry daily."

DONALD GAVAGAN JR.
He Lives On in This Miracle

Six weeks after Donald Gavagan Jr. died in the World Trade Center, his wife, Jacqueline, gave birth to their third child, Connor Liam. Connor's arrival brought some comfort to a family that feared for the health of Connor's older brother, Donald III, just a few months ago, and now must go on without the boys' father.

A bond broker for Cantor Fitzgerald, Gavagan, 35, was on the 104th floor of Tower One on September 11. Gavagan had recently received a new three-year contract, his wife said, and they decided to celebrate by renovating their home in Bay Ridge. "I feel so bad because he will never get a chance to enjoy it," his wife said.

Born and raised in Brooklyn, Donald served in the Navy and attended Long Island University. He met Jacqueline in March 1993 when they were introduced by a mutual friend, but it wasn't exactly love at first sight. "I actually didn't like him when I met him," Jacqueline said. "I thought she was crazy for introducing us." They met again four months later and "something just happened," Jacqueline recalled. "I just liked the way he ordered a bottle of wine."

They were married on October 14, 1995. After struggling to have children, Jacqueline gave birth to twins, Lara and Donald, now 2 years old. "We really and truly were so happy when we had our children," she said. But there were anxious moments. In March, their son had open-heart surgery. At the time, the family could hardly imagine a greater heartache. "It was an incredibly difficult time for Jacqueline and Donald, and they felt it was the hardest thing they would ever have to go through," said Dorothy Vaudo, Jacqueline's aunt.

The Gavagans have a second home in Montauk, where Donald kept his 1969 Chrysler and enjoyed riding a Jeep on the beach. A staunch Republican, he loved politics, fishing and boats—as well as golf, dining and entertaining at the Montauk house. "Anybody who knew Donald would say they learned something," his wife said. "That's how smart he was."

Connor's arrival at New York University Medical Center was greeted by a full complement of family members eager to find some joy after six weeks of hardship.

"Of course, there were tears of sadness that Connor will never know his wonderful daddy, but there were also tears of joy witnessing the miracle of this birth," Vaudo said. "He weighed 8 pounds, 13 ounces, and he looks like his daddy."

BRIAN TERRENZI
"I Have Part of Him Forever"

They were young and studying abroad for the first time. Rome was beautiful in the early fall. And they were in love.

The beginning of Brian and Jane Terrenzi's relationship in 1994 seemed almost too romantic to be true. "I told my mother," said Jane, 28. "I called her and said, 'I found my future husband.' And she said, 'OK. We'll see.'"

But four years later, the Terrenzis were indeed married. On the morning of September 11, they were expecting their first child, and their romance was still as fresh as when they explored Rome together seven years ago.

"I remember what he was wearing," Jane said. "Khaki pants and a Ralph Lauren golf shirt. I didn't always notice, but because he looked very handsome, I told him he did. And he told me he loved me, and I told him I loved him, too."

Then Brian Terrenzi, 28, left for work, on the 101st floor of the World Trade Center's Tower One.

A global network manager at Cantor Fitzgerald, he was one of about 700 lost from that company's offices in the terrorist attack that day.

His daughter, Elizabeth Brian Terrenzi, was born on December 9.

"She has a cleft chin like my husband did, and she has his nose, too," Jane said. "There's a lot of comfort in having his child. I have a part of him forever. I thank God for her every day. She makes me smile all the time, and she makes me laugh. She gives me hope for a better future."

That Brian at least knew he was to have a daughter is also some small consolation, Jane said. "He was just so excited," she said. "He wanted her to be daddy's little girl. She would have been, because he would have given her so much attention and love. Because that's what he did with me. He made me so happy," she added.

"My husband is different from a lot of men, I think," she added. For example, when she was sorting some of his files recently, she found one marked "Jane." "It was just cards that I made over the years, or any little note that I wrote, that might have said 'I love you' or something, he kept it. I don't think most men would do something like that."

It was especially painful to lose Brian at a time when everything seemed to be going so well for the couple. They had just bought a house in Hicksville, and Brian loved his job at Cantor Fitzgerald, which he started in February 2001. His wife said she likes to remember him as he was at a cookout at her mother's house a week before the attack. "He was always the one to barbecue the food," she said. "He was playing with my mom and my brother in the pool. They were playing volleyball and laughing."

Five months after her loss, Jane was allowing some joy back in her life. "I've always wanted to be a mother," she said, "so that wasn't taken away from me. I have our future to look forward to. And I'm not alone because I have my daughter."

A Faith Stronger Than Evil

JIMMY BRESLIN

Richard Allen

"How old?" the mother was asked.

"One month." She looked down at the pink bundle in her arms.

"This makes her first funeral," I said to the mother.

"I hope it's the last of these," she said.

She was standing inside the entrance to the packed St. Francis de Sales church in Belle Harbor. Through the doors and over the heads of the people standing, you could see the priests saying mass for firefighter Richard Allen.

The mother said the baby's name was Anna and that she was Connie Hickey. The father is Robert Hickey, a firefighter.

There was a much older man standing alongside her and he was looking down and shaking his head.

"I am trying to contemplate something that I no longer understand," he was saying. "Why do all these young people have to die? And die horribly, apparently. I usually don't question the religion, but there have been so many of these, all I see is notices for funerals for these young people, that I wonder why it has to be. Where is the justice?"

"I'm having the same trouble," I said. "One too many funerals or memorials or whatever you call them, and you start asking things that you never did before."

"You just have to have faith," the mother, Connie Hickey, said.

"Yes, but how do you explain people so young dying so horribly?" I said. "What's that about? What about inside here? Then there was a woman waiting for a bus outside the buildings and burning jet fuel came out of the sky on her. How do you explain God's mercy then?"

"Faith," Connie Hickey said.

"Does that answer for all these innocent people suffering and dying? What is that about?"

"It just makes your faith stronger," she said.

"How many Catholic schools did you go to for that?" I asked.

"None. I went to public schools. I believe that."

Usually, when I went into one of these moods of asking out loud—"If God is so great, why does he let a young guy get burned to death and leave children?"—I called my friend, Father Mychal Judge at St. Francis of Assisi church on West 31st Street. On September 11, when I was going down to the World Trade Center, I called him at the rectory and got his answering tape. I left a message asking him to call my house and leave a place where I could find him, and maybe we could say a prayer. I got there just in time for Tower Two to come down and kill thousands, including Father Judge.

I don't know when it was, days later, that my friend Norman Ochs called to tell me that Richie Allen was missing. He was the oldest son of Gail McGuire Allen. I know her family. Right away, Gail told me that she had registered with the medical examiner's office and then went to the pier that handles the missing persons and the fire department. "We're doing everything so they can find him," she said. "We have faith."

Her brother, Bobby, a firefighter, was at The Dig, as the workers call the former World Trade Center. He was going through rubble with his hands, looking for her oldest son, his nephew.

Every time I called her, she said, "We don't give up. We have faith."

One day Bobby changed from speaking of finding Richie Allen alive to finding his body so his mother could have "closure."

It is the common word of the times, and after digging for Richie Allen every day since September 11, he can say what he wants, but I writhe at the word *closure*. It is a fraud perpetrated by those whose hands touch nothing that is not at least a thousand miles from reality. No mother closes the feelings, as if a dresser drawer, on the sorrow and images of her oldest child suddenly dead.

But people use such words—and *faith* particularly—to get through the long, numbing days.

When there was no hope, the memorial was scheduled. The faces were those of Rockaway Beach through the decades. The talks by Richie Allen's friends were about beach life, surfing and lifeguards. "I sat on 36th Street, he sat on 38th. We always went in on saves together."

The difference was in the voice of a young woman, Judy, the sister. She stood up in the brand-new tradition of women speaking at funerals and she was pure thrilling Irish as she talked of her brother running up the staircase of the World Trade Center, lifted by the thought of saving.

Anna Hickey, age 1 month, was still in the entranceway in her mother's arms. She had gone through her first funeral from start to finish, gone through it sleeping in the arms of her mother, sleeping softly in the faith that her mother would keep her safe. And the mother holding her looked to the altar in faith that the horror of the young death had made only stronger.

Jimmy Breslin is a columnist for Newsday.

The List of the Lost

ABOUT THIS LIST

The following pages contain the names of the missing and deceased victims of the September 11 terrorist attacks. The names were obtained from airline manifests, the New York State Supreme Court, the New York City Medical Examiner's Office, the Associated Press, the Department of Defense, articles and death notices in area newspapers and World Trade Center company Web sites. At the time of this printing, New York City had not released an official list. So you may notice possible duplications or variations in the spelling of a name. Because of the evolving nature of this information, any changes and updates can be found online at http://www.newsday.com/911memorial.

WORLD TRADE CENTER OCCUPANTS

Gordon McCannel Aamoth, 32, New York, NY
Investment banker, Sandler O'Neill & Partners
Edelmiro Abad, 54, Brooklyn, NY
Banker/financial adviser, Fiduciary Trust Company International
Maria Rose Abad, 49, Syosset, NY
Investment banker, Keefe Bruyette & Woods
Andrew Anthony Abate, 37, Melville, NY
Investor, Cantor Fitzgerald
Vincent Abate, 40, Brooklyn, NY
Investor, Cantor Fitzgerald
Laurence Abel
Cantor Fitzgerald
William F. Abrahamson, 58, Cortland Manor, NY
Information technology specialist, Marsh & McLennan
Richard Anthony Aceto, 42, Wantagh, NY
Insurance brokerage, Marsh & McLennan
Heinrich B. Ackermann, 38, Manhattan, NY
Insurance brokerage, Aon Corp.
Paul Andrew Acquaviva, 29, Glen Rock, NJ
Corporate development, Cantor Fitzgerald
Donald Leroy Adams, 28, Chatham, NJ
Brokerage, Cantor Fitzgerald
Patrick Adams, 61, Brooklyn, NY
Security officer, Fuji Bank
Shannon Lewis Adams, 25, Long Island City, NY
Accountant, Cantor Fitzgerald
Stephen George Adams, 51, Manhattan, NY
Beverage management, Windows on the World
Ignatius Adanga, 62, Bronx, NY
Transportation, NY State Department of Transportation
Christy A. Addamo, 28, New Hyde Park, NY
Accountant, Marsh & McLennan
Terence E. Adderley Jr., 22, Bloomfield Hills, MI
Investment banking, Fred Alger Management
Sophia Buruwa Addo, 36, Bronx, NY
Housekeeper, Windows on the World
Lee Adler, 48, Springfield, NJ
Computer programming, Cantor Fitzgerald
Daniel Thomas Afflitto, 32, Manalapan, NJ
Brokerage, Cantor Fitzgerald
Emmanuel Afuakwah, 37, Bronx, NY
Alok Agarwal, 36, Kendall Park, NJ
Programmer, Cantor Fitzgerald
Mukul Agarwala, 37, Manhattan, NY
Researcher, Fiduciary Trust Company International

David S. Agnes, 46, New York, NY
Brokerage, Cantor Fitzgerald
Joao A.D. Aguiar Jr., 30, Red Bank, NJ
Investment banking, Keefe Bruyette & Woods
Jeremiah J. Ahern, 74, Cliffside Park, NJ
Auditor, New York State Department of Taxation & Finance
Joanne Ahladiotis, 27, Forest Hills, NY
Computer systems analyst, Cantor Fitzgerald
Shabbir Ahmed, 45, Brooklyn, NY
Waiter, Windows on the World
Terrance Andre Aiken, 30, Staten Island, NY
Computer consultant, Vital Computer Services/Marsh & McLennan
Godwin Ajala, 33, Jamaica, NY
Security officer, Summit Security Services
Nana Akwasi-Mienkah, New York, NY
Windows on the World
Gertrude Trudi M. Alagero, 37, Manhattan, NY
Client services, Marsh & McLennan
Andrew Alameno, 37, Westfield, NJ
Brokerage, Cantor Fitzgerald
Manuel A. Alarcon, Medford, NJ
Margaret Ann Jezycki "Peggy" Alario, 41, Staten Island, NY
Global products management, Zurich American
Gary Albero, 39, Emerson, NJ
Insurance brokerage, Aon Corp.
Jon L. Albert, 46, Upper Nyack, NY
Information technology, Marsh & McLennan
Peter Craig Alderman, 25, New York, NY
Financial service, Bloomberg LP
Jacquelyn Delaine Aldridge, 46, Staten Island, NY
Financial adviser, Marsh & McLennan
Grace Alegre-Cua, 40, Glen Rock, NJ
Accountant, Mitsui Bank of Japan
David Dewey Alger, 57, Manhattan, NY
Investor, Fred Alger Management
Boutros al-Hashim, 41
Ernest Alikakos, 43, Brooklyn, NY
New York State Department of Taxation & Finance
Edward L. Allegretto, 51, Colonia, NJ
Brokerage, Cantor Fitzgerald
Joseph Ryan Allen, 39, Manhattan, NY
Brokerage, Cantor Fitzgerald
Richard Allen, 30, Brooklyn, NY
Mail clerk, Marsh & McLennan

Christopher Edward Allingham, 36, River Edge, NJ
Brokerage, Cantor Fitzgerald
Janet M. Alonso, 41, Stony Point, NY
E-mail analyst, Marsh & McLennan
Anthony Alvarado, 31, Bronx, NY
Food service worker, Forte Food Service
Antonio Javier Alvarez, 23, Jackson Heights, NY
Grill cook, Windows on the World
Telmo Alvear, 25, Jackson Heights, NY
Waiter, Windows on the World
Cesar A. Alviar, 60, Bloomfield, NJ
Accountant, Marsh & McLennan
Tariq Amanullah, 40, Metuchen, NJ
Computer information technology, Fiduciary Trust Company International
Angelo Amaranto, 60, Brooklyn, NY
Janitor, ABM Industries
Joseph Amatuccio, 41, Ozone Park, NY
Maintenance supervisor, Port Authority of New York & New Jersey
Kazuhiro Anai, 42, Scarsdale, NY
Banker, The Nishi-Nippon Bank Ltd.
Jorge Octavio Santos Anaya, Aguascaliente, Mexico
Joseph Peter Anchundia, 26, Manhattan, NY
Investment banker, Sandler O'Neill & Partners
Kermit Charles Anderson, 57, Green Brook, NJ
Information technology, Marsh & McLennan
Yvette C. Anderson, 53, New York, NY
Keyboard specialist, New York State Department of Taxation & Finance
John Andreacchio, 52, New York, NY
Human resources, Fuji Bank
Michael Rourke Andrews, 34, Belle Harbor, NY
Brokerage, financial services, Cantor Fitzgerald
Jean Ann Andrucki, 42, Hoboken, NJ
Risk management, Port Authority of New York & New Jersey
Siew Nya Ang, 37, East Brunswick, NJ
Technical analyst, Marsh & McLennan
Laura Angilletta, 23, Staten Island, NY
Purchase and sales clerk, Cantor Fitzgerald
Doreen J. Angrisani, 44, Ridgewood, NY
Finance, Marsh & McLennan
Lorraine Del Carmen Antigua, 32, Middletown, NJ
Brokerage, Cantor Fitzgerald
Peter Paul Apollo, 26, Waretown, NJ
Brokerage, Cantor Fitzgerald
Frank Thomas "F.T." Aquilino, 26, Staten Island, NY
Brokerage, Cantor Fitzgerald
Patrick Michael Aranyos, 26, Manhattan, NY
Brokerage, EuroBrokers Inc.
Michael G. Arczynski, 45, Little Silver, NJ
Risk management, Aon Corp.
Adam P. Arias, 37, Staten Island, NY
Investor, EuroBrokers Inc.
Michael Joseph Armstrong, 34, Manhattan, NY
Investor, Cantor Fitzgerald
Jack Charles Aron, 52, Bergenfield, NJ
Information technology, Marsh & McLennan
Joshua Todd Aron, 29, New York, NY
Brokerage, Cantor Fitzgerald
Richard Avery Aronow, 48, Mahwah, NJ
Lawyer, Port Authority of New York & New Jersey
Japhet J. Aryee, 49, Spring Valley, NY
Tax auditor, New York State Department of Taxation & Finance
Michael A. Asciak, 47, Ridgefield, NJ
Investment banking, Carr Futures
Michael Edward Asher, 53, Monroe, NY
Computer software development, Cantor Fitzgerald
Janice M. Ashley, 25, Rockville Centre, NY
Researcher, Fred Alger Management
Thomas J. Ashton, 21, Woodside, NY
Student (apprentice electrician), World Trade Center

Manuel O. Asitimbay, 36, New York, NY
Cook, Windows on the World
James Audiffred, 38, Starret City, NY
Elevator operator, ABM Industries
Frank Louis Aversano Jr., 58, Manalapan, NJ
Insurance brokerage, Aon Corp.
Ezra Aviles, 41, Commack, NY
Geologist, Port Authority of New York & New Jersey
Samuel Sandy Ayala, 36, New York, NY
Banquet arranger, Windows on the World
Arlene T. Babakitis, 47, Secaucus, NJ
Secretary, Port Authority of New York & New Jersey
Eustace Rudy Bacchus, 48, Metuchen, NJ
Brokerage, self-employed
John James Badagliacca, 35, Staten Island, NY
Brokerage, Cantor Fitzgerald
Jane Ellen Baeszler, 43, Staten Island, NY
Brokerage, Cantor Fitzgerald
Robert John Baierwalter, 44, Albertson, NY
Insurance, F.M. Global
Andrew J. Bailey, 29, Queens, NY
Marsh & McLennan
Brett T. Bailey, 28, Bricktown, NJ
Brokerage, EuroBrokers Inc.
Tatyana Bakalinskaya, 43, Brooklyn, NY
Insurance, Marsh & McLennan
Michael S. Baksh, 36, Englewood, NJ
Insurance, Marsh & McLennan
Julio Minto Balanca
Sharon Balkcom, 43, White Plains, NY
Information technology, Marsh & McLennan
Michael Andrew Bane, 33, Yardley, PA
Insurance, Marsh & McLennan
Kathy Bantis, 44, Chicago, IL
Insurance, Marsh & McLennan
Walter Baran, 42, Staten Island, NY
Finance, Fiduciary Trust Company International
Paul V. Barbaro, 35, Holmdel, NJ
Engineering, Cantor Fitzgerald
James W. Barbella, 53, Oceanside, NY
Maintenance, Port Authority of New York & New Jersey
Ivan Kiryllos Fairbanks Barbosa, 30, Jersey City, NJ
Cantor Fitzgerald
Victor Daniel Barbosa, 23, Bronx, NY
Maintenance worker, Windows on the World
Colleen Ann (Meehan) Barkow, 26, East Windsor, NJ
Brokerage, financial services, Cantor Fitzgerald
David Michael Barkway, 34, Toronto, Ontario, Canada
Finance, BMO Nesbitt Burns of Toronto
Sheila Patricia Barnes, 55, Bay Shore, NY
Aon Corp.
Evan J. Baron, 38, Bridgewater, NJ
Finance, Carr Futures
Renee Barrett-Arjune, 41
Accountant, Cantor Fitzgerald
Diane G. Barry, 60, Staten Island, NY
Administrative assistant, Aon Corp.
Scott D. Bart, 28, Malverne, NY
Risk-management technology, Marsh & McLennan
Carlton W. Bartels, 44, Staten Island, NY
Brokerage, Cantor Fitzgerald
Guy Barzvi, 29, Queens, NY
Computer science, Cantor Fitzgerald
Inna Basina, 43, Brooklyn, NY
Finance, Cantor Fitzgerald
Alysia Basmajian, 23, Bayonne, NJ
Accounting, Cantor Fitzgerald
Kenneth William Basnicki, 47, Etobicoke, Ontario, Canada
Finance, BEA Systems Inc.
Paul James Battaglia, 22, Brooklyn, NY
Consulting, Marsh & McLennan
W. David Bauer, 45, Rumson, NJ
Sales, Cantor Fitzgerald

Ivhan Luis Carpio Bautista, 24, Ozone Park, NY
Restaurant worker, Windows on the World
Marlyn C. Bautista, 46, Iselin, NJ
Accountant, Marsh & McLennan
Jasper Baxter, 45, Philadelphia, PA
Career consultant, Lee Hecht Harrison
Michelle Beale, 37, Essex, Britain
Conference directing, Risk Waters Group
Paul F. Beatini, 40, Park Ridge, NJ
Engineer, F.M. Global
Jane S. Beatty, 53, Belford, NJ
Insurance, Marsh & McLennan
Lawrence I. Beck, 38, Baldwin, NY
Cantor Fitzgerald
Manette Marie Beckles, 43, Rahway, NJ
Michael E. Beekman, 39, Staten Island, NY
Trade clerk, LaBranche
Maria Asuncion Behr, 41, Milford, NJ
Finance, Cantor Fitzgerald
Yelena Helen Belilovsky, 38, Mamaroneck, NY
Investor, Fred Alger Management
Nina Patrice Bell, 39, Manhattan, NY
Insurance, Marsh & McLennan
Andrea Della Bella, 59, Jersey City, NJ
Insurance, Aon Corp.
Debbie S. Bellows, 30, East Windsor, NJ
Cantor Fitzgerald
Paul Michael Benedetti, 32, Queens, NY
Aon Corp.
Denise Lenore Benedetto, 40, Staten Island, NY
Aon Corp.
Bryan Craig Bennett, 25, Manhattan, NY
Salesman, Cantor Fitzgerald
Eric L. Bennett, 29, Brooklyn, NY
Alliance Consulting Group
Oliver Duncan Bennett, 29, Manhattan, NY
Journalist, Risk Waters Group
Margaret L. Benson, 52, Rockaway, NJ
Human resources, Port Authority of New York & New Jersey
Dominick J. Berardi, 25, Whitestone, NY
Finance, Cantor Fitzgerald
James Patrick Berger, 44, Lower Makefield, PA
Insurance, Aon Corp.
Steven Howard Berger, 45, Manalapan, NJ
Government/finance, New York State Department of Taxation
& Finance
Alvin Bergsohn, 48, Baldwin Harbor, NY
Finance, Cantor Fitzgerald
Daniel D. Bergstein, 38, Teaneck, NJ
Government, Port Authority of New York & New Jersey
Michael Berkeley, 38, Manhattan, NY
Finance, Berkeley Group
Donna Bernaerts-Kearns, 44, Hoboken, NJ
Computer programming, Accenture
Dave Bernard, 57, Chelmsford, MA
IRS
William H. "Bill" Bernstein, 44, Brooklyn, NY
Brokerage, Cantor Fitzgerald
David M. Berray, 39, Manhattan, NY
Finance, MoneyLine
David S. Berry, 43, Park Slope, NY
Keefe Bruyette & Woods
Joseph J. Berry, 55, Saddle River, NJ
Investment banking, Keefe Bruyette & Woods
William Reed Bethke, 36, Hamilton, NJ
Computer programming, Marsh & McLennan
Timothy D. Betterly, 42, Little Silver, NJ
Brokerage, Cantor Fitzgerald
Edward F. Beyea, 42, Manhattan, NY
Systems analyst, Empire Blue Cross/Blue Shield
Anil T. Bharvaney, 41, East Windsor, NJ
Media, Instinet (Reuters)

Bella Bhukan, 23, Union, NJ
Finance, Cantor Fitzgerald
Shimmy David Biegeleisen, 42, Brooklyn, NY
Finance, Fiduciary Trust Company International
William Biggart, 54, New York, NY
Freelance photojournalist, Impact Visuals Photo Agency
Ralph Bijoux
Gary Bird, 51, Tempe, AZ
Insurance, Marsh & McLennan
Joshua David Birnbaum, 24, Manhattan, NY
Trader, Cantor Fitzgerald
George John Bishop, 52, Granite Springs, NY
Insurance, Aon Corp.
Jeffrey D. Bittner, 27, Manhattan, NY
Keefe Bruyette & Woods
Balewa Albert Blackman, 26, Brooklyn, NY
Accountant, Cantor Fitzgerald
Susan L. Blair, 35, East Brunswick, NJ
Business administration, Aon Corp.
Harry Blanding Jr., 38, Blakeslee, PA
Insurance, Aon Corp.
Janice L. Blaney, 55, Williston Park, NY
Insurance, Marsh & McLennan
Craig Michael Blass, 27, Greenlawn, NY
Trader, Cantor Fitzgerald
Rita Blau, 52, Brooklyn, NY
Operator, Fiduciary Trust Company International
Richard M. Blood, 38, Ridgewood, NJ
Insurance brokerage, Aon Corp.
Michael Andrew Boccardi, 30, Bronxville, NY
Investment adviser, Fred Alger Management
John Paul Bocchi, 38, New Vernon, NJ
Brokerage, Cantor Fitzgerald
Susan Mary Bochino, 36, Staten Island, NY
Marketing, Aon Corp.
Bruce Douglas Boehm, 49, West Hempstead, NY
Brokerage, Cantor Fitzgerald
Mary Katherine Boffa, 45, Staten Island, NY
Insurance, Marsh & McLennan
Nicholas A. Bogdan, 34, Browns Mills, NJ
Information technology, Marsh & McLennan
Darren C. Bohan, 34, Queens, NY
Accountant, Aon Corp.
Lawrence Francis Boisseau, 36, Freehold, NJ
Port Authority of New York & New Jersey
Vincent M. Boland Jr., 25, Ringwood, NJ
Business analyst, Marsh & McLennan
Alan Bondarenko, 53, Flemington, NJ
Engineering/construction, Washington Group International
Andre Bonheur Jr., 40, Brooklyn, NY
Finance, Citigroup Inc.
Colin Arthur Bonnett, 39, Crown Heights, NY
Telecommunications technician, Marsh & McLennan
Yvonne L. Bonomo, 30, Jackson Heights, NY
Travel, American Express
Sean Booker, 35, Irvington, NJ
Xerox technician, Marsh & McLennan
Juan Jose Borda Leyva, 58, New York, NY
Self-employed
Sherry Ann Bordeaux, 38, Jersey City, NJ
Fiduciary Trust Company International
Krystine C. Bordenabe, 33, Old Bridge, NJ
Sales, Keefe Bruyette & Woods
Martin Boryczewski, 29, Parsippany, NJ
Insurance, Cantor Fitzgerald
Richard E. Bosco, 34, Suffern, NY
Citigroup Inc.
John Howard Boulton Jr., 29, New York, NY
Francisco E. Bourdier, 41, Jackson Heights, NY
Security officer, Deutsche Bank
Thomas H. Bowden Jr., 36, Wyckoff, NJ
Bond trader, Cantor Fitzgerald

Kimberly S. Bowers, 31, Islip, NY
Cantor Fitzgerald
Veronique Nicole Bowers, 28, Bronx, NY
Accountant, Windows on the World
Larry Bowman, 46, Brooklyn, NY
Security, Summit Security Services
Shawn Edward Bowman Jr., 28, Staten Island, NY
Personnel specialist, Cantor Fitzgerald
Kevin L. Bowser, 45, Philadelphia, PA
Software instructor, Marsh & McLennan
Gennady Boyarsky, 34, Far Rockaway, NY
Travel agent, American Express
Pamela Boyce, 43, Brooklyn, NY
Accountant, Carr Futures
Alfred J. Braca, 54, Leonardo, NJ
Bond trader, Cantor Fitzgerald
Sandra Conaty Brace, 60, Staten Island, NY
Administrative assistant, Risk Insurance Solutions
David Brian Brady, 41, Summit, NJ
Merrill Lynch
Alexander Braginsky, 38, Stamford, CT
Reuters
Nicholas W. Brandemarti, 21, West Deptford, NJ
Equity researcher, Keefe Bruyette & Woods
Michelle Renee Bratton, 23, Yonkers, NY
Executive assistant, Cantor Fitzgerald
Patrice Braut
Insurance, Marsh & McLennan
Lydia Estelle Bravo, 50, Dunellen, NJ
Insurance, Marsh & McLennan
Ronald Michael Breitweiser, 39, Middleton, NJ
Investments specialist, Fiduciary Trust Company
International
Edward A. "Ted" Brennan III, 37, Manhattan, NY
Finance, Cantor Fitzgerald
Frank H. Brennan, 50, Oak Beach, NY
Broker, Cantor Fitzgerald
Thomas M. Brennan, 32, Scarsdale, NY
Investment banking, Sandler O'Neill & Partners
Gary L. Bright, 36, Union City, NJ
Insurance, Aon Corp.
Jonathan Eric Briley, 43, Mount Vernon, NY
Technician, Windows on the World
Mark A. Brisman, 34, Armonk, NY
Lawyer, Harris Beach LLP
Paul Gary Bristow, 27, Brooklyn, NY
Finance, Risk Waters Group
Victoria Alvarez Brito, 38, Elmhurst, NY
Insurance, Marsh & McLennan
Mark Francis Broderick, 42, Old Bridge, NJ
Accountant, Cantor Fitzgerald
Herman Broghammer, 58, North Merrick, NY
Aon Corp.
Keith Broomfield, 49, Brooklyn, NY
Mechanical technician, Advent Corp.
Janice J. Brown, 35, Brooklyn, NY
Accountant, Marsh & McLennan
Lloyd Brown, 28, Bronxville, NY
Cantor Fitzgerald
Bettina Browne-Radburn, 49, Atlantic Beach, NY
Attorney, Aon Corp.
Mark Bruce, 40, Summit, NJ
Finance, Sandler O'Neill & Partners
Richard Bruehert, 38, Westbury, NY
Marsh & McLennan
Brandon J. Buchanan, 24, Manhattan, NY
Brokerage, Cantor Fitzgerald
Dennis Buckley, 38, Chatham, NJ
Brokerage, Cantor Fitzgerald
Nancy Bueche, 43, Hicksville, NY
Aon Corp.
Patrick Joseph Buhse, 36, Lincroft, NJ
Brokerage, Cantor Fitzgerald

John E. Bulaga Jr., 35, Haskell, NJ
Engineer, Cantor Fitzgerald
Stephen Bunin, 45
Finance, Cantor Fitzgerald
Matthew J. Burke, 28, Manhattan, NY
Trader, Cantor Fitzgerald
Thomas Daniel Burke, 38, Bedford Hills, NY
Bond trader, Cantor Fitzgerald
Kathleen A. Burns, 49, Staten Island, NY
Fiduciary Trust Company International
Keith James Burns, 39, East Rutherford, NJ
Finance, Cantor Fitzgerald
Irina Buslo, 32, Queens, NY
Milton Bustillo, 37, Staten Island, NY
Computer specialist, Cantor Fitzgerald
Timothy G. Byrne, 36, Manhattan, NY
Investment banking, Sandler O'Neill & Partners
Jesus N. Cabezas, 66, Brooklyn, NY
Cook, Windows on the World
Lillian Caceres, 48, Staten Island, NY
Technical analyst, Marsh & McLennan
Brian Joseph Cachia, 26, Fresh Meadows, NY
Cantor Fitzgerald
Steven Cafiero Jr., 31, Whitestone, NY
Client specialist, Aon Corp.
Richard M. Caggiano, 25, Brooklyn, NY
Cantor Fitzgerald
Cecile M. Caguicla, 55, Boonton, NJ
Accountant, Marsh & McLennan
Michael John Cahill, 37, East Williston, NY
Attorney, Marsh & McLennan
Scott Walter Cahill, 30, West Caldwell, NJ
Brokerage, Cantor Fitzgerald
Thomas J. Cahill, 36, Franklin Lakes, NJ
Trader, Cantor Fitzgerald
Joseph Calandrillo, 49, Hawley, PA
Insurance, Reinsurance Solutions Inc.
Philip V. Calcagno, 57, Staten Island, NY
Edward Calderon, 44, Jersey City, NJ
Operations manager, Port Authority of New York & New
Jersey
Kenneth Marcus Caldwell, 30, Brooklyn, NY
Sales, Alliance Consulting Group
Dominick E. Calia, 40, Manalapan, NJ
Brokerage, Cantor Fitzgerald
Bobby Calixte, 38, Springfield Gardens, NY
Air-conditioning maintenance, Bobby Calixte
Felix Calixte, 38, Brooklyn, NY
Luigi Gino Calvi, 34, East Rutherford, NJ
Brokerage, Cantor Fitzgerald
Roko Camaj, 60, Manhasset, NY
Maintenance personnel, ABM Industries
David Otey Campbell, 51, Basking Ridge, NJ
Brokerage, Keefe Bruyette & Woods
Geoffrey Thomas Campbell, 31, Manhattan, NY
Consulting, Reuters
Jill Marie Campbell, 31, Middle Village, NY
Administrative assistant, Baseline Financial Services
Robert Arthur Campbell, 25, Brooklyn, NY
Fine Painting and Decorating
Sandra Patricia Campbell, 45, Brooklyn, NY
Computer programmer, Cantor Fitzgerald
Juan Ortega Campos, 32, Brooklyn, NY
Food services worker
Sean T. Canavan, 39, Bay Ridge, NY
Carpenter, Installation Resources
John A. Candela, 42, Glen Ridge, NJ
Stock trader, Cantor Fitzgerald
Vincent Cangelosi, 30, Staten Island, NY
Stephen J. Cangialosi, 40, Middletown, NJ
Brokerage, Cantor Fitzgerald
Lisa B. Cannava, 30, Staten Island, NY
Finance, Carr Futures

Christopher Sean Canton, 34, Manhattan, NY
Michael R. Canty, 30, Schenectady, NY
Brokerage, Carr Futures
Louis A. Caporicci, 35, Staten Island, NY
Brokerage, Cantor Fitzgerald
Jonathan Neff Cappello, 23, Garden City, NY
Brokerage, Cantor Fitzgerald
James Christopher Cappers, 33, Wading River, NY
Brokerage, Marsh & McLennan
Richard M. Caproni, 34, Lynbrook, NY
Accountant, Marsh & McLennan
Jose Cardona, 35, Manhattan, NY
Finance, Carr Futures
Edward Carlino, 46, Brooklyn, NY
Finance, Marsh & McLennan
David G. Carlone, 46, Randolph, NJ
Account executive, FM Global
Rosemarie C. Carlson, 40, Brooklyn, NY
International Office Centers
Mark Stephen Carney, 41, Rahway, NJ
Recruiting, Association of Independent Recruiters
Joyce Ann Carpeneto, 40, Manhattan, NY
Client services, General Telecom
Alicia Acevedo Carranza, Teziutlan, Puebla, Mexico
Jeremy M. Carrington, 34, New York, NY
Finance, Cantor Fitzgerald
James J. Carson Jr., 32, Massapequa Park, NY
Engineer, Cantor Fitzgerald
Christopher Newton Carter, 52, Middletown, NJ
James Marcel Cartier, 26, Astoria, NY
Electrician, Aon Corp.
Joel Cartridge
Vivian Casalduc, 45, Brooklyn, NY
Insurance, Empire Blue Cross/Blue Shield
John F. Casazza, 38, Colts Neck, NJ
Finance, Cantor Fitzgerald
Paul Reegan Cascio, 23, Manhasset, NY
Finance, EuroBrokers Inc.
Margarito Casillas, Guadalajara, Jalisco, Mexico
William Otto Caspar, 57, Eatontown, NJ
Data-processing specialist, Marsh & McLennan
Alejandro Castano, 35, Edgewater, NJ
Delivery man, Empire Distribution
Arcelia Chela Castillo, 50, Elizabeth, NJ
Accountant, Marsh & McLennan
Leonard Castrianno, 30, New York, NY
Finance, Cantor Fitzgerald
Jose Ramon Castro, 37, Bronx, NY
Food service handler, Forte Food Service
Richard G. Catarelli, 47, Brooklyn, NY
Christopher Sean Caton, 34, Manhattan, NY
Finance, Cantor Fitzgerald
Robert J. Caufield, 49, Valley Stream, NY
Electrician, Denino Electric
Mary Teresa Caulfield, 58, Eastchester, NY
Judson Cavalier, 26, Huntington, NY
Investment banking, Sandler O'Neill & Partners
Jason David Cayne, 32, Morganville, NJ
Brokerage, Cantor Fitzgerald
Juan Armando Ceballos, 47, Queens, NY
Marcia G. Cecil-Carter, 34, Brooklyn, NY
Reconciliation clerk, Carr Futures
Jason Cefalu, 30, West Hempstead, NY
Brokerage, Cantor Fitzgerald
Thomas J. Celic, 43, Staten Island, NY
Business administration, Marsh & McLennan
Ana M. Centeno, 38, Bayonne, NJ
Accountant, Marsh & McLennan
Jeffrey M. Chairnoff, 35, Windsor, NJ
Mortgage financing, Sandler O'Neill & Partners
Swarna Chalasani, 33, Jersey City, NJ
Investment analyst, Fiduciary Trust Company International

William Chalcoff, 41, Roslyn, NY
Information technology, Marsh & McLennan
Eli Chalouh, 23, Brooklyn, NY
Government/finance, New York State Department of Taxation
& Finance
Charles Lawrence "Chip" Chan, 23, Manhattan, NY
Brokerage, Cantor Fitzgerald
Mandy Chang, 40, Manhattan, NY
Finance, First Commercial Bank
Mark L. Charette, 38, Millburn, NJ
Insurance brokerage, Marsh & McLennan
Gregorio Manuel Chavez, 48, Manhattan, NY
Restaurant worker, Windows on the World
Pedro Francisco Checo, 35, New York, NY
Finance, Fiduciary Trust Company International
Douglas MacMillan Cherry, 38, Maplewood, NJ
Insurance brokerage, Aon Corp.
Stephen Patrick Cherry, 41, Stamford, CT
Brokerage, Cantor Fitzgerald
Nestor Chevalier, 30, New York, NY
Finance, Cantor Fitzgerald
Swede Joseph Chevalier, 26, Locust, NJ
Brokerage, Cantor Fitzgerald
Alexander H. Chiang, 51, New York, NY
Information technology, Marsh & McLennan
Dorothy J. Chiarchiaro, 61, Glenwood, NY
File clerk, Fred Alger Management
Luis Alfonso Chimbo, 39, Corona, NY
Restaurant worker, Windows on the World
Robert Chin, 33, Brooklyn, NY
Account associate, Fiduciary Trust Company International
Wing Wai "Eddie" Ching, 29, Union, NJ
Finance, Cantor Fitzgerald
Peter A. Chirchirillo, 47, Langhorne, PA
Insurance, Marsh & McLennan
Catherine E. Chirls, 47, Princeton, NJ
Finance, Cantor Fitzgerald
Kyung Kaccy Cho, 30, Clifton, NJ
Insurance, Marsh & McLennan
Abdul K. Chowdhury, 30, New York, NY
Finance, Cantor Fitzgerald
Mohammad Salahuddin Chowdhury, 38, Woodside, NY
Restaurant worker, Windows on the World
Kirsten L. Christophe, 39, Maplewood, NJ
Attorney, Aon Corp.
Pamela Chu, 31, Manhattan, NY
Cantor Fitzgerald
Steven Paul Chucknick, 44, Cliffwood Beach, NJ
EuroBrokers Inc.
Wai-ching Chung, 36, New York, NY
Finance, UBS PaineWebber
Christopher Ciafardini, 30, Manhattan, NY
Finance, Fred Alger Management
Alex F. Ciccone, 38, New Rochelle, NY
Finance, Marsh & McLennan
Frances Ann Cilente, 26, Staten Island, NY
Administration, Cantor Fitzgerald
Elaine Cillo, 40, Brooklyn, NY
Insurance, Marsh & McLennan
Edna Cintron, 46, New York, NY
Administrative assistant, Marsh & McLennan
Nestor Andre Cintron, 26, Bronx, NY
Finance, Cantor Fitzgerald
Juan Pablo Cisneros, 24, Weehawken, NJ
Brokerage, Cantor Fitzgerald
Benjamin Keefe Clark, 39, Brooklyn, NY
Food services, Sodexho
Buddah Clark, Villanova, PA
Eugene Clark, 47, New York, NY
Administrative assistant, Aon Corp.
Gregory A. Clark, 40, Teaneck, NJ
Computer technology, Cantor Fitzgerald

Mannie Leroy Clark, 54, Bronx, NY
Thomas R. Clark, 37, Summit, NJ
Finance, Sandler O'Neill & Partners
Christopher Robert Clarke, 34, Philadelphia, PA
Finance, Sandler O'Neill & Partners
Donna Clarke, 39, New York, NY
Finance, Marsh & McLennan
Suria R.E. Clarke, 30, Brooklyn, NY
Media relations, Cantor Fitzgerald
Kevin F. Cleary, 38, New York, NY
Brokerage, EuroBrokers Inc.
James D. Cleere, 55, Newton, IA
Insurance, Marsh & McLennan
Geoffrey W. Cloud, 36, Stamford, CT
Attorney, Cantor Fitzgerald
Susan M. Clyne, 42, Lindenhurst, NY
Insurance, Marsh & McLennan
Jeffrey Coale, 31, Souderton, PA
Restaurant worker, Windows on the World
Patricia A. Cody, 46, Brigantine, NJ
Insurance brokerage, Marsh & McLennan
Daniel Michael Coffey, 54, Newburgh, NY
Insurance, Marsh & McLennan
Jason Matthew Coffey, 25, Newburgh, NY
Accountant, Marsh & McLennan
Florence Cohen, 62, New York, NY
Secretary, New York State Department of Taxation & Finance
Kevin Sanford Cohen, 28, Manhattan, NY
Computer technology, Cantor Fitzgerald
Anthony Joseph Coladonato III, 47, Staten Island, NY
Brokerage, Cantor Fitzgerald
Mark J. Colaio, 34, Manhattan, NY
Brokerage, Cantor Fitzgerald
Stephen J. Colaio, 32, Montauk, NY
Brokerage, Cantor Fitzgerald
Christopher M. Colasanti, 33, Hoboken, NJ
Finance, Cantor Fitzgerald
Kevin Nathaniel Colbert, 25, West Hempstead, NY
Brokerage, Keefe Bruyette & Woods
Michel Paris Colbert, 39, West New York, NJ
Finance, Cantor Fitzgerald
Keith Eugene Coleman, 34, Warren, NJ
Brokerage, Cantor Fitzgerald
Scott Thomas Coleman, 31, Manhattan, NY
Brokerage, Cantor Fitzgerald
Liam Colhoun, 49, Flushing, NY
Finance, Bank of America
Robert Dana Colin, 49, West Babylon, NY
Insurance brokerage, Aon Corp.
Robert Joseph Coll, 35, Glen Ridge, NJ
Brokerage, EuroBrokers Inc.
Jean Marie Collin, 42, Manhattan, NY
Michael Collins, 38, Upper Montclair, NJ
Brokerage, Cantor Fitzgerald
Thomas J. Collins, 36, New York, NY
Brokerage, Cantor Fitzgerald
Joseph Collison
Kidder Peabody Paine Webber
Patricia Malia Colodner, 39, Manhattan, NY
Secretary, Marsh & McLennan
Linda M. Colon, 46, Perrineville, NJ
Finance, Marsh & McLennan
Soledi E. Colon, 39, New York, NY
Insurance, Aon Corp.
Ronald Comer, 56, Huntington, NY
Brokerage, Marsh & McLennan
Jaime Concepcion, 46, Manhattan, NY
Restaurant worker, Windows on the World
Albert Conde, 62, Englishtown, NJ
Brokerage, AIG Corp.
Denease Conley, 44, New York, NY
Security, Summit Security Services

Susan Clancy Conlon, 41, Staten Island, NY
Banking, Bank of America
Margaret Mary Conner, 57, Brooklyn, NY
Receptionist, Cantor Fitzgerald
Cynthia L. Connolly, 40, Metuchen, NJ
John E. Connolly Jr., 46, Allenwood, NJ
Brokerage, EuroBrokers Inc.
James Lee Connor, 38, Summit, NJ
Investment banking, Sandler O'Neill & Partners
Jonathan "J.C." Connors, 55, Old Brookville, NY
Brokerage, Cantor Fitzgerald
Kevin P. Connors, 55, Greenwich, CT
Brokerage, EuroBrokers Inc.
Kevin Francis Conroy, 47, Brooklyn, NY
Accountant, Marsh & McLennan
Brenda E. Conway, 40, New York, NY
Insurance, Marsh & McLennan
Dennis Michael Cook, 33, Colts Neck, NJ
Brokerage, Cantor Fitzgerald
Helen D. Cook, 24, Bronx, NY
Telecommunications, General Telecom
John A. Cooper, 40, Bayonne, NJ
Account manager, SunGard Trading Systems
Joseph J. Coppo Jr., 47, New Canaan, CT
Brokerage, Cantor Fitzgerald
Gerard J. Coppola, 46, New Providence, NJ
Broadcast engineer, WNET-TV
Joseph Albert Corbett, 28, Islip, NY
Brokerage, Cantor Fitzgerald
Alejandro Cordero, 23, Manhattan, NY
Insurance, Marsh & McLennan
David Vargas Cordoba
Management, T&T Enterprises Intl.
Daniel A. Correa-Gutierrez, 25, Fairview, NJ
Accountant, Marsh & McLennan
Carlos Cortes, 57, Manhattan, NY
Washington Group International
Adianes Cortes-Oyolla, 23, Brooklyn, NY
Human resources, Fuji Bank
Kevin M. Cosgrove, 46, West Islip, NY
Insurance brokerage, Aon Corp.
Dolores Marie Costa, 52, Middletown, NJ
Fred Alger Management
Alexandra Digna Costanza, 25, Woodside, NY
Charles Gregory Costello, 46, Old Bridge, NJ
Construction worker, Thyssen Kropp
Michael S. Costello, 27, Hoboken, NJ
Finance, Cantor Fitzgerald
Conrod K.H. Cottoy Sr., 51, Brooklyn, NY
Brokerage, Carr Futures
Martin Coughlan, 54, County Tipperary, Ireland
Carpenter
Timothy John Coughlin, 42, Manhattan, NY
Brokerage, Cantor Fitzgerald
James E. Cove, 48, Rockville Centre, NY
Insurance, Aon Corp.
Andre Cox, 29, Canarsie, NY
Food services, Forte Food Service
Frederick John Cox, 27, Manhattan, NY
Finance, Sandler O'Neill & Partners
Michele Coyle-Eulau, 38, Garden City, NY
Consulting, Marsh & McLennan
Anne Martino Cramer, 47, Staten Island, NY
Finance, Fiduciary Trust Company International
Christopher S. Cramer, 34, Manahawkin, NJ
Finance, Fiduciary Trust Company International
Denise Crant, 46, Hackensack, NJ
Insurance, Marsh & McLennan
James Leslie Crawford Jr., 33, Madison, NJ
Brokerage, Cantor Fitzgerald
Joanne Cregan, 32, New York, NY
Finance, Cantor Fitzgerald

Lucia Crifasi, 51, Glendale, NY
Travel coordinator, American Express
Daniel Hal Crisman, 25, Manhattan, NY
Finance, Marsh & McLennan
Helen Crossin-Kittle, 34, Larchmont, NY
Computer technology, Cantor Fitzgerald
Kevin Raymond Crotty, 43, Summit, NJ
Brokerage, Sandler O'Neill & Partners
Thomas G. Crotty, 42, Rockville Centre, NY
Brokerage, Sandler O'Neill & Partners
John R. Crowe, 57, Rutherford, NJ
Insurance brokerage, Aon Corp.
Welles Remy Crowther, 24, Upper Nyack, NY
Brokerage, Sandler O'Neill & Partners
Robert Cruikshank, 64, New York, NY
Finance, Carr Futures
Francisco Cruz, 47, Staten Island, NY
Security officer, Summit Security Services
John Robert Cruz, 32, Jersey City, NJ
Kenneth John Cubas, 48, Staten Island, NY
Computer technology, Fiduciary Trust Company International
Francisco C. Cubero, 47, Staten Island, NY
Richard Joseph Cudina, 46, Glen Gardner, NJ
Brokerage, Cantor Fitzgerald
Neil James Cudmore, 38, Port Washington, NY
Sales, Risk Waters Group
Joan McConnell Cullinan, 47, Scarsdale, NY
Administration, Cantor Fitzgerald
Joyce Cummings, 65
Brian Thomas Cummins, 38, Manasquan, NJ
Brokerage, Cantor Fitzgerald
Nilton Albuquerque Fernao Cunha, 41
Michael "Micky" J. Cunningham, 39, West Windsor, NJ
Brokerage, EuroBrokers Inc.
Laurence Curia, 41, Garden City, NY
Brokerage, Cantor Fitzgerald
Paul Dario Curioli, 53, Norwalk, CT
Insurance brokerage, FM Global
Beverly Curry, 41, Staten Island, NY
Finance and management, Cantor Fitzgerald
Gavin Cushny, 47, Hoboken, NJ
Computer technology, Cantor Fitzgerald
Manuel J. Da Mota, 44, Valley Stream, NY
Builder, Bronx Builders
Caleb Arron Dack, 39, Montclair, NJ
Software developer, Encompys (visiting)
Carlos S. DaCosta, 41, Elizabeth, NJ
Electrical engineer, Port Authority of New York & New Jersey
Vincent D'Amadeo, 36, East Patchouge, NY
Brokerage, Cantor Fitzgerald
Thomas A. Damaskinos, 33, Matawan, NJ
Brokerage, Cantor Fitzgerald
Jack L. D'Ambrosi, 45, Woodcliff Lake, NJ
Bond trader, Cantor Fitzgerald
Jeannine Marie Damiani-Jones, 28, Brooklyn, NY
Cantor Fitzgerald
Patrick William Danahy, 35, Yorktown Heights, NY
Financial investor, Fiduciary Trust Company International
Mary Yolanda D'Antonio, 55, New York, NY
Marsh & McLennan
Dwight Donald Darcy, 55, Bronxville, NY
Attorney, Port Authority of New York & New Jersey
Elizabeth Ann Darling, 28, Newark, NJ
Business analyst, Marsh & McLennan
Anette Andrea Dataram, 25, South Ozone Park, NY
Accountant, Windows on the World
Julane Davidson, 26, Jersey City, NJ
Lawrence Davidson, 51, Brooklyn, NY
Brokerage, Aon Corp.
Michael Allen Davidson, 27, Westfield, NJ
Brokerage, Cantor Fitzgerald
Titus Davidson, 51, Brooklyn, NY
Security guard, Bowles Corporation/Morgan Stanley

Niurka Davila, 47, Manhattan, NY
Technology services, Port Authority of New York & New Jersey
Wayne Terrial Davis, 29, Fort Meade, MD
Computer systems, Callixa
Anthony Richard Dawson, 32, Southampton, Hampshire, England
Thales Contact Solutions
Calvin Dawson, 46, New York, NY
EuroBrokers Inc.
Jayceryll M. De Chavez, 24, Carteret, NJ
Financial analyst, Fiduciary Trust Company International
Nataly de la Cruz, New York, NY
Emerita Emily de la Pena, 32, Briarwood, NY
Administrative assistant, Fiduciary Trust Company International
Azucena de la Torre, 50, Staten Island, NY
Brokerage, Cantor Fitzgerald
Cristina de Laura
Oscar de Laura
Francis Albert De Martini, 49, Brooklyn, NY
Architect, Port Authority of New York & New Jersey
William T. Dean, 35, Floral Park, NY
Insurance brokerage, Marsh & McLennan
Robert J. DeAngelis Jr., 47, West Hempstead, NY
Engineering equipment buyer, Washington Group International
Ana Gloria Pocasangre DeBarrera, 49, Soyapango, El Salvador
Export
Tara Debek, 35, Babylon, NY
Insurance brokerage, Marsh & McLennan
Anna DeBin, 30, East Farmingdale, NY
Brokerage, Cantor Fitzgerald
James Vincent Deblase, 45, Manalapan, NJ
Brokerage, Cantor Fitzgerald
Paul DeCola, 39, Ridgewood, NY
Cantor Fitzgerald
Simon Dedvukaj, 26, Mohegan Lake, NY
ABM Industries
Jason DeFazio, 29, Staten Island, NY
Bond broker, Cantor Fitzgerald
David A. DeFeo, 37, Flushing, NY
Sandler O'Neill & Partners
Jennifer DeJesus, 23, Brooklyn, NY
Data entry, Morgan Stanley
Monique E. DeJesus, 28, Brooklyn, NY
Cantor Fitzgerald
Nereida DeJesus, 30, Bronx, NY
Insurance brokerage, Aon Corp.
Donald A. Delapenha, 37, Allendale, NJ
Bond trader, Keefe Bruyette & Woods
Vito Joseph DeLeo, 41, Staten Island, NY
Engineer, ABM Industries
Danielle Delie, 47, New York, NY
Joseph A. Della Pietra, 24, Brooklyn, NY
Brokerage, Cantor Fitzgerald
Palmina Delli Gatti, 33, Queens, NY
Marsh & McLennan
Colleen Ann Deloughery, 41, Bayonne, NJ
Insurance specialist, Aon Corp.
Anthony Demas, 61, New York, NY
Insurance brokerage, Aon Corp.
Francis X. Deming, 47, Franklin Lakes, NJ
Software developer, Oracle Corp.
Carol K. Demitz, 49, Manhattan, NY
Lawyer, Fiduciary Trust Company International
Kevin Dennis, 43, Peapack, NJ
Brokerage, Cantor Fitzgerald
Thomas F. Dennis, 43, Setauket, NY
Brokerage, Cantor Fitzgerald
Jean C. DePalma, 42, Newfoundland, NJ
Accountant, Marsh & McLennan
Jose Nicholas Depena, 42, Bronx, NY

Robert J. Deraney, 43, Manhattan, NY
Financial consultant, Self-employed
Michael DeRienzo, 37, Hoboken, NJ
Cantor Fitzgerald
Jemal Legesse DeSantis, 28, Jersey City, NJ
Brokerage, Cantor Fitzgerald
Christian D. DeSimone, 23, Ringwood, NJ
Accountant, Marsh & McLennan
Edward DeSimone III, 36, Atlantic Highlands, NJ
Bond trader, Cantor Fitzgerald
Michael Jude D'Esposito, 32, Morganville, NJ
Computer programmer, Self-employed
Cindy Ann Deuel, 28, Brooklyn, NY
Brokerage, Carr Futures
Melanie Louise DeVere, 30, Portsmouth, England
Publishing assistant, Risk Waters Group
Jerry DeVito, 66, Bronx, NY
Chauffeur, Fred Alger Management
Robert P. Devitt Jr., 36, Plainsboro, NJ
Cantor Fitzgerald
Simon Suleman Ali Kassamali Dhanani, 62, Hartsdale, NY
Insurance brokerage, Aon Corp.
Marisa Di Nardo Schorpp, 38, White Plains, NY
Trading, Cantor Fitzgerald
Michael L. Diagostino, 41, Garden City, NY
Brokerage, Cantor Fitzgerald
Matthew Diaz, 33, Brooklyn, NY
Carpenter, NY City District Council of Carpenters Local 2287
Nancy Diaz, 28, North Bronx, NY
Kitchen assistant, Windows on the World
Judith Berquis Diaz-Sierra, 32, Bay Shore, NY
Administrative assistant, Fiduciary Trust Company International
Patricia F. Dichiaro, 63, Queens, NY
Marsh & McLennan
Joseph Dermott Dickey Jr., 50, Manhasset, NY
Brokerage, Cantor Fitzgerald
Lawrence Patrick Dickinson, 35, Morganville, NJ
Brokerage, Harvey, Young & Yurman
Michael David Diehl, 48, Bricktown, NJ
Finance, Fiduciary Trust Company International
Michael Diez-Piedra III, 49
John DiFato, 39, Staten Island, NY
Business securities controller, Cantor Fitzgerald
Vincent Francis DiFazio, 43, Hampton, NJ
Brokerage, Cantor Fitzgerald
Carl DiFranco, 27, Staten Island, NY
Accountant, Marsh & McLennan
Donald J. DiFranco, 43, Brooklyn, NY
Engineer, WABC-TV
Debra Ann DiMartino, 36, Staten Island, NY
Trading, Keefe Bruyette & Woods
Stephen Patrick Dimino, 48, Basking Ridge, NJ
Brokerage, Cantor Fitzgerald
William J. Dimmling, 47, Garden City, NY
Marsh & McLennan
Christopher M. Dincuff, 31, Jersey City, NJ
Trading, Carr Futures
Jeffrey M. Dingle, 32, Bronx, NY
Computer technology, Encompys
Anthony Dionisio Jr., 38, Glen Rock, NJ
Brokerage, Cantor Fitzgerald
Joseph DiPilato, 57, Staten Island, NY
Electrician, Petrocelli Electric Co./Morgan Stanley
Douglas Frank DiStefano, 24, Hoboken, NJ
Cantor Fitzgerald
Ramzi A. Doany, 35, Bayonne, NJ
Insurance brokerage, Marsh & McLennan
John J. Doherty, 58, Hartsdale, NY
Aon Corp.
Melissa C. Doi, 32, Bronx, NY
IQ Financial Systems
Brendan Dolan, 37, Glen Rock, NJ
Oil futures brokerage, Carr Futures

Neil M. Dollard, 28, Hoboken, NJ
Brokerage, Cantor Fitzgerald
James Joseph Domanico, 56, New York, NY
New York State Department of Taxation & Finance
Benilda P. Domingo, 38, Elmhurst, NY
Janitor, ABM Industries
Charles "Carlos" Dominguez, 34, East Meadow, NY
Marsh & McLennan
Jacqueline Donovan, 34, Lynbrook, NY
Administrative assistant, Keefe Bruyette & Woods
Stephen S. Dorf, 39, New Milford, NJ
Maintenance and communications, EuroBrokers Inc.
Thomas Dowd, 37, Monroe, NY
Brokerage, Cantor Fitzgerald
Mary Yolanda Dowling, 46, Rosedale, NY
Insurance brokerage, Aon Corp.
Frank Joseph Doyle, 39, Englewood, NJ
Investment banking, Keefe Bruyette & Woods
Joseph M. Doyle, 25, Staten Island, NY
Brokerage, Cantor Fitzgerald
Randy Drake, 37, Lee's Summit, MO
Telecommunications, Siemens
Mirna A. Duarte, 31, Richmond Hill, NY
Aramark Corp.
Michelle Duberry, London, England
Risk Waters Group
Luke A. Dudek, 50, Livingston, NJ
Food and beverage controller, Windows on the World
Christopher Michael Duffy, 23, New York, NY
Brokerage, Keefe Bruyette & Woods
Michael Joseph Duffy, 29, Northport, NY
Brokerage, Keefe Bruyette & Woods
Thomas W. Duffy, 52, Pittsford, NY
Insurance brokerage, Marsh & McLennan
Antoinette Duger, 44, Belleville, NJ
Operations associate, First Union Bank
Jackie Sayegh Duggan, 34
Sales, Windows on the World
Sareve Dukat, 53, Manhattan, NY
Taxation, New York State Department of Taxation & Finance
Christopher Joseph Dunne, 28, Mineola, NY
Computer technology, Marsh & McLennan
Richard A. Dunstan, 54, New Providence, NJ
Brokerage, Aon Corp.
Patrick Thomas Dwyer, 37, Nissequogue, NY
Joseph Anthony Eacobacci, 26, Flushing, NY
Broker, Cantor Fitzgerald
John Bruce Eagleson, 53, Middlefield, CT
Management, Westfield Corp. Inc.
Catherine Eagon, Hull, NJ
Robert Eaton, 37, Manhasset, NY
Brokerage, Cantor Fitzgerald
Dean P. Eberling, 44, Cranford, NJ
Brokerage, Keefe Bruyette & Woods
Margaret Ruth Echtermann, 33, Hoboken, NJ
Regus Business Centers
Paul Robert Eckna, 28, West New York, NJ
Brokerage, Cantor Fitzgerald
Constantine Gus Economos, 41, Brooklyn, NY
Investment banking, Sandler O'Neill & Partners
Dennis Michael Edwards, 35, Huntington, NY
Brokerage, Cantor Fitzgerald
Michael Hardy Edwards, 33, Manhattan, NY
Sandler O'Neill & Partners
Christine Egan, 55, Winnipeg, Manitoba, Canada
Epidemiologist, U.S. government
Lisa Egan, 31, Cliffside Park, NJ
Business administration, Cantor Fitzgerald
Michael Egan, 51, Middletown, NJ
Insurance broker, Aon Corp.
Samantha Egan, 24, Jersey City, NJ
Finance, Cantor Fitzgerald

Carole Eggert, 60, Staten Island, NY
Accountant, Marsh & McLennan
Lisa Caren Ehrlich, 36, Brooklyn, NY
Insurance brokerage, Aon Corp.
John Ernst "Jack" Eichler, 69, Cedar Grove, NJ
Retired executive director, Cadwalader, Wickersham & Taft
Eric Adam Eisenberg, 32, Commack, NY
Insurance, Aon Corp.
Daphne F. Elder, 36, Newark, NJ
Insurance, Marsh & McLennan
Valerie Silver Ellis, 46, New York, NY
Brokerage, Cantor Fitzgerald
Albert Alfy William Elmarry, 30, North Brunswick, NJ
Computer engineer, Cantor Fitzgerald
Edgar H. Emery, 45, Clifton, NJ
Finance, Fiduciary Trust Company International
Doris Suk-Yuen Eng, 30, Flushing, NY
Manager, Windows on the World
Christopher S. Epps, 29
Accountant, Marsh & McLennan
Erwin L. Erker, 41, Farmingdale, NY
Computer technology, Marsh & McLennan
William John Erwin, 30, Verona, NJ
Brokerage, Cantor Fitzgerald
Sarah Ali Escarcega, 35, Balham, England
Marketing, Risk Waters Group
Jose Espinal, 31
Fanny M. Espinoza, 29, Teaneck, NJ
Brokerage, Cantor Fitzgerald
Brigette Ann Esposito, 34, Brooklyn, NY
Insurance, Marsh & McLennan
William Esposito, 52, Bellmore, NY
Brokerage, Cantor Fitzgerald
Ruben Esquilin Jr., 35, Manhattan, NY
Maintenance worker, Fiduciary Trust Company International
Sadie Ette, 36, Manhattan, NY
Account representative, Windows on the World
Barbara G. Etzold, 43, Jersey City, NJ
Receptionist, Fred Alger Management
Eric Brian Evans, 31, Weehawken, NJ
Insurance, Aon Corp.
Meredith Emily June Ewart, 29, Hoboken, NJ
Brokerage, Aon Corp.
Catherine K. Fagan, 58, New York, NY
Computer technology, Marsh & McLennan
Patricia M. Fagan, 55, Toms River, NJ
Insurance brokerage, Aon Corp.
William F. Fallon Jr., 53, Rocky Hill, NJ
Management, Port Authority of New York & New Jersey
William L. Fallon Jr., 38, Coram, NY
Computer science, Cantor Fitzgerald
Anthony J. Fallone Jr., 39, Manhattan, NY
Finance/brokerage, Cantor Fitzgerald
Dolores B. Fanelli, 38, Farmingville, NY
Insurance, Marsh & McLennan
Kathleen "Kit" Faragher, 33, Denver, CO
Systems consultant, Janus Capital Corp.
Nancy Carole Farley, 45, Jersey City, NJ
Insurace brokerage, Reinsurance Solutions Inc.
Elizabeth Ann "Betty" Farmer, 62, Manhattan, NY
Executive assistant, Cantor Fitzgerald
Douglas Farnum, 33, New York, NY
Software specialist, Marsh & McLennan
John Gerard Farrell, 32, Brooklyn, NY
Finance, Cantor Fitzgerald
John William Farrell, 41, Basking Ridge, NJ
Brokerage, Sandler O'Neill & Partners
Thomas P. Farrelly, 54, East Northport, NY
Syed Abdul Fatha, 54, Newark, NJ
Copy machine operator, Pitney Bowes
Christopher Faughnan, 37, South Orange, NJ
Brokerage, Cantor Fitzgerald

Wendy R. Faulkner, 47, Mason, OH
Insurance brokerage, Aon Corp.
Shannon M. Fava, 30, New York, NY
Brokerage, Cantor Fitzgerald
Bernard D. Favuzza, 52, Suffern, NY
Brokerage, Cantor Fitzgerald
Ronald Carl Fazio, 57, Closter, NJ
Accountant, Aon Corp.
Francis J. "Frank" Feely, 41, Middletown, NY
Insurance, Marsh & McLennan
Garth E. Feeney, 28, Manhattan, NY
Engineering, Datasynapse
Sean Fegan, 34, Manhattan, NY
Investment analyst, Fred Alger Management
Peter Feidelberg, 34, Hoboken, NJ
Insurance brokerage, Aon Corp.
Arnold Feinberg, Neptune, NJ
Rosa Maria Feliciano, 30, New York, NY
Insurance, Marsh & McLennan
Edward T. Fergus Jr., 40, Wilton, CT
Brokerage, Cantor Fitzgerald
George J. Ferguson, 54, Teaneck, NJ
Henry Fernandez, 23, New York, NY
Restaurant worker, Windows on the World
Jose Manuel Contreras Fernandez, El Aguacate, Jalisco, Mexico
Judy H. Fernandez, 27, Parlin, NJ
Cantor Fitzgerald
Elisa Giselle Ferraina, 27, London, England
Conference coordinator, Risk Waters Group
Anne Marie Sallerin Ferreira, 29, Jersey City, NJ
Finance, Cantor Fitzgerald
Robert John Ferris, 63, Garden City, NY
Insurance brokerage, Aon Corp.
David Francis Ferrugio, 46, Middletown, NJ
Brokerage, Cantor Fitzgerald
Louis V. Fersini, 38, Basking Ridge, NJ
Brokerage, Cantor Fitzgerald
Michael Ferugio, 37, Brooklyn Heights, NY
Insurance, Aon Corp.
Bradley James Fetchet, 24, Manhattan, NY
Brokerage, Keefe Bruyette & Woods
Jennifer Louise Fialko, 29, Teaneck, NJ
Computer technology, Aon Corp.
Kristen Fiedel, 27, Bronx, NY
Marsh & McLennan
Samuel Fields, 36, Manhattan, NY
Security, Summit Security Services
Michael Bradley Finnegan, 37, Basking Ridge, NJ
Brokerage, Cantor Fitzgerald
Timothy J. Finnerty, 33, Glen Rock, NJ
Brokerage, Cantor Fitzgerald
Stephen J. Fiorelli, 43, Aberdeen, NJ
Civil engineer, Port Authority of New York & New Jersey
Paul Fiori, 31, Yorktown Heights, NY
Finance, Cantor Fitzgerald
John Fiorito, 40, Stamford, CT
Brokerage, Cantor Fitzgerald
Andrew Fisher, 42, Manhattan, NY
Software sales, Imagine Software
Bennett Lawson Fisher, 58, Stamford, CT
Asset management, Fiduciary Trust Company International
John Roger Fisher, 46, Bayonne, NJ
Security consultant, Port Authority of New York & New Jersey
Thomas Joseph Fisher, 36, Union, NJ
Asset management, Fiduciary Trust Company International
Lucy Fishman, 37, Brooklyn, NY
Secretary, Aon Corp.
Ryan Daniel Fitzgerald, 26, Floral Park, NY
Trader, Fiduciary Trust Company International
Thomas Fitzpatrick, 35, Tuckahoe, NY
Investment banking, Sandler O'Neill & Partners

Richard P. Fitzsimons, 57, Lynbrook, NY
Fire security officer, OCS Security
Salvatore A. Fiumefreddo, 45, Manalapan, NJ
Telephone technician, IPC
Christina Donovan Flannery, 26, Middle Village, NY
Brokerage, Sandler O'Neill & Partners
Eileen Flecha, 33, Kew Gardens, NY
Finance, Fiduciary Trust Company International
Carl M. Flickinger, 38, Conyers, NY
Brokerage, Cantor Fitzgerald
Joseph W. Flounders, 46, East Stroudsburg, PA
Finance, EuroBrokers Inc.
David Lawrence William Fodor, 38, Garrison, NY
Accountant, Fiduciary Trust Company International
Stephen Mark Fogel, 40, Westfield, NJ
Attorney, Cantor Fitzgerald
Chih Min Dennis Foo, 40, Holmdel, NJ
Bobby Forbes, 37, Rahway, NJ
Del Rose Forbes-Cheatham, 48, New York, NY
Accountant, Cantor Fitzgerald
Godwin Forde, 39, Brooklyn, NY
Security, Bowles Corporate Services
Christopher Hugh Forsythe, 44, Basking Ridge, NJ
Finance, Cantor Fitzgerald
Claudia Alicia Martinez Foster, 26, Staten Island, NY
Broker, Cantor Fitzgerald
Noel J. Foster, 40, Bridgewater, NJ
Brokerage, Aon Corp.
Ana Fosteris, 58, Coram, NY
Aon Corp.
Yolette Fouchet
Jeffrey L. Fox, 40, Cranbury, NJ
Investment banking, Keefe Bruyette & Woods
Virginia Fox, 58, Manhattan, NY
Insurance, Marsh & McLennan
Joan Francis
Lucille Virgin Francis, 63, Brooklyn, NY
Housekeeping, Windows on the World
Pauline Francis, 57, New York, NY
Food service, Forte Food Service
Jean-Pierre Francois, 58, Brooklyn, NY
Restaurant worker, Windows on the World
Gary J. Frank, 35, South Amboy, NJ
Computer programming, Aon Corp.
Morton H. Frank, 31, Manhattan, NY
Brokerage, Cantor Fitzgerald
Peter Christopher Frank, 29, Manhattan, NY
Financial analyst, Fred Alger Management
Richard K. Fraser, 32, Manhattan, NY
Insurance brokerage, Aon Corp.
Kevin Joseph Frawley, 34, Bronxville, NY
Trader, EuroBrokers Inc.
Clyde Frazier Jr., 41, Jamaica, NY
Tax investigator, New York State Department of Taxation & Finance
Lillian Inez Frederick, 46, Teaneck, NJ
Aon Corp.
Tamitha Freeman, 35, Brooklyn, NY
Client services, Aon Corp.
Jamitha Freemen, 35, New York, NY
Insurance, Aon Corp.
Brett O. Freiman, 29, Roslyn, NY
Arlene E. Fried, 49, Roslyn Heights, NY
Attorney, Cantor Fitzgerald
Alan Wayne Friedlander, 52, Yorktown Heights, NY
Engineer, Aon Corp.
Andrew K. Friedman, 44, Woodbury, NY
Brokerage, Carr Futures
Peter Christian Fry, 36, Wilton, CT
Brokerage, EuroBrokers Inc.
Clement Fumando, 59, Staten Island, NY
Financier, Cantor Fitzgerald

Steven Elliot Furman, 40, Wesley Hills, NY
Finance, Cantor Fitzgerald
Paul James Furmato, 37, Colts Neck, NJ
Brokerage, Cantor Fitzgerald
Fredric Gabler, 30, Manhattan, NY
Brokerage, Cantor Fitzgerald
Richard S. Gabrielle, 50, West Haven, CT
Insurance brokerage, Aon Corp.
James Andrew Gadiel, 23, Manhattan, NY
Brokerage, Cantor Fitzgerald
Pamela Gaff, 51, Robinsville, NJ
Insurance brokerage, Aon Corp.
Ervin Vincent Gailliard, 42, Bronx, NY
Security officer, Summit Security Services
Deanna Galante, 32, Staten Island, NY
Brokerage, Cantor Fitzgerald
Grace Galante, 29, Staten Island, NY
Brokerage, Cantor Fitzgerald
German Castillo Galicia, Ozumba, Mexico
Anthony Edward Gallagher, 41, New York, NY
Brokerage, Cantor Fitzgerald
Daniel James Gallagher, 23, Red Bank, NJ
Brokerage, Cantor Fitzgerald
John Gallagher, 31, Yonkers, NY
Brokerage, Cantor Fitzgerald
Lourdes Galletti, 33, Bronx, NY
Executive secretary, Cantor Fitzgerald
Cono E. Gallo, 30, Maspeth, NY
Brokerage, Carr Futures
Vincenzo Gallucci, 36, Monroe, NJ
Insurance brokerage, Marsh & McLennan
Thomas Edward Galvin, 32, Manhattan, NY
Brokerage, Cantor Fitzgerald
Giovanna Genni Gambale, 27, Brooklyn, NY
Brokerage, Cantor Fitzgerald
Giann F. Gamboa, 26, New York, NY
Hospitality, Top of the World Cafe
Claude Michael Gann, 41, Roswell, GA
Risk-management software development, Algorithmics (visiting)
Cesar Garcia, 36, Staten Island, NY
Marsh & McLennan
David Garcia, 40, Freeport, NY
Computer programming, Alliance Consulting Group
Jorge Luis Morron Garcia, 38, Queens, NY
Security, Summit Security Services
Juan Garcia, 50, Brooklyn, NY
Food service, Forte Food Service
Marlyn Carmen Garcia, 21, Brooklyn, NY
Student, Marsh & McLennan
Christopher Gardner, 36, Darien, CT
Insurance brokerage, Aon Corp.
Douglas B. Gardner, 39, New York, NY
Electronic trading, Cantor Fitzgerald
Harvey Joseph Gardner III, 35, Lakewood, NJ
Telecommunications, General Telecom
Jeffrey Brian Gardner, 36, Hoboken, NJ
Brokerage, Marsh & McLennan
William Arthur "Bill" Gardner, 45, Lynbrook, NY
Finance, Cantor Fitzgerald
Francesco Garfi, 29, New York, NY
Finance, Cantor Fitzgerald
Rocco Gargano, 28, Bayside, NY
Finance, Cantor Fitzgerald
James Michael Gartenberg, 36, Manhattan, NY
Brokerage, Julien J. Studley Inc.
Boyd A. Gatton, 38, Jersey City, NJ
Finance, Fiduciary Trust Company International
Donald Richard Gavagan Jr., 35, Bay Ridge, NY
Brokerage, Cantor Fitzgerald
Terence D. Gazzani, 24, Brooklyn, NY
Brokerage, Cantor Fitzgerald

Paul Hamilton Geier, 33, Farmingdale, NY
Brokerage, Cantor Fitzgerald
Julie Geis, 44, Lee's Summit, MO
Insurance, Aon Corp.
Peter Gelinas, 34, Bronxville, NY
Brokerage, Cantor Fitzgerald
Steven Paul Geller, 52, Manhattan, NY
Brokerage, Cantor Fitzgerald
Howard G. Gelling Jr., 28, Manhattan, NY
Finance, Sandler O'Neill & Partners
Peter Victor Genco, 36, Rockville Centre, NY
Brokerage, Cantor Fitzgerald
Steven Gregory Genovese, 37, Basking Ridge, NJ
Brokerage, Cantor Fitzgerald
Alayne F. Gentul, 44, Mountain Lakes, NJ
Human resources, Fiduciary Trust Company
International
Suzanne Geraty, 30, New York, NY
Information technology, Cantor Fitzgerald
Ralph Gerhardt, 34, Manhattan, NY
Finance, Cantor Fitzgerald
Robert J. Gerlich, 56, Monroe, CT
Accountant, Reinsurance Solutions Inc.
Marina R. Gertsberg, 25, Brooklyn, NY
Finance, Cantor Fitzgerald
Susan M. Getzendanner, 57, New York, NY
Finance, Fiduciary Trust Company International
James "Jimmy" Gerald Geyer, 41, Rockville Centre, NY
Broker, Cantor Fitzgerald
Joseph M. Giaccone, 43, Monroe, NJ
Telecommunications, Cantor Fitzgerald
Debra L. Gibbon, 43, Hackettstown, NJ
Risk management, Aon Corp.
Craig Neil Gibson, 37, New York, NY
Insurance, Marsh & McLennan
Andrew Clive Gilbert IV, 39, Califon, NJ
Finance, Cantor Fitzgerald
Timothy Paul Gilbert, 35, Lebanon, NJ
Finance, Cantor Fitzgerald
Paul Stuart Gilbey, 39, Chatham, NJ
Brokerage, EuroBrokers Inc.
Mark Y. Gilles, 33, Brooklyn, NY
Cantor Fitzgerald
Evan H. Gillette, 40, New York, NY
Finance, Sandler O'Neill & Partners
Ronald Gilligan, 43, Norwalk, CT
Finance, Cantor Fitzgerald
Laura Gilly, 32, New York, NY
Information technology, Cantor Fitzgerald
Donna Marie Giordano, 44, Parlin, NJ
Brokerage, Aon Corp.
Steven A. Giorgetti, 43, Manhasset, NY
Insurance, Marsh & McLennan
Martin Giovinazzo Jr., 34, Staten Island, NY
Maintenance technician, Marsh & McLennan
Jinny Lady Giraldo, 27
Kum-Kum Girolamo, 41, Kew Gardens, NY
Insurance, Aon Corp.
Salvatore Gitto, 44, Manalapan, NJ
Insurance, Marsh & McLennan
Cynthia Giugliano, 46, Nesconset, NY
Technical specialist, Empire Blue Cross/Blue Shield
Mon Gjonbalaj, 66, Throgs Neck, NY
Janitor, ABM Industries
Dianne Gladstone, 55, Forest Hills, NY
New York State Department of Taxation & Finance
Thomas I. Glasser, 40, Summit, NJ
Investment banking, Sandler O'Neill & Partners
Harry Glenn, 38, Piscataway, NJ
Marsh & McLennan
Barry H. Glick, 55, Wayne, NJ
Finance, Port Authority of New York & New Jersey

Steven Lawrence Glick, 42, Greenwich, CT
Financial consultant, Credit Suisse-First Boston (visiting)
John Gnazzo, 32, New York, NY
Brokerage, Cantor Fitzgerald
William Robert "Bill" Godshalk, 35, Manhattan, NY
Investment, Keefe Bruyette & Woods
Michael Gogliormella, 43, New Providence, NJ
Finance, Cantor Fitzgerald
Brian Frederic Goldberg, 26, Union, NJ
Finance, Fiduciary Trust Company International
Jeffrey Grant Goldflam, 48, Melville, NY
Finance, Cantor Fitzgerald
Michelle Herman Goldstein, 31, Manhattan, NY
Insurance, Aon Corp.
Monica Goldstein, 25, Staten Island, NY
Brokerage, Cantor Fitzgerald
Steven Goldstein, 35, Princeton, NJ
Finance/technology, Cantor Fitzgerald
Andrew H. Golkin, 30, Manhattan, NY
Finance, Cantor Fitzgerald
Dennis James Gomes, 40, Richmond Hill, NY
Finance, Fiduciary Trust Company International
Enrique Antonio Gomez, 42, Brooklyn, NY
Cook, Windows on the World
Jose Bienvenido Gomez, 45, New York, NY
Cook, Windows on the World
Manuel Gomez, 42, Brooklyn, NY
Banking, Fuji Bank
Max Gomez
Wilder Gomez, 38, New York, NY
Restaurant worker, Windows on the World
Jenine Gonzalez, 27, Bronx, NY
Insurance, Aon Corp.
Joel Guevara Gonzalez, Aguacalientes, Mexico
Mauricio Gonzalez, 27, Manhattan, NY
Carpenter, Aon Corp.
Rosa Julia Gonzalez, 32, Jersey City, NJ
Secretary, Port Authority of New York & New Jersey
Tambi Gonzalez, 22, Yonkers, NY
Windows on the World
Calvin J. Gooding, 38, Riverdale, NY
Brokerage, Cantor Fitzgerald
Harry Goody, 50, Coney Island, NY
New York State Department of Taxation & Finance
Kiran Reddy Gopu, 24, Bridgeport, CT
Computer programmer, Marsh & McLennan
Catherine Carmen Gorayeb, 41, Manhattan, NY
Random Walk Computing
Kerene Gordon, 42, Far Rockaway, NY
Food service, Cantor Fitzgerald
Sebastian Gorki, 27, Manhattan, NY
Finance, Deutsche Bank
Kieran Gorman, 35, Yonkers, NY
Construction worker, Structure Tone
Michael Edward Gould, 29, Hoboken, NJ
Brokerage, Cantor Fitzgerald
Yuji Goya, 42, Rye, NY
Finance, Fuji Bank
Jon Grabowski, 33, Manhattan, NY
Technology information, Marsh & McLennan
Christopher Michael Grady, 39, Cranford, NJ
Finance, Cantor Fitzgerald
Edwin J. Graff III, 48, Rowayton, CT
Finance, Cantor Fitzgerald
David M. Graifman, 40, Manhattan, NY
Equity analyst, Keefe Bruyette & Woods
Gilbert Granados, 51, Hicksville, NY
Insurance, Aon Corp.
Elvira Granitto, 43, Bronx, NY
Empire Blue Cross/Blue Shield
Winston A. Grant, 60, West Hempstead, NY
Empire Blue Cross/Blue Shield

Christopher Stewart Gray, 32, Weehawken, NJ
Brokerage, Cantor Fitzgerald
Linda Mair Grayling, 44, New York, NY
Receptionist, Marsh & McLennan
John Michael Grazioso, 41, Middletown, NJ
Brokerage, Cantor Fitzgerald
Tim Grazioso, 42, Gulf Stream, FL
Brokerage, Cantor Fitzgerald
Derrick Arthur Green, 44, Bronx, NY
Construction worker

Wade Brian Green, 42, Westbury, NY
Telecommunications, Thomson Financial
Elaine Myra Greenberg, 56, Manhattan, NY
Technology, Compaq
Gayle R. Greene, 51, Montville, NJ
Insurance, Marsh & McLennan
James Arthur Greenleaf Jr., 32, New York, NY
Finance, Carr Futures
Eileen Marsha Greenstein, 52, Morris Plains, NJ
Insurance, Aon Corp.
Elizabeth Martin "Lisa" Gregg, 52, Brooklyn, NY
Finance, Fred Alger Management
Denise Gregory, 39, Queens, NY
Finance, Carr Futures
Donald H. Gregory, 62, Ramsey, NJ
Brokerage, Cantor Fitzgerald
Florence M. Gregory, 38, New York, NY
Marine insurance, Aon Corp.
Jack Gregory, 53, Manhattan, NY
Pedro Grehan, 35, Hoboken, NJ
Finance, Cantor Fitzgerald
John M. Griffin, 38, Waldwick, NJ
Real estate, Silverstein Properties
Tawanna Griffin, 30, Brooklyn, NY
Cashier, Cantor Fitzgerald
Joan Donna Griffith, 39, Willingboro, NJ
Finance, Fiduciary Trust Company International
Warren Grifka, 54, Brooklyn, NY
Information technology, Marsh & McLennan
Ramon Grijalvo, 58
Morgan Stanley
Joseph F. Grillo, 46, Staten Island, NY
Risk finance analyst, Port Authority of New York & New
Jersey
David Grimner, 51, Merrick, NY
Kenneth G. Grouzalis, 56, Lyndhurst, NJ
Property manager, Port Authority of New York & New Jersey
Matthew J. Grzymalski, 34, New Hyde Park, NY
Brokerage, Cantor Fitzgerald
Robert Joseph Gschaar, 55, Spring Valley, NY
Insurance brokerage, Aon Corp.
Liming Michael Gu, 34, Piscataway, NJ
Marsh & McLennan
Yan Z. "Cindy" Guan, 25, New York, NY
Accounting, New York State Department of Taxation &
Finance
Babita Guman, 33, Bronx, NY
Computer specialist, Fiduciary Trust Company International
Douglas B. Radianz Gurian, 38, Tenafly, NJ
Information technology, Radianz
Janet H. Gustafson, 48, New York, NY
Philip T. Guza, 54, Sea Bright, NJ
Insurance brokerage, Aon Corp.
Sabita Guzman
Barbara Guzzardo, 49, Glendale, NY
Insurance brokerage, Aon Corp.
Peter Mark Gyulavary, 44, Warwick, NY
Environmental engineer, Washington Group International
Gary Robert Haag, 36, Ossining, NY
Insurance brokerage, Marsh & McLennan
Andrea Lyn Haberman, 25, Chicago, IL
Finance, Carr Futures

Barbara M. Contarino Habib, 49, Staten Island, NY
Insurance brokerage, Marsh & McLennan
Philip Haentzler, 49, Staten Island, NY
Legal administration, Kidder Peabody Paine Webber
Nizam Ahmad Hafiz, 32, South Ozone Park, NY
Computer technology, Marsh & McLennan
Karen Hagerty, 34, Manhattan, NY
Insurance brokerage, Aon Corp.
Steven Michael Hagis, 31, Staten Island, NY
Brokerage, Cantor Fitzgerald
Mary Lou Hague, 26, Manhattan, NY
Brokerage, Keefe Bruyette & Woods
Maile Rachel Hale, 26, Cambridge, MA
Investments, Boston Investor Services
Richard Hall, 49, Purchase, NY
Insurance brokerage, Aon Corp.
Vaswald George Hall, 50, St. Albans, NY
Courier services
Robert John Halligan, 59, Basking Ridge, NJ
Insurance brokerage, Aon Corp.
James D. Halvorson, 56, Greenwich, CT
Insurance brokerage, Marsh & McLennan
Mohammed Salman Hamdani, 23, New York, NY
Research technician, Howard Hughes Medical Institute
Felicia Hamilton, 62, New York, NY
Finance, Fiduciary Trust Company International
Frederic Kim Han, 45, Marlboro, NJ
Brokerage, Cantor Fitzgerald
Christopher James Hanley, 34, Manhattan, NY
Sales, Radianz
Valerie Joan Hanna, 57, Freeville, NY
Brokerage, Marsh & McLennan
Kevin James Hannaford, 32, Basking Ridge, NJ
Brokerage, Cantor Fitzgerald
Michael L. Hannan, 34, Lynbrook, NY
Brokerage, Marsh & McLennan
Vassilios G. Haramis, 56, Staten Island, NY
Mechanical engineer, Washington Group International
James A. Haran, 41, Malverne, NY
Brokerage, Cantor Fitzgerald
Jeffrey P. Hardy, 46, Brooklyn, NY
Chef, Cantor Fitzgerald
Timothy John Hargrave, 38, Readington, NJ
Brokerage, Cantor Fitzgerald
Frances Haros, 76, Staten Island, NY
Receptionist, Keefe Bruyette & Woods
Aisha Harris, 22, Bronx, NY
Switch operator, General Telecom
Stewart Dennis Harris, 52, Marlboro, NJ
Brokerage, Cantor Fitzgerald
John Patrick Hart, 38, Danville, CA
Investments, Franklin Templeton Investments
John Clinton Hartz, 64, Basking Ridge, NJ
Brokerage, Fiduciary Trust Company International
Emeric J. Harvey, 56, Upper Montclair, NJ
Brokerage, Harvey, Young & Yurman
Joseph John Hasson III, 34, New York, NY
Brokerage, Cantor Fitzgerald
Leonard William Hatton, 45, Ridgefield Park, NJ
Law enforcement, Federal Bureau of Investigation
Timothy Aaron Haviland, 41, Oceanside, NY
Insurance brokerage, Marsh & McLennan
Donald G. Havlish Jr., 53, Yardley, PA
Insurance brokerage, Aon Corp.
Anthony Hawkins, 30, Bedford-Stuyvesant, NY
Maintenance, Cantor Fitzgerald
Nobuhiro Hayatsu, 36, Scarsdale, NY
Banking, Chuo Mitsui Trust & Banking Company
William Ward Haynes, 35, Rye, NY
Brokerage, Cantor Fitzgerald
Scott Hazelcorn, 29, Hoboken, NJ
Cantor Fitzgerald

Roberta Bernstein Heber, 60, New York, NY
Computer technology, Marsh & McLennan
Charles Francis Xavier Heeran, 23, Belle Harbor, NY
Brokerage, Cantor Fitzgerald
Howard Joseph Heller, 37, Ridgefield, CT
Brokerage, Carr Futures
JoAnn L. Heltibridle, 46, Springfield, NJ
Brokerage, Marsh & McLennan
Mark F. Hemschoot, 45, Red Bank, NJ
Insurance brokerage, Aon Corp.
Janet Hendricks
Insurance brokerage, Aon Corp.
Brian Hennessey, 35, Ringoes, NJ
Brokerage, Cantor Fitzgerald
Michelle Marie Henrique, 27, Staten Island, NY
Administration, Fiduciary Trust Company International
John C. Henwood, 35, New York, NY
Brokerage, Cantor Fitzgerald
Robert Allan Hepburn, 39, Union, NJ
Administration, Marsh & McLennan
Mary Molly Herencia, 47, New York, NY
Insurance brokerage, Aon Corp.
Lindsay Coates Herkness III, 58, Manhattan, NY
Brokerage, Morgan Stanley
Harvey Robert Hermer, 59, Manhattan, NY
Electrician, Forest Electric Corp.
Anabel Hernandez, 41
Banking, JP Morgan Chase
Claribel Hernandez, 31, Woodside, NY
Administration, Sybase Inc.
Eduardo Hernandez, 40
Banking, JP Morgan Chase
Norberto Hernandez, 42, New York, NY
Chef, Windows on the World
Raul Hernandez, 51, Washington Heights, NY
Maintenance supervisor, Cantor Fitzgerald
Gary Herold, 44, Farmingdale, NY
Insurance brokerage, Aon Corp.
Jeffrey A. Hersch, 53, New York, NY
Brokerage, Cantor Fitzgerald
Ysidro Hidalgo-Tejada, Dominican Republic
Food service, Windows on the World
Robert Higley II, 29, New Fairfield, CT
Insurance brokerage, Aon Corp.
Todd Russell Hill, 34, Boston, MA
Computer technology, QRS Corp.
Clara Victorine Hinds, 52, Far Rockaway, NY
Seamstress, Windows on the World
Neal Hinds, 28, Laurelton Gardens, NY
Banking, Bank of New York
Mark D. Hindy, 28, New York, NY
Brokerage, Cantor Fitzgerald
Katsuyuki Hirai, 32, Hartsdale, NY
Chuo Mitsui Trust & Banking Company
Heather Malia Ho, 32, Manhattan, NY
Chef, Windows on the World
Tara Yvette Hobbs, 31, New York, NY
Insurance brokerage, Aon Corp.
Thomas A. Hobbs, 41, Baldwin, NY
Brokerage, Cantor Fitzgerald
James L. Hobin, 47, Marlborough, CT
Brokerage, Marsh & McLennan
Robert Wayne Hobson III, 36, Jersey City, NJ
Brokerage, Cantor Fitzgerald
DaJuan Hodges, 29, New York, NY
Management services, Marsh & McLennan
Ronald George Hoerner, 58, Massapequa Park, NY
Security, Summit Security Services
Patrick Aloysius Hoey, 53, Middletown, NJ
Management, Port Authority of New York & New Jersey
Frederick J. Hoffman, 53, Freehold, NJ
Brokerage, Cantor Fitzgerald

Joseph Hoffman, 43
Marcia Hoffman, 52, Brooklyn, NY
Michele Lee Hoffman, 27, Freehold, NJ
Brokerage, Cantor Fitzgerald
Stephen G. Hoffman, 36, Long Beach, NY
Brokerage, Cantor Fitzgerald
Judith Florence Hofmiller, 53, Brookfield, CT
Database programmer, Marsh & McLennan
Thomas Warren Hohlweck Jr., 57, Harrison, NY
Insurance brokerage, Aon Corp.
John Holland, 30
Joseph Francis Holland, 32, Glen Rock, NJ
Brokerage, Carr Futures
Elizabeth Holmes, 42, Manhattan, NY
Communications, EuroBrokers Inc.
Bradley Hoorn, 22, New York, NY
Finance, Fred Alger Management
James Patrick Hopper, 52, Farmingdale, NY
Security officer, Cantor Fitzgerald
Montgomery McCullough "Monte" Hord, 46, Pelham, NY
Brokerage, Cantor Fitzgerald
Michael Horn, 27, Lynbrook, NY
Software technician, Cantor Fitzgerald
Matthew D. Horning, 26, Hoboken, NJ
Database administrator, Marsh & McLennan
Robert L. Horohoe Jr., 31, New York, NY
Brokerage/financial services, Cantor Fitzgerald
Aaron Horwitz, 24, New York, NY
Brokerage, Cantor Fitzgerald
Charles J. Houston, 42, New York, NY
Brokerage, EuroBrokers Inc.
Michael C. Howell, 60, Bayside, NY
Engineer, Fred Alger Management
Steven L. Howell, 36, Staten Island, NY
Computer technology, Marsh & McLennan
Jennifer L. Howley-Dorsey, 34, New Hyde Park, NY
Insurance brokerage, Aon Corp.
Milagros Millie Hromada, 35, Queens, NY
Aon Corp.
Marian Hrycak, 56, Flushing, NY
Tax investigator, New York State Department of Taxation &
Finance
Kris R. Hughes, 30, Nesconset, NY
Brokerage, Keefe Bruyette & Woods
Melissa Harrington Hughes, 31, San Francisco, CA
Trade relations, SRI
Paul Hughes, 38, Stamford, CT
Computer engineering, Marsh & McLennan
Robert Thomas "Bobby" Hughes, 23, Sayreville, NJ
Banking, Bank of America
Thomas F. Hughes Jr., 46, Spring Lake Heights, NJ
Self-employed, Colonial Arts Decorators
Timothy Robert Hughes, 43, Madison, NJ
Brokerage, Cantor Fitzgerald
Susan Huie, 43, Fair Lawn, NJ
Finance, Compaq
Lamar Hulse, 30, Manhattan, NY
Security officer, Port Authority of New York & New Jersey
Kathleen Casey Anne Hunt, 43, Middletown, NJ
Brokerage, Sandler O'Neill & Partners
William C. Hunt, 32, Norwalk, CT
Broker, EuroBrokers Inc.
Robert Hussa, 51, Roslyn, NY
Brokerage, Carr Futures
John Hynes, Norwalk, CT
Vestek
Thomas E. Hynes, 28, Norwalk, CT
Finance, Thomson Financial
Joseph Anthony Ianelli Jr., 28, Hoboken, NJ
Accounting, Marsh & McLennan
Zuhtu Ibis, 25, Clifton, NJ
Brokerage, Cantor Fitzgerald

Michael Patrick Iken, 37, Bronx, NY
Brokerage, EuroBrokers Inc.
Daniel Ilkanayev, 36, Brooklyn, NY
Cantor Fitzgerald
Abraham Nethanel Ilowitz, 51, Brooklyn, NY
Metropolitan Life Insurance
Louis Steven Inghilterra, 46, New Castle, NY
Fiduciary Trust Company International
Christopher N. Ingrassia, 28, Watchung, NJ
Brokerage, Cantor Fitzgerald
Paul William Innella, 33, East Brunswick, NJ
Computer programmer, Cantor Fitzgerald
Stephanie V. Irby, 38, St. Albans, NY
Accountant, Marsh & McLennan
Doug Irgang, 32, Manhattan, NY
Investment banking, Sandler O'Neill & Partners
Kristin A. Irvine-Ryan, 30, Manhattan, NY
Brokerage, Sandler O'Neill & Partners
Todd A. Isaac, 29, New York, NY
Brokerage, Cantor Fitzgerald
Erik Hans Isbrandtsen, 30, New York, NY
Brokerage, Cantor Fitzgerald
William Iselepis, 33
Taizo Ishikawa, 50
Fuji Bank
Aram Iskenderian, 41, Merrick, NY
Brokerage, Cantor Fitzgerald
John F. Iskyan, 41, Wilton, CT
Brokerage, Cantor Fitzgerald
Kazushige Ito, 35, New York, NY
Fuji Bank
Aleksander Valeryerich Ivantsov, 23, New York, NY
Cantor Fitzgerald
Virginia M. Jablonski, 49, Matawan, NJ
Insurance brokerage, Marsh & McLennan
Brooke Alexandra Jackman, 23, Manhattan, NY
Brokerage, Cantor Fitzgerald
Aaron Jacobs, 27, Manhattan, NY
Brokerage, Cantor Fitzgerald
Ariel Louis Jacobs, 29, Briarcliff Manor, NY
Cantor Fitzgerald
Jason Kyle Jacobs, 32, Mendham, NJ
Fiduciary Trust Company International
Michael Grady Jacobs, 54, Danbury, CT
Accountant, Fiduciary Trust Company International
Steven A. Jacobson, 53, Manhattan, NY
Engineer, WPIX-Channel 11
Ricknauth Jaggernauth, 58, New York, NY
Construction worker, NTX Interiors
Jake Denis Jagoda, 24, Huntington, NY
Brokerage, Cantor Fitzgerald
Yudh V.S. Jain, 54, New City, NY
Brokerage, Cantor Fitzgerald
Maria Jakubiak, 41, Ridgewood, NY
Accountant, Marsh & McLennan
Ernest James, 40, Manhattan, NY
Risk management, Marsh & McLennan
Gricelda E. James, 44, Willingboro, NJ
International Office Centers
Mark Jardim, 39, New York, NY
Zurich Scudder Investments
Mohammed Jawara
MAS Security
Maxima Jean-Pierre, 40, Bellport, NY
Food server, Forte Food Service
Paul E. Jeffers, 39, New York, NY
Joseph Jenkins, 47, New York, NY
Alan K. Jensen, 49, Wyckoff, NJ
Prem Nath Jerath, 57, Edison, NJ
Engineering, Port Authority of New York & New Jersey
Farah Jeudy, 32, Spring Valley, NY
Administrative assistant, Aon Corp.

Hweidar Jian, 42, East Brunswick, NJ
Brokerage, Cantor Fitzgerald
Eliezer Jiminez Jr., 38, New York, NY
Chef's assistant, Windows on the World
Luis Jimenez, 25, Corona, NY
Accountant, Marsh & McLennan
Charles Gregory John, 44, Brooklyn, NY
Nicholas John, 42, Manhattan, NY
Banking, JP Morgan Chase
LaShawana Johnson, 27, Brooklyn, NY
Telecommunications, General Telecom
Scott Michael Johnson, 26, Manhattan, NY
Investment analyst, Keefe Bruyette & Woods
Allison Horstmann Jones, 31, Manhattan, NY
Brokerage, Sandler O'Neill & Partners
Arthur Joseph Jones III, 37, Ossining, NY
Carr Futures
Brian L. Jones, 44, Kew Gardens, NY
Systems administrator, Fiduciary Trust Company International
Christopher D. Jones, 53, Huntington, NY
Brokerage, Cantor Fitzgerald
Donald Thomas Jones II, 39, Livingston, NJ
Brokerage, Cantor Fitzgerald
Donald W. Jones, 43, Fairless Hills, PA
Brokerage/financial services, Cantor Fitzgerald
Linda Jones, 50, New York, NY
Aon Corp.
Mary S. Jones, 72, New York, NY
Clerical, Port Authority of New York & New Jersey
Robert Thomas Jordan, 34, East Williston, NY
Brokerage, Cantor Fitzgerald
Albert Joseph, 79, Manhattan, NY
Maintenance, Morgan Stanley
Ingeborg Joseph, 60, Germany
Shipping, Rhode & Liesenfeld
Robert Joseph, Spring Valley, NY
Stephen Joseph, 39, Franklin Park, NJ
Fiduciary Trust Company International
Jane Eileen Josiah, 47, Bellmore, NY
Fiduciary Trust Company International
Karen Susan Juday, 52, Brooklyn, NY
Administrative assistant, Cantor Fitzgerald
Shashikiran Lakshmikantha Kadaba, 25, Hackensack, NJ
Computer engineer, Marsh & McLennan
Roya Kafaie, New York, NY
Gavkharoy Mukhometovna Kamardinova, 26, Brooklyn, NY
Shari Kandell, 27, Wyckoff, NJ
Brokerage, Cantor Fitzgerald
Howard Lee Kane, 40, Hazlet, NJ
Accountant, Windows on the World
Jennifer Lynn Kane, 26, Fair Lawn, NJ
Accountant, Marsh & McLennan
Joon Koo Kang, 34, Riverdale, NJ
Brokerage, Cantor Fitzgerald
Sheldon R. Kanter, 53, Edison, NJ
Systems analyst, Cantor Fitzgerald
Deborah H. Kaplan, 45, Paramus, NJ
Port Authority of New York & New Jersey
Alvin Peter Kappelman Jr., 57, Greenbrook, NJ
Insurance executive, Royal and Sun Alliance (visiting)
Charles Karczewski, 34, Union, NJ
Insurance consultant, Aon Corp.
William Tony A. Karnes, 37, Manhattan, NY
Software instructor, Marsh & McLennan
Douglas G. Karpiloff, 53, Mamaroneck, NY
Security, Port Authority of New York & New Jersey
Andrew Keith Kates, 37, Manhattan, NY
Brokerage, Cantor Fitzgerald
John Katsimatides, 31, East Marion, NY
Brokerage, Cantor Fitzgerald
Don Jerome Kauth Jr., 51, Saratoga Springs, NY
Bank analyst, Keefe Bruyette & Woods

Hideya Kawauchi, 36, Fort Lee, NJ
Banker, Fuji Bank
Edward Thomas Keane, 66, West Caldwell, NJ
Engineer, Port Authority of New York & New Jersey
Richard M. Keane, 54, Wethersfield, CT
Insurance, risk management, Marsh & McLennan
Lisa Kearney-Griffin, 35, Jamaica, NY
Travel, American Express
Karol Ann Keasler, 42, Brooklyn, NY
Event planner, Keefe Bruyette & Woods
Leo Russell Keene III, 34, Westfield, NJ
Equity analyst, Keefe Bruyette & Woods
Joseph J. Keller, 31, Park Ridge, NJ
Hospitality, Marriott World Trade Center Hotel
Peter Rodney Kellerman, 35, New York, NY
Brokerage, Cantor Fitzgerald
Joseph P. Kellett, 37, Riverdale, NY
Brokerage, Carr Futures
Frederick H. Kelley, 57, Huntington, NY
Brokerage, Cantor Fitzgerald
James Joseph "Kells" Kelly, 39, Oceanside, NY
Brokerage, Cantor Fitzgerald
Joseph Anthony Kelly, 40, Oyster Bay, NY
Brokerage, Cantor Fitzgerald
Maurice Patrick Kelly, 41, Bronx, NY
Carpenter, National Acoustics Inc.
Thomas Michael Kelly, 41, Wyckoff, NJ
Timothy C. Kelly, 37, Port Washington, NY
Brokerage, Cantor Fitzgerald
William Hill Kelly Jr., 30, Manhattan, NY
Bloomberg LP
Robert C. Kennedy, 55, Toms River, NJ
Brokerage, Marsh & McLennan
John Keohane, 41, Jersey City, NJ
Attorney, Zurich Insurance Co.
Howard L. Kestenbaum, 56, Upper Montclair, NJ
Insurance brokerage, Aon Corp.
Douglas D. Ketcham, 27, Manhattan, NY
Brokerage, Cantor Fitzgerald
Ruth E. Ketler, 42, New York, NY
Investment banking, Fiduciary Trust Company
International
Boris Khalif, 30, Sheepshead Bay, NY
Computer consultant, Marsh & McLennan
Sarah Khan, 32, Queens, NY
Taimour Firaz Khan, 29, Manhattan, NY
Brokerage, Carr Futures
Rajesh Khandelwal, 33, South Plainfield, NJ
Computer programmer, Marsh & McLennan
Bhowanie Devi Khemraj, Jersey City, NJ
Seilai Khoo, 38, Jersey City, NJ
Investment, Fred Alger Management
Satoshi Kikuchihara, 43, Scarsdale, NY
Andrew Jay-Hoon Kim, 26, Leonia, NJ
Financial analyst, Fred Alger Management
Lawrence Donald Kim, 31, Blue Bell, PA
Marsh & McLennan
Mary Jo Kimelman, 34, Manhattan, NY
Brokerage, Cantor Fitzgerald
Andrew Marshall King, 42, Princeton, NJ
Brokerage, Cantor Fitzgerald
Lucille King, 59, Ridgewood, NJ
Aon Corp.
Lisa M. King-Johnson, 34, New York, NY
Keefe Bruyette & Woods
Takashi Kinoshita, 46
Capital Markets Corp.
Chris Michael Kirby, 21, Bronx, NY
Howard Barry Kirschbaum, 53, Staten Island, NY
Risk and insurance, Marsh & McLennan
Glenn Davis Kirwin, 40, Scarsdale, NY
Brokerage, Cantor Fitzgerald

Richard J. Klares, 59, Somers, NY
Insurance, Marsh & McLennan
Peter A. Klein, 35, Weehawken, NJ
Marsh & McLennan
Alan David Kleinberg, 39, East Brunswick, NJ
Brokerage, Cantor Fitzgerald
Karen Joyce Klitzman, 38, Manhattan, NY
Energy specialist, Cantor Fitzgerald
Eugeuni Kniazev, 46, New York, NY
Windows on the World
Andrew Knox, 30, Adelaide, Australia
Thomas Patrick Knox, 31, Hoboken, NJ
Cantor Fitzgerald
Rebecca Koborie, 48, Guttenberg, NJ
Secretary, Marsh & McLennan
Deborah Kobus, 36, Brooklyn, NY
Chuo Mitsui Trust & Banking Company
Gary Edward Koecheler, 57, Harrison, NY
Brokerage, EuroBrokers Inc.
Frank J. Koestner, 48, Ridgewood, NJ
Brokerage, Cantor Fitzgerald
Ryan Kohart, 26, Manhattan, NY
Brokerage, Cantor Fitzgerald
Vanessa Lynn Kolpak, 21, New York, NY
Keefe Bruyette & Woods
Irina Kolpakova, 37, Brooklyn, NY
Lawyer's assistant, Harris Beach LLP
Suzanne Kondratenko, 28, Chicago, IL
Financial, Keane Consulting Group
Abdoulaye Kone, 37, New York, NY
Windows on the World
Bon-seok Koo, 32, River Edge, NJ
Insurance brokerage, LG Insurance Co.
Dorota Kopiczko, 26, Nutley, NJ
Marsh & McLennan
Bojan Kostic, 34, Manhattan, NY
Brokerage, Cantor Fitzgerald
Danielle Kousoulis, 29, Manhattan, NY
Brokerage, Cantor Fitzgerald
John J. Kren, 52
Lyudmila Ksido, 46, Brooklyn, NY
Computer programming, Accenture
Shekhar Kumar, 30, New York, NY
Frederick Kuo Jr., 53, Great Neck, NY
Mechanical engineer, Washington Group International
Patricia Kuras, 42, New York, NY
Nauka Kushitani, 44, New York, NY
Fiduciary Trust Company International
Victor Kwarkye, 35, New York, NY
Kui Fai Kwok, 31, New York, NY
Brokerage/financial services, Cantor Fitzgerald
Angela R. Kyte, 49, Boonton Township, NJ
Insurance brokerage, Marsh & McLennan
Amarnauth Lachhman, 42, Valley Stream, NY
Masonry, PM Contracting
Andrew LaCorte, 61, Jersey City, NJ
Brokerage, Carr Futures
Ganesh K. Ladkat, 27, Somerset, NJ
Information technology, Cantor Fitzgerald
James Patrick Ladley, 41, Colts Neck, NJ
Brokerage, Cantor Fitzgerald
Joseph A. Lafalce, 54, Queens, NY
Cantor Fitzgerald
Jeanette LaFond-Menichino, 49, New York, NY
Insurance brokerage, Marsh & McLennan
Michael Patrick LaForte, 39, Holmdel, NJ
Brokerage, Cantor Fitzgerald
Alan Lafranco, 43
Audio-visual technology, Windows on the World
Juan Lafuente, 61, Poughkeepsie, NY
Computer technology, Citigroup Inc.

Neil K. Lai, 59, East Windsor, NJ
Accounting, New York State Department of Taxation & Finance
Vincent Anthony Laieta, 31, Edison, NJ
Accounting, Aon Corp.
Franco Lalama, 45, Nutley, NJ
Engineer, Port Authority of New York & New Jersey
Chow Kwan Lam, 48, Maywood, NJ
Accounting, New York State Department of Taxation & Finance

Steven LaMantia, 38, Darien, CT
Brokerage, Cantor Fitzgerald
Amy Hope Lamonsoff, 29, Brooklyn, NY
Events manager, Risk Waters Group
Brendan M. Lang, 30, Red Bank, NJ
Construction, Structure Tone
Rosanne P. Lang, 42, Middletown, NJ
Brokerage, Cantor Fitzgerald
Vanessa Lang Langer, 29, Yonkers, NY
Administration, Regus Business Centers
Mary Lou Langley, 53, Staten Island, NY
Insurance brokerage, Aon Corp.
Michele B. Lanza, 36, Staten Island, NY
Administration, Fiduciary Trust Company International
Ruth Sheila Lapin, 53, East Windsor, NJ
Finance, Baseline Financial Services
Carol Ann LaPlante, 59, New York, NY
Marsh & McLennan
Ingeborg Astrid Desiree Lariby, 42, Manhattan, NY
Employment services, Regus Business Centers
Robin Blair Larkey, 48, Chatham, NJ
Brokerage, Cantor Fitzgerald
Christopher Randall Larrabee, 26, New York, NY
Brokerage, Cantor Fitzgerald
Hamidou S. Larry, 37, New York, NY
Marsh & McLennan
John Adam Larson, 37, Woodbridge, NJ
Insurance brokerage, Aon Corp.
Gary E. Lasko, 49, Memphis, TN
Insurance brokerage, Marsh & McLennan
Nicholas C. Lassman, 28, Cliffside Park, NJ
Computer technology, Cantor Fitzgerald
Jeffrey Latouche, 49, Jamaica, NY
Culinary arts, Windows on the World
Charles Laurencin, 61, Bedford-Stuyvesant, NY
Security officer, Morgan Stanley
Stephen James Lauria, 39, Staten Island, NY
Information technology, Marsh & McLennan
Maria LaVache, 60, Brooklyn, NY
Receptionist, Marsh & McLennan
Denis F. Lavelle, 42, Yonkers, NY
Accounting, Marsh & McLennan
Jeannine M. Laverde, 36, Staten Island, NY
Administration, Keefe Bruyette & Woods
Anna A. Laverty, 52, Middletown, NJ
Finance, Fiduciary Trust Company International
Steven Lawn, 28, West Windsor, NJ
Fiduciary Trust Company International
Robert A. Lawrence, 41, Summit, NJ
Investment banking, Sandler O'Neill & Partners
Nathaniel Lawson, 61, Brooklyn, NY
Food service, Cantor Fitzgerald
Eugen Lazar, 27, Glendale, NY
Computer engineering, Cantor Fitzgerald
Leon Lebor, 51, Jersey City, NJ
Janitor, ABM Industries
Kenneth Charles Ledee, 38, Monmouth Junction, NJ
Software administration, Marsh & McLennan
Alan J. Lederman, 43, Manhattan, NY
Insurance brokerage, Aon Corp.
Elena Ledesma, 36, Williamsburg, NY
Maintenance coordinating, Marsh & McLennan

Alexis Leduc, 45, New York, NY
Maintenance, Fiduciary Trust Company International
David Shufee Lee, 37, West Orange, NJ
Finance, Fiduciary Trust Company International
Gary H. Lee, 62, Lindenhurst, NY
Telecommunications, Cantor Fitzgerald
Hyun-joon Paul Lee, 32, New York, NY
Accounting, New York State Department of Taxation & Finance
Jong-min Lee
Juanita Lee, 44, New York, NY
Kathryn Blair Lee, 55, Brooklyn, NY
Information technology, Marsh & McLennan
Linda C. Lee, 34, Manhattan, NY
Finance, Jennison Associates
Lorraine Lee, 37, Staten Island, NY
Administration, Aon Corp.
Myung Woo Lee, 41, Lyndhurst, NJ
Accounting, New York State Department of Taxation & Finance
Richard Yun Choon Lee, 34, Great Neck, NY
Computer technology, Cantor Fitzgerald
Stuart Soo-Jin Lee, 30, New York, NY
Finance, Datasynapse
Yang-Der Lee, 63, Staten Island, NY
Delivery clerk, Windows on the World
Stephen Paul Lefkowitz, 50, Belle Harbor, NY
Mediation, New York State Department of Taxation & Finance
Adriana Legro, 32, Elmhurst, NY
Brokerage, Carr Futures
Edward J. Lehman, 41, Glen Cove, NY
Insurance brokerage, Aon Corp.
Eric Andrew Lehrfeld, 32, Brooklyn, NY
Finance, Random Walk Computing
David Ralph Leistman, 43, Garden City, NY
Brokerage, Cantor Fitzgerald
Joseph A. Lenihan, 41, Cos Cob, CT
Brokerage, Keefe Bruyette & Woods
John Robinson Lenoir, 38, Locust Valley, NY
Investment banking, Sandler O'Neill & Partners
Jorge Luis Leon, 43, Union City, NJ
Cantor Fitzgerald
Matthew Gerard Leonard, 38, Brooklyn, NY
Attorney, Cantor Fitzgerald
Michael Lepore, 39, Bronxville, NY
Information technology, Marsh & McLennan
Charles Antoine Lesperance, 55, Brooklyn, NY
Information technology, New York State Department of Taxation & Finance
Jeffrey Earle LeVeen, 55, Manhasset, NY
Brokerage, Cantor Fitzgerald
Alisha Caren Levin, 33, Manhattan, NY
Administration, Fuji Bank
Neil D. Levin, 46, Manhattan, NY
Attorney, Port Authority of New York & New Jersey
Robert "Bobby" Levine, West Babylon, NY
Finance, Thomson Financial
Robert M. Levine, 66, Edgewater, NJ
Shai Levinhar, 29, Manhattan, NY
Brokerage, Cantor Fitzgerald
Adam J. Lewis, 36, Fairfield, CT
Brokerage, Keefe Bruyette & Woods
Margaret Susan Lewis, 49, Elizabeth, NJ
Legal secretary, Port Authority of New York & New Jersey
Ye Wei Liang, 27, Woodside, NY
Information technology, Marsh & McLennan
Orasri Liangthanasarn, 26, Bayonne, NJ
Windows on the World
Ralph M. Licciardi, 30, West Hempstead, NY
Electrician, P.E. Stone Electric
Edward Lichtschein, 35, Park Slope, NY
Software engineering, Cantor Fitzgerald

Steven B. Lillianthal, 38, Millburn, NJ
Cantor Fitzgerald
Craig Damian Lilore, 30, Lyndhurst, NJ
Brokerage and law, Cantor Fitzgerald
Arnold A. Lim, 28
Computer technology, Fiduciary Trust Company International
Darya Lin, 32, Chicago, IL
Engineering and industrial operations, Keane Consulting
Group
Wei Rong Lin, 31, Jersey City, NJ
President, Frank W. Lin & Company
Tomas Gallegos Linares, Queretaro, Mexico
Nickie L. Lindo, 31, Brooklyn, NY
Thomas V. Linehan Jr., 39, Montville, NJ
Brokerage, Marsh & McLennan
Alan Linton Jr., 26, Jersey City, NJ
Investment banking, Sandler O'Neill & Partners
Diane Theresa Lipari, 42, Manhattan, NY
Brokerage, Carr Futures
Kenneth P. Lira, 28, Paterson, NJ
Genuity
Lorraine Lisi, 44, New York, NY
Fiduciary Trust Company International
Paul Lisson, 45, Brooklyn, NY
Clerk, Pitney Bowes
Vincent M. Litto, 52, Staten Island, NY
Brokerage, Cantor Fitzgerald
Ming-Hao Liu, 41, Livingston, NJ
Engineering, Washington Group International
Joseph Livera, 67
Nancy Liz, 39, New York, NY
Aon Corp.
Harold Lizcano, 31, East Elmhurst, NY
Accounting, Carr Futures
Martin Lizzul, 31, Manhattan, NY
Information technology consulting, Kestrel Technologies
George Llanes, 33, New York, NY
Brokerage, Carr Futures
Elizabeth Claire "Beth" Logler, 31, Rockville Centre, NY
Brokerage, Cantor Fitzgerald
Catherine Lisa LoGuidice, 30, New York, NY
Brokerage, Cantor Fitzgerald
Jerome Robert Lohez, 30, Jersey City, NJ
Software engineering, Empire Blue Cross/Blue Shield
Michael Lomax, 37, New York, NY
Insurance brokerage, Aon Corp.
Laura M. Longing, 35, Pearl River, NY
Brokerage, Marsh & McLennan
Salvatore Lopes, Franklin Square, NY
Investment banking, Sandler O'Neill & Partners
Daniel Lopez, 39, Greenpoint, NY
Brokerage, Carr Futures
George Lopez, 40, Stroudsburg, PA
Finance, Fiduciary Trust Company International
Luis M. Lopez, 38, New York, NY
Manuel L. "Manny" Lopez, 54, Jersey City, NJ
Accounting, Marsh & McLennan
Joseph Lostrangio, 48, Langhorne, PA
Finance, Devonshire Group
Chet Louie, 45, Manhattan, NY
Cantor Fitzgerald
Stuart Seid Louis, 43, East Brunswick, NJ
Investment banking, Sandler O'Neill & Partners
Michael W. Lowe, 48, Brooklyn, NY
Delivery man, Liberty Electric Co.
Garry Lozier, 47, Darien, CT
Investment banking, Sandler O'Neill & Partners
John Peter Lozowsky, 45, Astoria, NY
Self-employed
Charles Peter Lucania, 34, East Atlantic Beach, NY
Electrician, P.E. Stone Electric
Edward "Ted" Hobbs Luckett II, 40, Fair Haven, NJ
Brokerage, Cantor Fitzgerald

Mark G. Ludvigsen, 32, Manhattan, NY
Brokerage, Keefe Bruyette & Woods
Lee Charles Ludwig, 49, Staten Island, NY
Investment banking, Fiduciary Trust Company
International
Sean Thomas Lugano, 28, Manhattan, NY
Brokerage, Keefe Bruyette & Woods
Daniel Lugo, 45, Manhattan, NY
Security officer, Summit Security Services
Marie Lukas, 32, Staten Island, NY
Brokerage, Cantor Fitzgerald
William Lum Jr., 45, Manhattan, NY
Insurance brokerage, Marsh & McLennan
Michael P. Lunden, 37, Manhattan, NY
Brokerage, Cantor Fitzgerald
Christopher Lunder, 34, Wall, NJ
Brokerage, Cantor Fitzgerald
Anthony Luparello, 63, New York, NY
Janitor, ABM Industries
Gary Lutnick, 36, New York, NY
Brokerage, Cantor Fitzgerald
Linda Luzzicone, 33, Staten Island, NY
Brokerage, Cantor Fitzgerald
Alexander Lygin, 28, Brooklyn, NY
Computer programming, Cantor Fitzgerald
Farrell Peter Lynch, 39, Centerport, NY
Brokerage, Cantor Fitzgerald
Louise A. Lynch, 58, Amityville, NY
Brokerage, Marsh & McLennan
Michael Lynch, 34
Brokerage, Cantor Fitzgerald
Richard Dennis Lynch, 30, Bedford Hills, NY
Brokerage, EuroBrokers Inc.
Robert H. Lynch Jr., 44, Cranford, NJ
Administration, Port Authority of New York & New Jersey
Sean Lynch, 34, New York, NY
Brokerage, Cantor Fitzgerald
Sean Patrick Lynch, 36, Morristown, NJ
Brokerage, Cantor Fitzgerald
Monica Lyons, 53, Kew Gardens, NY
Administration, Marsh & McLennan
Robert Francis Mace, 43, Manhattan, NY
Lawyer, Cantor Fitzgerald
Jan Maciejewski, 37, Long Island City, NY
Waiter/computer consultant, Windows on the World
Catherine Fairfax MacRae, 23, Manhattan, NY
Brokerage, Fred Alger Management
Richard B. Madden, 35, Westfield, NJ
Insurance brokerage, Aon Corp.
Simon Maddison, 40, Florham Park, NJ
Computer programming, S.M.C.K./Cantor Fitzgerald
Noell C. Maerz, 29, Long Beach, NY
Brokerage, EuroBrokers Inc.
Jennieann Maffeo, 40, Bensonhurst, NY
Brokerage, UBS PaineWebber
Jay Robert Magazine, 48, Suffern, NY
Chef/catering, Windows on the World
Brian Magee, 52, Floral Park, NY
Compaq
Charles Wilson Magee, 51, Wantagh, NY
Engineer, World Trade Center
Joseph Maggitti, 47, Abington, MD
Marsh & McLennan
Ronald E. Magnuson, 57, Park Ridge, NJ
Finance, Cantor Fitzgerald
Daniel L. Maher, 50, Hamilton, NJ
Insurance brokerage, Marsh & McLennan
Thomas A. Mahon, 37, East Norwich, NY
Brokerage, Cantor Fitzgerald
Joseph Maio, 32, Roslyn Harbor, NY
Brokerage, Cantor Fitzgerald
Takashi Makimoto, 49
Fuji Bank

Abdu Malahi, 37, Brooklyn, NY
Marriott World Trade Center Hotel
Debora I. Maldonado, 47, South Ozone Park, NY
Secretary, Marsh & McLennan
Myrna T. Maldonado-Agosto, 49, Bronx, NY
Technology services, Port Authority of New York & New Jersey
Alfred R. Maler, 39, Convent Station, NJ
Cantor Fitzgerald
Gregory James Malone, 42, Hoboken, NJ
Brokerage, EuroBrokers Inc.
Edward Francis "Teddy" Maloney, 32, Norwalk, CT
Brokerage, Cantor Fitzgerald
Gene E. Maloy, 41, Bay Ridge, NY
Marsh & McLennan
Christian Hartwell Maltby, 37, Chatham, NJ
Brokerage, Cantor Fitzgerald
Francisco Mancini, 26, Astoria, NY
Construction, Local 79
Joseph Mangano, 53, Jackson, NJ
Software engineer, Marsh & McLennan
Sara Elizabeth Manley, 31, New York, NY
Investment adviser, Fred Alger Management
Debra M. Mannetta, 31, Islip, NY
Carr Futures
Marion Victoria "Vickie" Manning, 27, Rochdale Village, NY
Secretary, Marsh & McLennan
Terence J. Manning, 36, Point Lookout, NY
Computer consultant, ARC Partners (visiting)
James Maounis, 42, Brooklyn, NY
Laura A. Giglio Marchese, 35, Oceanside, NY
Alliance Consulting Group
Peter Edward Mardikian, 29, Manhattan, NY
Imagine Software
Edward Joseph Mardovich, 42, Lloyd Harbor, NY
Brokerage, EuroBrokers Inc.
Lester Vincent Marino, 57, Massapequa, NY
Electrician, Forest Electric Corp.
Vita Marino, 49, Manhattan, NY
Investment banking, Sandler O'Neill & Partners
Kevin D. Marlo, 28, Manhattan, NY
Brokerage, Sandler O'Neill & Partners
Jose J. Marrero, 32, Old Bridge, NJ
Investment, EuroBrokers Inc.
James Martello, 41, Rumson, NJ
Brokerage, Cantor Fitzgerald
Michael A. Marti, 26, Glendale, NY
Brokerage, Cantor Fitzgerald
William J. Martin, 35, Denville, NJ
Brokerage, Cantor Fitzgerald
Brian E. Martineau, 37, Edison, NJ
Insurance brokerage, Aon Corp.
Betsy Martinez, 33, New York, NY
Brokerage, Cantor Fitzgerald
Edward J. Martinez, 60, New York, NY
Brokerage, Cantor Fitzgerald
Jose Martinez, 49, Hauppauge, NY
Electrician, Forest Electric Corp.
Robert Gabriel Martinez, 24, Long Island City, NY
Security guard, Summit Security Services
Lizie Martinez-Calderon, 32, Washington Heights, NY
Secretary, Aon Corp.
Bernard Mascarenhas, 54, Newmarket, Ontario, Canada
Insurance brokerage, Marsh & McLennan
Stephen F. Masi, 55, New York, NY
Cantor Fitzgerald
Nicholas "Nick" Massa, 65, Manhattan, NY
Insurance brokerage, Aon Corp.
Patricia A. Massari, 25, Glendale, NY
Insurance brokerage, Marsh & McLennan
Michael Massaroli, 38, Staten Island, NY
Brokerage, Cantor Fitzgerald

Philip W. Mastrandrea, 42, Chatham, NJ
Cantor Fitzgerald
Rudolph Mastrocinque, 43, Kings Park, NY
Insurance brokerage, Marsh & McLennan
Joseph Mathai, 49, Arlington, MA
Cambridge Technology Partners
Charles William Mathers, 61, Sea Girt, NJ
Insurance brokerage, Marsh & McLennan
William A. Mathesen, 40, Morris Township, NJ
Brokerage, EuroBrokers Inc.
Margaret Elaine Mattic, 51, Brooklyn, NY
Customer service representative, General Telecom
Marcello Mattricciano, 31, New York, NY
Cantor Fitzgerald
Robert D. Mattson, 54, Green Pond, NJ
Banker, Fiduciary Trust Company International
Walter Matuza, 39, Staten Island, NY
Brokerage, Carr Futures
Charles A. Mauro, 65, Eltingville, NY
Aon Corp.
Charles J. Mauro, 38, Eltingville, NY
Windows on the World
Dorothy Mauro, 55, New York, NY
Marsh & McLennan
Nancy T. Mauro, 51, Forest Hills, NY
Insurance brokerage, Marsh & McLennan
Tyrone May, 44, Rahway, NJ
Tax auditor, New York State Department of Taxation & Finance
Robert J. Mayo, 46, Morganville, NJ
Fire safety, OSC Group
Edward Mazzella Jr., 62, Monroe, NY
Brokerage, Cantor Fitzgerald
Jennifer Mazzotta, 23, Maspeth, NY
Cantor Fitzgerald
Kaaria Mbaya, 39, Edison, NJ
Computer analyst, Cantor Fitzgerald
James J. McAlary, 42, Spring Lake Heights, NJ
Brokerage, Carr Futures
Patricia A. McAneney, 50, Pomona, NJ
Insurance brokerage, Marsh & McLennan
Colin Richard McArthur, 52, Howell, NJ
Aon Corp.
Kenneth M. McBrayer, 49, Manhattan, NY
Sandler O'Neill & Partners
Brendan F. McCabe, 40, Sayville, NY
Brokerage, Fiduciary Trust Company International
Charlie McCabe, 46
Michael Justin McCabe, 42, Rumson, NJ
Brokerage, Cantor Fitzgerald
Justin McCarthy, 30, Port Washington, NY
Brokerage, Cantor Fitzgerald
Kevin McCarthy, 42, Fairfield, CT
Brokerage, Cantor Fitzgerald
Michael Desmond McCarthy, 33, Huntington, NY
Brokerage, Carr Futures
Robert Garvin McCarthy, 33, Stony Point, NY
Brokerage, Cantor Fitzgerald
Stanley McCaskill, 47, Manhattan, NY
Security guard, Advantage Security
Katie McCloskey, 25, Mount Vernon, NY
Marsh & McLennan
Tara McCloud-Gray, 30, Brooklyn, NY
Engineer, General Telecom
Charles Austin McCrann, 55, Manhattan, NY
Insurance brokerage, Marsh & McLennan
Tonyell McDay, 25, Colonia, NJ
Information technology, Marsh & McLennan
Matthew T. McDermott, 34, Basking Ridge, NJ
Brokerage, Cantor Fitzgerald
Joseph P. McDonald, 43, Livingston, NJ
Brokerage, Cantor Fitzgerald

Michael Patrick McDonnell, 34, Red Bank, NJ
Accountant, Keefe Bruyette & Woods
John F. McDowell Jr., 33, Manhattan, NY
Brokerage, Sandler O'Neill & Partners
Eamon J. McEneaney, 46, New Canaan, CT
Brokerage, Cantor Fitzgerald
John Thomas McErlean Jr., 39, Larchmont, NY
Brokerage, Cantor Fitzgerald
Katherine "Katie" McGarry-Noack, 30, Hoboken, NJ
Financial consultant, Telekurs USA (visiting)
Daniel F. McGinley, 40, Ridgewood, NJ
Brokerage, Keefe Bruyette & Woods
Mark Ryan McGinly, 26, Manhattan, NY
Brokerage, Carr Futures
Thomas Henry McGinnis, 41, Oakland, NJ
Brokerage, Carr Futures
Michael Gregory McGinty, 42, Foxboro, MA
Insurance brokerage, Marsh & McLennan
Ann McGovern, 67, East Meadow, NY
Insurance brokerage, Aon Corp.
Scott Martin McGovern, 35, Wyckoff, NJ
Brokerage, EuroBrokers Inc.
Stacey S. McGowan, 38, Basking Ridge, NJ
Brokerage, Sandler O'Neill & Partners
Francis Noel McGuinn, 48, Rye, NY
Brokerage, Cantor Fitzgerald
Patrick J. McGuire, 40, Madison, NJ
Brokerage, EuroBrokers Inc.
Thomas McHale, 33, Huntington, NY
Cantor Fitzgerald
Keith McHeffey, 31, Monmouth Beach, NJ
Brokerage, Cantor Fitzgerald
Ann M. McHugh, 35, New York, NY
EuroBrokers Inc.
Denis J. McHugh, 36, Manhattan, NY
Brokerage, EuroBrokers Inc.
Michael Edward McHugh Jr., 35, Tuckahoe, NY
Brokerage, Cantor Fitzgerald
Robert G. McIlvaine, 26, Manhattan, NY
Media relations, Merrill Lynch
Stephanie McKenna, 45, Staten Island, NY
Accountant, Reinsurance Solutions Inc.
Barry J. McKeon, 47, Yorktown Heights, NY
Brokerage, Fiduciary Trust Company International
Darryl Leron McKinney, 26, New York, NY
Brokerage clerk, Cantor Fitzgerald
George Patrick McLaughlin Jr., 36, Hoboken, NJ
Carr Futures
Robert Carroll McLaughlin Jr., 29, Westchester, NY
Brokerage, Cantor Fitzgerald
Gavin McMahon, 35, Bayonne, NJ
Insurance brokerage, Aon Corp.
Edmund M. McNally, 40, Fair Haven, NJ
Brokerage, Fiduciary Trust Company International
Daniel McNeal, 29, NJ
Investment banking, Sandler O'Neill & Partners
Christine Sheila McNulty, 42, Peterborough, England
Visiting from England
Sean Peter McNulty, 30, New York, NY
Cantor Fitzgerald
Rocco Medaglia, 49, Melville, NY
Construction, Cantor Fitzgerald
Abigail Medina, 46, New York, NY
Brokerage, Guy Carpenter Reinsurance
Ana Iris Medina, 39, New York, NY
Damien Meehan, 32, Glen Rock, NJ
Brokerage, Cantor Fitzgerald
William J. Meehan Jr., 49, Darien, CT
Brokerage, Cantor Fitzgerald
Alok Mehta, 23, Hempstead, NY
Cantor Fitzgerald
Manuel Emilio Mejia, 54, Manhattan, NY
Food service, Windows on the World

Eskedar Melaku, 31, New York, NY
Insurance brokerage, Marsh & McLennan
Antonio Melendez, 30, Bronx, NY
Windows on the World
Mary Melendez, 44, Stroudsburg, PA
Assistant secretary, Fiduciary Trust Company International
Yelena Melnichenko, 28, New York, NY
Marsh & McLennan
Stuart Todd Meltzer, 32, Syosset, NY
Brokerage, Cantor Fitzgerald
Diarelia Jovannah Mena, 30, Brooklyn, NY
Computer programming, Cantor Fitzgerald
Lizette Mendoza, 33, North Bergen, NJ
Aon Corp.
Shevonne Mentis, 25, Brooklyn, NY
Receptionist, Marsh & McLennan
Wesley Mercer, 70, Manhattan, NY
Security, Morgan Stanley
Ralph Joseph Mercurio, 47, Rockville Centre, NY
Brokerage, Cantor Fitzgerald
Alan H. Merdinger, 47, Allentown, PA
Accountant, Cantor Fitzgerald
George C. Merino, 39, Bayside, NY
Brokerage, Fiduciary Trust Company International
George Merkouris, 35, Levittown, NY
Carr Futures
Deborah Merrick, 45
Port Authority of New York & New Jersey
Raymond J. Metz III, 37, Trumbull, CT
Brokerage, EuroBrokers Inc.
Jill A. Metzler, 32, Franklin Square, NY
Aon Corp.
David R. Meyer, 57, Glen Rock, NJ
Brokerage, Cantor Fitzgerald
Nurul Huq Miah, 36, Bay Ridge, NY
Audio-visual technology, Marsh & McLennan
Shakila Yasmin Miah, 26, Bay Ridge, NY
Information technology, Marsh & McLennan
William Edward Micciulli, 30, Matawan, NJ
Brokerage, Cantor Fitzgerald
Martin Paul Michelstein, 57, Morristown, NJ
Luis Clodoldo Revilla Mier, 54
Washington Group International
Peter Teague Milano, 43, Middletown, NJ
Brokerage, Cantor Fitzgerald
Gregory Milanowycz, 25, Cranford, NJ
Insurance brokerage, Aon Corp.
Lukasz Milewski, 21, Kew Gardens, NY
Food server, Windows on the World
Corey Peter Miller, 34, New York, NY
Brokerage, Cantor Fitzgerald
Craig James Miller, 29, VA
U.S. Secret Service
Joel Miller, 55, Baldwin, NY
Insurance brokerage, Marsh & McLennan
Michael Matthew Miller, 39, Englewood, NJ
Brokerage, Cantor Fitzgerald
Phillip D. Miller, 53, Staten Island, NY
Aon Corp.
Robert Alan Miller, 46, Matawan, NJ
Taxation, New York State Department of Taxation & Finance
Robert C. Miller Jr., 55, Hasbrouck Heights, NJ
Aon Corp.
Benjamin Millman, 40, Staten Island, NY
Independent carpenter, Aon Corp.
Charles M. Mills, 61, Brentwood, NY
Taxation, New York State Department of Taxation & Finance
Ronald Keith Milstein, 54, Queens, NY
Administrator, Fiduciary Trust Company International
William G. Minardi, 46, Bedford, NY
Brokerage, Cantor Fitzgerald
Louis Joseph Minervino, 54, Middletown, NJ
Insurance brokerage, Marsh & McLennan

Wilbert Miraille, 29, New York, NY
Mailroom employee, Cantor Fitzgerald
Domenick Mircovich, 40, Closter, NJ
Accountant, EuroBrokers Inc.
Rajesh A. Mirpuri, 30, Englewood Cliffs, NJ
Business development, Data Synapse
Joseph Mistrulli, 47, Wantagh, NY
Carpenter, Island Acoustics/Windows on the World
Susan Miszkowicz, 37, Brooklyn, NY
Engineering, Port Authority of New York & New Jersey
Richard Miuccio, 55, Staten Island, NY
Auditor, New York State Department of Taxation & Finance
Frank V. Moccia, 57, Hauppauge, NY
Facility planner, Washington Group International
Mubarak Mohammad, 23, East Orange, NJ
Boyie Mohammed, 50, New York, NY
Brokerage, Carr Futures
Fernando Jiminez Molina, Oaxaca, Mexico
Kleber Rolando Molina, 44, New York, NY
Manuel Dejesus Molina, 31, New York, NY
ABM Industries
Justin J. Molisani Jr., 42, Middletown Township, NJ
Brokerage, EuroBrokers Inc.
Brian Patrick Monaghan, 21, New York, NY
Apprentice carpenter, Certified Installation Service
Franklin Monahan, 45, Roxbury, NY
Cantor Fitzgerald
John G. Monahan, 47, Ocean Township, NJ
Accountant, Cantor Fitzgerald
Kristen Montanaro, 34, Staten Island, NY
Administrative assistant, Marsh & McLennan
Craig D. Montano, 38, Glen Ridge, NJ
Brokerage, Cantor Fitzgerald
Cheryl Ann Monyak, 43, Greenwich, CT
Insurance brokerage, Marsh & McLennan
Sharon Moore, 37, Queens, NY
Investment, Sandler O'Neill & Partners
Krishna V. Moorthy, 59, Briarcliff Manor, NY
Programmer, Fiduciary Trust Company International
Abner Morales, 37, Ozone Park, NY
Programming, Fiduciary Trust Company International
Carlos Morales, 29, New York, NY
Computer technician, Cantor Fitzgerald
Paula Morales, 42, Richmond Hill, NY
Finance, Aon Corp.
John Christopher Moran, 38, Haslemere, Surrey, England
Kathleen Moran, 42, Brooklyn, NY
Lindsay S. Morehouse, 24, Manhattan, NY
Investment, Keefe Bruyette & Woods
George Morell, 47, Mt. Kisco, NY
Brokerage, Cantor Fitzgerald
Steven P. Morello, 52, Bayonne, NJ
Facilities management, Marsh & McLennan
Arturo Alva Moreno, Mexico City, Mexico
Food service, Windows on the World
Yvette Nicole Moreno, 25, New York, NY
Receptionist, Carr Futures
Dorothy Morgan, 47, Hempstead, NY
Insurance brokerage, Marsh & McLennan
Richard J. Morgan, 66, Glen Rock, NJ
Emergency management, Consolidated Edison
Nancy Morgenstern, 32
Travel agent, Cantor Fitzgerald
Sanae Mori, Tokyo, Japan
Nomura Research Institute
Blanca Morocho, 26, New York, NY
Kitchen worker, Windows on the World
Leonel Morocho, 36, Brooklyn, NY
Chef, Windows on the World
Dennis G. Moroney, 39, Tuckahoe, NY
Brokerage, Cantor Fitzgerald
Lynne Irene Morris, 22, Monroe, NY
Brokerage, Cantor Fitzgerald

Seth A. Morris, 35, Kinnelon, NJ
Brokerage, Cantor Fitzgerald
Stephen Philip Morris, 31, Ormond Beach, FL
Christopher Morrison, 34, Charlestown, MA
Investment, Zurich Scudder Investments (visiting)
William David Moskal, 50, Brecksville, OH
Insurance brokerage, Marsh & McLennan
Marco Motroni Sr., 57, Fort Lee, NJ
Brokerage, Carr Futures
Cynthia Motus-Wilson, 52, Bronx, NY
Receptionist, International Office Centers
Chung Mou
Iouri Mouchinski, 55, Brooklyn, NY
Jude J. Moussa, 35, Manhattan, NY
Brokerage, Cantor Fitzgerald
Peter C. Moutos, 44, Chatham, NJ
Information technology, Marsh & McLennan
Damion Mowatt, 21, Brooklyn, NY
Food service, Forte Food Service
Stephen V. Mulderry, 33, Manhattan, NY
Brokerage, Keefe Bruyette & Woods
Peter James Mulligan, 28, Manhattan, NY
Cantor Fitzgerald
Michael Joseph Mullin, 27, Hoboken, NJ
Brokerage, Cantor Fitzgerald
James Donald Munhall, 45, Ridgewood, NJ
Brokerage, Sandler O'Neill & Partners
Nancy Muniz, 45, Ridgewood, NY
Administrative assistant, Port Authority of New York & New Jersey
Carlos Mario Munoz, 43
Food service, Windows on the World
Theresa "Terry" Munson, 54, New York, NY
Technical assistant, Aon Corp.
Robert M. Murach, 45, Montclair, NJ
Brokerage, Cantor Fitzgerald
Cesar Augusto Murillo, 32, Manhattan, NY
Brokerage, Cantor Fitzgerald
Marc A. Murolo, 28, Maywood, NJ
Brokerage, Cantor Fitzgerald
Brian Joseph Murphy, 41, New York, NY
Brokerage, Cantor Fitzgerald
Charles A. Murphy, 36, Ridgewood, NJ
Brokerage, Cantor Fitzgerald
Christopher William White Murphy, 35, Stamford, CT
Research analyst, Keefe Bruyette & Woods
Edward C. Murphy, 42, Clifton, NJ
Brokerage, Cantor Fitzgerald
James Francis Murphy IV, 30, Garden City, NY
Investment, Thomson Financial
James Thomas Murphy, 35, Middletown, NJ
Brokerage, Cantor Fitzgerald
Kevin James Murphy, 40, Northport, NY
Insurance brokerage, Marsh & McLennan
Patrick Sean Murphy, 36, Millburn, NJ
Information technology, Marsh & McLennan
Robert Murphy, 56, Hollis, NY
John J. Murray, 32, Hoboken, NJ
Brokerage, Cantor Fitzgerald
John Joseph "Jack" Murray, 52, Colts Neck, NJ
Banker, Industrial Bank of Japan (meeting)
Susan D. Murray, 54, Summit, NJ
Marsh & McLennan
Valerie Victoria Murray, 65, Queens, NY
Administration, Ohrenstein & Brown
Yuriy Mushynskyi, 55
Richard Todd Myhre, 37, Staten Island, NY
Finance, Cantor Fitzgerald
Takuya Nakamura, 30, Tuckahoe, NY
Nishi-Nippon
Alexander J.R. Napier Jr., 38, Morris Township, NJ
Aon Corp.

Frank Joseph Naples III, 29, Cliffside Park, NJ
Brokerage, Cantor Fitzgerald
Catherine Nardella, 40, Bloomfield, NJ
Insurance brokerage, Aon Corp.
Mario Nardone, 32, Staten Island, NY
Brokerage, EuroBrokers Inc.
Manika Narula, 22, Kings Park, NY
Brokerage, financial services, Cantor Fitzgerald
Narendra Nath, 33, Colonia, NJ
Karen S. Navarro, 30, Bayside, NY
Carr Futures
Francis Nazario, 28, Jersey City, NJ
Brokerage, Cantor Fitzgerald
Glenroy Neblett, 42, New York, NY
Marsh & McLennan
Marcus R. Neblett, 31, Roslyn Heights, NY
Insurance brokerage, Aon Corp.
Jerome O. Nedd, 39, New York, NY
Windows on the World
Laurence Nedell, 52, Lindenhurst, NY
Risk-management specialist, Aon Corp.
Luke G. Nee, 44, Stony Point, NY
Brokerage, Cantor Fitzgerald
Pete Negron, 34, Bergenfield, NJ
Architecture, Port Authority of New York & New Jersey
Ann Nicole Nelson, 30, Manhattan, NY
Brokerage, Cantor Fitzgerald
David William Nelson, 50, Park Slope, NY
Brokerage, Carr Futures
Michele Ann Nelson, 27, Valley Stream, NY
Brokerage, Cantor Fitzgerald
Oscar Nesbitt, 58, New York, NY
New York State Department of Taxation & Finance
Nancy Yuen Ngo, 36, Harrington Park, NJ
Computer technology, Marsh & McLennan
Jody Tepedino Nichilo, 39, New York, NY
Cantor Fitzgerald
Martin Stewart Niederer, 23, Hoboken, NJ
Brokerage, Cantor Fitzgerald
Frank John Niestadt Jr., 55, Ronkonkoma, NY
Insurance brokerage, Aon Corp.
Gloria Nieves, 48, Jackson Heights, NY
Fiduciary Trust Company International
Juan Nieves Jr., 56, Bronx, NY
Salad chef, Windows on the World
Troy Edward Nilsen, 33, Staten Island, NY
Engineering, Cantor Fitzgerald
Paul R. Nimbley, 42, Middletown, NJ
Brokerage, Cantor Fitzgerald
John Ballantine Niven, 44, Oyster Bay, NY
Insurance brokerage, Aon Corp.
Curtis Terrence Noel, 22, Bronx, NY
Telecommunications, General Telecom
Daniel Robert Nolan, 44, Lake Hopatcong, NJ
Brokerage, Marsh & McLennan
Robert Walter Noonan, 36, Norwalk, CT
Brokerage, Cantor Fitzgerald
Daniela R. Notaro, 25, New York, NY
Administration, Carr Futures
Brian Novotny, 33, Hoboken, NJ
Brokerage, Cantor Fitzgerald
Soichi Numata, 45, Irvington, NY
Banking, Fuji Bank
Brian Felix Nunez, 29, Staten Island, NY
Administration, Cantor Fitzgerald
Jose R. Nunez, 42, Bronx, NY
Food service, Windows on the World
Jeffrey Nussbaum, 37, Oceanside, NY
Brokerage, Carr Futures
James A. Oakley, 52, Cortlandt Manor, NY
Information technology, Marsh & McLennan
James P. O'Brien, 33, New York, NY
Brokerage, Cantor Fitzgerald

Michael O'Brien, 42, Cedar Knolls, NJ
Brokerage, Cantor Fitzgerald
Scott J. O'Brien, 40, Brooklyn, NY
Sales, Slam Dunk Networks
Timothy Michael O'Brien, 40, Brookville, NY
Brokerage, Cantor Fitzgerald
Jefferson Ocampo, 28
Dennis J. O'Connor Jr., 34, Manhattan, NY
Finance, Cantor Fitzgerald
Diana J. O'Connor, 38, Eastchester, NY
Finance, Sandler O'Neill & Partners
Keith Kevin O'Connor, 28, Hoboken, NJ
Brokerage, Keefe Bruyette & Woods
Richard J. O'Connor, 49, Poughkeepsie, NY
Brokerage, Marsh & McLennan
Amy O'Doherty, 23, New York, NY
Brokerage, Cantor Fitzgerald
Marni Pont O'Doherty, 31, Armonk, NY
Brokerage, Keefe Bruyette & Woods
Takashi Ogawa, 37, Tokyo, Japan
Research, Nomura Research Institute
Albert Ogletree, 49, Manhattan, NY
Food service handler, Forte Food Service
Philip Paul Ognibene, 39, Manhattan, NY
Brokerage, Keefe Bruyette & Woods
James Andrew O'Grady, 32, Harrington Park, NJ
Investment banking, Sandler O'Neill & Partners
Gerald Michael Olcott, 55, New Hyde Park, NY
Insurance brokerage, Marsh & McLennan
Gerald O'Leary, 34, Stony Point, NY
Chef, Cantor Fitzgerald
Christine Anne Olender, 39, Manhattan, NY
Administration, Windows on the World
Linda Mary Oliva, 44, Staten Island, NY
Brokerage, Carr Futures
Edward K. Oliver, 31, Jackson, NJ
Brokerage, Carr Futures
Leah E. Oliver, 24, Brooklyn Heights, NY
Sales, Marsh & McLennan
Maureen L. "Rene" Olson, 50, Rockville Centre, NY
Insurance brokerage, Marsh & McLennan
Matthew Timothy O'Mahony, 39, Manhattan, NY
Brokerage, Cantor Fitzgerald
Toshihiro Onda, 39
Banking, Fuji Bank
Seamus L. O'Neal, 52, Brooklyn, NY
Computers, Cantor Fitzgerald
John P. O'Neill, 49, Ventnor City, NJ
Security personnel, World Trade Center
Peter J. O'Neill Jr., 21, Amityville, NY
Brokerage, Sandler O'Neill & Partners
Sean Gordon Corbett O'Neill, 34, Rye, NY
Brokerage, Cantor Fitzgerald
Michael C. Opperman, 45, Selden, NY
Insurance brokerage, Aon Corp.
Ken O'Reilly, 26, Ireland
Business software
Christopher Orgielewicz, 35, Larchmont, NY
Research analyst, Sandler O'Neill & Partners
Margaret Q. Orloske, 50, Windsor, CT
Management, Marsh & McLennan
Virginia Ginger Ormiston-Kenworthy, 42, Manhattan, NY
Insurance brokerage, Marsh & McLennan
Juan Romero Orozco, Acatian de Osorio, Puebla, Mexico
Ronald Orsini, 59, Hillsdale, NJ
Brokerage, Cantor Fitzgerald
Peter K. Ortale, 37, Manhattan, NY
Brokerage, EuroBrokers Inc.
Alexander Ortiz, 36, Ridgewood, NY
Security officer, Empire Health Choice
David Ortiz, 37, Nanuet, NY
Locksmith, Port Authority of New York & New Jersey

Emilio Peter Ortiz Jr., 38, Corona, NY
Brokerage, Carr Futures
Pablo Ortiz, 49, Staten Island, NY
Construction, Port Authority of New York & New Jersey
Paul Ortiz Jr., 21, Brooklyn, NY
Computer technology, Bloomberg LP
Sonia Ortiz, 58, Flushing, NY
Janitorial services, ABM Industries
Masaru Ose, 36, Fort Lee, NJ
Brokerage, Mizuho Capital Markets Corp.
Patrick J. O'Shea, 45, Farmingdale, NY
Brokerage, Carr Futures
Robert W. O'Shea, 47, Wall, NJ
Brokerage, Carr Futures
Elsy Carolina Osorio-Oliva, 27, Queens, NY
Engineering, General Telecom
James Robert Ostrowski, 37, Garden City, NY
Brokerage, Cantor Fitzgerald
Timothy F. O'Sullivan, 68, Albrightsville, PA
Consulting, Cultural Institution of Retirement System Trusts
Jason Douglas Oswald, 28, Manhattan, NY
Accounting, Cantor Fitzgerald
Isidro Ottenwalder, 35, Queens, NY
Windows on the World
Michael Ou, 53, New York, NY
New York State Department of Taxation & Finance
Todd Joseph Ouida, 25, River Edge, NJ
Brokerage, Cantor Fitzgerald
Jesus Ovalles, 60, Manhattan, NY
Windows on the World
Peter J. Owens, Williston Park, NY
Cantor Fitzgerald
Adianes Oyola, 23, Brooklyn, NY
Human resources personnel, Fuji Bank
Angel M. "Chic" Pabon, 54, Brooklyn, NY
Brokerage, Cantor Fitzgerald
Israel Pabon, 31, Harlem, NY
Food service handler, Forte Food Service
Roland Pacheco, 25, Brooklyn, NY
Administration, Alliance Consulting Group
Michael Benjamin Packer, 45, New York, NY
Mechanical engineering, Merrill Lynch
Deepa K. Pakkala, 31, Stewartsville, NJ
Computer programming, Oracle Corp.
Thomas Anthony Palazzo, 44, Armonk, NY
Brokerage, Cantor Fitzgerald
Richard Palazzolo, 39, Manhattan, NY
Brokerage, Cantor Fitzgerald
Alan Palumbo, 42, Staten Island, NY
Brokerage, Cantor Fitzgerald
Christopher M. Panatier, 36, Rockville Centre, NY
Brokerage, Cantor Fitzgerald
Dominique Lisa Pandolfo, 27, Hoboken, NJ
Computer technology, Marsh & McLennan
Edward J. Papa, 47, Oyster Bay, NY
Brokerage, Cantor Fitzgerald
Salvatore Papasso, 34, Staten Island, NY
Criminal justice, New York State Department of Taxation & Finance
Vinod K. Parakat, 34, Sayreville, NJ
Software programming, Cantor Fitzgerald
Vijayashankar Paramsothy, 23, Astoria, NY
Insurance, Aon Corp.
Nitin Ramesh Parandkar, 28, Woodbridge, NJ
Software consulting, Marsh & McLennan
Hardai Casey Parbhu, 42, New York, NY
Insurance, Aon Corp.
Debra "Debbie" Paris, 48, Brooklyn, NY
Executive assistant, Sandler O'Neill & Partners
George Paris, 33, New York, NY
Finance, Cantor Fitzgerald
Gye-Hyong Park, 28, Flushing, NY
Insurance sales, Metropolitan Life Insurance

Philip L. Parker, 53, Skillman, NJ
Insurance brokerage, Aon Corp.
Michael A. Parkes, 27, East Flatbush, NY
Accounting, Marsh & McLennan
Robert Emmett Parks Jr., 47, Middletown, NJ
Brokerage, Cantor Fitzgerald
Hasmukh Chuckulal Parmar, 48, Warren, NJ
Computer technology, Cantor Fitzgerald
Diane Marie Moore Parsons, 58, Malta, NY
New York State Department of Taxation & Finance
Leobardo Lopez Pascual, 41, New York, NY
Food service, Windows on the World
Michael J. Pascuma, 50, Massapequa Park, NY
Brokerage, Harvey, Young & Yurman
Jerrold H. Paskins, 56, Anaheim Hills, CA
Insurance brokerage, Devonshire Group
Horace Robert Passananti, 55, Manhattan, NY
Insurance brokerage, Marsh & McLennan
Suzanne H. Passaro, 38, East Brunswick, NJ
Insurance, Aon Corp.
Victor Antonio Martinez Pastrana, Tlachichuca, Puebla, Mexico
Food service
Avnish Ramanbhai Patel, 28, Manhattan, NY
Brokerage, Fred Alger Management
Dipti Patel, 38, New Hyde Park, NY
Administration, Cantor Fitzgerald
Manish K. Patel, 29, Edison, NJ
Finance, EuroBrokers Inc.
Steven B. Paterson, 40, Ridgewood, NJ
Brokerage, Cantor Fitzgerald
James Matthew Patrick, 30, Norwalk, CT
Brokerage, Cantor Fitzgerald
Lawrence Patrick, Manalapan, NJ
Manuel Patrocino, 34
Food service, Windows on the World
Bernard E. "Bernie" Patterson, 46, Upper Brookville, NY
Brokerage, Cantor Fitzgerald
Cira Marie Patti, 40, Staten Island, NY
Brokerage, Keefe Bruyette & Woods
Robert Edward Pattison, 40, Manhattan, NY
James Robert Paul, 58, New York, NY
Brokerage, Carr Futures
Patrice Sobin Paz, 52, New York, NY
Aon Corp.
Sharon Cristina Millan Paz, 31, Manhattan, NY
Administration, Harris Beach LLP
Victor Paz-Gutierrez, 43, Queens, NY
Chef, Windows on the World
Stacey Lynn Peak, 36, Manhattan, NY
Brokerage, Cantor Fitzgerald
Thomas E. Pedicini, 30, Hicksville, NY
Brokerage, Cantor Fitzgerald
Todd D. Pelino, 34, Fair Haven, NJ
Brokerage, Cantor Fitzgerald
Michel Adrian Pelletier, 36, Greenwich, CT
Brokerage, Cantor Fitzgerald
Anthony Peluso, 46, Brooklyn, NY
Angel Ramon Pena, 45, River Vale, NJ
Attorney, Aon Corp.
Jose D. Pena
Food service, Windows on the World
Richard Al Penny, 53, Brooklyn, NY
Recyclable-waste collector, Project Renewal
Salvatore Pepe, 45, Elmhurst, NY
Technology management, Marsh & McLennan
Carl Allen Peralta, 37, Staten Island, NY
Brokerage, Cantor Fitzgerald
Robert David Peraza, 30, New York, NY
Brokerage, Cantor Fitzgerald
Marie Vola Percoco, 37, Brooklyn, NY
Administration, Aon Corp.

Jon Anthony Perconti, 32, Brick, NJ
Brokerage, Cantor Fitzgerald
Alejo Perez, 66, Union City, NJ
Food service, Windows on the World
Angel Perez, 43, Jersey City, NJ
Cantor Fitzgerald
Angela Susan Perez, 35, New York, NY
Cantor Fitzgerald
Anthony Perez, 33, Locust Valley, NY
Computer technology, Cantor Fitzgerald
Ivan A. Perez, 37, Ozone Park, NY
Brokerage, Fiduciary Trust Company International
Nancy E. Perez, 36, Secaucus, NJ
Management, Port Authority of New York & New Jersey
Joseph John Perroncino, 33, Smithtown, NY
Brokerage, Cantor Fitzgerald
Edward Joseph Perrotta, 43, Mount Sinai, NY
Brokerage, Cantor Fitzgerald
Emelda Perry, 52, Elmont, NY
Washington Group International
Franklin Allan Pershep, 59, Bensonhurst, NY
Insurance brokerage, Aon Corp.
Danny Pesce, 34, Staten Island, NY
Brokerage, Cantor Fitzgerald
Michael J. Pescherine, 32, Manhattan, NY
Brokerage, Keefe Bruyette & Woods
Davin Peterson, 25, Manhattan, NY
Brokerage, Cantor Fitzgerald
William Russel Peterson, 46, New York, NY
Marsh & McLennan
Mark Petrocelli, 29, Staten Island, NY
Brokerage, Carr Futures
Matthew Petterno, 38, Jersey City, NJ
Kaleen E. Pezzuti, 28, Fair Haven, NJ
Brokerage, Cantor Fitzgerald
Tu-Anh Pham, 42, Princeton, NJ
Brokerage, Fred Alger Management
Eugenia Piantieri, 55, Bronx, NY
Software technology, Marsh & McLennan
Ludwig J. Picarro, 44, Basking Ridge, NJ
Insurance brokerage, Zurich Insurance Co.
Matthew Picerno, 44, Holmdel, NJ
Brokerage, Cantor Fitzgerald
Joseph O. Pick, 40, Hoboken, NJ
Brokerage, Fiduciary Trust Company International
Dennis J. Pierce, 54, Queens, NY
New York State Department of Taxation & Finance
Bernard T. Pietronico, 39, Matawan, NJ
Brokerage, Cantor Fitzgerald
Nicholas P. Pietrunti, 38, Belford, NJ
Brokerage, Cantor Fitzgerald
Theodoros Pigis, 60, Brooklyn, NY
One Source
Susan Elizabeth Ancona Pinto, 44, Staten Island, NY
Brokerage, Cantor Fitzgerald
Joseph Piskadlo, 58, North Arlington, NJ
Carpentry, ABM Industries
Christopher Todd Pitman, 30, Manhattan, NY
Brokerage, Cantor Fitzgerald
Josh Piver, 42, Stonington, CT
Brokerage, Cantor Fitzgerald
Joseph Plumitallo, 45, Manalapan, NJ
Brokerage, Cantor Fitzgerald
John M. Pocher, 36, Middletown, NJ
Brokerage, Cantor Fitzgerald
William H. Pohlmann, 56, Ardsley, NY
Attorney, New York State Department of Taxation & Finance
Laurence M. Polatsch, 32, Manhattan, NY
Brokerage, Cantor Fitzgerald
Thomas H. Polhemus, 39, Morris Plains, NJ
Computer programming, Accenture

Steve Pollicino, 48, Plainview, NY
Brokerage, Cantor Fitzgerald
Susan M. Pollio, 45, Long Beach Township, NJ
Brokerage, EuroBrokers Inc.
Eric Thomas Popiteau, 34
Joshua Poptean, 37, North Flushing, NY
Construction, Bronx Builders
Giovanna Porras, 24, Richmond Hill, NY
Accounting, General Telecom
Anthony Portillo, 48, Brooklyn, NY
Architect, Raytheon
James Edward Potorti, 52, Plainsboro, NJ
Brokerage, Marsh & McLennan
Daphne Pouletsos, 47, Westwood, NJ
Aon Corp.
Richard Poulos, 55, Levittown, NY
Security officer, Cantor Fitzgerald
Stephen E. Poulos, 45, Basking Ridge, NJ
Information technology, Aon Corp.
Brandon Jerome Powell, 26, Bronx, NY
Food service handler, Forte Food Service
Tony Pratt, 43, New York, NY
Food service handler, Forte Food Service
Gregory M. Preziose, 34, Holmdel, NJ
Brokerage, Cantor Fitzgerald
Wanda Astol Prince, 30, Staten Island, NY
Brokerage, Fiduciary Trust Company International
Everett Martin "Marty" Proctor III, 44, New York, NY
Brokerage, Cantor Fitzgerald
Carrie B. Progen, 25, Brooklyn, NY
Administrative assistant, Aon Corp.
David Lee Pruim, 53, Upper Montclair, NJ
Insurance brokerage, Aon Corp.
John F. Puckett, 47, Glen Cove, NY
Engineering, All Digital Audio
Robert D. Pugliese, 47, East Fishkill, NY
Brokerage, Marsh & McLennan
Edward F. Pullis, 34, Hazlet, NJ
Insurance consulting, Aon Corp.
Patricia Ann Puma, 33, Staten Island, NY
Administration, Julien J. Studley Inc.
Hemanth Kumar Puttur, 26, White Plains, NY
Software engineering, Windows on the World
Edward Richard Pykon, 33, Princeton Junction, NJ
Brokerage, Fred Alger Management
Christopher Quackenbush, 44, Manhasset, NY
Lawyer/investment banker, Sandler O'Neill & Partners
Lars P. Qualben, 49, New York, NY
Insurance brokerage, Marsh & McLennan
Beth Ann Quigley, 25, New York, NY
Brokerage, Cantor Fitzgerald
James Francis Quinn, 23, Brooklyn, NY
Brokerage, Cantor Fitzgerald
Carol Rabalais, 38, Brooklyn, NY
Insurance brokerage assistant, Aon Corp.
Christopher Peter A. Racaniello, 30, Little Neck, NY
Accountant, Cantor Fitzgerald
Eugene J. Raggio, 55, Staten Island, NY
Operations supervisor, Port Authority of New York & New Jersey
Laura Marie Ragonese-Snik, 41, Bangor, PA
Insurance brokerage, Aon Corp.
Peter F. Raimondi, 46, Staten Island, NY
Brokerage, Carr Futures
Harry A. Raines, 37, Bethpage, NY
Cantor Fitzgerald
Ehtesham U. Raja, 28, Clifton, NJ
Information technology, TCG Software
Valsa Raju, 39, Yonkers, NY
Brokerage, Carr Futures
Lukas "Luke" Rambousek, 27, Brooklyn, NY
Information technology, Cantor Fitzgerald

Julio Fernandez Ramirez, 47, New York, NY
Painter, Hudson-Shantz Painting Co.
Maria Isabel Ramirez, 25, Canarsie, NY
Secretary, Langan Engineering and Environmental Services Inc.
Ulf Ramm-Ericson, 79, Greenwich, CT
Civil engineer, Washington Group International
Harry Ramos, 45, Newark, NJ
Brokerage, May Davis Group
Vishnoo Ramsaroop, 44, Jackson Heights, NY
Elevator operator, ABM Industries
Lorenzo Ramzey, 48, East Northport, NY
Insurance brokerage, Aon Corp.
Alfred Todd Rancke, 42, Summit, NJ
Investment banking, Sandler O'Neill & Partners
Jonathan C. Randall, 42, Brooklyn, NY
Insurance brokerage, Marsh & McLennan
Srinivasa Shreyas Ranganath, 26, Hackensack, NJ
Software development, Marsh & McLennan
Anne T. Ransom, 45, Edgewater, NJ
American Express
Faina Rapoport, 45, Brooklyn, NY
Insurance brokerage, Marsh & McLennan
Robert Arthur Rasmussen, 42, Hinsdale, IL
Financial analyst, Vestek
Ameenia Rasool, 33, Staten Island, NY
Accountant, Marsh & McLennan
Roger Mark Rasweiler, 53, Flemington, NJ
Insurance brokerage, Marsh & McLennan
David Alan James Rathkey, 47, Mountain Lakes, NJ
Financial investment, IQ Financial Systems
William R. Raub, 38, Saddle River, NJ
Brokerage, Cantor Fitzgerald
Gerard Rauzi, 42, Flushing, NY
New York State Department of Taxation & Finance
Alexey Razuvaev, 40, Brooklyn, NY
Computer programming, EuroBrokers Inc.
Gregory Reda, 33, New Hyde Park, NY
Insurance brokerage, Marsh & McLennan
Sarah (Prothero) Redheffer, 35, London, England
Conferences operations manager, Risk Waters Group
Michele Marie Reed, 26, Ringoes, NJ
Insurance brokerage, Aon Corp.
Judith A. Reese, 56, Kearny, NJ
Administrative assistant, LJ Gonzer Associates
Thomas M. Regan, 43, Cranford, NJ
Aon Corp.
Howard Reich, 59, Forest Hills, NY
Mail clerk, Pitney Bowes
Gregory Reidy, 26, Holmdel, NJ
Brokerage, Cantor Fitzgerald
James B. Reilly, 25, Huntington Station, NY
Brokerage, Keefe Bruyette & Woods
Timothy E. Reilly, 40, Brooklyn, NY
Insurance brokerage, Marsh & McLennan
Joseph Reina, 32, Staten Island, NY
Brokerage, Cantor Fitzgerald
Thomas Barnes Reinig, 48, Bernardsville, NJ
Investment banking, Cantor Fitzgerald
Frank B. Reisman, 41, Princeton, NJ
Brokerage, Cantor Fitzgerald
Joshua Scott Reiss, 23, Manhattan, NY
Brokerage, Cantor Fitzgerald
Karen C. Renda, 52, Staten Island, NY
Travel agent, American Express
John Armand Reo, 28, Larchmont, NY
Brokerage, Cantor Fitzgerald
Richard C. Rescorla, 62, Morristown, NJ
Security, Morgan Stanley
John Thomas Resta, 40, Bayside, NY
Investment, Carr Futures
Sylvia San Pio Resta, 27, Bayside, NY
Brokerage, Carr Futures

Eduvigis Eddie Reyes, 37, St. Albans, NY
Shipping, Rhode & Liesenfeld
John Frederick Rhodes Jr., 57, Howell, NJ
Insurance brokerage, Aon Corp.
Francis S. Riccardelli, 40, Westwood, NJ
Elevator technician, Port Authority of New York & New Jersey
Rudolph N. Riccio, 50, Bronx, NY
Computer programming, Cantor Fitzgerald
AnnMarie Davi Riccoboni, 58, Queens, NY
Billing supervisor, Ohrenstein & Brown
David Rice, 31, New York, NY
Investment banking, Sandler O'Neill & Partners
Eileen Mary Rice, 57, New York, NY
Executive assistant, Marsh & McLennan
Kenneth F. Rice III, 34, Hicksville, NY
Technology, Marsh & McLennan
Gregory Richards, 30, New York, NY
Corporate development, Cantor Fitzgerald
Michael Richards, 38, Jamaica, NY
Sculptor
Venesha O. Richards, 26, North Brunswick, NJ
Insurance brokerage, Marsh & McLennan
Alan Jay Richman, 44, Long Island City, NY
Insurance brokerage, Marsh & McLennan
John M. Rigo, 48, New York, NY
Insurance brokerage, Marsh & McLennan
James Riley, 25, Manhattan, NY
Theresa Ginger Risco, 48, Manhattan, NY
Fred Alger Management
Rose Mary Riso, 55, Queens, NY
Moises N. Rivas, 29, Manhattan, NY
Chef, Windows on the World
Carmen Alicia Rivera, 33, Westtown, NY
Brokerage, Fiduciary Trust Company International
Isaias Rivera, 51, Perth Amboy, NJ
Maintenance engineer, CBS
Juan William Rivera, 27, Bronx, NY
Engineer, General Telecom
Linda I. Rivera, 26, Far Rockaway, NY
Human resources management, Marsh & McLennan
David E. Rivers, 40, Manhattan, NY
Editorial director, Risk Waters Group
Joseph R. Riverso, 34, White Plains, NY
Brokerage, Cantor Fitzgerald
Paul V. Rizza, 34, Park Ridge, NJ
Investment, Fiduciary Trust Company International
John Frank Rizzo, 50, Brooklyn, NY
Stephen Louis Roach, 36, Verona, NJ
Brokerage, Cantor Fitzgerald
Joseph Roberto, 37, Midland Park, NJ
Research analyst, Keefe Bruyette & Woods
Leo Roberts, 44, Wayne, NJ
Brokerage, Cantor Fitzgerald
Donald Walter Robertson Jr., 38, Rumson, NJ
Brokerage, Cantor Fitzgerald
Catherina Robinson, 45, Bronx, NY
First Union Bank
Jeffrey Robinson, 38, Monmouth Junction, NJ
Systems analyst, Marsh & McLennan
Michell Lee Robotham, 32, Kearny, NJ
Aon Corp.
Donald Arthur Robson, 52, Manhasset, NY
Brokerage, Cantor Fitzgerald
Antonio Augusto Tome Rocha, 34, East Hanover, NJ
Brokerage, Cantor Fitzgerald
Raymond J. Rocha, 29, Malden, MA
Brokerage, Cantor Fitzgerald
Laura Rockefeller, 41, Manhattan, NY
Conference coordinator, Risk Waters Group
John M. Rodak, 39, Mantua, NJ
Investment, Sandler O'Neill & Partners
Carlos Cortez Rodriguez

Carmen Milagros Rodriguez, 46, Freehold, NJ
Aon Corp.
Gregory Rodriguez, 31, White Plains, NY
Brokerage, financial services, Cantor Fitzgerald
Marsha A. Rodriguez, 41, West Paterson, NJ
David B. Rodriguez-Vargas, 44, Manhattan, NY
Windows on the World
Karlie Barbara Rogers, 26, London, England
Divisional sponsorship manager, Risk Waters Group
Scott Rohner, 22, Hoboken, NJ
Brokerage, Cantor Fitzgerald
Joseph M. Romagnolo, 37, Coram, NY
Brokerage, financial services, Cantor Fitzgerald
Efrain Franco Romero Sr., 57, Hazleton, PA
Fine Painting
Elvin Santiago Romero, 34, Matawan, NJ
Brokerage, Cantor Fitzgerald
Sean Rooney, 50, Stamford, CT
Aon Corp.
Eric Thomas Ropiteau, 24, Brooklyn, NY
Aida Rosario, 42, Jersey City, NJ
Risk and insurance, Marsh & McLennan
Angela Rosario, 27, Manhattan, NY
Mark Harlan Rosen, 45, West Islip, NY
Investment banking, Sandler O'Neill & Partners
Brooke David Rosenbaum, 31, Franklin Square, NY
Cantor Fitzgerald
Linda Rosenbaum, 41, Little Falls, NJ
Sheryl Lynn Rosenbaum, 33, Warren, NJ
Brokerage, financial services, Cantor Fitzgerald
Lloyd D. Rosenberg, 31, Morganville, NJ
Brokerage, Cantor Fitzgerald
Mark Louis Rosenberg, 26, Teaneck, NJ
Marsh & McLennan
Andrew I. Rosenblum, 45, Rockville Centre, NY
Brokerage, financial services, Cantor Fitzgerald
Joshua M. Rosenblum, 28, Hoboken, NJ
Brokerage, financial services, Cantor Fitzgerald
Joshua Rosenthal, 44, Manhattan, NY
Investment banking, Fiduciary Trust Company
International
Richard David Rosenthal, 50, Fair Lawn, NJ
Brokerage, financial services, Cantor Fitzgerald
Daniel Rossetti, 32, Bloomfield, NJ
Construction, Certified Installation Services
Norman S. Rossinow, 39, Cedar Grove, NJ
Risk management, insurance, Aon Corp.
Michael Craig Rothberg, 39, Old Greenwich, CT
Brokerage, financial services, Cantor Fitzgerald
Donna Marie Rothenberg, 53, New York, NY
Risk management, insurance, Aon Corp.
Nicholas Rowe, 29, Hoboken, NJ
Software designing, UmeVoice, Inc.
Behzad Roya, 37, New York, NY
Ronald J. Ruben, 36, Hoboken, NJ
Brokerage, Keefe Bruyette & Woods
Joanne Rubino, 45, New York, NY
Risk and insurance, Marsh & McLennan
David M. Ruddle, 31, New York, NY
Reliable
Bart Joseph Ruggiere, 32, Manhattan, NY
Brokerage, Cantor Fitzgerald
Susan Ann Ruggiero, 30, Plainview, NY
Risk management, insurance, Marsh & McLennan
Adam K. Ruhalter, 40, Plainview, NY
Finance, Cantor Fitzgerald
Gilbert Ruiz, 45, New York, NY
Restaurants, Windows on the World
Obdulio Ruiz-Diaz, 44, Valley Stream, NY
Architecture/construction, Bronx Builders
Steven Harris Russin, 32, Mendham, NJ
Brokerage, Cantor Fitzgerald

Wayne Alan Russo, 37, Union, NJ
Insurance, Marsh & McLennan
Edward Ryan, 42, Scarsdale, NY
Brokerage, Carr Futures
John Joseph Ryan, 45, Princeton Junction, NJ
Brokerage, Keefe Bruyette & Woods
Jonathan Stephan Ryan, 32, Bayville, NY
Brokerage, EuroBrokers Inc.
Tatiana Ryjova, 36, South Salem, NY
Office leasing, business services, Regus Business Centers
Christina Sunga Ryook, 25, Manhattan, NY
Human resources, Cantor Fitzgerald
Jason E. Sabbag, 26, New York, NY
Finance, Fiduciary Trust Company International
Scott Saber, 38, New York, NY
Finance, UBS PaineWebber
Joseph F. Sacerdote, 48, Freehold, NJ
Finance, Cantor Fitzgerald
Francis John Sadocha, 41, Huntington Station, NY
Jude Elias Safi, 24, Brooklyn, NY
Finance, Cantor Fitzgerald
Brock Joel Safronoff, 26, Brooklyn, NY
Computer programmer, Marsh & McLennan
Edward Saiya, 49, Brooklyn, NY
Telecommunications engineer, Genuity
Kalyan K. Sakar, Westwood, NJ
Port Authority employee, Port Authority of New York & New
Jersey
John Patrick Salamone, 37, North Caldwell, NJ
Finance, Cantor Fitzgerald
Hernando R. Salas, 71, Flushing, NY
Clerk, New York City Civilian Complaint Review Board
Juan Salas, 35, Manhattan, NY
Restaurant worker, Windows on the World
Esmerlin Salcedo, 36, Bronx, NY
Security, Summit Security Services
John Salvatore Salerno, 31, Westfield, NJ
Brokerage, Cantor Fitzgerald
Richard L. Salinardi, 32, Hoboken, NJ
Food services, Aramark Corp.
Wayne Saloman, 43, Seaford, NY
Finance, Cantor Fitzgerald
Nolbert Salomon, 33, Brooklyn, NY
Security, Morgan Stanley
Catherine Patricia Salter, 37, New York, NY
Insurance, Aon Corp.
Frank G. Salvaterra, 41, Manhasset, NY
Finance, Sandler O'Neill & Partners
Paul Salvio, 27, New York, NY
Brokerage, Carr Futures
Samuel R. Salvo, 59, Yonkers, NY
Insurance, Aon Corp.
Carlos Samaniego, 29, Richmond Hill, NY
Finance, Cantor Fitzgerald
Rena Sam-Dinnoo, 28, Brooklyn, NY
Accounting, Marsh & McLennan
James Kenneth Samuel Jr., 29, Hoboken, NJ
Finance, Carr Futures
Michael V. San Phillip, 55, Ridgewood, NJ
Finance, Sandler O'Neill & Partners
Hugo Sanay-Perafiel, 41, New York, NY
Chef, EuroBrokers Inc.
Alva Jeffries Sanchez, 41, Hempstead, NY
Finance, Marsh & McLennan
Erick Sanchez, 41
Floor covering installer, Soundtone
Jacquelyn P. Sanchez, 23, Manhattan, NY
Law, Cantor Fitzgerald
Eric Sand, 36, Hawthorne, NY
Finance, Cantor Fitzgerald
Stacey Leigh Sanders, 25, New York, NY
Insurance, Marsh & McLennan

Herman S. Sandler, 57, New York, NY
Investment banking, Sandler O'Neill & Partners
James Sands Jr., 39, Bricktown, NJ
Finance/technology, Cantor Fitzgerald
Ayleen J. Santiago, 40, Borough Park, NY
Consultant, Elcom Services
Kirsten Santiago, 26, Bronx, NY
Human resources/insurance, American Multiline Corp.
Maria Theresa Santillan, 27, Morris Plains, NJ
Customer service, Cantor Fitzgerald
Susan G. Santo, 24, New York, NY
Insurance, Marsh & McLennan
Rafael Humberto Santos, 42, New York, NY
Finance, Cantor Fitzgerald
Rufino Condrado F. "Roy" Santos, 37, Manhattan, NY
Computer consultant, Accenture
Kalyan K. Sarkar, 53, Westwood, NJ
Engineer, Port Authority of New York & New Jersey
Chapelle Sarker
Computer specialist, Marsh & McLennan
Paul F. Sarle, 38, Babylon, NY
Finance, Cantor Fitzgerald
Deepika Kumar Sattaluri, 33, Edison, NJ
Accountant, Marsh & McLennan
Susan Sauer, 48, Chicago, IL
Insurance, Marsh & McLennan
Anthony Savas, 72, Astoria, NY
Inspector, Port Authority of New York & New Jersey
Vladimir Savinkin, 21, Brooklyn, NY
Accounting, Cantor Fitzgerald
John Sbarbaro, 45, New York, NY
Finance, Cantor Fitzgerald
Robert Louis "Rob" Scandole, 36, Pelham Manor, NY
Finance, Cantor Fitzgerald
Thomas Scaracio, 35, Astoria, NY
Michelle Scarpitta, 26, New York, NY
Finance, EuroBrokers Inc.
John G. Scharf, 29, Manorville, NY
Technician, Liebert Global Services
Angela Susan Scheinberg, 46, Staten Island, NY
Manager, Empire Blue Cross/Blue Shield
Scott M. Schertzer, 28, Edison, NJ
Human resources, Cantor Fitzgerald
Sean Schielke, 27, Manhattan, NY
Finance, Cantor Fitzgerald
Steven Francis Schlag, 41, Franklin Lakes, NJ
Finance, Cantor Fitzgerald
Jon S. Schlissel, 51, Jersey City, NJ
Finance/government, New York State Department of
Taxation & Finance
Karen Helene Schmidt, 42, Bellmore, NY
Ian Schneider, 45, Short Hills, NJ
Finance, Cantor Fitzgerald
Frank G. Schott, 39, Massapequa, NY
Insurance/technology, Marsh & McLennan
Jeffrey Schreier, 48, Brooklyn, NY
Mailroom clerk, Cantor Fitzgerald
John T. Schroeder, 31, Hoboken, NJ
Finance, Fred Alger Management
Susan Lee Kennedy Schuler, 55, Allentown, NJ
Consultant, Singer Frumento LLP
Edward W. Schunk, 54, Baldwin, NY
Finance, Cantor Fitzgerald
Mark E. Schurmeier, 44, McLean, VA
Finance/technology, Federal HomeLoan Mortgage Corp.
Clarin Shellie Schwartz, 51, New York, NY
Insurance brokerage, Aon Corp.
John Burkhart Schwartz, 49, Goshen, CT
Finance, Cantor Fitzgerald
Adrianne Scibetta, 31, Staten Island, NY
Accounting, Cantor Fitzgerald
Raphael Scorca, 61, Beachwood, NJ
Insurance, Marsh & McLennan

Randolph Scott, 48, Stamford, CT
Finance, EuroBrokers Inc.
Christopher Scudder, 34, Monsey, NY
Computer technician, En Pointe Technologies
Arthur Warren Scullin, 57, Flushing, NY
Insurance, Marsh & McLennan
Michael H. Seaman, 41, Manhasset, NY
Finance, Cantor Fitzgerald
Margaret Seeliger, 34, Manhattan, NY
Insurance brokerage, Aon Corp.
Anthony Segarra, 52, New York, NY
Electrical worker, Proven Electrical Contracting Inc.
Carlos Segarra, 54, Brooklyn, NY
Jason Sekzer, 31, New York, NY
Finance, Cantor Fitzgerald
Matthew Carmen Sellitto, 23, Morristown, NJ
Finance, Cantor Fitzgerald
Howard Selwyn, 47, Hewlett, NY
Finance, EuroBrokers Inc.
Larry John Senko, 34, Yardley, PA
Technology, Alliance Consulting Group
Arturo Angelo Sereno, 29, Brooklyn, NY
Frankie Serrano, 23, Elizabeth, NJ
Telecommunications, Genuity
Alena Sesinova, 57, Brooklyn Heights, NY
Information technology, Marsh & McLennan
Adele Sessa, 36, Staten Island, NY
Finance, Cantor Fitzgerald
Situ Nermalla Sewnarine, 37, Brooklyn, NY
Information technology, Fiduciary Trust Company International
Karen Lynn Seymour-Dietrich, 40, Millington, NJ
Technology specialist, Garban Intercapital
Davis G. "Deeg" Sezna Jr., 22, New York, NY
Finance, Sandler O'Neill & Partners
Thomas J. Sgroi, 45, Staten Island, NY
Insurance, Marsh & McLennan
Jayesh Shah, 38, Edgewater, NJ
Finance, Cantor Fitzgerald
Khalid Mohammad Shahid, 35, Union, NJ
Finance, Cantor Fitzgerald
Mohammed Shajahan, 41, Spring Valley, NY
Computer administrator, Marsh & McLennan
Gary Shamay, 23, New York, NY
Technology, Cantor Fitzgerald
Earl Richard Shanahan, 50, Flushing, NY
Shiv Shankar, New York, NY
Insurance, Aon Corp.
Huang Shaoxiang, China
Liang Shaozhen, China
Wang Shaozshang, China
Neil G. Shastri, 25, Ho-Ho-Kus, NJ
Consultant, Scient Company
Kathryn Anne Shatzoff, 37, Bronx, NY
Consultant assistant, Marsh & McLennan
Barbara A. Shaw, 57, Morristown, NJ
Computer executive, Compaq
Jeffery James Shaw, 42, Levittown, NY
Electrician, Forest Electric Corp.
Robert John Shay Jr., 27, Staten Island, NY
Bond trader, Cantor Fitzgerald
Daniel James Shea, 37, Pelham Manor, NY
Finance, Cantor Fitzgerald
Joseph Patrick Shea, 47, Pelham Manor, NY
Finance, Cantor Fitzgerald
Linda Sheehan, 40, White Plains, NY
Finance, Sandler O'Neill & Partners
Hagay Shefi, 34, Tenafly, NJ
Technology, GoldTier Technologies Inc.
Terrance H. Shefield, 34, Newark, NJ
John Anthony Sherry, 34, Rockville Centre, NY
Finance, EuroBrokers Inc.
Sean Shielke, 27, New York, NY
Finance, Cantor Fitzgerald

Atsushi Shiratori, 36, Manhattan, NY
Trader, Cantor Fitzgerald
Thomas Joseph Shubert, 43, Flushing, NY
Brokerage, Cantor Fitzgerald
Mark Shulman, 44, Old Bridge, NJ
Consultant, Marsh & McLennan
See-Wong Shum, 44, Westfield, NJ
Information technology, New York Metropolitan
Transportation Council
Allan Shwartzstein, 37, Chappaqua, NY
Trader, Cantor Fitzgerald
Johanna Sigmund, 25, Wyndmoor, PA
Finance, Fred Alger Management
Dianne T. Signer, 32, Middle Village, NY
Finance, Fred Alger Management
David Silver, 35, New Rochelle, NY
Finance, Cantor Fitzgerald
Craig A. Silverstein, 41, Wyckoff, NJ
Finance, Sandler O'Neill & Partners
Nasima H. Simjee, 38, New York, NY
Finance, Fiduciary Trust Company International
Bruce Edward Simmons, 41, Ridgewood, NJ
Finance, Sandler O'Neill & Partners
Arthur Simon, 57, Thiells, NY
Finance, Fred Alger Management
Kenneth Alan Simon, 34, Secaucus, NJ
Finance, Cantor Fitzgerald
Michael John Simon, 40, Harrington Park, NJ
Finance, Cantor Fitzgerald
Paul Joseph Simon, 54, Staten Island, NY
Computer consultant, Marsh & McLennan
Marianne Simone, 62, Staten Island, NY
Computer consultant, Cantor Fitzgerald
Barry Simowitz, 64, Manhattan, NY
Accounting, New York State Department of Taxation &
Finance
Jeff Simpson, 38, Lake Ridge, VA
Project manager, Oracle Corp.
George V. Sims, 46, Newark, NJ
Khamladai K. "Khami" Singh, 25, New York, NY
Restaurant management, Windows on the World
Roshan R. "Sean" Singh, 21, Woodhaven, NY
Audio-visual specialist, Windows on the World
Thomas Edison Sinton III, 44, Croton-on-Hudson, NY
Finance, Cantor Fitzgerald
Peter A. Siracuse, 29, Manhattan, NY
Finance, Cantor Fitzgerald
Muriel F. Siskopoulos, 60, Brooklyn, NY
Secretary, Keefe Bruyette & Woods
Joseph M. Sisolak, 35, New York, NY
Insurance, Marsh & McLennan
Francis J. Skidmore Jr., 58, Mendham, NJ
Trader, EuroBrokers Inc.
Toyena C. Skinner, 27, Kingston, NJ
Secretary, First Union Securities
Paul Skrzypek, 37, Manhattan, NY
Brokerage/financial services, Cantor Fitzgerald
Christopher Paul Slattery, 31, Manhattan, NY
Finance, Cantor Fitzgerald
Vincent R. Slavin, 41, Belle Harbor, NY
Brokerage, Cantor Fitzgerald
Robert Sliwak, 42, Wantagh, NY
Finance, Cantor Fitzgerald
Paul K. Sloan, 26, Manhattan, NY
Finance, Keefe Bruyette & Woods
Wendy L. Small, 26, New York, NY
Secretary, Cantor Fitzgerald
Catherine T. Smith, 44, West Haverstraw, NY
Finance, Marsh & McLennan
Daniel Laurence Smith, 47, Northport, NY
Finance, EuroBrokers Inc.
George Eric Smith, 38, West Chester, PA
Finance, SunGard Trading Systems

James G. Smith, 43, Garden City, NY
Trader, Cantor Fitzgerald
Jeffrey Randall Smith, 36, Manhattan, NY
Equity research analyst, Sandler O'Neill & Partners
Joyce Smith, 55, Queens, NY
Cantor Fitzgerald
Karl Trumbull Smith, 44, Little Silver, NJ
Cantor Fitzgerald
Rosemary A. Smith, 61, Staten Island, NY
Sidley Austin Brown and Wood
Sandra Fajardo Smith, 37, Queens, NY
Accounting, Marsh & McLennan
Bonnie Smithwick, 54, Quogue, NY
Fred Alger Management
Rochelle Monique Snell, 24, Mount Vernon, NY
Administration, The Regus Co.
Leonard Joseph Snyder, 35, Cranford, NJ
Aon Corp.
Astrid Elizabeth Sohan, 32, Freehold, NJ
Insurance brokerage, Marsh & McLennan
Sushil Solanki, 35, New York, NY
Cantor Fitzgerald
Ruben Solares, 51, Queens, NY
Cantor Fitzgerald
Naomi Leah Solomon, 52, Manhattan, NY
Finance, Callixa
Daniel W. Song, 34, New York, NY
Brokerage, Cantor Fitzgerald
Michael C. Sorresse, 34, Morris Plains, NJ
Finance, Marsh & McLennan
Fabian Soto, 31, Harrison, NJ
ABM Industries
Timothy Patrick Soulas, 35, Basking Ridge, NJ
Brokerage/financial services, Cantor Fitzgerald
Gregory T. Spagnoletti, 32, Manhattan, NY
Banking, financial services, Keefe Bruyette & Woods
Donald Spampinato, 39, Manhasset, NY
Brokerage, financial services, Cantor Fitzgerald
Thomas Sparacio, 35, Staten Island, NY
Brokerage, EuroBrokers Inc.
Georgia Sparks, New York, NY
John Anthony Spataro, 32, Mineola, NY
Insurance/financial, Marsh & McLennan
Maynard S. Spence, 42, Douglasville, GA
Consultant, Marsh & McLennan
George E. Spencer III, 50, West Norwalk, CT
Brokerage, EuroBrokers Inc.
Robert Andrew Spencer, 35, Red Bank, NJ
Brokerage, Cantor Fitzgerald
Mary Rubina Sperando, 39, Queens, NY
High-Tech, Encompys
Frank J. Spinelli, 44, Short Hills, NJ
Brokerage, financial services, Cantor Fitzgerald
William E. Spitz, 49, Oceanside, NY
Cantor Fitzgerald
Klaus Johannes Sprockamp, 42, Muhltal, Germany
Biological information technology, Lion Bioscience AG
Saranya Srinuan, 23, Manhattan, NY
Brokerage, financial services, Cantor Fitzgerald
Fitzroy St. Rose, 40, South Bronx, NY
Information technology, General Telecom
Michael F. Stabile, 50, Staten Island, NY
Brokerage, EuroBrokers Inc.
Richard James Stadelberger, 55, Middletown, NJ
Brokerage, Fiduciary Trust Company International
Eric A. Stahlman, 43, Holmdel Township, NJ
Brokerage, Cantor Fitzgerald
Alexandru Liviu Stan, 34, Queens, NY
Brokerage, Cantor Fitzgerald
Corina Stan, 31, Middle Village, NY
Brokerage, Cantor Fitzgerald
Mary D. Stanley, 53, Jamacia, NY
Insurance, financial, Marsh & McLennan

Joyce Stanton

Patricia Stanton

Anthony M. Starita, 35, Westfield, NJ
Brokerage, Cantor Fitzgerald

Derek James Statkevicus, 30, Norwalk, CT
Keefe Bruyette & Woods

Craig William Staub, 30, Basking Ridge, NJ
Keefe Bruyette & Woods

William V. Steckman, 56, West Hempstead, NY
NBC

Eric Thomas Steen, 32, New York, NY
Brokerage, EuroBrokers Inc.

William R. Steiner, 56, New Hope, PA
Information technology, Marsh & McLennan

Alexander Robbins Steinman, 32, Hoboken, NJ
Brokerage, Cantor Fitzgerald

Andrew Stergiopoulos, 23, Manhattan, NY
Finance, Cantor Fitzgerald

Andrew Stern, 45, Bellmore, NY
Cantor Fitzgerald

Martha Stevens
Aon Corp.

Michael J. Stewart, 42, New York, NY
Finance, Carr Futures

Richard H. Stewart Jr., 35, Manhattan, NY
Brokerage, Cantor Fitzgerald

Sanford "Sandy" M. Stoller, 54, Brooklyn, NY
Accenture

Lonny Jay Stone, 43, Bellmore, NY
Carr Futures

Jimmy Nevill Storey, 58, Katy, TX
Marsh & McLennan

Timothy C. Stout, 42, Dobbs Ferry, NY
Cantor Fitzgerald

Thomas S. Strada, 41, Chatham, NJ
Brokerage, Cantor Fitzgerald

James J. Straine Jr., 36, Oceanport, NJ
Cantor Fitzgerald

Edward W. Straub, 48, Convent Station, NJ
Aon Corp.

George J. Strauch Jr., 53, Avon-by-the-Sea, NJ
Aon Corp.

Edward T. Strauss, 44, Edison, NJ
Port Authority of New York & New Jersey

Steven R. Strauss, 51, Fresh Meadows, NY
Electrician, Petrocelli Electric Co./Morgan Stanley

Steven F. Strobert, 33, Ridgewood, NJ
Cantor Fitzgerald

David Scott Suarez, 24, Princeton, NJ
Information technology, Deloitte & Touche (for Marsh)

Yoichi Sugiyama, 34, Fort Lee, NJ
Banking, Fuji Bank

William C. Sugra, 30, Manhattan, NY
Finance, Cantor Fitzgerald

Patrick Sullivan, 32, Breezy Point, NY
Cantor Fitzgerald

Thomas Sullivan, 38, Kearney, NJ
Harvey, Young & Yurman

Hilario Soriano "Larry" Sumaya, 42, Staten Island, NY
Information technology, Marsh & McLennan

James Joseph Suozzo, 47, Hauppauge, NY
Cantor Fitzgerald

Colleen Supinski, 27, Manhattan, NY
Brokerage, Sandler O'Neill & Partners

Robert Sutcliffe Jr., 39, Huntington, NY
Harvey, Young & Yurman

Seline Selina Sutter, 63, Manhattan, NY
First Liberty Investment Group

Claudia Suzette Sutton, 34, Brooklyn, NY
Cantor Fitzgerald

John F. Swaine, 36, Larchmont, NY
Brokerage, Cantor Fitzgerald

Valerie Swanson, 23, Harrison, NJ

Kristine M. Swearson, 34, Manhattan, NY
Information technology, Cantor Fitzgerald

Kenneth J. Swensen, 40, Chatham, NJ
Brokerage, Cantor Fitzgerald

Thomas F. Swift, 30, Jersey City, NJ
Finance, Morgan Stanley

Derek O. Sword, 29, Manhattan, NY
Keefe Bruyette & Woods

Kevin T. Szocik, 27, Garden City, NY
Keefe Bruyette & Woods

Gina Sztejnberg, 52, Ridgewood, NJ
Marsh & McLennan

Norbert P. Szurkowski, 31, Brooklyn, NY
Mechanic and carpenter (LU 608), union carpenter/wallpaper

Harry Taback, 56, Staten Island, NY
Marsh & McLennan

Joann Tabeek, 41, Staten Island, NY
Cantor Fitzgerald

Norma C. Taddei, 64, Woodside, NY
Marsh & McLennan

Michael Taddonio, 39, Huntington, NY
EuroBrokers Inc.

Keiichiro Takahashi, 53, Port Washington, NY
EuroBrokers Inc.

Keiji Takahashi, 42, Tenafly, NJ
EuroBrokers Inc.

Phyllis Talbot, 53, New York, NY
Marsh & McLennan

Robert R. Talhami, 40, Shrewsbury, NJ
Trader, Cantor Fitzgerald

Maurita Tam, 22, Staten Island, NY
Aon Corp.

Rachel Tamares, 30, Bronx, NY
Aon Corp.

Hector Tamayo, 51, Holliswood, NY
Carpenter, Vanderbilt Group

Michael Andrew Tamuccio, 37, Pelham Manor, NY
Brokerage, Fred Alger Management

Kenichiro Tanaka, 52, Rye Brook, NY
Fuji Bank

Rhondelle Cherie Tankard, 31, Devonshire, Bermuda
Aon Corp.

Michael Anthony Tanner, 44, Secaucus, NJ
Trader, Cantor Fitzgerald

Dennis Gerard Taormina, 36, Montville, NJ
Financier/volunteer firefighter, Marsh & McLennan

Kenneth Joseph Tarantino, 39, Bayonne, NJ
Cantor Fitzgerald

Ronald Tartaro, 38, Bridgewater, NJ
Fred Alger Management

Darryl A. Taylor, 52, Staten Island, NY
Information technology, General Telecom

Donnie Brooks Taylor, 40, New York, NY
Aon Corp.

Lorisa Ceylon Taylor, 31, East Flatbush, NY
Insurance, Marsh & McLennan

Michael M. Taylor, 42, New York, NY
Brokerage, Cantor Fitzgerald

Yesh Tembe, 59, Piscataway, NJ
Accounting, New York State Department of Taxation & Finance

Anthony Tempesta, 38, Elizabeth, NJ
Brokerage, Cantor Fitzgerald

Dorothy Temple, 52, New York, NY
New York State Department of Taxation & Finance

David Tengelin, 25, Manhattan, NY
Accounting, Marsh & McLennan

Brian J. Terrenzi, 28, Hicksville, NY
Global network manager, Cantor Fitzgerald

Lisa Marie Terry, 42, Rochester, MI
Marsh & McLennan

Goumatie Thackurdeen, 35, South Ozone Park, NY
Fiduciary Trust Company International

Harshad Sham Thatte, 30, Norcross, GA
Marsh & McLennan
Thomas F. Theurkauf Jr., 44, Stamford, CT
Bank analyst, Keefe Bruyette & Woods
Saada Thierry, 27, Manhattan, NY
Cantor Fitzgerald
Lesley Thomas-O'Keefe, 40, Hoboken, NJ
Brokerage, Cantor Fitzgerald
Brian T. Thompson, 42, Dix Hills, NY
Fuji Bank
Clive Thompson, 43, Summit, NJ
International bank loans, EuroBrokers Inc.
Glenn Thompson, 44, New York, NY
Brokerage, Cantor Fitzgerald
Nigel Bruce Thompson, 33, New York, NY
Brokerage, Cantor Fitzgerald
Perry Anthony Thompson, 36, Mount Laurel, NJ
Insurance adjuster, Aon Corp.
Vanavah Alexi Thompson, 26, Bronx, NY
ABM Industries
Eric Raymond Thorpe, 35, Manhattan, NY
Brokerage, Keefe Bruyette & Woods
Nichola A. Thorpe, 22, Brooklyn, NY
Accounting, Keefe Bruyette & Woods
Sal E. Tieri Jr., 40, Shrewsbury, NJ
Marsh & McLennan
Mary Ellen Tiesi, 38, Jersey City, NJ
William Randolph Tieste, 54, Basking Ridge, NJ
Trader, Cantor Fitzgerald
Stephen Edward Tighe, 41, Rockville Centre, NY
Securities trader, Cantor Fitzgerald
Scott C. Timmes, 28, Ridgewood, NY
Carr Futures
Michael E. Tinley, 56, Dallas, TX
Insurance executive, Marsh & McLennan
Jennifer Marie Tino, 29, West Caldwell, NJ
Marsh & McLennan
Robert Frank Tipaldi, 25, Dyker Heights, NY
Brokerage, Cantor Fitzgerald
David Lawrence Tirado, 26, Brooklyn, NY
Computer technology, Rent-a-PC
Michelle Titolo, 34, Copiague, NY
Brokerage, Cantor Fitzgerald
John J. Tobin, 47, Kenilworth, NJ
Marsh & McLennan
Richard J. Todisco, 61, Wyckoff, NJ
Sandler O'Neill & Partners
Vladimir Tomasevic, 36, Etobicoke, Ontario, Canada
Software development, Optus e-business solutions
Stephen K. Tompsett, 39, Garden City, NY
Computer scientist, Instinet (Reuters)
Thomas Tong, 31, Manhattan, NY
Doris Torres, 32
Luis Eduardo Torres, 31
Cantor Fitzgerald
Amy E. Toyen, 24, Newton, MA
Marketing, Thomson Financial
Christopher M. Traina, 25, Bricktown, NJ
Finance, Carr Futures
Daniel Patrick Trant, 40, Northport, NY
Bond broker, Cantor Fitzgerald
Abdoul Karim Traore, 41, New York, NY
Food service, Windows on the World
Glenn J. Travers, 53, Tenafly, NJ
Electrician, Forest Electric Corp.
Walter P. "Wally" Travers, 44, Upper Saddle River, NJ
Finance, Cantor Fitzgerald
Felicia Traylor-Bass, 38, Brooklyn, NY
Office manager, Alliance Consulting Group
Lisa L. Trerotola, 36, Hazlet, NJ
Port Authority of New York & New Jersey
Karamo Trerra, 40, Manhattan, NY
Computer technician, Fiduciary Trust Company International

Michael Trinidad, 33, Jamaica, NY
Accounting, Cantor Fitzgerald
Francis Joseph Trombino, 68, Clifton, NJ
Security guard/armored-car driver, Brinks Security
Gregory J. Trost, 26, Manhattan, NY
Finance, Keefe Bruyette & Woods
William Tselepis, 33, New Providence, NJ
Cantor Fitzgerald
Zhanetta Tsoy, 32, Jersey City, NJ
Accountant, Marsh & McLennan
Michael Patrick Tucker, 40, Rumson, NJ
Trader, Cantor Fitzgerald
Pauline Tull-Francis, 56
Food service, Cantor Fitzgerald
Lance Richard Tumulty, 32, Bridgewater, NJ
Trader, EuroBrokers Inc.
Ching Ping Tung, 43, Queens, NY
Simon James Turner, 39, London, England
Risk Waters Group
Donald Joseph Tuzio, 51, Goshen, NY
Attending an employment seminar
Robert T. Twomey, 48, Brooklyn, NY
Stock trader, Harvey, Young & Yurman
Jennifer Tzemis, 26, Staten Island, NY
Fred Alger Management
John G. Ueltzhoeffer, 36, Roselle Park, NJ
Programmer, Marsh & McLennan
Tyler V. Ugolyn, 23, Manhattan, NY
Fred Alger Management
Michael A. Uliano, 42, Aberdeen, NJ
Brokerage, Cantor Fitzgerald
Jonathan J. Uman, 33, Westport, CT
Cantor Fitzgerald
Anil Shivhari Umarkar, 34, Hackensack, NJ
Cantor Fitzgerald
Allen V. Upton, 44, New York, NY
Corporate bonds, Cantor Fitzgerald
Diane Maria Urban, 50, Malverne, NY
New York State Department of Taxation & Finance
John Damien Vaccacio, 30, New York, NY
Bradley Hodges Vadas, 37, Westport, CT
Keefe Bruyette & Woods
Mayra Valdes-Rodriguez, 39, Brooklyn, NY
Aon Corp.
Felix Antonio Vale, 29, New York, NY
Brokerage, Cantor Fitzgerald
Ivan Vale, 27, New York, NY
Information technology, Cantor Fitzgerald
Benito Valentin, 33, Bronx, NY
Travel, American Express
Carlton F. Valvo, 38, New York, NY
Brokerage, Cantor Fitzgerald
Erica Van Acker, 62, New York, NY
Consultant, Aon Corp.
Kenneth W. Van Auken, 47, East Brunswick, NJ
Brokerage, Cantor Fitzgerald
Daniel M. Van Laere, 46, Glen Rock, NJ
Risk and insurance, Aon Corp.
Edward Raymond Vanacore, 29, Jersey City, NJ
Fiduciary Trust Company International
Jon C. Vandevander, 44, Ridgewood, NJ
Brokerage, Carr Futures
Frederick T. Varacchi, 35, Greenwich, CT
Brokerage, Cantor Fitzgerald
Gopalakrishnan Varadhan, 32, New York, NY
Brokerage, Cantor Fitzgerald
David Vargas, 46, Queens, NY
Customer service, Pitney Bowes
Scott C. Vasel, 32, Park Ridge, NJ
Computer technician, Marsh & McLennan
Azael Ismael Vasquez, 21, New York, NY
Food service, Forte Food Service
Santos Vasquez, 55, New York, NY

Arcangel Vazquez, 47, Brooklyn, NY

Sankara Velamuri, 63, Avenel, NJ
Accounting, State of New York

Jorge Velazquez, 47, Passaic, NJ
Brokerage, Morgan Stanley

Anthony M. Ventura, 41, Middletown, NJ

David Vera, 41, Brooklyn, NY
Telecommunications, EuroBrokers Inc.

Loretta A. Vero, 51, Nanuet, NY

Christopher Vialonga, 30, Demarest, NJ
Brokerage, Carr Futures

Matthew Gilbert Vianna, 23, Manhasset, NY
Cantor Fitzgerald

Robert A. Vicario, 40, Weehawken, NJ
Contractor

Celeste Torres Victoria, 41, Manhattan, NY
Conference telesales, Risk Waters Group

Joanna Vidal, 26, Yonkers, NY
Marketing, Risk Waters Group

Frank J. Vignola Jr., 44, Merrick, NY
Brokerage, Cantor Fitzgerald

Joseph B. Vilardo, 44, Stanhope, NJ
Brokerage, Cantor Fitzgerald

Chantal Vincelli, 38, Harlem, NY
Marketing, Data Synapse

Melissa Renee Vincent, 28, Hoboken, NJ
Recruiter, Alliance Consulting Group

Francine A. Virgilio, 48, Staten Island, NY
Insurance brokerage, Aon Corp.

Joseph G. Visciano, 22, Staten Island, NY
Brokerage, Keefe Bruyette & Woods

Joshua S. Vitale, 28, Great Neck, NY
Brokerage, Cantor Fitzgerald

Lynette D. Vosges, 48, New York, NY
Aon Corp.

Garo H. Voskerijian, 43, Valley Stream, NY
Risk and insurance services, Marsh & McLennan

Alfred Vukosa, 37, Brooklyn, NY
Computer technician, Cantor Fitzgerald

Gregory Kamal Bruno Wachtler, 25, Ramsey, NJ
Finance, Fred Alger Management

Gabriela Waisman, 33, Elmhurst, NY
Sybase Inc.

Wendy Alice Rosario Wakeford, 40, Freehold, NJ
Finance, Cantor Fitzgerald

Courtney Wainsworth Walcott, 37, Hackensack, NJ
Business consultant, IQ Financial Systems

Victor Wald, 49, Manhattan, NY
Stockbroker, Aon Corp.

Benjamin Walker, 41, Suffern, NY
Marsh & McLennan

Glen James Wall, 38, Rumson, NJ
Collateralized mortgage obligation, Cantor Fitzgerald

Peter Guyder Wallace, 66, Lincoln Park, NJ
Insurance, Marsh & McLennan

Roy M. Wallace, 42, Wyckoff, NJ
Broker, Cantor Fitzgerald

Jean Marie Wallendorf, 23, Brooklyn Heights, NY
Keefe Bruyette & Woods

Matthew Blake Wallens, 31, New York, NY
Brokerage, Cantor Fitzgerald

John Wallice Jr., 43, Huntington, NY
Broker, Cantor Fitzgerald

Barbara P. Walsh, 59, Staten Island, NY
Secretary, Marsh & McLennan

James Walsh, 37, Scotch Plains, NJ
Computer programmer, Cantor Fitzgerald

Ching Wang, 59, Queens, NY
First Commercial Bank

Weibin Wang, 41, Orangeburg, NY
Computer systems, Cantor Fitzgerald

Stephen Gordon Ward, 33, Gorham, ME
Accounting, Cantor Fitzgerald

James A. Waring, 49, Bayside, NY
Cantor Fitzgerald

Brian Gerald Warner, 32, Morganville, NJ
Technology/finance, Cantor Fitzgerald

Derrick Christopher Washington, 33, Calverton, NY
Telecommunications technician, Verizon

Charles Waters, 44, New York, NY
Financier, Cantor Fitzgerald

James Thomas "Muddy" Waters Jr., 39, Manhattan, NY
Finance technology, Keefe Bruyette & Woods

Michael H. Waye, 38, Morganville, NJ
Computer technician, Marsh & McLennan

Todd C. Weaver, 30, New York, NY
Financier, Fiduciary Trust Company International

Glenn Webber, 35, Wales
Business technology

Dinah Webster, 50
Ad sales, Risk Waters Group

Joanne Flora Weil, 39, Manhattan, NY
Attorney, Harris Beach LLP

Steven Jay Weinberg, 41, New City, NY
Accounting, Baseline Financial Services

Scott Jeffrey Weingard, 29, New York, NY
Financier, Cantor Fitzgerald

Steven Weinstein, 50, New York, NY

Simon Weiser, 65, Brooklyn, NY
Port Authority of New York & New Jersey

David Thomas Weiss, 50, New York, NY
Technology/finance/environmental, Cantor Fitzgerald

Vincent Michael Wells, 22, Redbridge, England
Financial consulting, Cantor Fitzgerald

Christian Hans Rudolph Wemmers, 43, San Francisco, CA
Information technology, Callixa

Ssu-Hui Vanessa Wen, 23, New York, NY
Information technology, Cantor Fitzgerald

Oleh D. Wengerchuk, 56, Centerport, NY
Transportation designer, Washington Group
International

Peter Matthew West, 54, Pottersville, NJ
Cantor Fitzgerald

Whitfield West, 41, New York, NY
Cantor Fitzgerald

Meredith L. Whalen, 23, Hoboken, NJ
Fred Alger Management

Adam S. White, 26, Brooklyn, NY
Environmental technologist, Cantor Fitzgerald

James Patrick White, 34, Hoboken, NJ
Bond broker, Cantor Fitzgerald

John S. White, 48, Brooklyn, NY
Elevator operator, ABM Industries

Kenneth W. White, 50, Staten Island, NY
Telephone technician, Cantor Fitzgerald

Leonard Anthony White, 57, Brooklyn, NY
Technician, Verizon

Malissa White, 37, East Flatbush, NY
Human resources, Marsh & McLennan

Wayne White, 38, New York, NY
Marsh & McLennan

Leanne Marie Whiteside, 31, Manhattan, NY
Lawyer, Aon Corp.

Mary Lenz Wieman, 43, Rockville Centre, NY
Marketing, Aon Corp.

Jeffrey David Wiener, 33, New York, NY
Risk technologies, Marsh & McLennan

William Joseph Wik, 44, Crestwood, NY
Risk-management services, Aon Corp.

Allison Marie Wildman, 30, Manhattan, NY
Stockbroker, Carr Futures

John C. Willett, 29, Jersey City, NJ
Analyst, Cantor Fitzgerald

Brian Patrick Williams, 29, New York, NY
Finance, Cantor Fitzgerald

Crossley Williams Jr., 28, Uniondale, NY
Financier, Fiduciary Trust Company International
David Williams, 34, Bronx, NY
Engineer, ABM Industries
Deborah Lynn Williams, 35, Hoboken, NJ
Aon Corp.
Kevin Michael Williams, 24, Manhattan, NY
Bond sales, Sandler O'Neill & Partners
Louie Anthony Williams, 44, Manhattan, NY
Labor & Law Dept.
Louis Calvin Williams III, 53, Mandeville, LA
Consultant, Vestek
Donna Wilson, 48, Williston Park, NY
Financial reporter, Aon Corp.
William Eben Wilson, 55, Manhattan, NY
Insurance broker, Aon Corp.
David H. Winton, 29, Brooklyn, NY
Finance, Keefe Bruyette & Woods
Thomas Francis Wise, 43, New York, NY
Technology, Marsh & McLennan
Alan L. Wisniewski, 47, Howell, NJ
Investment banking/technology, Sandler O'Neill & Partners
Frank Thomas "Paul" Wisniewski, 54, Basking Ridge, NJ
Finance, Cantor Fitzgerald
David Wiswall, 54, North Massapequa, NY
Aon Corp.
Sigrid Charlotte Wiswe, 41, Manhattan, NY
American Express
Michael Robert Wittenstein, 34, Hoboken, NJ
Finance, Cantor Fitzgerald
Christopher W. Wodenshek, 35, Ridgewood, NJ
Brokerage operations, Cantor Fitzgerald
Martin P. Wohlforth, 47, Greenwich, CT
Sandler O'Neill & Partners
Katherine S. Wolf, 40, Manhattan, NY
Executive assistant, Marsh & McLennan
Jennifer Y. Wong, 26, Whitestone, NY
Technologist, Marsh & McLennan
Jenny Seu Kueng Low Wong, 25, New York, NY
Information analyst, Marsh & McLennan
Siu Cheung Wong, 34, Jersey City, NJ
Insurance consultant, Marsh & McLennan
Yin Ping "Steven" Wong, 34, Jersey City, NJ
Technologist, Aon Corp.
Yuk Ping Winnie Wong, 47, New York, NY
New York State Department of Taxation & Finance
Brent James Woodall, 31, Oradell, NJ
Finance, Keefe Bruyette & Woods
James J. Woods, 26, Pearl River, NY
Financier, Cantor Fitzgerald
Patrick Woods, 36, Staten Island, NY
Carpenter, Aon Corp.
Richard Herron Woodwell, 44, Ho-Ho-Kus, NJ
Finance, Keefe Bruyette & Woods
John Bentley Works, 36, Darien, CT
Finance, Keefe Bruyette & Woods
Martin M. Wortley, 29, Park Ridge, NJ
Finance, Cantor Fitzgerald
Rodney J. Wotton, 36, Middletown, NJ
Technologist, Fiduciary Trust Company International
William Wren, 61, Lynbrook, NJ
Fire security officer, OCS Security
John Wright, 33, Rockville Centre, NY
Financier, Sandler O'Neill & Partners
Neil Robbin Wright, 30, Bethlehem, NJ
Financier, Cantor Fitzgerald
Sandra Wright, 57, Langhorne, PA
Facilities manager, Aon Corp.

Jupiter Yambem, 41, Beacon, NY
Restaurant management, Windows on the World
Suresh Yanamadala, 33, Plainsboro, NJ
Marsh & McLennan
Matthew David Yarnell, 26, Jersey City, NJ
Fiduciary Trust Company International
Myrna Yaskulka, 59, Staten Island, NY
Executive assistant, Fred Alger Management
Olabisi Layeni Yee, 38, Staten Island, NY
Office manager, International Office Centers
Edward Phillip York, 45, Wilton, CT
Human resources director, Cantor Fitzgerald
Kevin Patrick York, 41, Princeton Township, NJ
Financier, EuroBrokers Inc.
Suzanne Youmans, 60, Brooklyn, NY
Aon Corp.
Barrington L. Young, 35, Rosedale, NY
Telecommunications systems manager, EuroBrokers Inc.
Jacqueline "Jakki" Young, 37, New York, NY
Marsh & McLennan
Elkin Yuen, 32, Flushing, NY
Floor broker, Carr Futures
Joseph Zaccoli, 39, Valley Stream, NY
Financier, Cantor Fitzgerald
Adel Agayby Zakhary, 50, North Arlington, NJ
Accountant, Carr Futures
Arkady Zaltsman, 45, Brooklyn, NY
Architect, Skidmore Owings & Merrill
Edwin J. Zambrana Jr., 24, Brooklyn, NY
Robert Alan "Robbie" Zampieri, 30, Saddle River, NJ
Financier, Carr Futures
Mark Zangrilli, 36, Pompton Plains, NJ
Insurance underwriter, Kemper Insurance
Ira Zaslow, 55, North Woodmere, NY
Financial analyst, Lehman Brothers
Aurelio Zedillo, Mexico
Kenneth Albert Zelman, 36, Succasunna, NJ
Computer consultant, self-employed
Abraham J. Zelmanowitz, 55, Brooklyn, NY
Computer programmer, Empire Blue Cross/Blue Shield
Martin Morales Zempoaltecatl, 22, Queens, NY
Chef, Windows on the World
Zhe Zack Zeng, 28, Brooklyn, NY
Banker, Bank of New York
Marc Scott Zeplin, 33, West Harrison, NY
Financier, Cantor Fitzgerald
Jie Yao Justin Zhao, 27, Manhattan, NY
Computer technician, Aon Corp.
Ivelin Ziminski, 40, Tarrytown, NY
Marsh & McLennan
Michael Joseph Zinzi, 37, Newfoundland, NJ
Accountant, Marsh & McLennan
Charles A. Zion, 54, Greenwich, CT
Finance executive, Cantor Fitzgerald
Julie Lynne Zipper, 44, Paramus, NJ
Product manager, SunGard Trading Systems
Salvatore J. Zisa, 45, Hawthorne, NJ
Senior VP, Marsh & McLennan
Prokopios Paul Zois, 46, Lynbrook, NY
Corporate travel planner, American Express
Joseph J. Zuccala, 54, Croton-on-Hudson, NY
Computer technician, Fuji Bank
Andrew Steven Zucker, 27, Riverdale, NY
Lawyer, Harris Beach LLP
Igor Zukelman, 29, Queens, NY
Computer technician, Fiduciary Trust Company International

PENTAGON OCCUPANTS

Samantha Lightbourn Allen, 36, Hillside, MD
Budget analyst, U.S. Army

Craig Amundson, 28, Fort Belvoir, VA
Multimedia illustrator for deputy chief of staff of personnel, U.S. Army

Melissa Rose Barnes, 27, Redlands, CA
Yeoman second class, U.S. Navy

Max Beilke, 69, Laurel, MD
Civilian employee, U.S. Army

Kris Romeo Bishundat, 23, Waldorf, MD
Information systems technician second class, U.S. Navy

Carrie Blagburn, 48, Temple Hills, MD
Civilian budget analyst, U.S. Army

Canfield D. "Buddy" Boone, 54, Clifton, VA
U.S. Army

Donna Bowen, 42, Waldorf, MD
Pentagon communications representative, Verizon

Allen Boyle, 30, Fredericksburg, VA
Defense Department contractor, U.S. Defense Department

Christopher Lee Burford, 23, Hubert, NC
Electronics technician third class, U.S. Navy

Daniel Martin Caballero, 21, Houston, TX
Electronics technician third class, U.S. Navy

Jose Orlando Calderon, 44, Annandale, VA
U.S. Army

Angelene C. Carter, 51, Forrestville, MD
Accountant, U.S. Army

Sharon Carver, 38, Waldorf, MD
Civilian employee, U.S. Army

John J. Chada, 55, Manassas, VA
Civilian employee, U.S. Army

Rosa Maria "Rosemary" Chapa, 64, Springfield, VA
Civilian employee, Defense Intelligence Agency

Julian Cooper, 39, Springdale, MD
Department of the Navy contractor, U.S. Navy

Eric Allen Cranford, 32, Drexel, NC
U.S. Navy

Ada Davis, 57, Camp Springs, MD
Civilian employee, U.S. Army

Diana Borrero de Padro, 55, Woodbridge, VA
Civilian employee, U.S. Army

Gerald Francis Deconto, 44, Sandwich, MA
Director of current operations and plans, U.S. Navy

Jerry Don Dickerson, 41, Durant, MS
U.S. Army

Johnnie Doctor Jr., 32, Jacksonville, FL
Information systems technician first class, U.S. Navy

Robert Edward Dolan, 43, Alexandria, VA
Head of strategy and concepts branch, U.S. Navy

William Howard Donovan, 37, Nunda, NY
Commander, U.S. Navy

Patrick S. Dunn, 39, Springfield, VA
Surface warfare officer, U.S. Navy

Edward Thomas Earhart, 26, Salt Lick, KY
Aerographer's mate first class, U.S. Navy

Robert Randolph "Bob" Elseth, 37, Vestal, NY
Lieutenant commander, U.S. Navy

Jamie Lynn Fallon, 23, Woodbridge, VA
Storekeeper third class, U.S. Navy

Amelia Virginia Fields, 36, Dumfries, VA
Civilian employee, U.S. Army

Gerald P. Fisher, 57, Potomac, MD
Consultant, Booz-Allen & Hamilton Inc.

Matthew Michael Flocco, 21, Newark, DE
Aerographer's mate second class, U.S. Navy

Sandra N. Foster, 41, Clinton, MD
Civilian employee, U.S. Defense Department

Lawrence Daniel Getzfred, 57, Elgin, NE
Officer in the Navy command center at the Pentagon, U.S. Navy

Cortz Ghee, 54, Reisterstown, MD
Civilian employee, U.S. Army

Brenda C. Gibson, 59, Falls Church, VA
Civilian employee, U.S. Army

Ron Golinski, 60, Columbia, MD
Civilian employee, U.S. Army

Diane M. Hale-McKinzy, 38, Alexandria, VA
Civilian employee, U.S. Army

Carolyn B. Halmon, 49, Washington, DC
Budget analyst, U.S. Army

Sheila Hein, 51, University Park, MD
Budget and management specialist, U.S. Army

Ronald John Hemenway, 37, Shawnee, KS
Electronics technician first class, U.S. Navy

Wallace Cole Hogan, 40, Alexandria, VA
U.S. Army

Jimmie Ira Holley, 54, Lanham, MD
Civilian accountant, U.S. Army

Angela Houtz, 27, La Plata, MD
Civilian employee, U.S. Navy

Brady Kay Howell, 26, Arlington, VA
Management intern for chief of intelligence, U.S. Navy

Peggie Hurt, 36, Crewe, VA
Accountant, U.S. Army

Stephen Neil Hyland, 45, Burke, VA
Personnel issues, U.S. Army

Robert J. Hymel, 55, Woodbridge, VA
Civilian management analyst, Pentagon

Lacey B. Ivory, 43, Woodbridge, VA
Sergeant major, U.S. Army

Dennis M. Johnson, 48, Port Edwards, WI
Lieutenant colonel, U.S. Army

Judith Jones, 53, Woodbridge, VA
Civilian employee, U.S. Navy

Brenda Kegler, 49, Washington, DC
Budget analyst, U.S. Army

Michael Scott Lamana, 31, Baton Rouge, LA
Lieutenant, U.S. Navy

David W. Laychak, 40, Manassas, VA
Civilian budget analyst, U.S. Army

Stephen V. Long, 39, Alexandria, VA
Major, U.S. Army

James Lynch, 55, Manassas, VA
Civilian employee, U.S. Navy

Terence M. Lynch, 49, Alexandria, VA
Consultant, Booz-Allen & Hamilton Inc.

Nehamon Lyons IV, 30, Mobile, AL
Operations specialist second class, U.S. Navy

Shelley A. Marshall, 37, Marbury, MD
Budget analyst, Defense Intelligence Agency

Teresa M. Martin, 45, Stafford, VA
Civilian employee, U.S. Army

Ada L. Mason, 50, Springfield, VA
Civilian employee, U.S. Army

Dean E. Mattson, 57, Alexandria, VA
Lieutenant colonel, U.S. Army

Timothy Maude, 53, Fort Myer, VA
Deputy chief of staff for personnel, U.S. Army

Robert J. Maxwell, 53, Manassas, VA
Civilian employee, U.S. Army

Molly Hornberger McKenzie, 38, Dale City, VA
Civilian employee, U.S. Army

Patricia E. "Patti" Mickley, 41, Springfield, VA
Financial manager, U.S. Defense Department

Ronald D. Milam, 33, Washington, DC
Assistant to the Secretary, U.S. Army

Gerard P. "Jerry" Moran, 39, Upper Marlboro, MD
Engineering contractor, U.S. Navy

Odessa V. Morris, 54, Upper Marlboro, MD
Budget analyst, U.S. Army

Brian Anthony Moss, 34, Sperry, OK
Electronics technician second class, U.S. Navy
Teddington Hamm "Ted" Moy, 48, Silver Spring, MD
Civilian employee, U.S. Army
Patrick Jude Murphy, 38, Flossmoor, IL
U.S. Navy
Khang Nguyen, 41, Fairfax, VA
Contractor, U.S. Navy
Michael Allen Noeth, 30, Jackson Heights, NY
Illustrator/draftsman second class, U.S. Navy
Chin Sun Pak, 24, Lawton, OK
Specialist, U.S. Army
Jonas Martin Panik, 26, Mingoville, PA
Lieutenant, U.S. Navy
Clifford L. Patterson, 33, Alexandria, VA
Major, U.S. Army
Darin Howard Pontell, 26, Columbia, MD
Lieutenant j.g., U.S. Navy
Scott Powell, 35, Silver Spring, MD
BTG Inc.
Jack Punches, 51, Clifton, VA
Civilian employee, U.S. Navy
Joseph John Pycior Jr., 39, Carlstadt, NJ
Aviation warfare systems operator first class, U.S. Navy
Deborah Ramsaur, 45, Annandale, VA
Civilian employee, U.S. Army
Rhonda Ridge Rasmussen, 44, Woodbridge, VA
Civilian employee, U.S. Army
Marsha Dianah Ratchford, 34, Prichard, AL
Information systems technician first class, U.S. Navy
Martha Reszke, 36, Stafford, VA
Budget analyst, U.S. Army
Cecelia E. Richard, 41, Fort Washington, MD
Accounting technician, U.S. Army
Edward V. Rowenhorst, 32, Lake Ridge, VA
Civilian employee, U.S. Army
Judy Rowlett, 44, Woodbridge, VA
Civilian employee, U.S. Army
Robert E. Russell, 52, Oxon Hill, MD
Civilian budgetary supervisor, U.S. Army
William R. Ruth, 57, Mount Airy, MD
Chief warrant officer fourth class, U.S. Army
Charles E. Sabin, 54, Burke, VA
Civilian employee, U.S. Defense Department
Marjorie C. Salamone, 53, Springfield, VA
Budget program analyst, U.S. Army
David M. Scales, 44, Berea, OH
Lieutenant colonel, U.S. Army
Robert Allan Schlegel, 38, Alexandria, VA
Commander, U.S. Navy
Janice Scott, 46, Springfield, VA
Civilian employee, U.S. Army
Michael L. Selves, 53, Fairfax, VA
Information management support center director, U.S. Army
Marion Serva, 47, Stafford, VA
Civilian employee, U.S. Army
Dan Frederic Shanower, 40, Naperville, IL
Commander, U.S. Navy

Antoinette "Toni" Sherman, 35, Forest Heights, MD
Budget analyst, U.S. Army
Donald Dean Simmons, 58, Dumfries, VA
Civilian employee, U.S. Army
Cheryle D. Sincock, 53, Dale City, VA
Administrative assistant, U.S. Army
Gregg Harold Smallwood, 44, Overland Park, KS
Chief information systems technician, U.S. Navy
Gary F. Smith, 55, Alexandria, VA
Civilian employee, U.S. Army
Patricia J. Statz, 41, Tacoma Park, MD
Civilian employee, U.S. Army
Edna L. Stephens, 53, Washington, DC
Budget analyst, U.S. Army
Larry Strickland, 52, Woodbridge, VA
Senior adviser on personnel issues to the Joint Chiefs of Staff, U.S. Army
Kip P. Taylor, 38, McLean, VA
Adjutant general's corps, U.S. Army
Sandra Carol Taylor, 50, Alexandria, VA
Civilian employee, U.S. Army
Karl W. Teepe, 57, Centreville, VA
Civilian employee, Defense Information Agency
Tamara C. Thurman, 25, Brewton, AL
Classified employee, U.S. Army
Otis Vincent Tolbert, 38, Lemoore, CA
U.S. Navy
Willie Q. Troy, 51, Aberdeen Proving Ground, MD
Program analyst, U.S. Army
Ronald James Vauk, 37, Nampa, ID
Watch commander, U.S. Navy
Karen Wagner, 40, Houston, TX
Lieutenant colonel, U.S. Army
Meta L. Waller, 60, Alexandria, VA
Civilian employee, U.S. Army
Maudlyn A. White, 38, Ft. Belvoir, VA
Staff sergeant, U.S. Army
Sandra Letitia White, 44, Dumfries, VA
Civilian employee, U.S. Army
Ernest M. Willcher, 62, North Potomac, MD
Consultant, Booz-Allen & Hamilton Inc.
David Lucian Williams, 32, Newport, OR
Lieutenant commander, U.S. Navy
Dwayne Williams, 40, Jacksonville, AL
Major, U.S. Army
Marvin R. Woods, 58, Great Mills, MD
Civilian communications manager, U.S. Navy
Kevin Wayne Yokum, 27, Lake Charles, LA
Information systems technician second class, U.S. Navy
Donald McArthur Young, 41, Roanoke, VA
Chief information systems technician, U.S. Navy
Edmond Young, 22, Owings, MD
Information technology specialist, BTG Inc.
Lisa L. Young, 36, Germantown, MD
Civilian employee, U.S. Army

EMERGENCY/RESCUE PERSONNEL

Joseph Agnello, 35, Belle Harbor, NY
Firefighter, FDNY
Brian G. Ahearn, 43, Huntington, NY
Firefighter, FDNY
Eric Allen, 41, New York, NY
Firefighter, FDNY
Richard D. Allen, 31, Belle Harbor, NY
Firefighter, FDNY
James M. Amato, 43, Ronkonkoma, NY
Firefighter, FDNY

Christopher C. Amoroso, 29, Staten Island, NY
Police officer, Port Authority of New York & New Jersey
Calixto Charlie Anaya Jr., 35, Suffern, NY
Firefighter, FDNY
Joseph Angelini Jr., 38, Lindenhurst, NY
Firefighter, FDNY
Joseph Angelini Sr., 63, Lindenhurst, NY
Firefighter, FDNY
Faustino Apostol Jr., 55, Staten Island, NY
Firefighter, FDNY

David Arce, 36, New York, NY
Firefighter, FDNY

Louis Arena, 32, Staten Island, NY
Firefighter, FDNY

Carl Asaro, 39, Middletown, NY
Firefighter, FDNY

Gregg Arthur Atlas, 45, Howells, NY
Firefighter, FDNY

Gerald Atwood, 38, Brooklyn, NY
Firefighter, FDNY

Gerard Jean Baptiste, 35, Riverdale, NY
Firefighter, FDNY

Gerard A. Barbara, 53, Staten Island, NY
Firefighter, FDNY

Matthew Barnes, Monroe, NY
Firefighter, FDNY

Arthur T. Barry, 35, Staten Island, NY
Firefighter, FDNY

Maurice Vincent "Moe" Barry, 48, Rutherford, NJ
Police officer, Port Authority of New York & New Jersey

Steven J. Bates, 42, Glendale, NY
Firefighter, FDNY

Carl Bedigian, 35, Flushing, NY
Firefighter, FDNY

Stephen Belson, 51, Far Rockaway, NY
Firefighter, FDNY

John P. Bergin, 39, Staten Island, NY
Firefighter, FDNY

Paul Michael Beyer, 37, Staten Island, NY
Firefighter, FDNY

Peter Alexander Bielfeld, 44, Bronx, NY
Firefighter, FDNY

Brian Bilcher, 36, Staten Island, NY
Firefighter, FDNY

Carl Vincent Bini, 44, Staten Island, NY
Firefighter, FDNY

Christopher Joseph Blackwell, 42, Putnam Lake, NY
Firefighter, FDNY

Michael L. Bocchino, 45, New York, NY
Firefighter, FDNY

Frank Bonomo, 42, Port Jefferson, NY
Firefighter, FDNY

Gary R. Box, 37, North Bellmore, NY
Firefighter, FDNY

Michael Boyle, 37, Westbury, NY
Firefighter, FDNY

Kevin H. Bracken, 37, Manhattan, NY
Firefighter, FDNY

Michael Emmett Brennan, 27, Long Island City, NY
Firefighter, FDNY

Peter Brennan, 30, Ronkonkoma, NY
Firefighter, FDNY

Daniel J. Brethel, 43, Farmingville, NY
Firefighter, FDNY

Patrick J. Brown, 48, Manhattan, NY
Firefighter, FDNY

Andrew Brunn, 28
Firefighter, FDNY

Vincent Brunton, New York, NY
Firefighter, FDNY

Ronald Paul Bucca, 47, Tuckahoe, NY
Firefighter, FDNY

Gregory Joseph Buck, 37, Brooklyn, NY
Firefighter, FDNY

William F. Burke Jr., 46, New York, NY
Firefighter, FDNY

Donald James Burns, 61, Nissequogue, NY
Firefighter, FDNY

John Patrick Burnside, 36, Manhattan, NY
Firefighter, FDNY

Thomas M. Butler, 37, Kings Park, NY
Firefighter, FDNY

Patrick Byrne, New York, NY
Firefighter, FDNY

George Cain, 35, Massapequa, NY
Firefighter, FDNY

Salvatore Calabro, 38, Staten Island, NY
Firefighter, FDNY

Frank Callahan
Firefighter, FDNY

Liam Callahan, 44, Rockaway, NJ
Port Authority officer, Port Authority of New York & New Jersey

Michael Cammarata, 22, Staten Island, NY
Firefighter, FDNY

Brian Cannizzaro, 30, Staten Island, NY
Firefighter, FDNY

Dennis M. Carey, 51, Wantagh, NY
Firefighter, FDNY

Michael Scott Carlo, 34, Whitestone, NY
Firefighter, FDNY

Michael T. Carroll, 39, New York, NY
Firefighter, FDNY

Peter J. Carroll, 42, Staten Island, NY
Firefighter, FDNY

Thomas Anthony Casoria, 29, Whitestone, NY
Firefighter, FDNY

Michael Joseph Cawley, 32, Bellmore, NY
Firefighter, FDNY

Vernon Paul Cherry, 49, Queens, NY
Firefighter, FDNY

Nicholas P. Chiofalo Jr., 39, Selden, NY
Firefighter, FDNY

John Chipura, 39, Staten Island, NY
Firefighter, FDNY

Robert D. Cirri, 39, Nutley, NJ
Police officer, Port Authority of New York & New Jersey

Michael Clarke, 27, Prince's Bay, NY
Firefighter, FDNY

Steven Coakley, 36, Deer Park, NY
Firefighter, FDNY

Tarel Coleman, 32, Rochdale Village, NY
Firefighter, FDNY

John Michael Collins, 42, Bronx, NY
Firefighter, FDNY

Robert Cordice, 28, Staten Island, NY
Firefighter, FDNY

Ruben D. Correa, 44, Staten Island, NY
Firefighter, FDNY

James Corrigan, 60, Little Neck, NY
Fire and safety operations, World Trade Center

John Gerard Coughlin, 43, Pomona, NY
Police officer, NYPD

James Raymond Coyle, 26, New York, NY
Firefighter, FDNY

Robert James Crawford, 62, Brooklyn, NY
Firefighter, FDNY

John Crisci, 48, Holbrook, NY
Firefighter, FDNY

Dennis A. Cross, 60, Islip Terrace, NY
Firefighter, FDNY

Thomas Patrick Cullen III, 31, Staten Island, NY
Firefighter, FDNY

Robert Curatolo, 31, Staten Island, NY
Firefighter, FDNY

Michael Sean Curtin, 45, Medford, NY
Police officer, NYPD

John Dallara, 47, Pearl River, NY
Police officer, NYPD

Vincent G. Danz, 38, Farmingdale, NY
Police officer, NYPD

Edward Alexander D'Atri, 38, Staten Island, NY
Firefighter, FDNY

Michael D. D'Auria, 25, Staten Island, NY
Firefighter, FDNY

Scott Matthew Davidson, 33, New York, NY
Firefighter, FDNY
Clinton Davis, 38, Flushing, NY
Police officer, Port Authority of New York & New Jersey
Edward James Day, 45, Staten Island, NY
Firefighter, FDNY
Thomas P. DeAngelis, 51, Westbury, NY
Firefighter, FDNY
Manuel Del Valle Jr., 32, Bronx, NY
Firefighter, FDNY
Martin N. DeMeo, 47, Farmingville, NY
Firefighter, FDNY
David Paul Derubbio, 38, Bensonhurst, NY
Firefighter, FDNY
Andrew J. Desperito, 44, East Patchogue, NY
Firefighter, FDNY
Dennis Lawrence Devlin, 51, Washingtonville, NY
Firefighter, FDNY
Gerard Dewan, 35, New York, NY
Firefighter, FDNY
George DiPasquale, 33, Staten Island, NY
Firefighter, FDNY
Jerome Mark Patrick Dominguez, 37, West Islip, NY
Police officer, NYPD
Kevin W. Donnelly, 43, Seaford, NY
Firefighter, FDNY
Kevin Dowdell, 46, Breezy Point, NY
Firefighter, FDNY
Ray M. Downey, 63, Deer Park, NY
Firefighter, FDNY
Stephen Patrick Driscoll, 38, Lake Carmel, NY
Emergency services, North Bronx Emergency Services Unit
Gerard Duffy, 53, Manorville, NY
Firefighter, FDNY
Martin J. Egan Jr., 36, Staten Island, NY
Firefighter, FDNY
Michael J. Elferis, 27, College Point, NY
Firefighter, FDNY
Mark J. Ellis, 26, Huntington, NY
Police officer, NYPD
Francis Esposito, 32, Staten Island, NY
Firefighter, FDNY
Michael Esposito, 43, Staten Island, NY
Firefighter, FDNY
Robert "Bobby" Evans, 36, Franklin Square, NY
Firefighter, FDNY
Keith G. Fairben, 24, Floral Park, NY
Emergency medical technician, New York Presbyterian
Hospital
John Joseph "Jack" Fanning, 54, West Hempstead, NY
Firefighter, FDNY
Thomas J. Farino, 37, South Ozone Park, NY
Firefighter, FDNY
Terrence Patrick Farrell, 45, Huntington, NY
Firefighter, FDNY
Joseph Farrelly, 47, Staten Island, NY
Firefighter, FDNY
Robert Fazio, 41, Freeport, NY
Police officer, NYPD
William M. Feehan, 71, Flushing, NY
Firefighter, FDNY
Lee Fehling, 28, Wantagh, NY
Firefighter, FDNY
Alan D. Feinberg, 48, Marlboro, NJ
Firefighter, FDNY
Michael Curtis Fiore, 46, Staten Island, NY
Firefighter, FDNY
John R. Fischer, 46, Staten Island, NY
Firefighter, FDNY
Andre G. Fletcher, 37, North Babylon, NY
Firefighter, FDNY
John Joseph Florio, 33, Oceanside, NY
Firefighter, FDNY

Michael N. Fodor, 53, Warwick, NY
Firefighter, FDNY
Thomas Foley, 32, West Nyack, NY
Firefighter, FDNY
David Fontana, 37, New York, NY
Firefighter, FDNY
Donald A. Foreman, 53, Staten Island, NY
Police officer, Port Authority of New York & New Jersey
Robert Joseph Foti, 42, Albertson, NY
Firefighter, FDNY
Andrew Fredericks, 40, Suffern, NY
Firefighter, FDNY
Peter L. Freund, 45, Westtown, NY
Firefighter, FDNY
Gregg J. Froehner, 46, Chester, NJ
Police officer, Port Authority of New York & New Jersey
Thomas Gambino Jr., 48, Babylon, NY
Firefighter, FDNY
Peter Ganci, 54, North Massapequa, NY
Firefighter, FDNY
Charles William Garbarini, 43, Pleasantville, NY
Firefighter, FDNY
Thomas A. Gardner, 39, Oceanside, NY
Firefighter, FDNY
Matthew David Garvey, 37
Firefighter, FDNY
Bruce H. Gary, 51, Bellmore, NY
Firefighter, FDNY
Gary Geidel, New York, NY
Firefighter, FDNY
Edward F. Geraghty, 45, Rockville Centre, NY
Firefighter, FDNY
Denis Germain, 33, Tuxedo Park, NY
Firefighter, FDNY
Vincent Francis Giammona, 40, Valley Stream, NY
Firefighter, FDNY
James A. Giberson, 43, Staten Island, NY
Firefighter, FDNY
Ronnie E. Gies, 43, Merrick, NY
Firefighter, Merrick Fire Department
Paul John Gill, 34, Queens, NY
Firefighter, FDNY
Rodney C. Gillis, 34, Brooklyn, NY
Police officer, NYPD
John F. Ginley, 37, Warwick, NY
Firefighter, FDNY
Jeffrey John Giordano, 46, Staten Island, NY
Firefighter, FDNY
John J. Giordano, 46, Newburgh, NY
Firefighter, FDNY
Keith Glascoe, 39, New York, NY
Firefighter, FDNY
Thomas E. Gorman, 41, Middlesex, NJ
Emergency services, Port Authority of New York & New
Jersey
James Michael Gray, 34, Staten Island, NY
Firefighter, FDNY
Joseph Grzelak, 52, Staten Island, NY
Firefighter, FDNY
Jose Antonio Guadalupe, 37, Rochdale Village, NY
Firefighter, FDNY
Geoffrey E. Guja, 47, Lindenhurst, NY
Firefighter, FDNY
Joseph Gullickson, 37, Staten Island, NY
Firefighter, FDNY
David Halderman Jr., 40, New York, NY
Firefighter, FDNY
Vincent Gerard Halloran, 43, North Salem, NY
Firefighter, FDNY
Robert Hamilton, 43, Washingtonville, NY
Firefighter, FDNY
Sean Hanley, 35, New York, NY
Firefighter, FDNY

Thomas Hannafin, 36, Staten Island, NY
Firefighter, FDNY
Dana Hannon, 29, Suffern, NY
Firefighter, FDNY
Daniel Harlin, 41, Kent, NY
Firefighter, FDNY
Harvey L. Harrell, 49, Staten Island, NY
Firefighter, FDNY
Stephen Gary Harrell, 44, Staten Island, NY
Firefighter, FDNY
Thomas Theodore Haskell, 37, Massapequa, NY
Firefighter, FDNY
Timothy Haskell, 34, Seaford, NY
Firefighter, FDNY
Terence S. Hatton, 41, Manhattan, NY
Firefighter, FDNY
Michael Helmut Haub, 34, Franklin Square, NY
Firefighter, FDNY
Philip Thomas Hayes, 67, East Northport, NY
Firefighter, FDNY
Michael K. Healey, 42, East Patchogue, NY
Firefighter, FDNY
John E. Heffernan, 37, New York, NY
Firefighter, FDNY
Ronnie Lee Henderson, 52, Newburgh, NJ
Firefighter, FDNY
Joseph P. Henry, 25, New York, NY
Firefighter, FDNY
William Henry, 49, Springfield Gardens, NY
Firefighter, FDNY
Thomas Hetzel, 33, Elmont, NY
Firefighter, FDNY
Brian Hickey, 47, Bethpage, NY
Firefighter, FDNY
Timothy B. Higgins, 43, Farmingville, NY
Firefighter, FDNY
Jonathan R. Hohmann, 48, Staten Island, NY
Firefighter, FDNY
Thomas P. Holohan, 36, Chester, NY
Firefighter, FDNY
Uhuru Houston, 32, Englewood, NJ
Port Authority officer, Port Authority of New York & New Jersey
George Gerald Howard, 45, Hicksville, NY
Police officer, Port Authority of New York & New Jersey
Stephen Huczko Jr., 44, Hampton, NJ
Police officer, Port Authority of New York & New Jersey
Joseph G. Hunter, 32, South Hempstead, NY
Firefighter, FDNY
Walter G. Hynes, 36, Belle Harbor, NY
Firefighter and attorney, FDNY
Jonathan Lee Ielpi, 29, Great Neck, NY
Firefighter, FDNY
Frederick III Jr., 49, Pearl River, NY
Firefighter, FDNY
Anthony P. Infante Jr., 47, Mountainside, NJ
Police officer, Port Authority of New York & New Jersey
William Johnston, 31, North Babylon, NY
Firefighter, FDNY
Andrew Jordan, 35, Remsenburg, NY
Firefighter, FDNY
Karl Henry Joseph, 25, Brooklyn, NY
Firefighter, FDNY
Anthony Jovic, 39, Massapequa Park, NY
Firefighter, FDNY
Angel C. Juarbe Jr., 35, Bronx, NY
Firefighter, FDNY
Mychal Judge, 68, Manhattan, NY
Chaplain, FDNY
Paul William Jurgens, 47, Levittown, NY
Police officer, Port Authority of New York & New Jersey
Thomas Edward Jurgens, 26, Lawrence, NY
Court officer, New York State Supreme Court

Vincent D. Kane, 37, Manhattan, NY
Firefighter, FDNY
Charles L. Kasper, 54, Staten Island, NY
Firefighter, FDNY
Robert M. Kaulfers, 49, Kenilworth, NJ
Police officer, Port Authority of New York & New Jersey
Paul H. Keating, 38, Manhattan, NY
Firefighter, FDNY
Richard John Kelly Jr., 50, Staten Island, NY
Firefighter, FDNY
Thomas Richard Kelly, 38, Riverhead, NY
Firefighter, FDNY
Thomas W. Kelly, 51, Staten Island, NY
Firefighter, FDNY
Thomas J. Kennedy, 36, Islip Terrace, NY
Firefighter, FDNY
Ronald T. Kerwin, 42, Levittown, NY
Firefighter, FDNY
Michael Kiefer, 25, Franklin Square, NY
Firefighter, FDNY
Robert King Jr., 36
Firefighter, FDNY
Ronald Phillip Kloepfer, 39, Franklin Square, NY
Police officer, NYPD
Scott Kopytko, 32, Oakland Gardens, NY
Firefighter, FDNY
William Krukowski, 36, New York, NY
Firefighter, FDNY
Kenneth Kumpel, 42, Cornwall, NY
Firefighter, FDNY
Thomas Kuveikis, 48, Carmel, NY
Firefighter, FDNY
David LaForge, 50, Staten Island, NY
Firefighter, FDNY
William David Lake, 44, Bay Ridge, NY
Firefighter, FDNY
Robert T. Lane, 28, Staten Island, NY
Firefighter, FDNY
Peter J. Langone, 41, Roslyn Heights, NY
Firefighter, FDNY
Thomas Michael Langone, 39, Williston Park, NY
Police officer, NYPD
Scott Larsen, Queens, NY
Firefighter, FDNY
Paul Laszczynski, 49, Paramus, NJ
Police officer, Port Authority of New York & New Jersey
James Leahy, 38, Staten Island, NY
Police officer, NYPD
Joseph Gerard Leavey, 45, Pelham, NY
Firefighter, FDNY
Neil Leavy, 34, Staten Island, NY
Firefighter, FDNY
David Prudencio Lemagne, 27, North Bergen, NJ
Police officer, Port Authority of New York & New Jersey
John Joseph "Jay" Lennon Jr., 44, Howell, NJ
Police officer, Port Authority of New York & New Jersey
John Dennis Levi, 50, Brooklyn, NY
Police officer, Port Authority of New York & New Jersey
Daniel F. Libretti, 43, Staten Island, NY
Firefighter, FDNY
Carlos R. Lillo, 37, Babylon, NY
Emergency medical technician, FDNY
Robert Thomas Linnane, 33, West Hempstead, NY
Firefighter, FDNY
Joseph Lovero, 60, Jersey City, NJ
Civilian fire dispatcher, New Jersey Fire Department
James Francis Lynch, 47, Woodbridge, NJ
Police officer, Port Authority of New York & New Jersey
Michael F. Lynch, 33, New Hyde Park, NY
Firefighter, FDNY
Michael Francis Lynch, 30, Bronx, NY
Firefighter, FDNY

Michael J. Lyons, 32, Hawthorne, NY
Firefighter, FDNY
Patrick Lyons, 34, South Setauket, NY
Firefighter, FDNY
Joseph Maffeo, 30, Staten Island, NY
Firefighter, FDNY
William J. Mahoney, 38, Bohemia, NY
Firefighter, FDNY
Joseph E. Maloney, 46, Farmingville, NY
Firefighter, FDNY
Joseph Ross Marchbanks Jr., 47, Nanuet, NY
Firefighter, FDNY
Charles Joseph Margiotta, 44, Staten Island, NY
Firefighter, FDNY
Kenneth Joseph Marino, 40, Monroe, NY
Firefighter, FDNY
John Marshall, 35, Congers, NY
Firefighter, FDNY
Peter C. Martin, 43, Miller Place, NY
Firefighter, FDNY
Paul Richard Martini, 37, Brooklyn, NY
Firefighter, FDNY
Joseph A. Mascali, 44, Staten Island, NY
Firefighter, FDNY
Keithroy Maynard, 30, Brooklyn, NY
Firefighter, FDNY
Kathy Nancy Mazza-Delosh, 46, Farmingdale, NY
Police officer, Port Authority of New York & New Jersey
Brian G. McAleese, 36, Baldwin, NY
Firefighter, FDNY
John McAvoy, 47, Staten Island, NY
Firefighter, FDNY
Thomas McCann, 46, Woodside, NY
Firefighter, FDNY
Brian G. McDonnell, 38, Wantagh, NY
Police officer, NY Emergency Service Unit
William E. McGinn, 43, Bronx, NY
Firefighter, FDNY
William J. McGovern, 49, Smithtown, NY
Firefighter, FDNY
Dennis P. McHugh, 34, Sparkill, NY
Firefighter, FDNY
Donald James McIntyre, 38, New City, NY
Police officer, Port Authority of New York & New Jersey
Robert Dismas McMahon, 35, Woodside, NY
Firefighter, FDNY
Walter Arthur McNeil, 53, East Stroudsburg, PA
Police officer, Port Authority of New York & New Jersey
Robert William McPadden, 30, Pearl River, NY
Firefighter, FDNY
Terence McShane, 37, West Islip, NY
Firefighter, FDNY
Timothy Patrick McSweeney, 37, Staten Island, NY
Firefighter, FDNY
Martin Edward McWilliams, 35, Kings Park, NY
Firefighter, FDNY
Raymond Meisenheimer, 46, West Babylon, NY
Firefighter, FDNY
Charles Mendez, 38, Floral Park, NY
Firefighter, FDNY
Steve Mercado, 38, Bronx, NY
Firefighter, FDNY
Yamel Merino, 24, Yonkers, NY
Emergency medical technician, MetroCare Ambulance Group
Douglas C. Miller Jr., 34, Port Jervis, NY
Firefighter, FDNY
Henry Miller Jr., 52, Massapequa, NY
Firefighter, FDNY
Robert Minara, 54, Carmel, NY
Firefighter, FDNY
Thomas Mingione
Firefighter, FDNY

Paul Thomas Mitchell, 46, Staten Island, NY
Firefighter, FDNY
Louis Joseph Modafferi, 45, Staten Island, NY
Firefighter, FDNY
Dennis Mojica, 50, Brooklyn, NY
Firefighter, FDNY
Manuel Mojica, 37, Bellmore, NY
Firefighter, FDNY
Carl Molinaro, 32, Staten Island, NY
Firefighter, FDNY
Michael G. Montesi, 39, Highland Mills, NY
Firefighter, FDNY
Thomas Moody, 45, Stony Brook, NY
Firefighter, FDNY
John Moran, 43, Rockaway, NY
Firefighter, FDNY
Vincent S. Morello, 34, Middle Village, NY
Firefighter, FDNY
Ferdinand V. Morrone, 63, Lakewood, NJ
Police officer, Port Authority of New York & New Jersey
Christopher Mozzillo, 27, Staten Island, NY
Firefighter, FDNY
Richard Muldowney Jr., 40, Babylon, NY
Firefighter, FDNY
Michael Dermott Mullan, 34, Flushing, NY
Firefighter, FDNY
Dennis Michael Mulligan, 32, Bronx, NY
Firefighter, FDNY
Raymond E. Murphy, 46, New York, NY
Firefighter, FDNY
Robert Nagel, 55, Manhattan, NY
Firefighter, FDNY
John Napolitano, 33, Ronkonkoma, NY
Firefighter, FDNY
Joseph Michael Navas, 44, Paramus, NJ
Police officer, Port Authority of New York & New Jersey
James Arthur Nelson, 40, Clark, NJ
Police officer, Port Authority of New York & New Jersey
Peter Allen Nelson, 42, Huntington Station, NY
Firefighter, FDNY
Gerard Terence Nevins, 46, Campbell Hall, NY
Firefighter, FDNY
Alfonse Joseph Niedermeyer III, 40, Manasquan, NJ
Police officer, Port Authority of New York & New Jersey
Dennis O'Berg, Babylon, NY
Firefighter, FDNY
Daniel O'Callaghan, 42, Smithtown, NY
Firefighter, FDNY
Douglas Oelschlager, 36, St. James, NY
Firefighter, FDNY
Joseph J. Ogren, 30, Staten Island, NY
Firefighter, FDNY
Thomas O'Hagan, 43, New York, NY
Firefighter, FDNY
Samuel Oitice, 45, Peekskill, NY
Firefighter, FDNY
Patrick J. O'Keefe, 44, Oakdale, NY
Firefighter, FDNY
William O'Keefe, 49, Staten Island, NY
Firefighter, FDNY
Eric Taube Olsen, 41, Staten Island, NY
Firefighter, FDNY
Jeffrey James Olsen, 31, Staten Island, NY
Firefighter, FDNY
Steven John Olson, 38, Staten Island, NY
Firefighter, FDNY
Kevin M. O'Rourke, 44, Hewlett, NY
Firefighter, FDNY
Michael Otten, 42, East Islip, NY
Firefighter, FDNY
Jeffrey Matthew Palazzo, 33, Staten Island, NY
Firefighter, FDNY

Orio Joseph Palmer, 45, Valley Stream, NY
Firefighter, FDNY

Frank A. Palombo, 46, Brooklyn, NY
Firefighter, FDNY

Paul Pansini, 34, Staten Island, NY
Firefighter, FDNY

John M. Paolillo, 51, Glen Head, NY
Firefighter, FDNY

James N. Pappageorge, 29, Yonkers, NY
Firefighter, FDNY

James W. Parham, 32, Jackson Heights, NY
Police officer, Port Authority of New York & New Jersey

Robert Parro, 35, Levittown, NY
Firefighter, FDNY

Richard Allen Pearlman, 18, Howard Beach, NY
Volunteer emergency medical technician, Forest Hills
Ambulance Corp.

Durrell V. Pearsall, 38, Hempstead, NY
Firefighter, FDNY

Glenn C. Perry, 41, Monroe, NY
Firefighter, FDNY

John William Perry, 38, Manhattan, NY
Police officer, NYPD

Philip Scott Petti, 43, Staten Island, NY
Firefighter, FDNY

Glen K. Pettit, 30, Oakdale, NY
Police officer/photographer, NYPD

Dominick A. Pezzulo, 36, Bronx, NY
Police officer, Port Authority of New York & New Jersey

Kevin Pfeifer, 42, Middle Village, NY
Firefighter, FDNY

Kenneth Phelan, 41, Maspeth, NY
Firefighter, FDNY

Christopher Pickford, 32, Forest Hills, NY
Firefighter, FDNY

Shawn Edward Powell, 32, Brooklyn, NY
Firefighter, FDNY

Vincent Princiotta, 39, Orangeburg, NY
Firefighter, FDNY

Kevin M. Prior, 28, Bellmore, NY
Firefighter, FDNY

Richard Prunty, 57, Sayville, NY
Firefighter, FDNY

Lincoln Quappe, 38, Sayville, NY
Firefighter, FDNY

Michael Quilty, 42, Staten Island, NY
Firefighter, FDNY

Ricardo Quinn, 40, Bayside, NY
Emergency medical technician, FDNY

Leonard Ragaglia, 36, Staten Island, NY
Firefighter, FDNY

Michael Ragusa, 29, New York, NY
Firefighter, FDNY

Edward J. Rall, 44, Holbrook, NY
Firefighter, FDNY

Adam David Rand, 30, Bellmore, NY
Firefighter, FDNY

Donald J. Regan, 47, Wallkill, NY
Firefighter, FDNY

Robert Regan, 48, Floral Park, NY
Firefighter, FDNY

Christian Michael Otto Regenhard, 28, Bronx, NY
Firefighter, FDNY

Kevin O. Reilly, 28, Manhattan, NY
Firefighter, FDNY

Bruce A. Reynolds, 41, Columbia, NJ
Police officer, Port Authority of New York & New Jersey

Vernon Allan Richard, 53, Nanuet, NY
Firefighter, FDNY

Claude D. Richards, 46, New York, NY
Police officer, NYPD

James Riches, 29, Bay Ridge, NY
Firefighter, FDNY

Joseph Rivelli Jr., 43, Manhattan, NY
Firefighter, FDNY

Michael Edward Roberts, 31, New York, NY
Firefighter, FDNY

Antonio Jose Carrusca Rodrigues, 35, Port Washington, NY
Police officer, Port Authority of New York & New Jersey

Anthony Rodriguez, 37, Staten Island, NY
Firefighter, FDNY

Richard Rodriguez, 31, Cliffwood, NJ
Police officer, Port Authority of New York & New Jersey

Matthew Rogan, 37, West Islip, NY
Firefighter, FDNY

Keith Roma, 27, Staten Island, NY
Fire patrol officer, FDNY

James A. Romito, 51, Westwood, NJ
Chief of Port Authority Police Department, Port Authority of
New York & New Jersey

Nicholas Rossomando, 35, Staten Island, NY
Firefighter, FDNY

Timothy Alan Roy Sr., 36, Massapequa Park, NY
Police officer, NYPD

Paul G. Ruback, 50, Newburgh, NY
Firefighter, FDNY

Stephen P. Russell, 40, Rockaway Beach, NY
Firefighter, FDNY

Michael Thomas Russo Sr., 44, Nesconset, NY
Firefighter, FDNY

Matthew Lancelot Ryan, 54, Seaford, NY
Firefighter, FDNY

Thomas E. Sabella, 44, Staten Island, NY
Firefighter, FDNY

Christopher Santora, 23, New York, NY
Firefighter, FDNY

John Santore, 49, Staten Island, NY
Firefighter, FDNY

Mario L. Santoro, 28, Manhattan, NY
Emergency medical technician, New York Presbyterian
Hospital

Dominick Santos, 36, Bronx, NY
Police officer, Port Authority of New York & New Jersey

Gregory Thomas Saucedo, 31, Old Mill Basin, NY
Firefighter, FDNY

Dennis Scauso, 46, Dix Hills, NY
Firefighter, FDNY

John A. Schardt, 34, Staten Island, NY
Firefighter, FDNY

Fred Claude Scheffold Jr., 57, Piermont, NY
Firefighter, FDNY

Thomas G. Schoales, 27, Stony Point, NY
Firefighter, FDNY

Gerard P. Schrang, 45, Holbrook, NY
Firefighter, FDNY

Mark Schwartz, 50, West Hempstead, NY
Emergency response, City Office of Emergency Management

Gregory Sikorsky, 34, Spring Valley, NY
Firefighter, FDNY

Stephen Siller, 34, Staten Island, NY
Firefighter, FDNY

John P. Skala, 31, Clifton, NJ
Police officer, Port Authority of New York & New Jersey

Stanley S. Smagala, 36, Holbrook, NY
Firefighter, FDNY

Kevin Smith, 47, Mastic, NY
Firefighter, FDNY

Leon Smith Jr., 48, Brooklyn, NY
Firefighter, FDNY

Moira Smith, 38, Queens, NY
Police officer, NYPD

Robert W. Spear Jr., 30, Valley Cottage, NY
Firefighter, FDNY

Joseph P. Spor, 35, Yorktown Heights, NY
Firefighter, FDNY

Lawrence T. Stack, 58, Lake Ronkonkoma, NY
Firefighter, FDNY
Timothy Stackpole, 42, Brooklyn, NY
Firefighter, FDNY
Gregory Stajk, 46, Long Beach, NY
Firefighter, FDNY
Jeffrey Stark, 30, Staten Island, NY
Firefighter, FDNY
Walwyn W. Stuart Jr., 28, Valley Stream, NY
Police officer, Port Authority of New York & New Jersey
Benjamin Suarez, 36, New York, NY
Firefighter, FDNY
Ramon Suarez, 45, Ridgewood, NY
Transit police, NYC Transit
Daniel Suhr, 37, Neponsit, NY
Firefighter, FDNY
David Marc Sullins, 30, Glendale, NY
Paramedic, Cabrini Medical Center
Christopher P. Sullivan, 38, Massapequa, NY
Firefighter, FDNY
Brian Edward Sweeney, 29, Merrick, NY
Firefighter, FDNY
Sean Patrick Tallon, 26, Yonkers, NY
Firefighter, FDNY
Paul Talty, 40, Wantagh, NY
Police officer, NYPD
Allan Tarasiewicz, 45, Staten Island, NY
Firefighter, FDNY
Paul A. Tegtmeier, 41, Hyde Park, NY
Firefighter, FDNY
William Harry Thompson, 51, New York, NY
Court officer and instructor, NYS
John Patrick Tierney, 27, Staten Island, NY
Firefighter, FDNY
Kenneth F. Tietjen, 31, Matawan, NJ
Law enforcement, Port Authority of New York & New Jersey
John J. Tipping II, 33, Port Jefferson, NY
Firefighter, FDNY
Hector Luis Tirado Jr., 30, Bronx, NY
Firefighter, FDNY
Santos Valentin Jr., 39, Richmond Hill, NY
Law enforcement, NYPD
Richard Bruce Van Hine, 48, Greenwood Lake, NY
Firefighter, FDNY
Peter Anthony Vega, 36, Brooklyn, NY
Firefighter, FDNY
Lawrence Veling, 44, Gerritsen Beach, NY
Firefighter, FDNY

John T. Vigiano II, 36, West Islip, NY
Firefighter, FDNY
Joseph Vincent Vigiano, 34, Medford, NY
Police officer, NYPD
Sergio Villanueva, 33, Jackson Heights, NY
Firefighter, FDNY
Lawrence Virgilio, 38
Firefighter, FDNY
Mitchel Scott Wallace, 34, Mineola, NY
Court officer, NYS
Robert F. Wallace, 43, Woodhaven, NY
Firefighter, FDNY
Jeffrey Patrick Walz, 37, Tuckahoe, NY
Firefighter, FDNY
Michael Warchola, 51, Middle Village, NY
Firefighter, FDNY
Patrick J. Waters, 44, Queens, NY
Firefighter, FDNY
Kenneth Thomas Watson, 39, Smithtown, NY
Firefighter, FDNY
Walter E. Weaver, 30, Centereach, NY
Police officer, NYPD
Nathaniel Webb, 56, Jersey City, NJ
Police officer, Port Authority of New York & New Jersey
Michael T. Weinberg, 34, Maspeth, NY
Firefighter, FDNY
David Martin Weiss, 41, Maybrook, NY
Firefighter, FDNY
Timothy Welty, 34, Yonkers, NY
Firefighter, FDNY
Eugene Whelan, 31, Rockaway, NY
Firefighter, FDNY
Edward James White, 30, Queens, NY
Firefighter, FDNY
Mark Whitford, 33, Salisbury Mills, NY
Firefighter, FDNY
Michael T. Wholey, 34, Westwood, NJ
Police officer, Port Authority of New York & New Jersey
Glenn E. Wilkinson, 46, Bayport, NY
Firefighter, FDNY
John P. Williamson, 46, Warwick, NY
Firefighter, FDNY
Glenn J. Winuk, 40, Manhattan, NY
Lawyer/volunteer firefighter, FDNY
David Terence Wooley, 54, Nanuet, NY
Firefighter, FDNY
Raymond R. York, 45, Valley Stream, NY
Firefighter, FDNY

233

American
Airlines
Flight 11
(WTC North
Tower)

AMERICAN AIRLINES FLIGHT 11 (WTC NORTH TOWER)

Anna Williams Allison, 49, Stoneham, MA
Software consultant
David Lawrence Angell, 54, Pasadena, CA
Executive producer, NBC
Lynn Angell, 52, Pasadena, CA
Retired librarian/philanthropist
Seima Aoyama, 48, Culver City, CA
Accountant, SGI-USA Buddhist Association
Barbara Jean Arestigui, 38, Marstons Mills, MA
Flight attendant, American Airlines
Myra Joy Aronson, 50, Charleston, MA
Press-analyst relations, Compuware Corp.
Christine Barbuto, 32, Brookline, MA
Retail buyer, TJX Companies
Carolyn Beug, 48, Santa Monica, CA
Filmmaker, video producer and author
Kelly Ann Booms, 24, Brookline, MA
Accounting, Pricewaterhouse Coopers
Carol Marie Bouchard, 43, Warwick, RI
Secretary, Kent Hospital

Neilie Anne Heffernan Casey, 32, Wellesley, MA
Retail management, TJX Companies
Jeffrey Dwayne Collman, 41, Novato, CA
Flight attendant, American Airlines
Jeffrey Coombs, 42, Abington, MA
Computer technology, Compaq
Tara Kathleen Creamer, 30, Worcester, MA
Merchandise manager, TJX Companies
Thelma Cuccinello, 71, Wilmot Flat, NH
Retired
Patrick Currivan, 52, Winchester, MA
Technology specialist, AtosEuronext
Brian Paul Dale, 43, Warren, NJ
Investor, Blue Capital Management
David DiMeglio, 22, Wakefield, MA
Electrician apprentice
Donald Americo DiTullio, 49, Peabody, MA
Endoscopy, Smith & Nephew Inc.
Alberto Dominguez, 66, Lidcombe, New South Wales,
Australia
Baggage handler/disk jockey, Qantas Airlines

234

American
Airlines
Flight 11
(WTC North
Tower)

Paige Farley-Hackel, 46, Newton, MA
Counselor
Alexander M. Filipov, 70, Concord, MA
Engineer
Carol Flyzik, 40, Plaistow, NH
Software sales, Meditech
Paul J. Friedman, 45, Belmont, MA
Consulting, Emergence Consulting
Karleton D.B. Fyfe, 31, Brookline, MA
Senior analyst, John Hancock
Peter Allan Gay, 54, Tewksbury, MA
Plant manager, Raytheon
Linda M. George, 27, Westboro, MA
Buyer, TJX Companies
Edmund Glazer, 41, Wellesley, MA
Telecommunications, MRV Communications
Lisa Reinhart Fenn Gordenstein, 41, Needham, MA
Merchandise management, TJX Companies
Andrew Peter Charles Curry Green, 34, Santa Monica, CA
Business development, eLogic
Peter Paul Hashem, 40, Tewksbury, MA
Engineer, Teradyne Inc.
Robert Jay Hayes, 38, Amesbury, MA
Marketing, Netstal
Edward R. "Ted" Hennessy Jr., 35, Belmont, MA
Consulting, Emergence Consulting
John Hofer, 45, Bellflower, CA
Self-employed, John's Sharpening Center
Cora Hidalgo Holland, 52, Sudbury, MA
Sudbury Food Pantry, Our Lady of Fatima Church
John Nicholas Humber Jr., 60, Newton, MA
Mechanical engineering, Enron Wind Corporation
Waleed Iskandar, 34, London, England
Business strategy consultant, Monitor Group
John Charles Jenkins, 45, Cambridge, MA
Economics and business consulting, Charles River Associates
Charles E. Jones, 48, Bedford, MA
Defense contractor, BAE Systems
Robin Kaplan, 33, Westboro, MA
Equipment specialist, TJX Companies
Barbara Keating, 72, Palm Springs, CA
Retired, St. Theresa Catholic Church
David Kovalcin, 42, Hudson, NH
Engineer, Raytheon
Judy Larocque, 50, Framingham, MA
Technology consulting, Market Perspectives Inc.
Natalie Janis Lasden, 46, Peabody, MA
Research and testing, General Electric
Daniel John Lee, 34, Van Nuys, CA
Carpenter, Backstreet Boys Tour
Daniel C. Lewin, 31, Charlestown, MA
Computer technology, Akamai Technologies Inc.
Sara Low, 28, Batesville, AR
Flight attendant, American Airlines
Susan A. MacKay, 44, Wellesley, MA
Retailer, TJX Companies
Karen Martin, 40, Amherst, MA
Flight attendant, American Airlines
Thomas F. McGuinness Jr., 42, Portsmouth, NH
Pilot, American Airlines
Christopher D. Mello, 25, Boston, MA
Financial analyst, Alta Communications
Jeff Mladenik, 43, Hinsdale, IL
Publishing, Cahners Publishing (eLogic)
Carlos Alberto Montoya, 36, Belmont, MA
Laura Lee Morabito, 34, Framingham, MA
National sales manager, Qantas Airways

Mildred Naiman, 81, Andover, MA
Retired
Laurie Ann Neira, 48, Los Angeles, CA
Transcriber, Your Office Genie
Renee Lucille Newell, 37, Cranston, RI
Customer service, American Airlines
Kathleen Ann Nicosia, 54, Winthrop, MA
Flight attendant, American Airlines
Jacqueline Norton, 60, Lubec, ME
Retired
Robert Grant Norton, 85, Lubec, ME
Retired engineer
John Ogonowski, 52, Dracut, MA
Pilot, American Airlines
Betty Ann Ong, 45, Andover, MA
Flight attendant, American Airlines
Jane Orth, 49, Haverhill, MA
Retired
Thomas Nicholas Pecorelli, 31, Topanga, CA
Cameraman, Fox Sports Net
Berry Berenson Perkins, 53, Los Angeles, CA
Photographer and actress
Sonia Morales Puopolo, 58, Dover, MA
Philanthropy
David E. Retik, 33, Needham, MA
Communications, Alta Communications
Jean Destrehan Roger, 24, Longmeadow, MA
Flight attendant, American Airlines
Philip Rosenzweig, 47, Acton, MA
Engineering/computer networking, Sun Microsystems
Richard Barry Ross, 58, Newton, MA
President and chief executive, The Ross Group
Jessica Leigh Sachs, 23, Billerica, MA
Accounting, Pricewaterhouse Coopers
Rahma Salie, 28, Boston, MA
Computer consultant
Heather Lee Smith, 30, Boston, MA
Financial analyst, Beacon Capital Partners
Dianne Bullis Snyder, 42, Westport Point, MA
Flight attendant, American Airlines
Douglas J. Stone, 54, Dover, NH
Self-employed
Xavier Suarez, 41, Chino Hills, CA
Engineering
Madeline Amy Sweeney, 35, Acton, MA
Flight attendant, American Airlines
Michael Theodoridis, 32, Boston, MA
Computer consultant
James Trentini, 65, Everett, MA
Retired teacher and assistant principal
Mary Trentini, 67, Everett, MA
Retired secretary
Antonio Jesus Montoya Valdes, 46, East Boston, MA
Houseman, Boston Harbor Hotel
Pendyala Vamsikrishna, 30, Los Angeles, CA
Software technician, DTI Technologies
Mary Alice Wahlstrom, 75, Kaysville, UT
Retired loan officer
Kenneth Waldie, 46, Methuen, MA
Senior quality control engineer, Raytheon
John Joseph Wenckus, 46, Torrance, CA
Mechanical engineering and tax consulting, Lockhart Industries
Candace Lee Williams, 20, Danbury, CT
Student
Christopher Rudolph Zarba, 47, Hopkinton, MA
Software engineer, Concord Communications

UNITED AIRLINES FLIGHT 175 (WTC SOUTH TOWER)

Alona Avraham, 30, Ashdod, Israel
Manufacturing engineer, Applied Materials
Garnet Edward "Ace" Bailey, 54, Lynnfield, MA
Professional hockey scout, Los Angeles Kings
Mark Lawrence Bavis, 31, West Newton, MA
Professional hockey scout, Los Angeles Kings
Graham Andrew Berkeley, 37, Wellesley, MA
Director of e-commerce solutions, Compuware Corp.
Touri Bolourchi, 69, Beverly Hills, CA
Retired nurse
Klaus Bothe, 31, Linkenheim, Baden-Wurttemberg, Germany
Software development, BCT Technology AG
Daniel R. Brandhorst, 42, Los Angeles, CA
Attorney and accountant, Pricewaterhouse Coopers
David Reed Gamboa Brandhorst, 3, Los Angeles, CA
John Brett Cahill, 56, Wellesley, MA
Executive, Xerox
Christoffer Mikael Carstanjen, 33, Turner Falls, MA
Computer research analyst, University of Massachusetts
John Jay Corcoran, 45, Norwell, MA
Engineer
Dorothy Dearaujo, 82, Long Beach, CA
Artist
Robert J. Fangman, 33, Claymont, DE
Flight attendant, United Airlines
Lisa Frost, 22, Rancho Santa Margarita, CA
Sales and marketing associate
Ronald Gamboa, 33, Los Angeles, CA
Business management, Gap
Lynn Catherine Goodchild, 25, Attleboro, MA
Administrator, Putnam Investments
Peter Morgan Goodrich, 33, Sudbury, MA
Product manager, MKS Inc.
Douglas A. Gowell, 52, Methuen, MA
New business development, Avid Technologies
Francis Grogan, 76, Easton, MA
Priest, Holy Cross Church
Carl Max Hammond Jr., 37, Derry, NH
Physicist, Massachusetts Institute of Technology
Christine Hanson, 2, Groton, MA
Peter Hanson, 32, Groton, MA
Technology sales, Timetrade
Sue Kim Hanson, 35, Groton, MA
Genealogist, Boston University
Gerald F. Hardacre, 62, Carlsbad, CA
Environmental engineer
Eric Samadikan Hartono, 20, Boston, MA
Student
James E. Hayden, 47, Westford, MA
Software Technology, Netegrity Inc.
Herbert W. Homer, 48, Milford, MA
Contract management, Raytheon Corp.
Michael R. Horrocks, 38, Glen Mills, PA
Pilot, United Airlines
Robert Adrien Jalbert, 61, Swampscott, MA
Salesman, Rogers Foam Corp.
Amy N. Jarret, 28, North Smithfield, RI
Flight attendant, United Airlines

Ralph Kershaw, 52, Manchester-by-the-Sea, MA
Marine surveyor
Heinrich Kimmig, 43, Willstaett, Germany
Mechanical engineer, BCT Technology AG
Amy R. King, 29, Stafford Springs, CT
Flight attendant, United Airlines
Brian Kinney, 29, Lowell, MA
Auditor, Pricewaterhouse Coopers
Kathryn L. LaBorie, 44, Providence, RI
Flight attendant, United Airlines
Robert George LeBlanc, 70, Lee, NH
Educator, University of New Hampshire
Maclovio Joe Lopez, 41, Los Angeles, CA
Construction, Spiniello Companies
Marianne MacFarlane, 34, Revere, MA
Passenger service representative, United Airlines
Alfred Gilles Padre Joseph Marchand, 44, Alamogordo, NM
Flight attendant, United Airlines
Louis Neil Mariani, 59, Derry, NH
Retired
Juliana Valentine McCourt, 4, New London, CT
Ruth Magdaline McCourt, 45, New London, CT
Salon owner/beauty specialist, Clifford Classique Day Spa
Deborah Medwig, 46, Dedham, MA
Systems analyst, NStar
Wolfgang Peter Menzel, 59, Willstaett, Germany
Software development, BCT Technology AG
Shawn Nassaney, 25, Pawtucket, RI
Sales, American Power Conversion
Marie Pappalardo, 53, Paramount, CA
Director of finance & production, ALA Foods
Patrick J. Quigley IV, 40, Wellesley Hills, MA
Partner, Pricewaterhouse Coopers
Frederick Charles Rimmele III, 32, Marblehead, MA
Doctor, Beverly Hospital
James M. Roux, 43, Portland, ME
Lawyer
Jesus Sanchez, 45, Hudson, MA
Flight attendant, United Airlines
Victor J. Saracini, 51, Lower Makefield Township, PA
Pilot, United Airlines
Mary Kathleen Shearer, 61, Dover, NH
Retired doll store owner
Robert Michael Shearer, 63, Dover, NH
Retired engineer
Jane Louise Simpkin, 36, Wayland, MA
Representative of rock bands
Brian D. Sweeney, 38, Barnstable, MA
Business consultant, Brandes Associates
Michael C. Tarrou, 38, Stafford Springs, CT
Flight attendant, United Airlines
Alicia N. Titus, 28, San Francisco, CA
Flight attendant, United Airlines
Timothy Ray Ward, 38, San Diego, CA
Restaurant executive, Rubio's restaurants
William M. Weems, 46, Marblehead, MA
TV producer

AMERICAN AIRLINES FLIGHT 77 (PENTAGON)

Paul Ambrose, 32, Washington, DC
Senior clinical adviser, Office of the Surgeon General
Yeneneh Betru, 35, Burbank, CA
Director of medical affairs, IPC
Mary Jane "MJ" Booth, 64, Falls Church, VA
Secretary to American Airlines' general manager at Dulles International Airport, American Airlines

Bernard Curtis Brown, 11, Washington, DC
Student, Leckie Elementary School (Washington)
Charles "Chick" Burlingame III, 51, Herndon, VA
Captain, American Airlines
Suzanne Calley, 42, San Martin, CA
Strategic marketing, Cisco Systems Inc.
William E. Caswell, 54, Silver Spring, MD
Physicist, U.S. Navy

David M. Charlebois, 39, Washington, DC
First officer, American Airlines
Sarah Clark, 65, Columbia, MD
Sixth-grade teacher, Backus Middle School (Washington)
Asia Cottom, 11, Washington, DC
Student, Backus Middle School (Washington)
James Daniel Debeuneure, 58, Upper Marlboro, MD
Fifth-grade teacher, Ketcham Elementary School (Washington)
Rodney Dickens, 11, Washington, DC
Student, Ketcham Elementary School (Washington)
Eddie Dillard, 54, Alexandria, VA
Retired marketing manager, Philip Morris
Charles Droz, 52, Springfield, VA
Vice president for software development, EM Solutions Inc.
Barbara G. Edwards, 58, Las Vegas, NV
Teacher, Palo Verde High School
Charles S. Falkenberg, 45, University Park, MD
Research director, ECOlogic Corp.
Dana Falkenberg, 3, University Park, MD
Zoe Falkenberg, 8, University Park, MD
James Joe Ferguson, 39, Washington, DC
Educational outreach director, National Geographic Society
Darlene Dee Flagg, 63, Millwood, VA
Wilson Bud Flagg, 63, Millwood, VA
Retired Navy admiral and pilot, American Airlines
Richard P. Gabriel, 54, Great Falls, VA
Managing partner, Stratin Consulting
Ian J. Gray, 55, Columbia, MD
President, McBee Associates
Stanley Hall, 68, Rancho Palos Verdes, CA
Director of program management, Raytheon Co.
Michele Heidenberger, 57, Chevy Chase, MD
Flight attendant, American Airlines
Bryan Creed Jack, 48, Alexandria, VA
Budget analyst/director of the programming and fiscal
economics division, U.S. Defense Department
Steven D. "Jake" Jacoby, 43, Alexandria, VA
Chief operating officer, Metrocall Inc.
Ann Judge, 49, Great Falls, VA
Travel office manager, National Geographic Society
Chandler Chad Keller, 29, El Segundo, CA
Propulsion engineer, Boeing Co.
Yvonne Kennedy, 62, Sydney, New South Wales, Australia
Retired, Australian Red Cross
Norma Cruz Khan, 45, Reston, VA
Manager of member services, Plumbing-Heating-Cooling
Contractors National Association
Karen A. Kincaid, 40, Washington, DC
Lawyer, Wiley Rein & Fielding (Washington)
Dong Lee, 48, Leesburg, VA
Engineer, Boeing Co.

Jennifer Lewis, 38, Culpeper, VA
Flight attendant, American Airlines
Kenneth Lewis, 49, Culpeper, VA
Flight attendant, American Airlines
Renee May, 39, Baltimore, MD
Flight attendant, American Airlines
Dora M. Menchaca, 45, Santa Monica, CA
Associate director of clinical research, Amgen Inc.
Christopher Newton, 38, Ashburn, VA
Executive, WorkLife Benefits
Barbara Olson, 45, Great Falls, VA
TV commentator, author and lawyer
Ruben Ornedo, 39, Los Angeles, CA
Propulsion engineer, Boeing Co.
Robert Penniger, 63, Poway, CA
Electrical engineer, BAE Systems
Robert R. Ploger, 59, Annandale, VA
Software architect, Lockheed Martin Corp.
Zandra Cooper Ploger, 48, Annandale, VA
Marketing brand manager, IBM
Lisa J. Raines, 42, Great Falls, VA
Senior vice president, Genzyme Corp.
Todd Reuben, 40, Potomac, MD
Tax and business lawyer, Venable, Baetjer, Howard & Civiletti
John Sammartino, 37, Annandale, VA
Technical manager, XonTech Inc.
Diane M. Simmons, Great Falls, VA
Retired, Xerox
George Simmons, Great Falls, VA
Retired manager of sales training, Xerox
Mari-Rae Sopper, 35, Santa Barbara, CA
Women's gymnastics coach, UC Santa Barbara
Robert Speisman, 47, Irvington, NY
Executive vice president, Lazar Kaplan International
Norma Lang Steuerle, 54, Alexandria, VA
Clinical psychologist
Hilda E. Taylor, 62, Forestville, MD
Sixth-grade teacher, Leckie Elementary School (Washington)
Leonard Taylor, 45, Reston, VA
Technical group manager, XonTech Inc.
Sandra Teague, 31, Fairfax, VA
Physical therapist, Georgetown University Hospital
Leslie A. Whittington, 45, University Park, MD
Professor, Georgetown University
John D. Yamnicky, 71, Waldorf, MD
Defense contractor, Veridian Corp.
Vicki C. Yancey, 43, Springfield, VA
Defense contractor, Vredenburg Co.
Shuyin Yang, 61, Beijing, China
Retired pediatrician
Zheng Yuguang, 65, Beijing, China
Retired chemist

UNITED AIRLINES FLIGHT 93 (PENNSYLVANIA)

Christian Adams, 37, Biebelsheim, Germany
Foreign sales manager, German Wine Fund
Lorraine Grace Bay, 58, Hightstown, NJ
Flight attendant, United Airlines
Todd Beamer, 32, Cranbury, NJ
Account manager, Oracle Corp.
Alan Beaven, 48, Oakland, CA
Environmental lawyer
Mark K. Bingham, 31, San Francisco, CA
Owner, The Bingham Group
Deora Frances Bodley, 20, Santa Clara, CA
University student, Santa Clara (Calif.) University
Sandra W. Bradshaw, 38, Greensboro, NC
Flight attendant, United Airlines
Marion Ruth Britton, 53, Bay Ridge, NY
Assistant regional director, U.S. Census Bureau

Thomas E. Burnett Jr., 38, San Ramon, CA
Senior vice president and chief operating officer, Thoratec
Corp.
William Joseph Cashman, 57, North Bergen, NJ
Construction worker
Georgine Rose Corrigan, 56, Honolulu, HI
Antiques and collectibles dealer
Patricia Cushing, 69, Bayonne, NJ
Retired
Jason Dahl, 43, Denver, CO
Captain, United Airlines
Joseph DeLuca, 52, Ledgewood, NJ
Systems business consultant, Pfizer Inc.
Patrick Joseph Driscoll, 70, Manalapan, NJ
Retired research director, Bell Communications

Edward Porter Felt, 41, Matawan, NJ
Technology director, BEA Systems
Jane C. Folger, 73, Bayonne, NJ
Retired
Colleen Laura Fraser, 51, Elizabeth, NJ
Chairwoman, New Jersey Developmental Disabilities Council
Andrew Garcia, 62, Portola Valley, CA
Salesman
Jeremy Glick, 31, West Milford, NJ
Lauren Grandcolas, 36, San Rafael, CA
Sales worker, Good Housekeeping magazine
Wanda Anita Green, 49, Linden, NJ
Flight attendant, United Airlines
Donald F. Greene, 52, Greenwich, CT
Executive vice president, Safe Flight Instrument Corp.
Linda Gronlund, 46, Greenwood Lake, NY
Environmental compliance, BMW
Richard Jerry Guadagno, 38, Eureka, CA
Manager, Humboldt Bay National Wildlife Refuge
LeRoy Homer, 36, Marlton, NJ
First officer, United Airlines
Toshiya Kuge, 20, Tokyo, Japan
Student
CeeCee Lyles, 33, Fort Myers, FL
Flight attendant, United Airlines
Hilda Marcin, 79, Budd Lake, NJ
Retired teacher's aide

Waleska Martinez Rivera, 38, Jersey City, NJ
Automation specialist, U.S. Census Bureau
Nicole Miller, 21, San Jose, CA
Student, West Valley College
Louis J. Nacke, 42, New Hope, PA
Distribution center director, Kay-Bee Toys
Donald Arthur Peterson, 66, Spring Lake, NJ
Retired president, Continental Electric Co.
Jean Hoadley Peterson, 55, Spring Lake, NJ
Mark "Mickey" Rothenberg, Scotch Plains, NJ
Owner, MDR Global Resources
Christine Anne Snyder, 32, Kailua, HI
Arborist, Outdoor Circle
John Talignani, 74, New York, NY
Retired restaurant worker
Honor Elizabeth Wainio, 27, Watchung, NJ
District manager, Discovery Channel stores
Deborah A. Welsh, 49, Manhattan, NY
Flight attendant, United Airlines
Olga Kristin Gould White, 65, New York, NY
Freelance medical journalist

To search Newsday's *interactive database for the names of victims of the September 11 terrorist attacks, as well as to see photos and stories, go to*
http://www.newsday.com/911memorial.

Contributors and Staff

SPECIAL WRITER: Indrani Sen

CONTRIBUTING WRITERS:

Newsday—Stacey Altherr, Rhoda Amon, Devi Athiappan, Fred Aun, Deborah Barfield, Pat Burson, Robert Cassidy, Richard J. Dalton Jr., Brian Donovan, Emi Endo, Alan H. Fallick, Robert Fresco, Sean Gardiner, Joe Haberstroh, Noel Holston, Nick Iyer, Bart Jones, S. Mitra Kalita, Bill Kaufman, Kathleen Kerr, Ann L. Kim, Steven Kreytak, Eden Laikin, Melanie Lefkowitz, Herbert Lowe, Carl MacGowan, Elizabeth Moore, Keiko Morris, Christian Murray, Collin Nash, Hoa Nguyen, J. Jioni Palmer, Rocco Parascandola, Sandra Peddie, Victor Manuel Ramos, Sumathi Reddy, Nedra Rhone, Michael Rothfeld, Ken Schacter, Dionne Searcy, Jennifer Smith, Jamie Talan, Michael Their, Katie Thomas, Kathryn Wellin, Steve Wick

Baltimore Sun—Sandy Alexander, Lynda Anderson, Athima Chansanchai, Michael Dresser, Rob Hiaasen, Chris Kaltenbach, Patricia Meisol, Michael Ollove, Jonathan Pitts, Michael Scarcella

Chicago Tribune—Rudolph Bush, Julie Deardorff, Eric Ferkenhoff, Liam Ford, Ted Gregory, Sean Hamill, Robert L. Kaiser, John Keilman, Jeff Long, Flynn McRoberts, Ray Quintanilla, Letitia Stein, Dawn Turner Trice, Brad Webber

The Daily Press—Fred Carroll

Hartford Courant—Josh Kovner

Los Angeles Times—Rob Fernas, Eric Lichtblau, Robert A. Rosenblatt

Morning Call—Christine Schiavo

Orlando Sentinel—Harry Wessel

Sun Sentinel—Kathleen Kerricky

CONTRIBUTING EDITORS: B. Monica Quintanilla, Monica Norton, Beth DeCarbo

Newsday Books

EXECUTIVE EDITOR: Phyllis Singer
EDITOR: Harvey Aronson
NEWS EDITOR: Rick Green

Photo Credits

The gathering of photographs of the victims could not have been done without the contribution of family members and the genuine concern of several organizations, businesses, and Web sites. New York City Police and Fire Department officials provided countless images of their fallen brethren. Media sources gathered forces and helped share images.

The display photographs appearing in this book were taken by *Newsday* photographers. The photograph of the flag that flew at the World Trade Center towers, which appears in the opening page of each chapter, was taken by Audrey C. Tiernan when the flag was flown at Yankee Stadium during the World Series.

Other photo credits are as follows:

Pages 2 and 113, Ari Mintz

Page 6, Bruce Gilbert

Page 62, Thomas A. Ferrara

Page 114, Mayita Mendez

Page 156, J. Conrad Williams Jr.

Page 189, Audrey C. Tiernan

Pages 190 and 193, Kathy Kmonicek

Page 194, Michael E. Ach

Index